priceless

3

Priceless Vol.3
Created by Young-You Lee

Translation - Grace Min
English Adaptation - Hope Donovan
Copy Editor - Stephanie Duchin
Retouch and Lettering - Amit Gogia
Production Artist - Mike Estacio
Cover Design - Christian Lownds

Editor - Bryce P. Coleman
Digital Imaging Manager - Chris Buford
Pre-Production Supervisor - Erika Terriquez
Art Director - Anne Marie Horne
Managing Editor - Vy Nguyen
Production Manager - Elisabeth Brizzi
VP of Production - Ron Klamert
Editor-in-Chief - Rob Tokar
Publisher - Mike Kiley
President and C.O.O. - John Parker
C.E.O. and Chief Creative Officer - Stuart Levy

A  Manga

TOKYOPOP Inc.
5900 Wilshire Blvd. Suite 2000
Los Angeles, CA 90036

E-mail: info@TOKYOPOP.com
Come visit us online at www.TOKYOPOP.com

ISBN: 1-59816-311-6

First TOKYOPOP printing: December 2006
10 9 8 7 6 5 4 3 2 1
Printed in the USA

Volume 3

Young-You Lee

HAMBURG // LONDON // LOS ANGELES // TOKYO

SO FAR IN

POOR LANG-BEE HAS TO WORK 24-7 TO
PAY OFF DEBTS LEFT BY HER ABSENTEE MOM.
TO MAKE MATTERS WORSE, A YOUNG CON ARTIST
NAMED JIMMY HAS SHOWN UP CLAIMING TO BE
HER STEPFATHER! IN AN ATTEMPT TO EASE HER
FINANCIAL PROBLEMS, LANG-BEE HAS SET HER
SIGHTS ON THE LOCAL RICH KID, DAN WON, AND IT
SEEMS TO BE WORKING...DAN IS TOTALLY SMITTEN
BY LANG-BEE! PROBLEM SOLVED, RIGHT? WRONG!

IT SEEMS LANG-BEE'S ARCHRIVAL, YUKA, WANTS
DAN ALL TO HERSELF. PLUS, JIMMY IS TAKING THE
WHOLE "DAD" THINK A BIT TOO SERIOUSLY, GOING
SO FAR AS TO ENROLL IN LANG-BEE'S SCHOOL
TO KEEP CLOSER TABS ON HER!

WHAT'S A YOUNG GOLD DIGGER TO DO...?

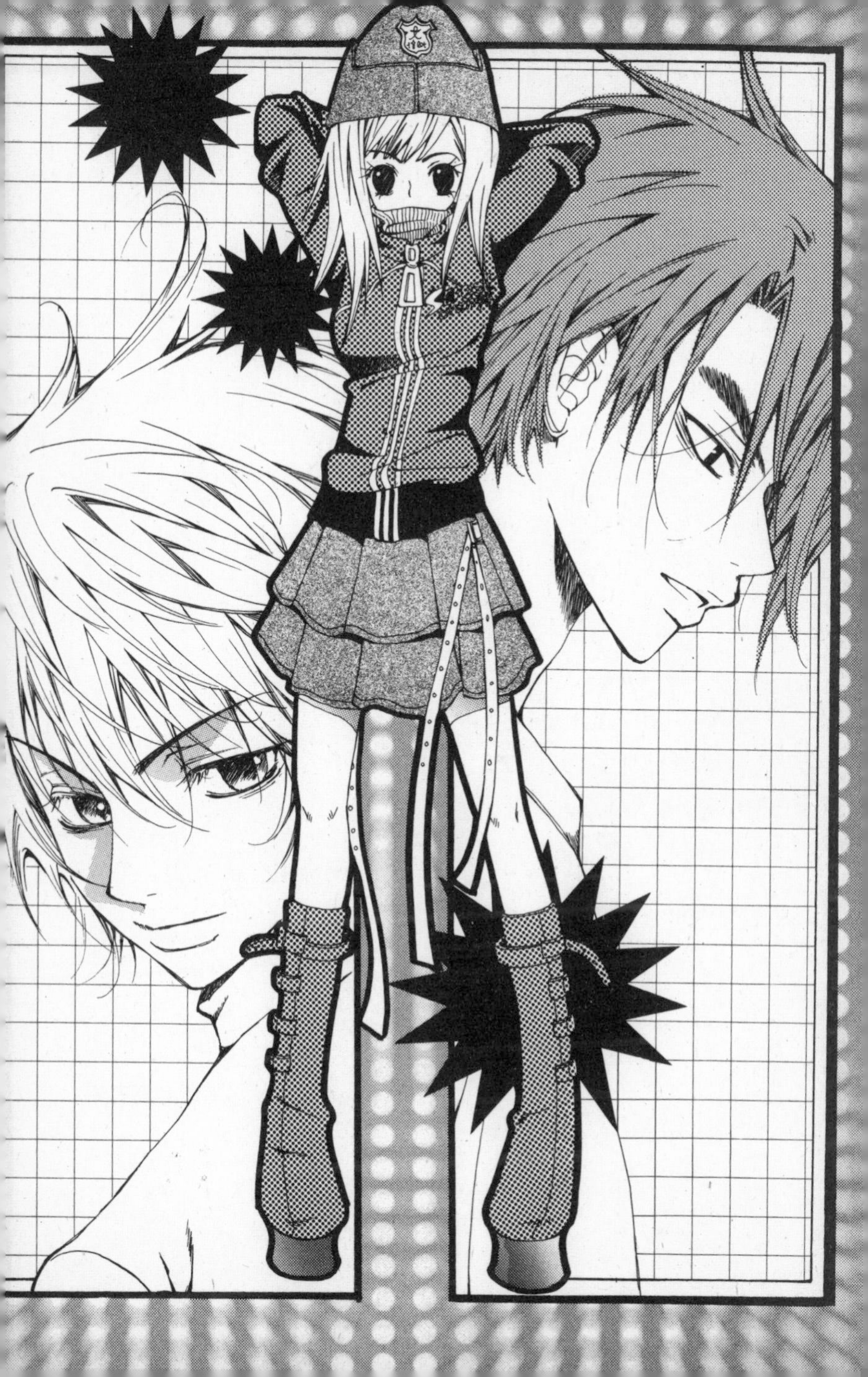

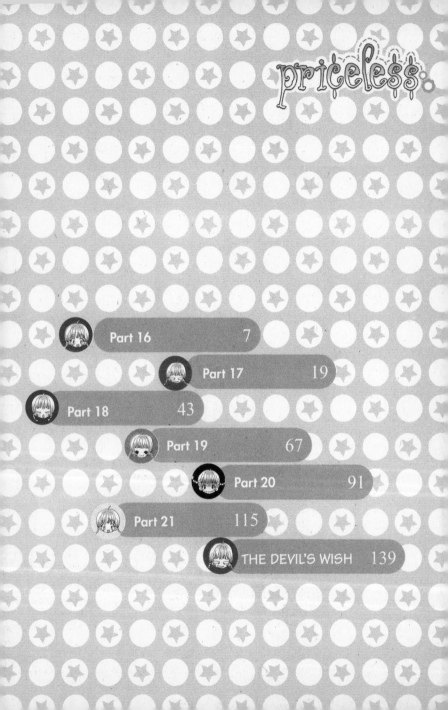

priceless

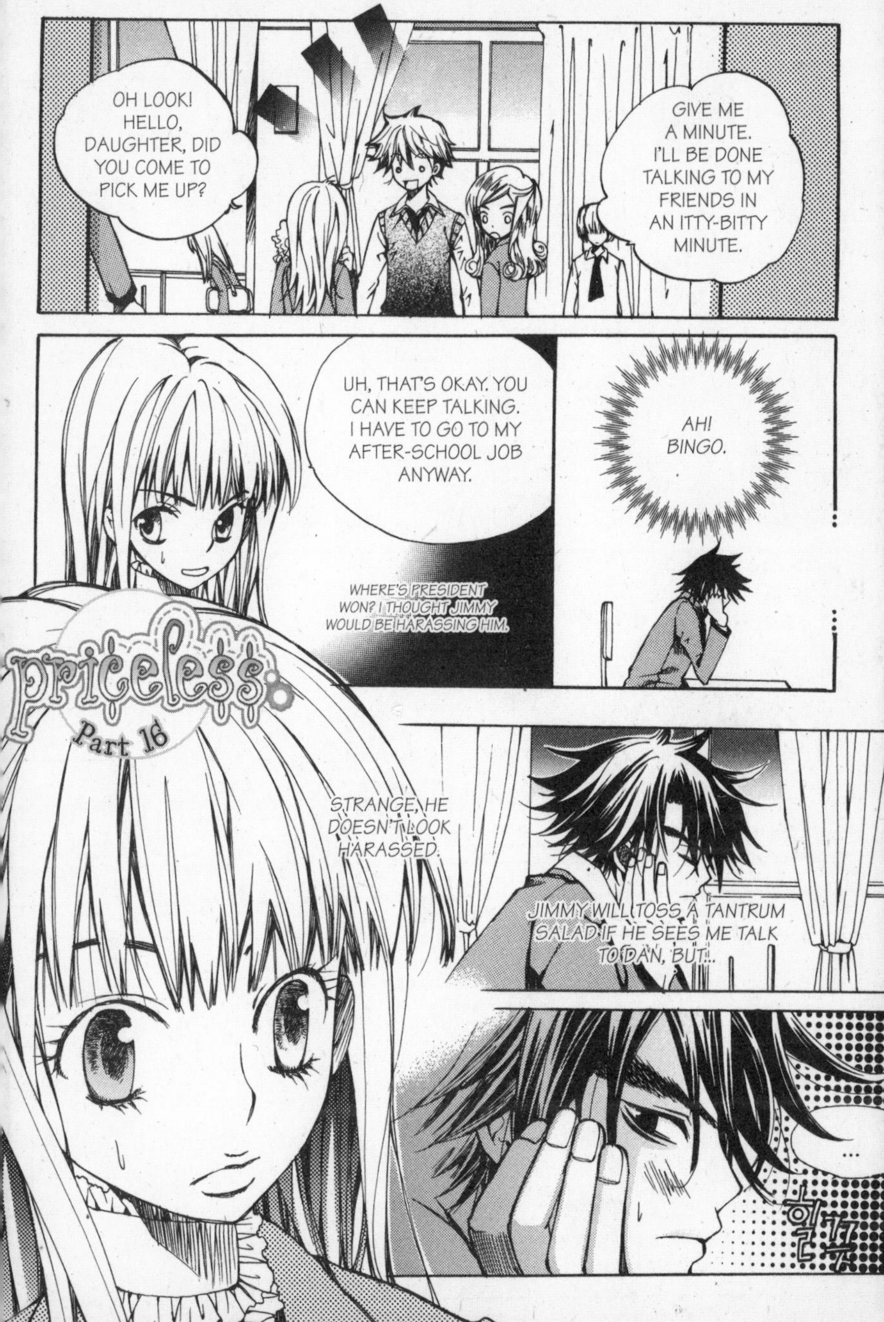
OH LOOK! HELLO, DAUGHTER, DID YOU COME TO PICK ME UP?
GIVE ME A MINUTE. I'LL BE DONE TALKING TO MY FRIENDS IN AN ITTY-BITTY MINUTE.
UH, THAT'S OKAY. YOU CAN KEEP TALKING. I HAVE TO GO TO MY AFTER-SCHOOL JOB ANYWAY.
WHERE'S PRESIDENT WON? I THOUGHT JIMMY WOULD BE HARASSING HIM.
AH! BINGO.
priceless
Part 16
STRANGE, HE DOESN'T LOOK HARASSED.
JIMMY WILL TOSS A TANTRUM SALAD IF HE SEES ME TALK TO DAN, BUT...
...
힐끗

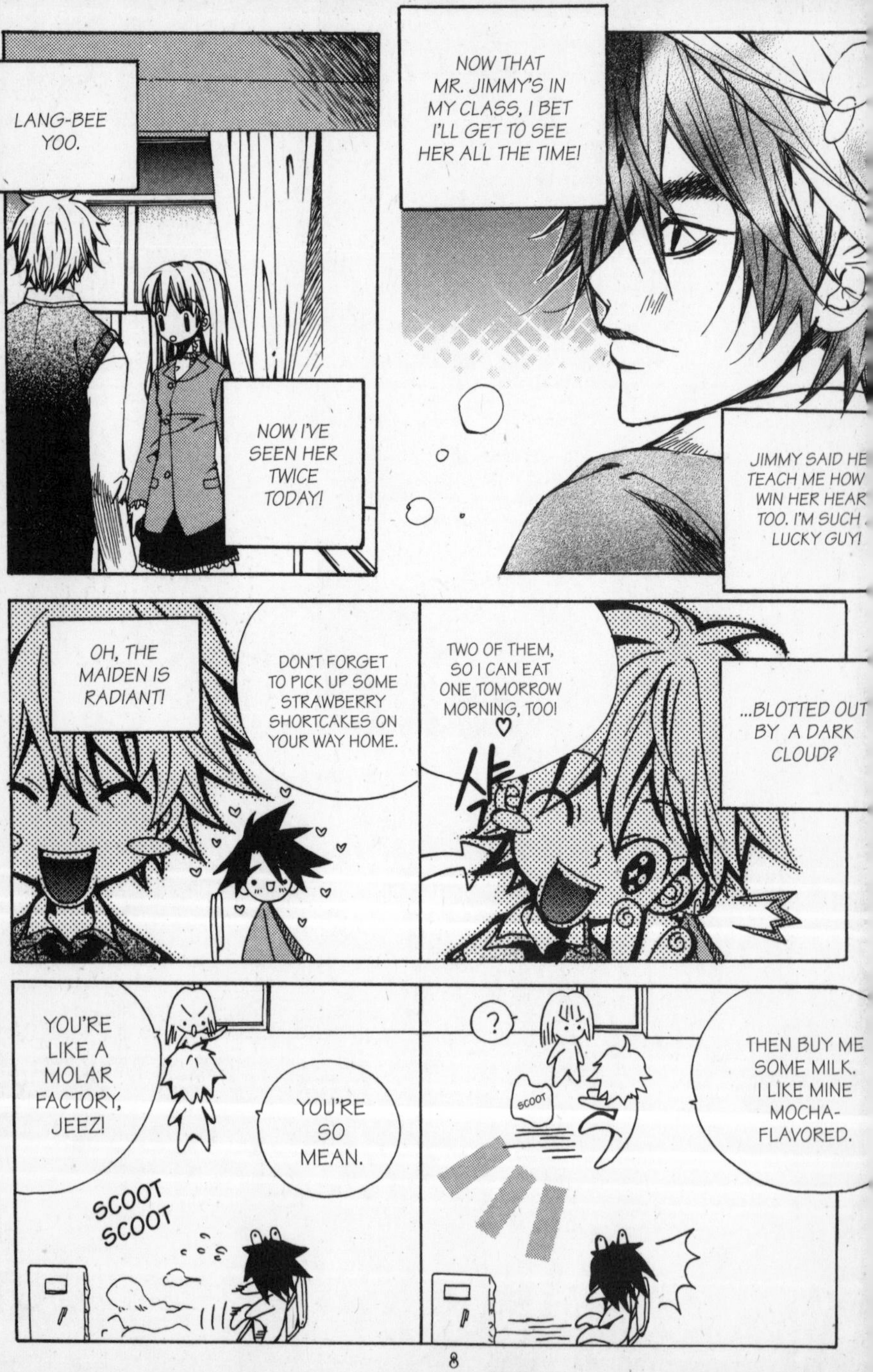
LANG-BEE YOO.
NOW I'VE SEEN HER TWICE TODAY!
NOW THAT MR. JIMMY'S IN MY CLASS, I BET I'LL GET TO SEE HER ALL THE TIME!
JIMMY SAID HE TEACH ME HOW WIN HER HEAR TOO. I'M SUCH LUCKY GUY!
OH, THE MAIDEN IS RADIANT!
DON'T FORGET TO PICK UP SOME STRAWBERRY SHORTCAKES ON YOUR WAY HOME.
TWO OF THEM, SO I CAN EAT ONE TOMORROW MORNING, TOO! ♡
...BLOTTED OUT BY A DARK CLOUD?
YOU'RE LIKE A MOLAR FACTORY, JEEZ!
YOU'RE SO MEAN.
SCOOT SCOOT
?
SCOOT
THEN BUY ME SOME MILK. I LIKE MINE MOCHA-FLAVORED.

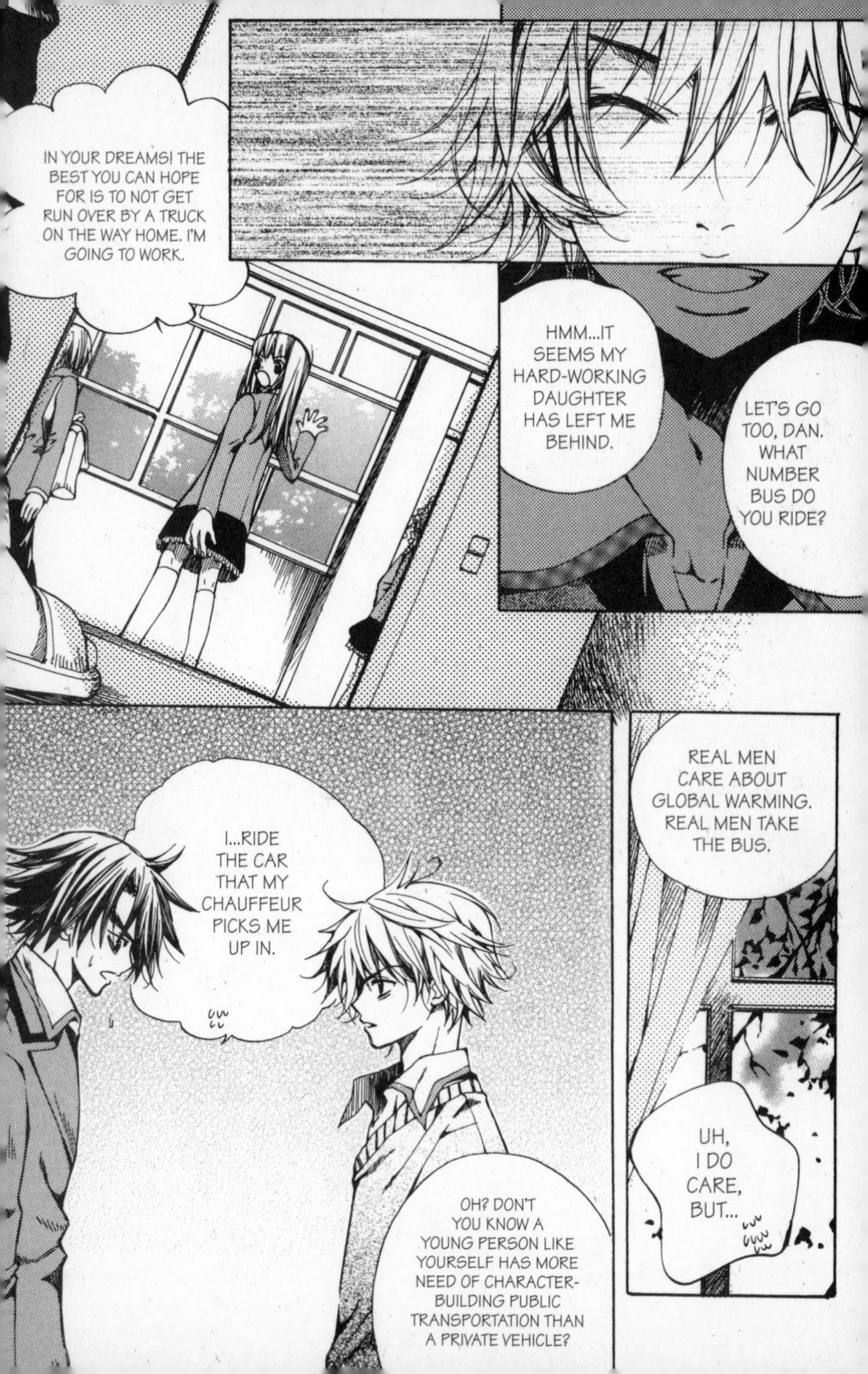
IN YOUR DREAMS! THE BEST YOU CAN HOPE FOR IS TO NOT GET RUN OVER BY A TRUCK ON THE WAY HOME. I'M GOING TO WORK.
HMM...IT SEEMS MY HARD-WORKING DAUGHTER HAS LEFT ME BEHIND.
LET'S GO TOO, DAN. WHAT NUMBER BUS DO YOU RIDE?
I...RIDE THE CAR THAT MY CHAUFFEUR PICKS ME UP IN.
OH? DON'T YOU KNOW A YOUNG PERSON LIKE YOURSELF HAS MORE NEED OF CHARACTER-BUILDING PUBLIC TRANSPORTATION THAN A PRIVATE VEHICLE?
REAL MEN CARE ABOUT GLOBAL WARMING. REAL MEN TAKE THE BUS.
UH, I DO CARE, BUT...

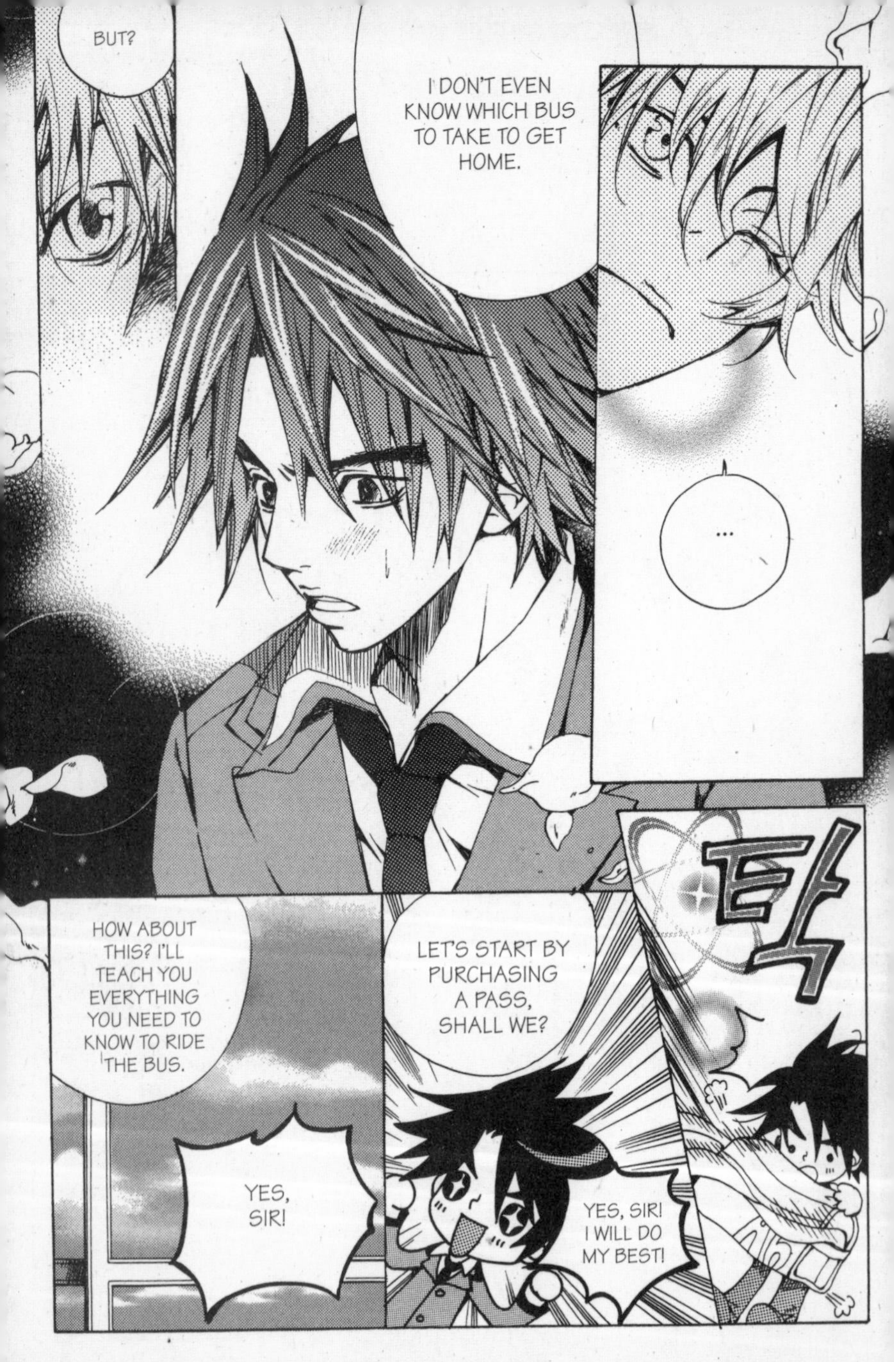
BUT?
I DON'T EVEN KNOW WHICH BUS TO TAKE TO GET HOME.
...
HOW ABOUT THIS? I'LL TEACH YOU EVERYTHING YOU NEED TO KNOW TO RIDE THE BUS.
YES, SIR!
LET'S START BY PURCHASING A PASS, SHALL WE?
YES, SIR! I WILL DO MY BEST!

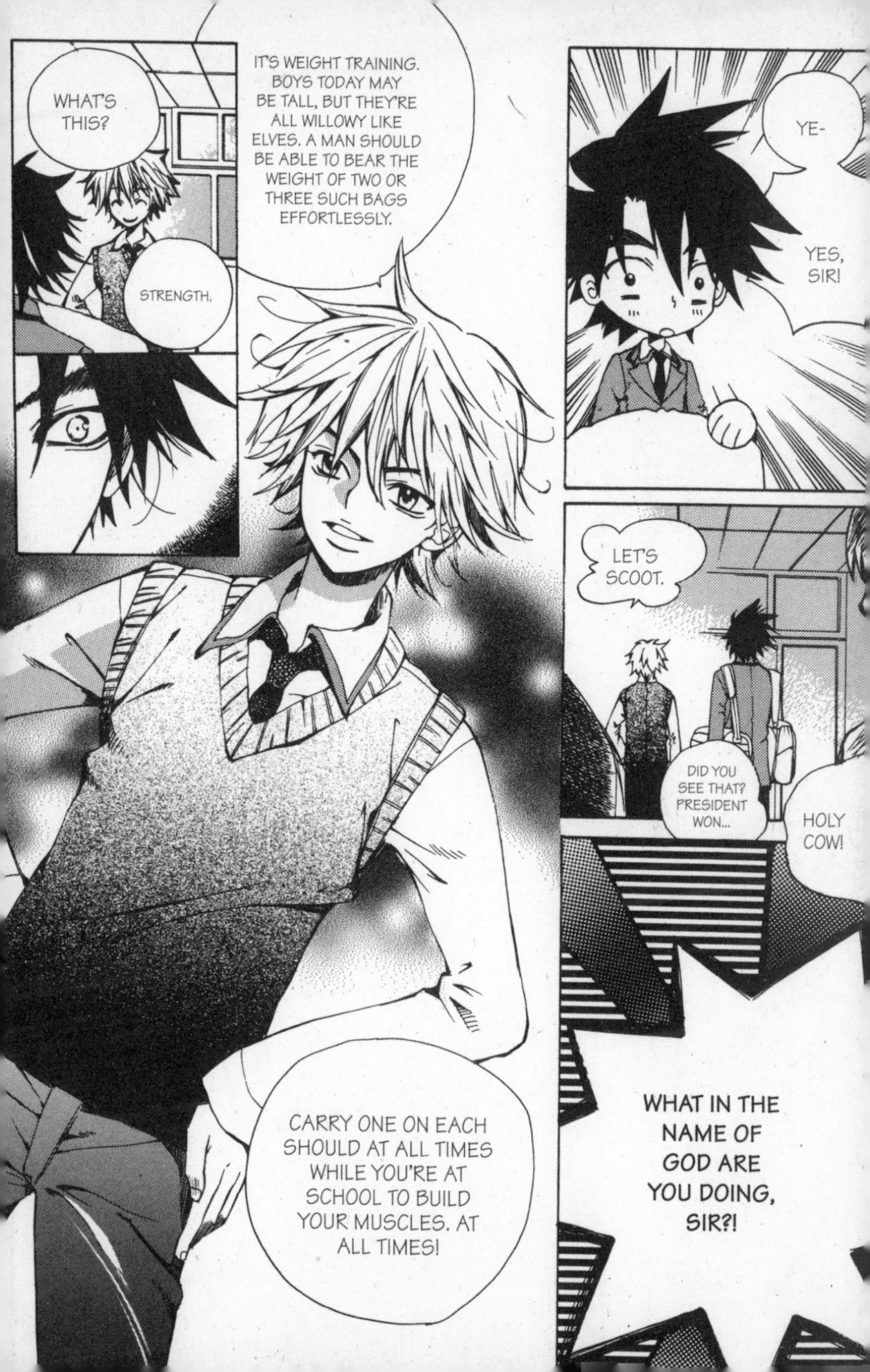
WHAT'S THIS?
IT'S WEIGHT TRAINING. BOYS TODAY MAY BE TALL, BUT THEY'RE ALL WILLOWY LIKE ELVES. A MAN SHOULD BE ABLE TO BEAR THE WEIGHT OF TWO OR THREE SUCH BAGS EFFORTLESSLY.
STRENGTH.
CARRY ONE ON EACH SHOULD AT ALL TIMES WHILE YOU'RE AT SCHOOL TO BUILD YOUR MUSCLES. AT ALL TIMES!
YE-
YES, SIR!
LET'S SCOOT.
DID YOU SEE THAT? PRESIDENT WON...
HOLY COW!
WHAT IN THE NAME OF GOD ARE YOU DOING, SIR?!

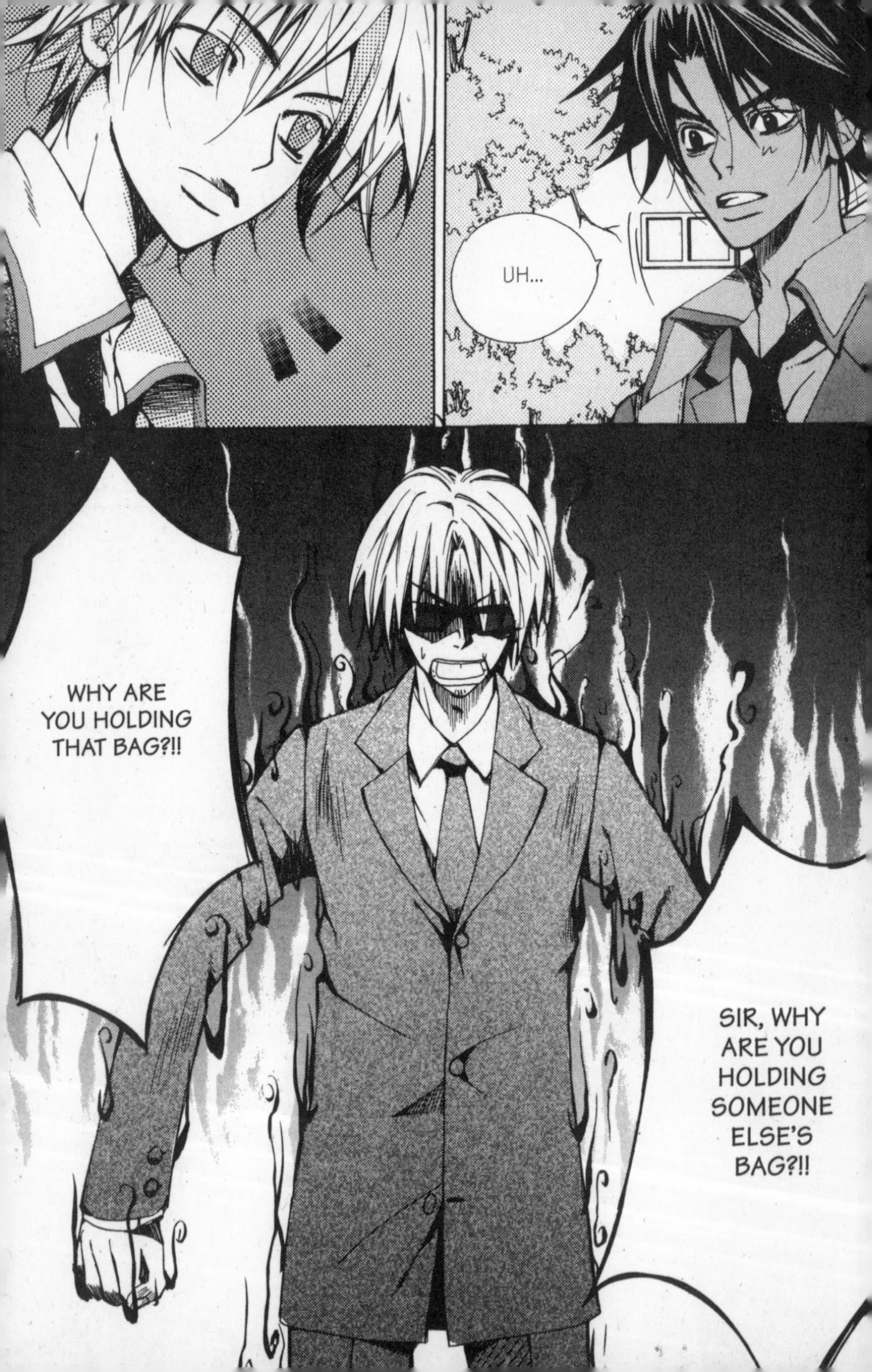
UH...
WHY ARE YOU HOLDING THAT BAG?!!
SIR, WHY ARE YOU HOLDING SOMEONE ELSE'S BAG?!!

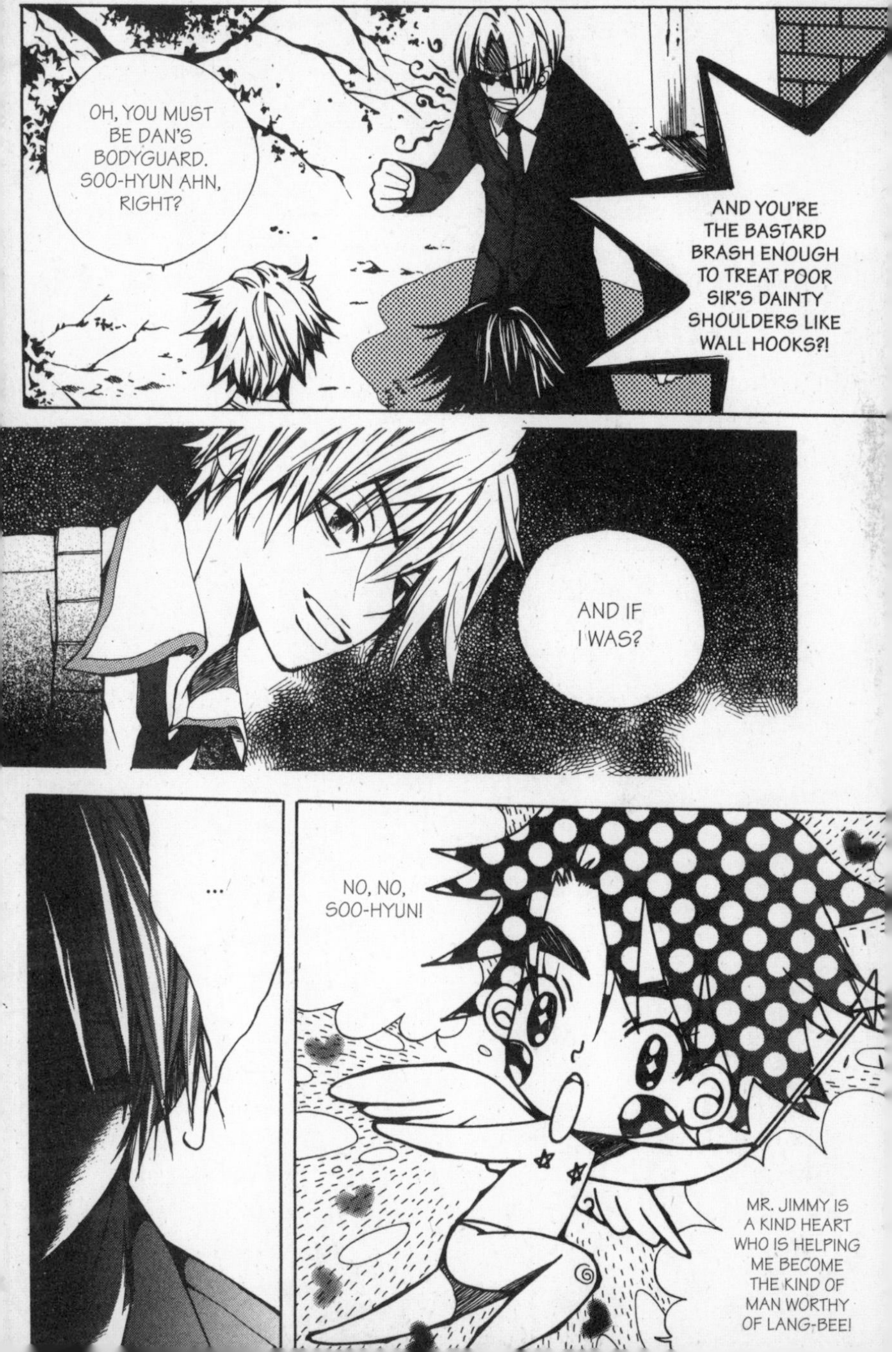
OH, YOU MUST BE DAN'S BODYGUARD. SOO-HYUN AHN, RIGHT?
AND YOU'RE THE BASTARD BRASH ENOUGH TO TREAT POOR SIR'S DAINTY SHOULDERS LIKE WALL HOOKS?!
AND IF I WAS?
...
NO, NO, SOO-HYUN!
MR. JIMMY IS A KIND HEART WHO IS HELPING ME BECOME THE KIND OF MAN WORTHY OF LANG-BEE!

EXCUSE ME?

IT'S WEIGHT TRAINING! DON'T GET THE WRONG IDEA, SILLY! TEE HEE!

WHAT THE...?!

THAT'S NOT WEIGHT TRAINING!! HE'S PLAYING YOU FOR A FOOL!

HOW STUPID CAN YOU BE, SIR?!

GO AHEAD! SHOW YOUR APPRECIATION TOO, SOO-HYUN!

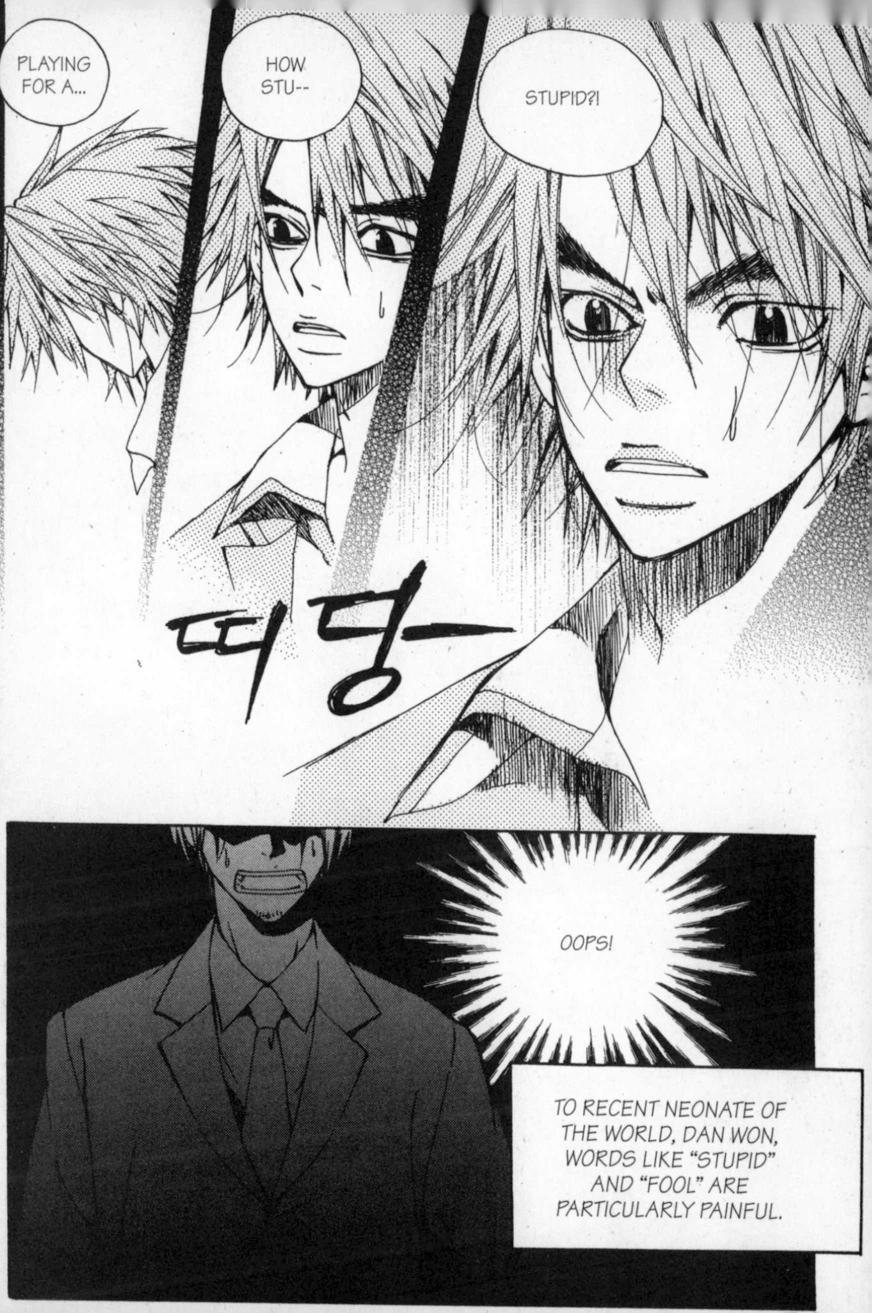
PLAYING FOR A...
HOW STU--
STUPID?!
띠딩—
OOPS!
TO RECENT NEONATE OF THE WORLD, DAN WON, WORDS LIKE "STUPID" AND "FOOL" ARE PARTICULARLY PAINFUL.

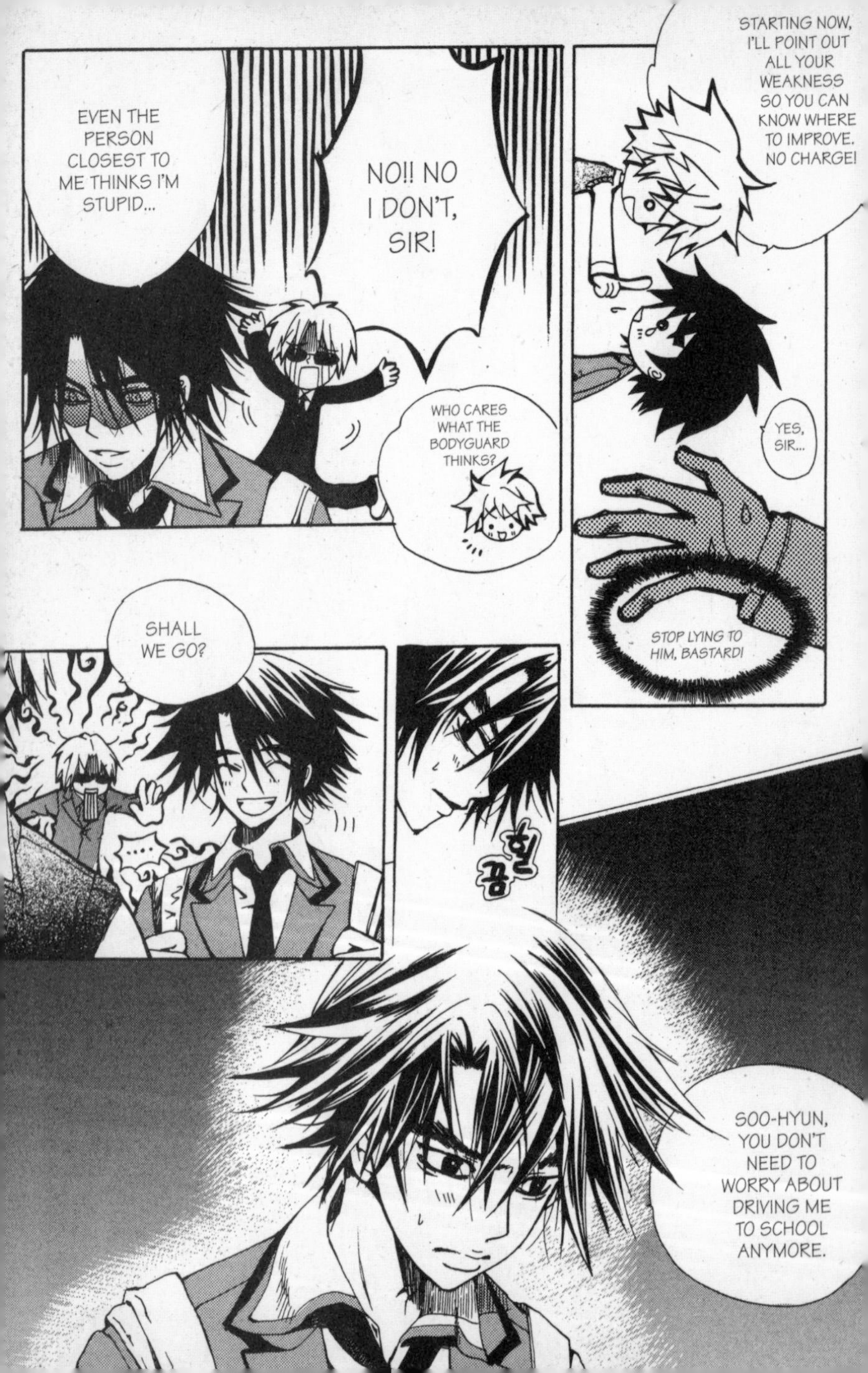
EVEN THE PERSON CLOSEST TO ME THINKS I'M STUPID...
NO!! NO I DON'T, SIR!
WHO CARES WHAT THE BODYGUARD THINKS?
STARTING NOW, I'LL POINT OUT ALL YOUR WEAKNESS SO YOU CAN KNOW WHERE TO IMPROVE. NO CHARGE!
YES, SIR...
STOP LYING TO HIM, BASTARD!
SHALL WE GO?
....
힐끔
SOO-HYUN, YOU DON'T NEED TO WORRY ABOUT DRIVING ME TO SCHOOL ANYMORE.

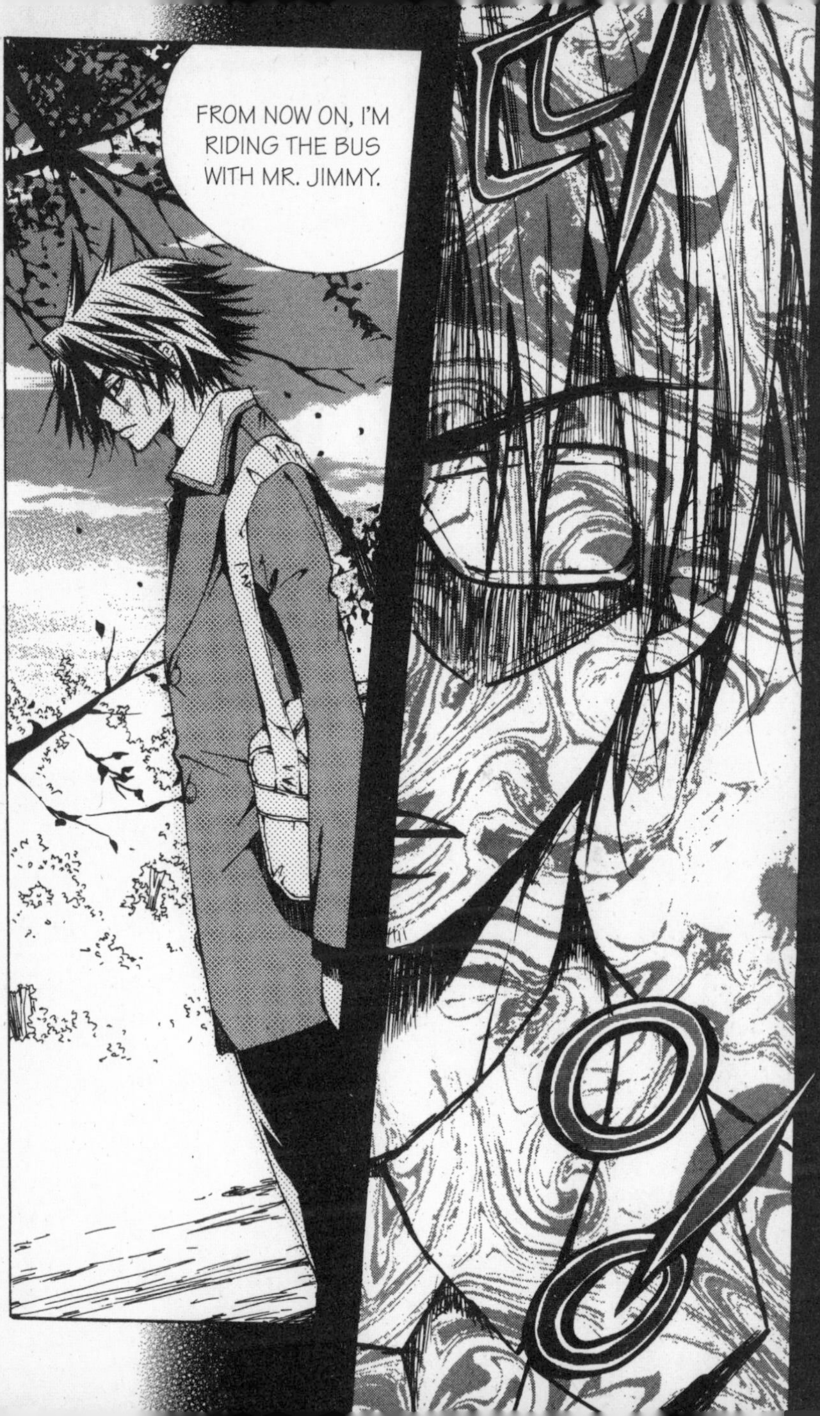
FROM NOW ON, I'M RIDING THE BUS WITH MR. JIMMY.

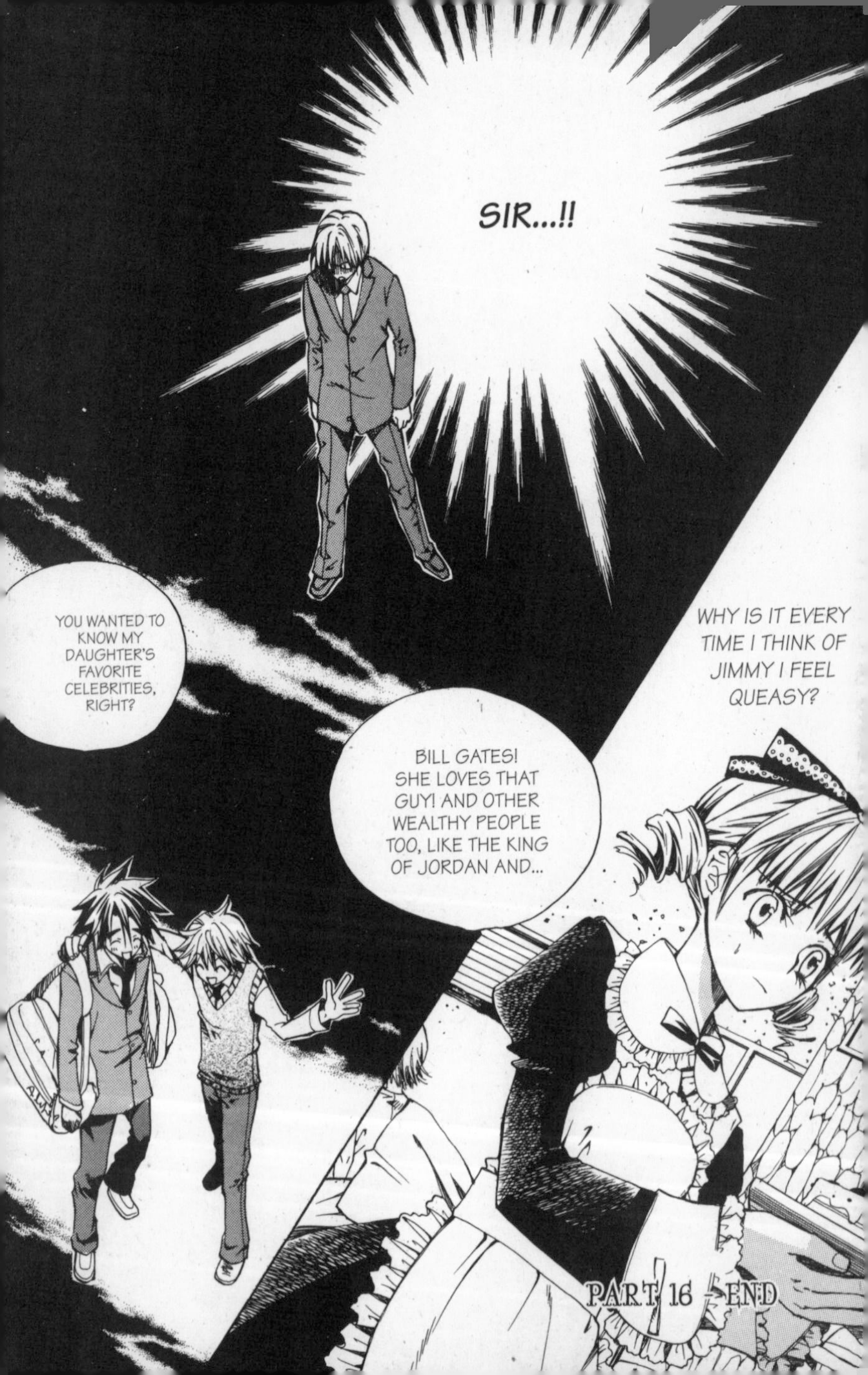
SIR...!!
YOU WANTED TO KNOW MY DAUGHTER'S FAVORITE CELEBRITIES, RIGHT?
BILL GATES! SHE LOVES THAT GUY! AND OTHER WEALTHY PEOPLE TOO, LIKE THE KING OF JORDAN AND...
WHY IS IT EVERY TIME I THINK OF JIMMY I FEEL QUEASY?
PART 16 - END

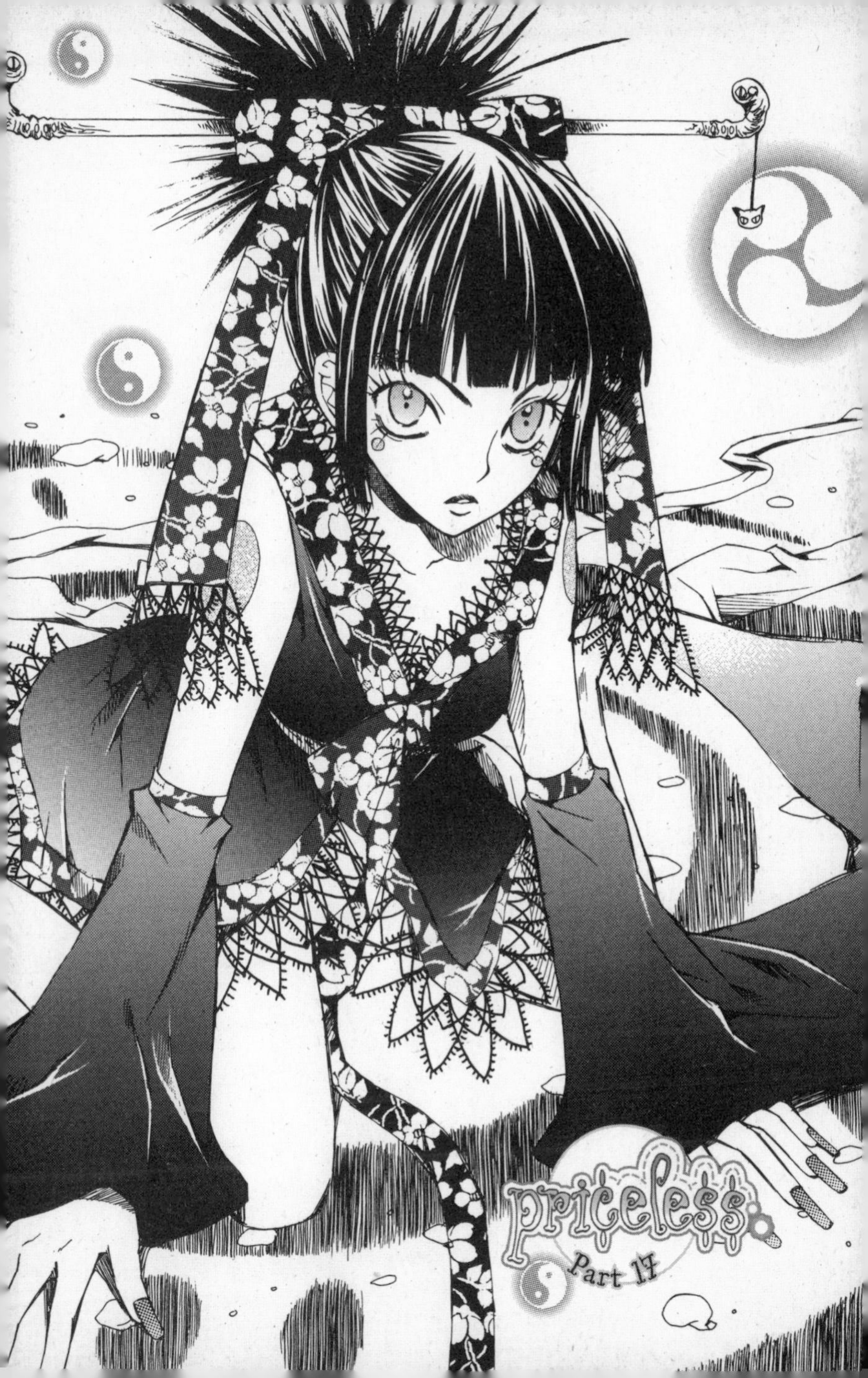
priceless
Part 17

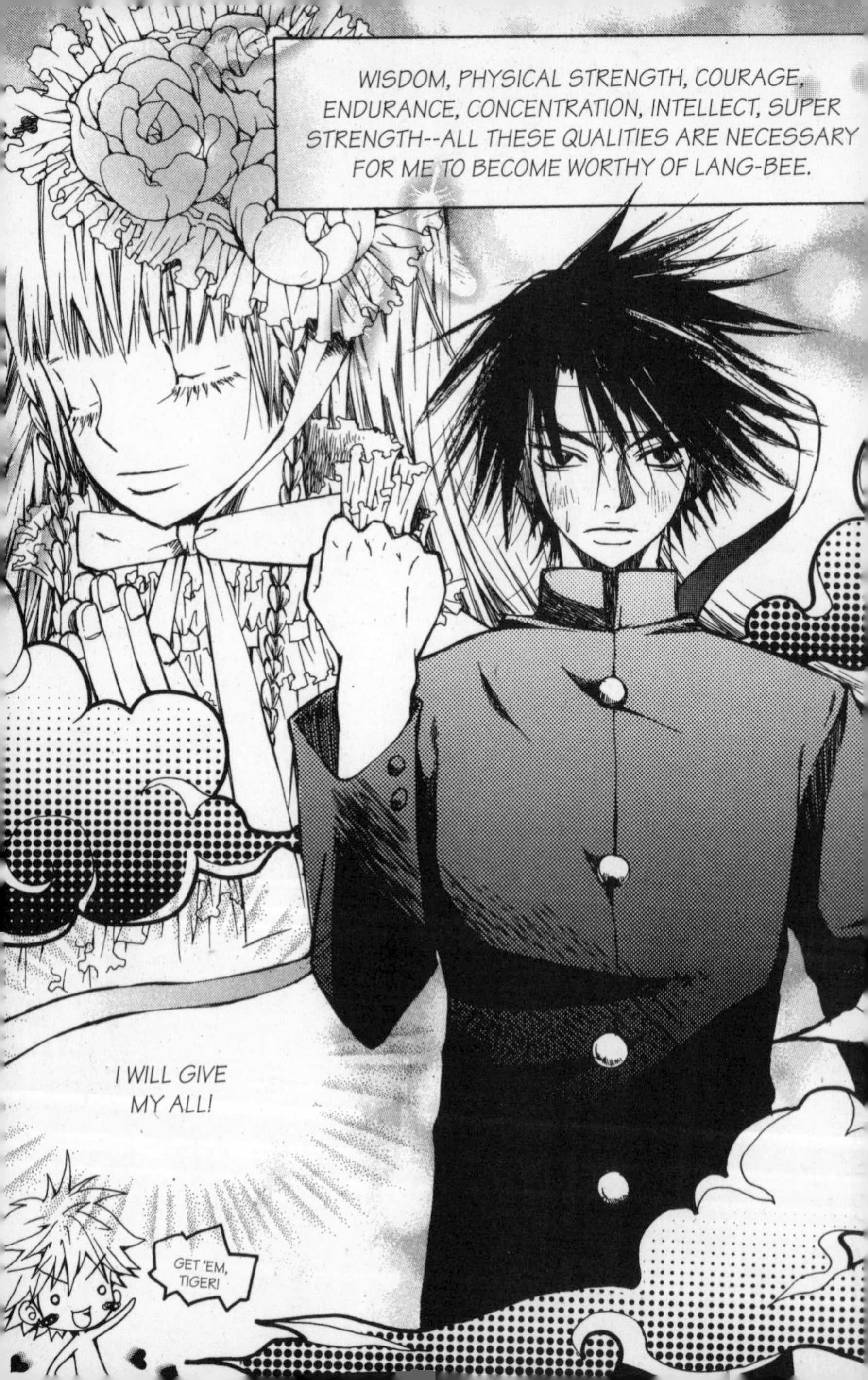
WISDOM, PHYSICAL STRENGTH, COURAGE, ENDURANCE, CONCENTRATION, INTELLECT, SUPER STRENGTH--ALL THESE QUALITIES ARE NECESSARY FOR ME TO BECOME WORTHY OF LANG-BEE.
I WILL GIVE MY ALL!
GET 'EM, TIGER!

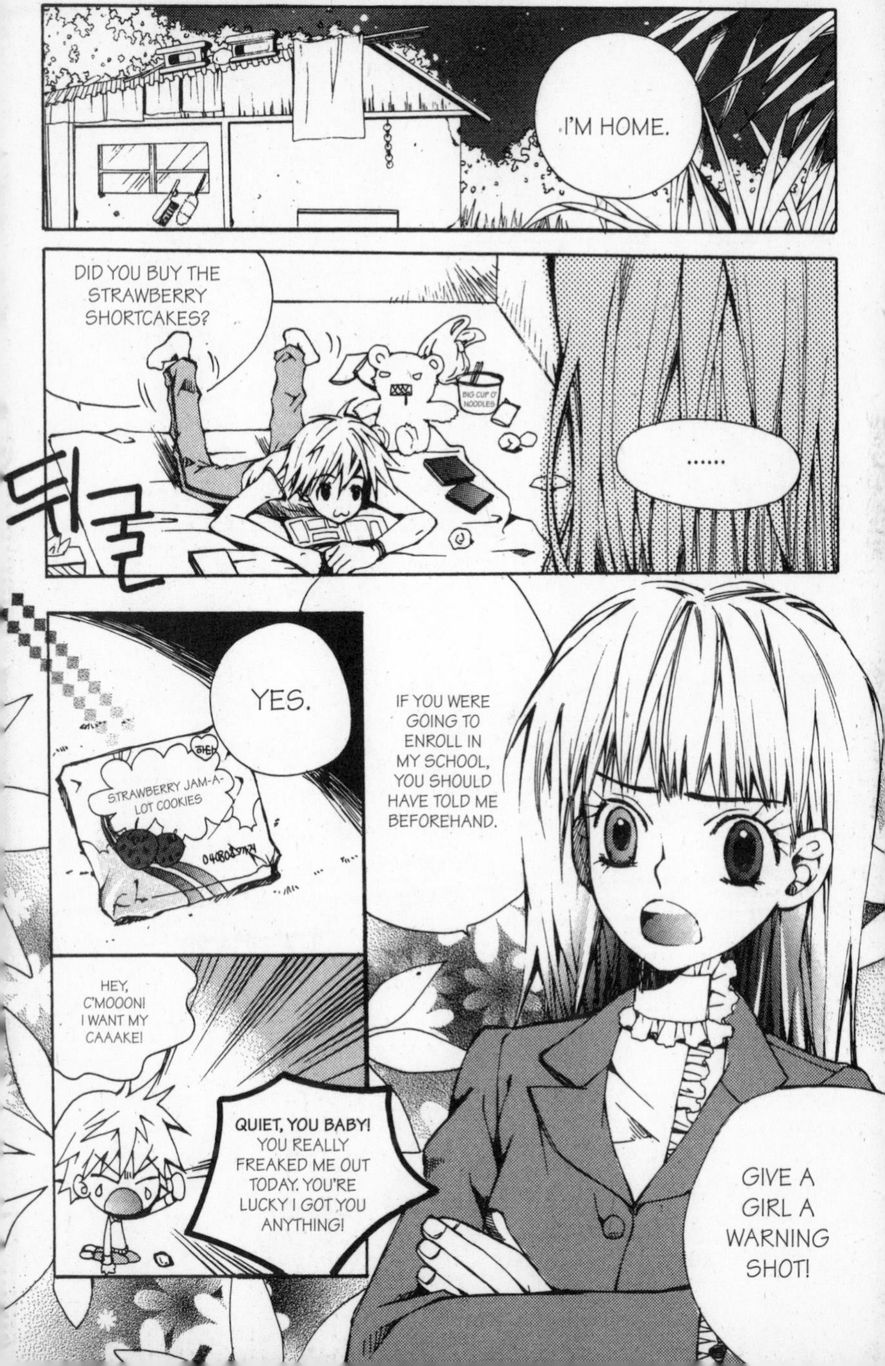

I'M HOME.
DID YOU BUY THE STRAWBERRY SHORTCAKES?
BIG CUP O' NOODLES
뒤굴
......
YES.
STRAWBERRY JAM-A-LOT COOKIES
HEY, C'MOOON! I WANT MY CAAAKE!
QUIET, YOU BABY! YOU REALLY FREAKED ME OUT TODAY. YOU'RE LUCKY I GOT YOU ANYTHING!
IF YOU WERE GOING TO ENROLL IN MY SCHOOL, YOU SHOULD HAVE TOLD ME BEFOREHAND.
GIVE A GIRL A WARNING SHOT!

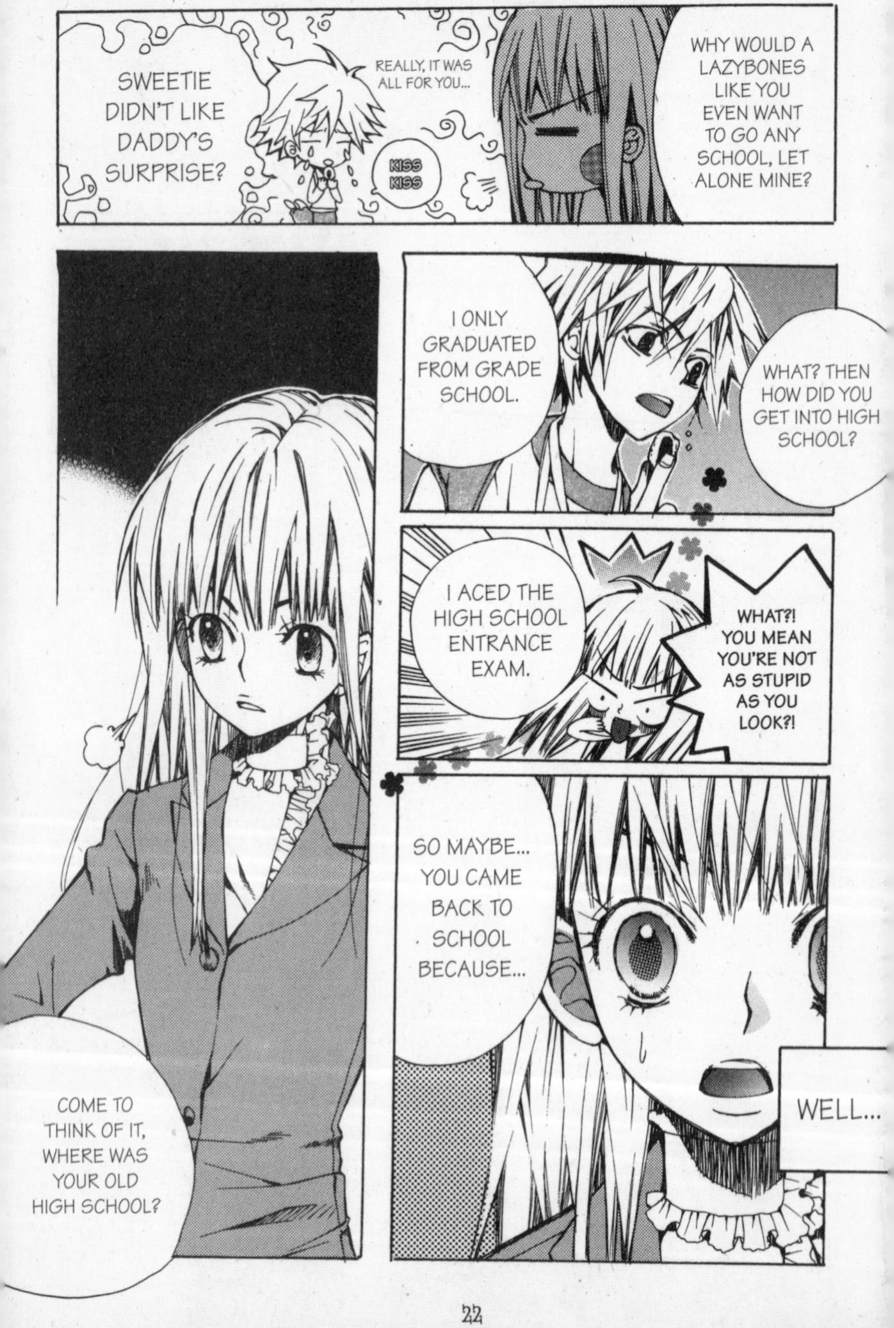
SWEETIE DIDN'T LIKE DADDY'S SURPRISE?
REALLY, IT WAS ALL FOR YOU...
KISS KISS
WHY WOULD A LAZYBONES LIKE YOU EVEN WANT TO GO ANY SCHOOL, LET ALONE MINE?
COME TO THINK OF IT, WHERE WAS YOUR OLD HIGH SCHOOL?
I ONLY GRADUATED FROM GRADE SCHOOL.
WHAT? THEN HOW DID YOU GET INTO HIGH SCHOOL?
I ACED THE HIGH SCHOOL ENTRANCE EXAM.
WHAT?! YOU MEAN YOU'RE NOT AS STUPID AS YOU LOOK?!
SO MAYBE... YOU CAME BACK TO SCHOOL BECAUSE...
WELL...

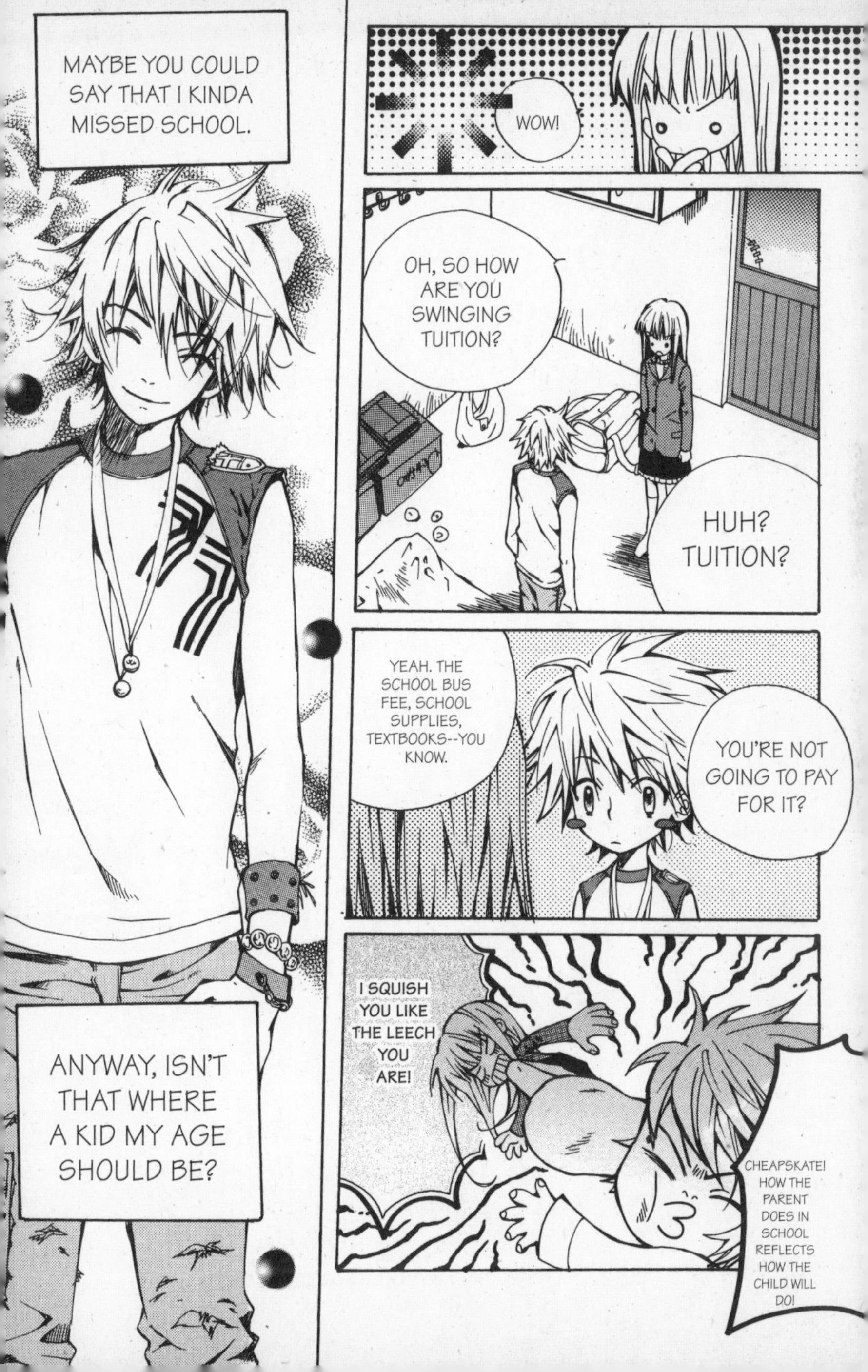
MAYBE YOU COULD SAY THAT I KINDA MISSED SCHOOL.
ANYWAY, ISN'T THAT WHERE A KID MY AGE SHOULD BE?
WOW!
OH, SO HOW ARE YOU SWINGING TUITION?
HUH? TUITION?
YEAH. THE SCHOOL BUS FEE, SCHOOL SUPPLIES, TEXTBOOKS--YOU KNOW.
YOU'RE NOT GOING TO PAY FOR IT?
I SQUISH YOU LIKE THE LEECH YOU ARE!
CHEAPSKATE! HOW THE PARENT DOES IN SCHOOL REFLECTS HOW THE CHILD WILL DO!

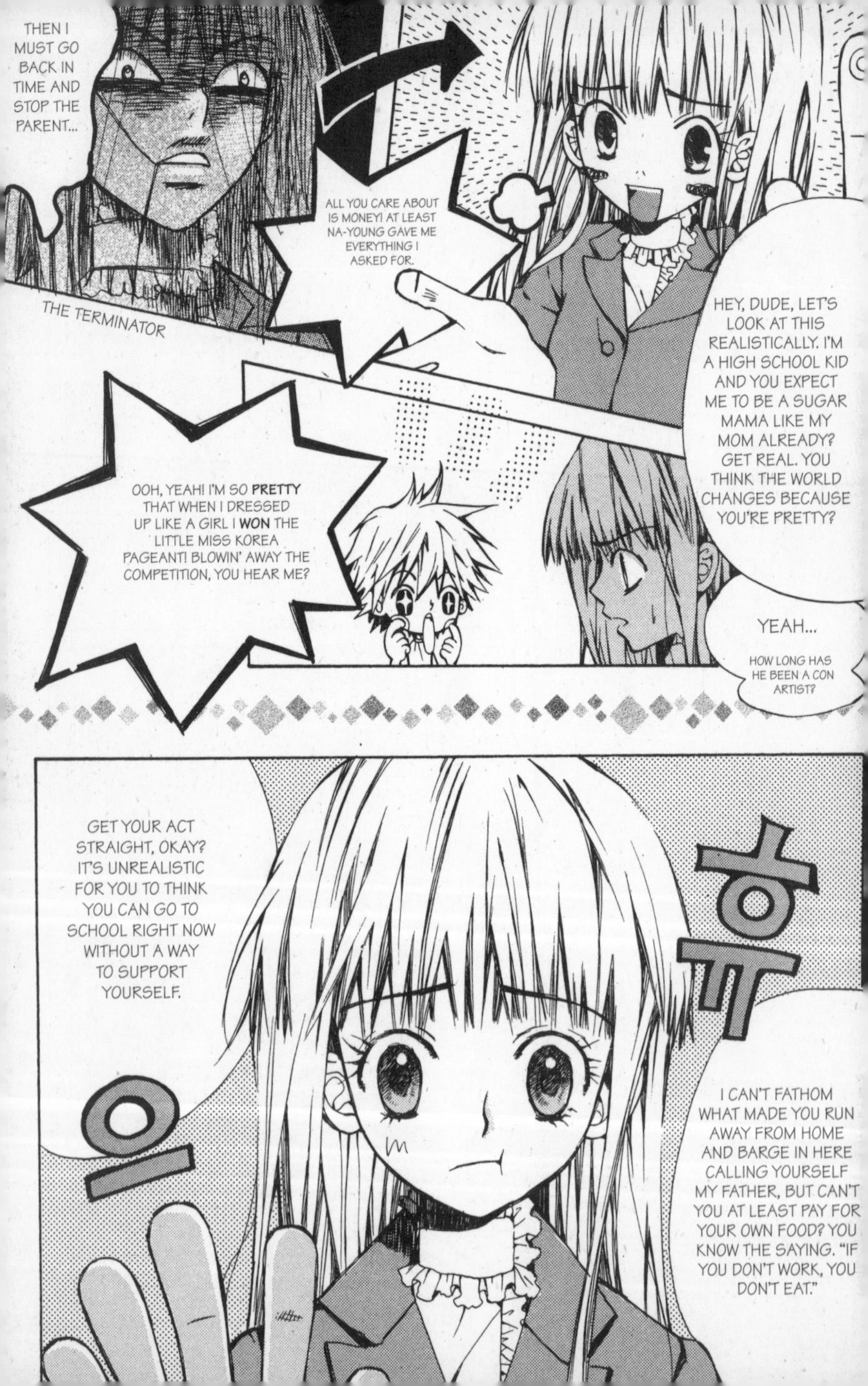
THEN I MUST GO BACK IN TIME AND STOP THE PARENT...
THE TERMINATOR
ALL YOU CARE ABOUT IS MONEY! AT LEAST NA-YOUNG GAVE ME EVERYTHING I ASKED FOR.
HEY, DUDE, LET'S LOOK AT THIS REALISTICALLY. I'M A HIGH SCHOOL KID AND YOU EXPECT ME TO BE A SUGAR MAMA LIKE MY MOM ALREADY? GET REAL. YOU THINK THE WORLD CHANGES BECAUSE YOU'RE PRETTY?
OOH, YEAH! I'M SO **PRETTY** THAT WHEN I DRESSED UP LIKE A GIRL I **WON** THE LITTLE MISS KOREA PAGEANT! BLOWIN' AWAY THE COMPETITION, YOU HEAR ME?
YEAH...
HOW LONG HAS HE BEEN A CON ARTIST?
GET YOUR ACT STRAIGHT, OKAY? IT'S UNREALISTIC FOR YOU TO THINK YOU CAN GO TO SCHOOL RIGHT NOW WITHOUT A WAY TO SUPPORT YOURSELF.
I CAN'T FATHOM WHAT MADE YOU RUN AWAY FROM HOME AND BARGE IN HERE CALLING YOURSELF MY FATHER, BUT CAN'T YOU AT LEAST PAY FOR YOUR OWN FOOD? YOU KNOW THE SAYING. "IF YOU DON'T WORK, YOU DON'T EAT."

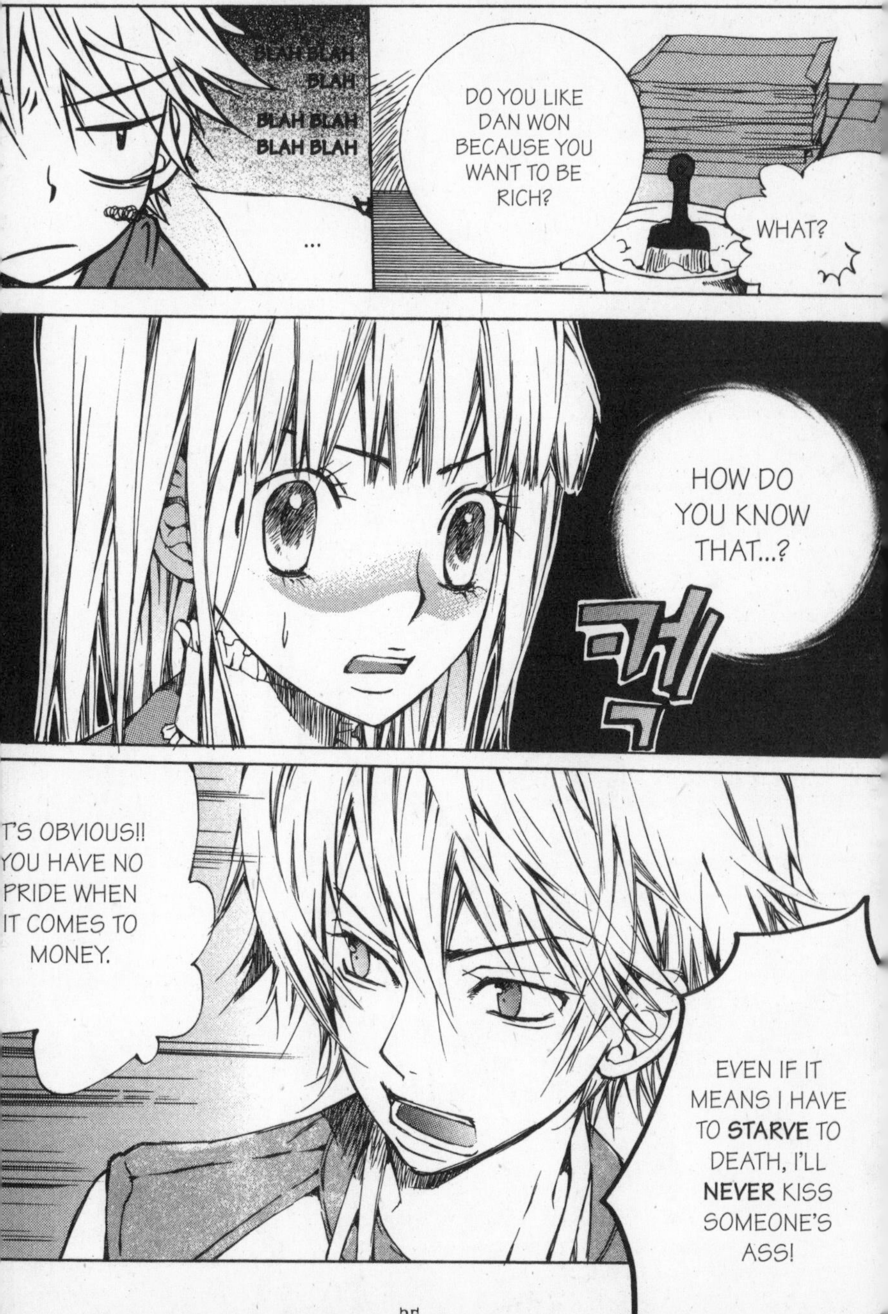

BLAH BLAH BLAH
BLAH BLAH BLAH BLAH
...
DO YOU LIKE DAN WON BECAUSE YOU WANT TO BE RICH?
WHAT?
HOW DO YOU KNOW THAT...?
T'S OBVIOUS!! YOU HAVE NO PRIDE WHEN IT COMES TO MONEY.
EVEN IF IT MEANS I HAVE TO **STARVE** TO DEATH, I'LL **NEVER** KISS SOMEONE'S ASS!

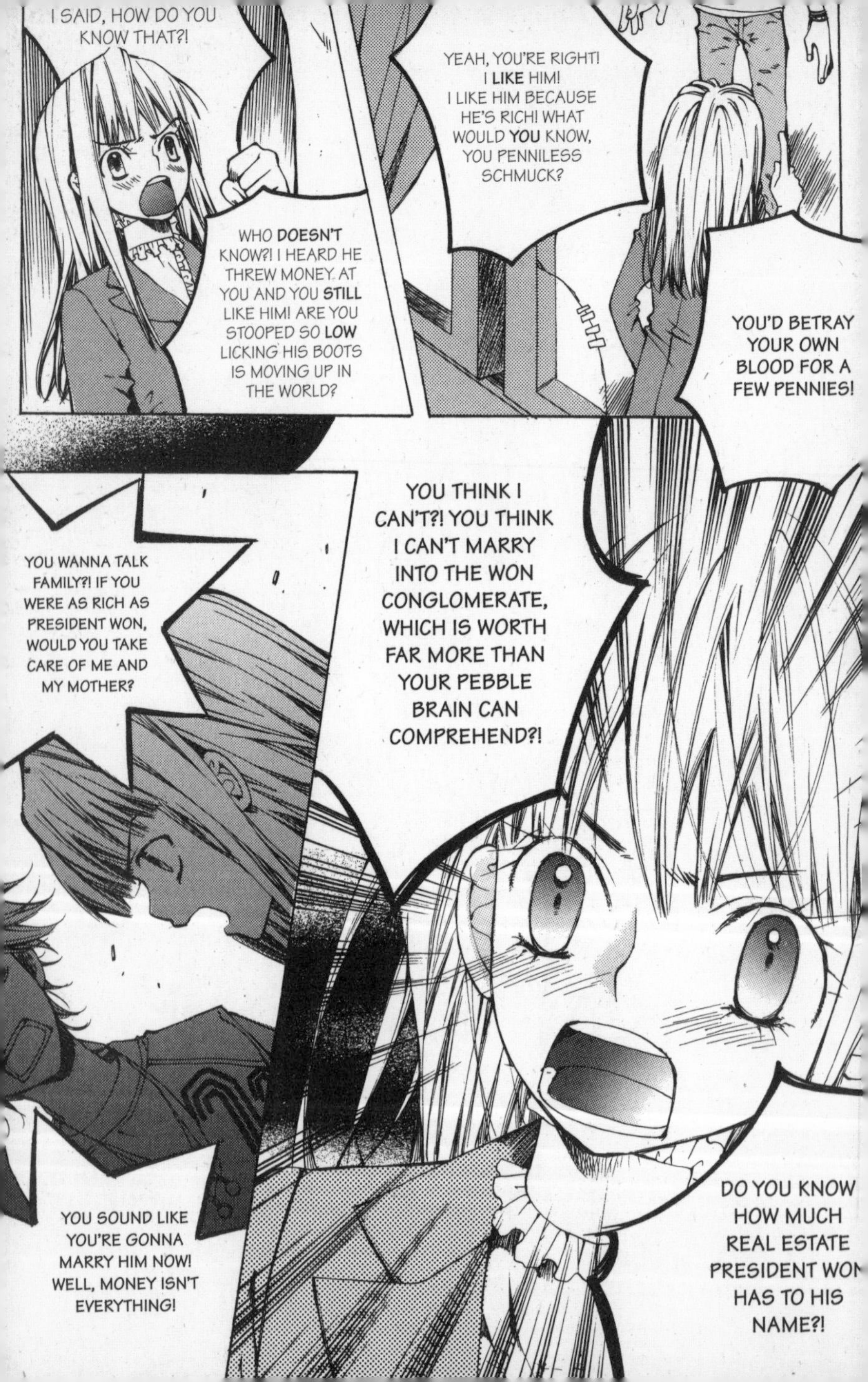
I SAID, HOW DO YOU KNOW THAT?!
WHO DOESN'T KNOW?! I HEARD HE THREW MONEY AT YOU AND YOU STILL LIKE HIM! ARE YOU STOOPED SO LOW LICKING HIS BOOTS IS MOVING UP IN THE WORLD?
YEAH, YOU'RE RIGHT! I LIKE HIM! I LIKE HIM BECAUSE HE'S RICH! WHAT WOULD YOU KNOW, YOU PENNILESS SCHMUCK?
YOU'D BETRAY YOUR OWN BLOOD FOR A FEW PENNIES!
YOU WANNA TALK FAMILY?! IF YOU WERE AS RICH AS PRESIDENT WON, WOULD YOU TAKE CARE OF ME AND MY MOTHER?
YOU SOUND LIKE YOU'RE GONNA MARRY HIM NOW! WELL, MONEY ISN'T EVERYTHING!
YOU THINK I CAN'T?! YOU THINK I CAN'T MARRY INTO THE WON CONGLOMERATE, WHICH IS WORTH FAR MORE THAN YOUR PEBBLE BRAIN CAN COMPREHEND?!
DO YOU KNOW HOW MUCH REAL ESTATE PRESIDENT WON HAS TO HIS NAME?!

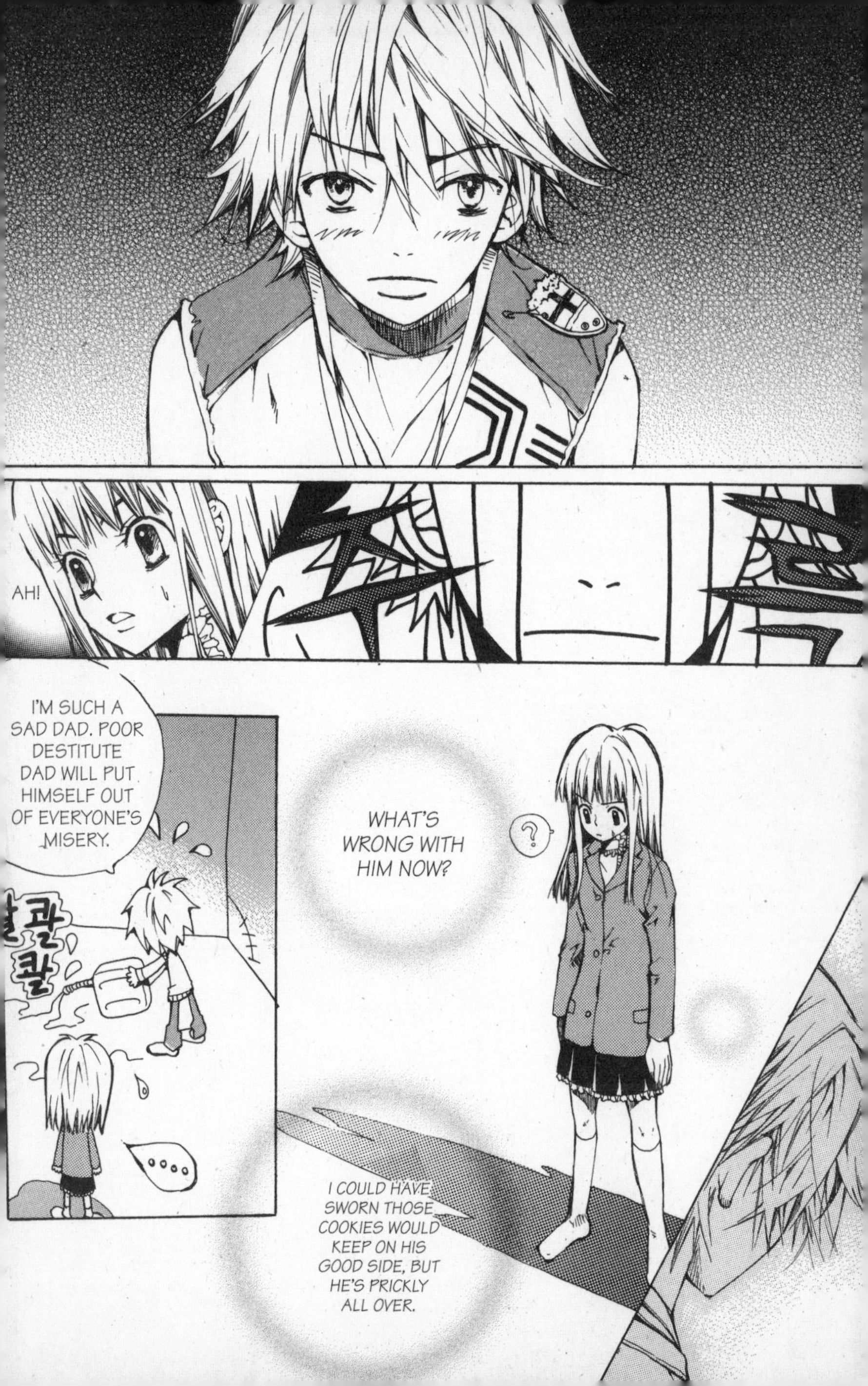
AH!
I'M SUCH A SAD DAD. POOR DESTITUTE DAD WILL PUT HIMSELF OUT OF EVERYONE'S MISERY.
콸콸
....
WHAT'S WRONG WITH HIM NOW?
?
I COULD HAVE SWORN THOSE COOKIES WOULD KEEP ON HIS GOOD SIDE, BUT HE'S PRICKLY ALL OVER.

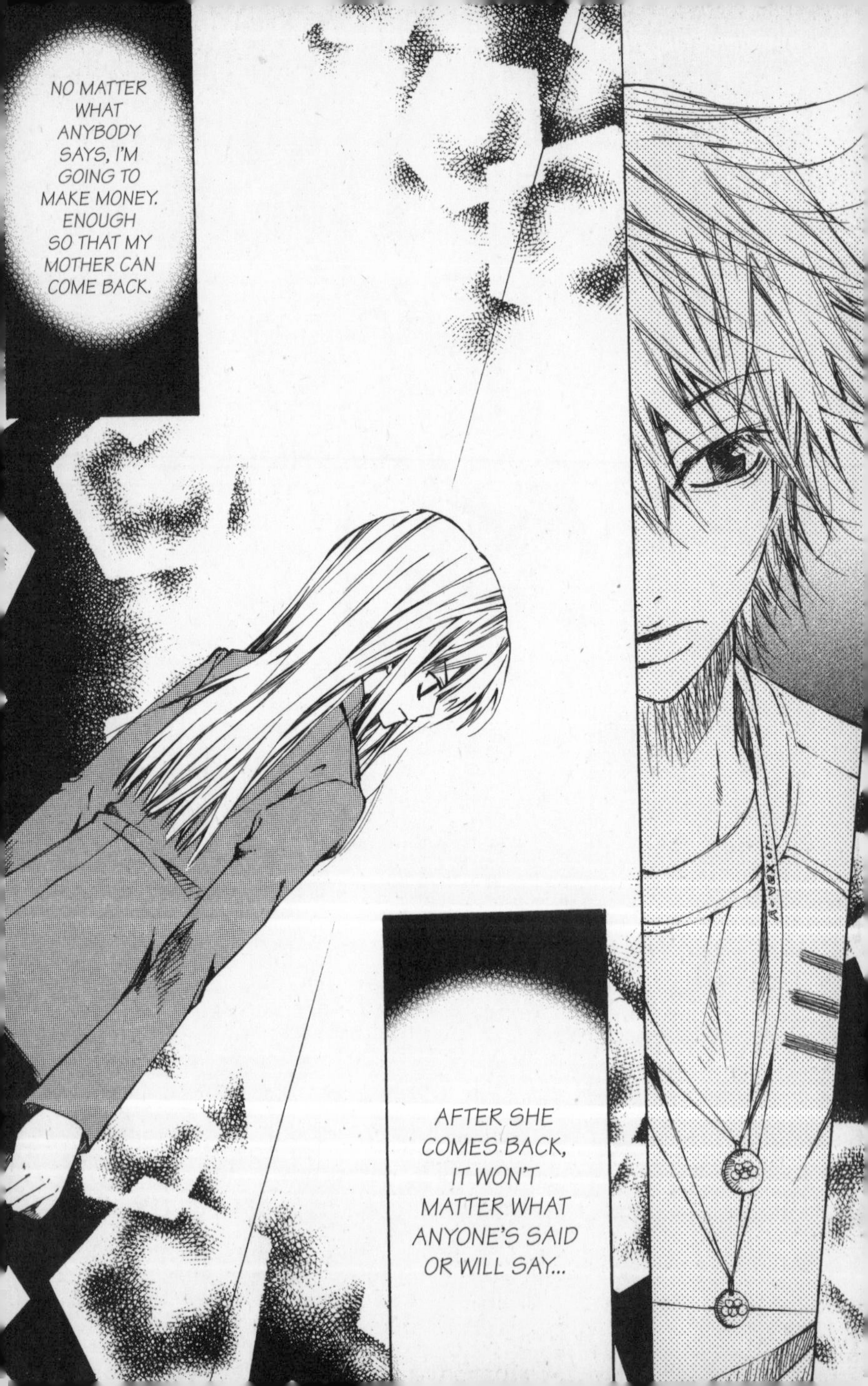
NO MATTER WHAT ANYBODY SAYS, I'M GOING TO MAKE MONEY. ENOUGH SO THAT MY MOTHER CAN COME BACK.
AFTER SHE COMES BACK, IT WON'T MATTER WHAT ANYONE'S SAID OR WILL SAY...

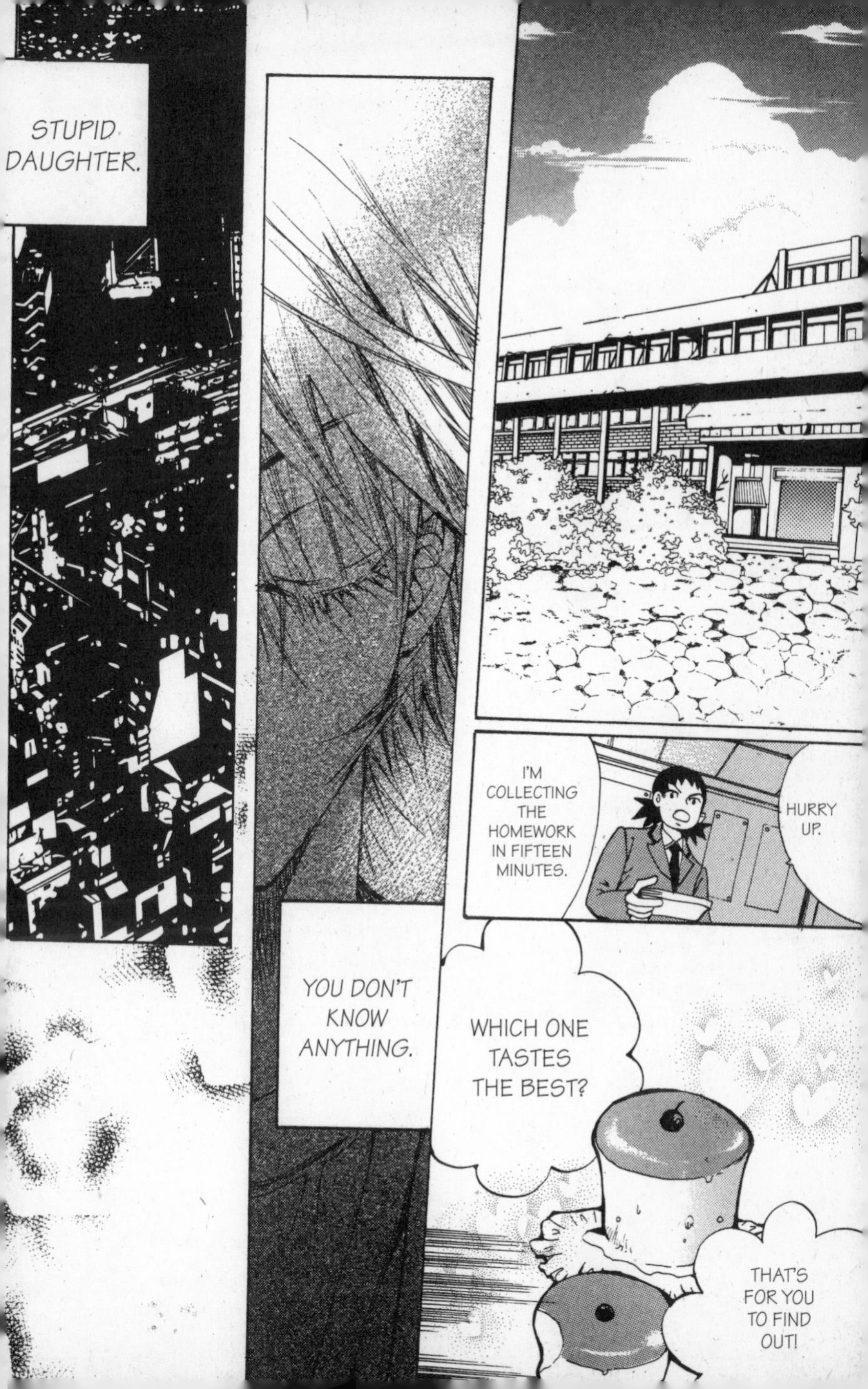
STUPID DAUGHTER.
YOU DON'T KNOW ANYTHING.
I'M COLLECTING THE HOMEWORK IN FIFTEEN MINUTES.
HURRY UP.
WHICH ONE TASTES THE BEST?
THAT'S FOR YOU TO FIND OUT!

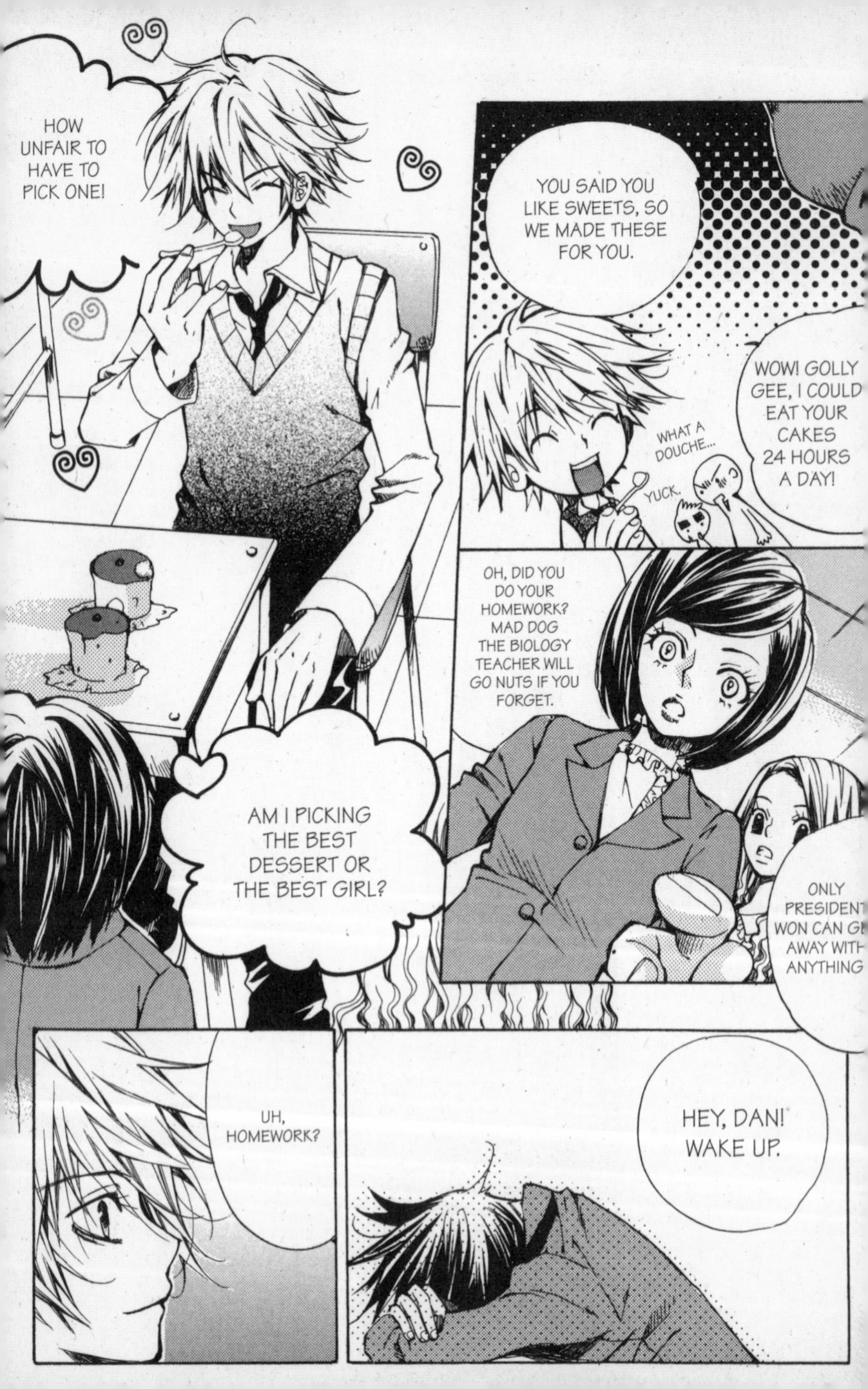
HOW UNFAIR TO HAVE TO PICK ONE!
AM I PICKING THE BEST DESSERT OR THE BEST GIRL?
YOU SAID YOU LIKE SWEETS, SO WE MADE THESE FOR YOU.
WOW! GOLLY GEE, I COULD EAT YOUR CAKES 24 HOURS A DAY!
WHAT A DOUCHE...
YUCK.
OH, DID YOU DO YOUR HOMEWORK? MAD DOG THE BIOLOGY TEACHER WILL GO NUTS IF YOU FORGET.
ONLY PRESIDENT WON CAN G AWAY WITH ANYTHING
UH, HOMEWORK?
HEY, DAN! WAKE UP.

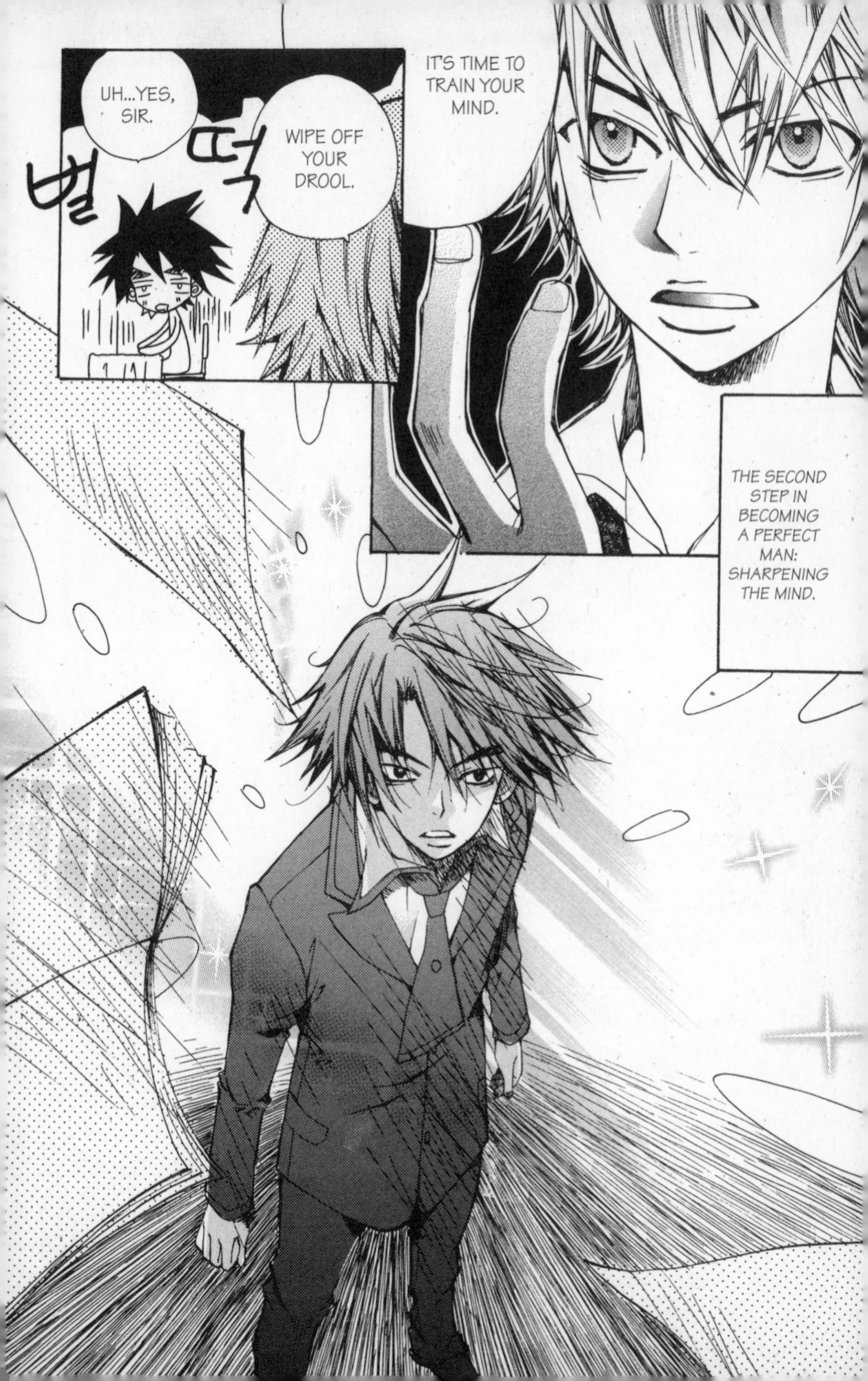
UH...YES, SIR.
벌떡
WIPE OFF YOUR DROOL.
IT'S TIME TO TRAIN YOUR MIND.
THE SECOND STEP IN BECOMING A PERFECT MAN: SHARPENING THE MIND.

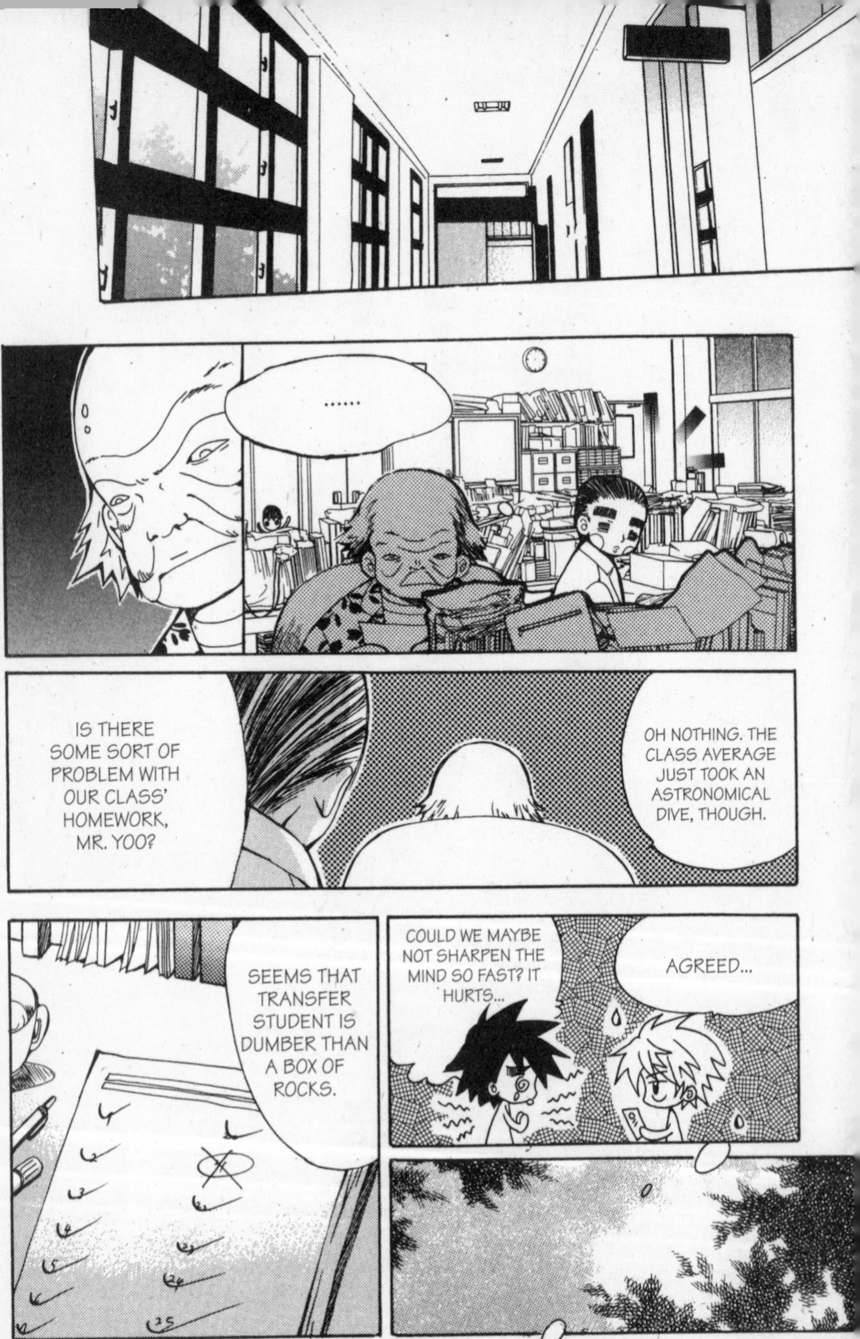
......
IS THERE SOME SORT OF PROBLEM WITH OUR CLASS' HOMEWORK, MR. YOO?
OH NOTHING. THE CLASS AVERAGE JUST TOOK AN ASTRONOMICAL DIVE, THOUGH.
SEEMS THAT TRANSFER STUDENT IS DUMBER THAN A BOX OF ROCKS.
COULD WE MAYBE NOT SHARPEN THE MIND SO FAST? IT HURTS...
AGREED...

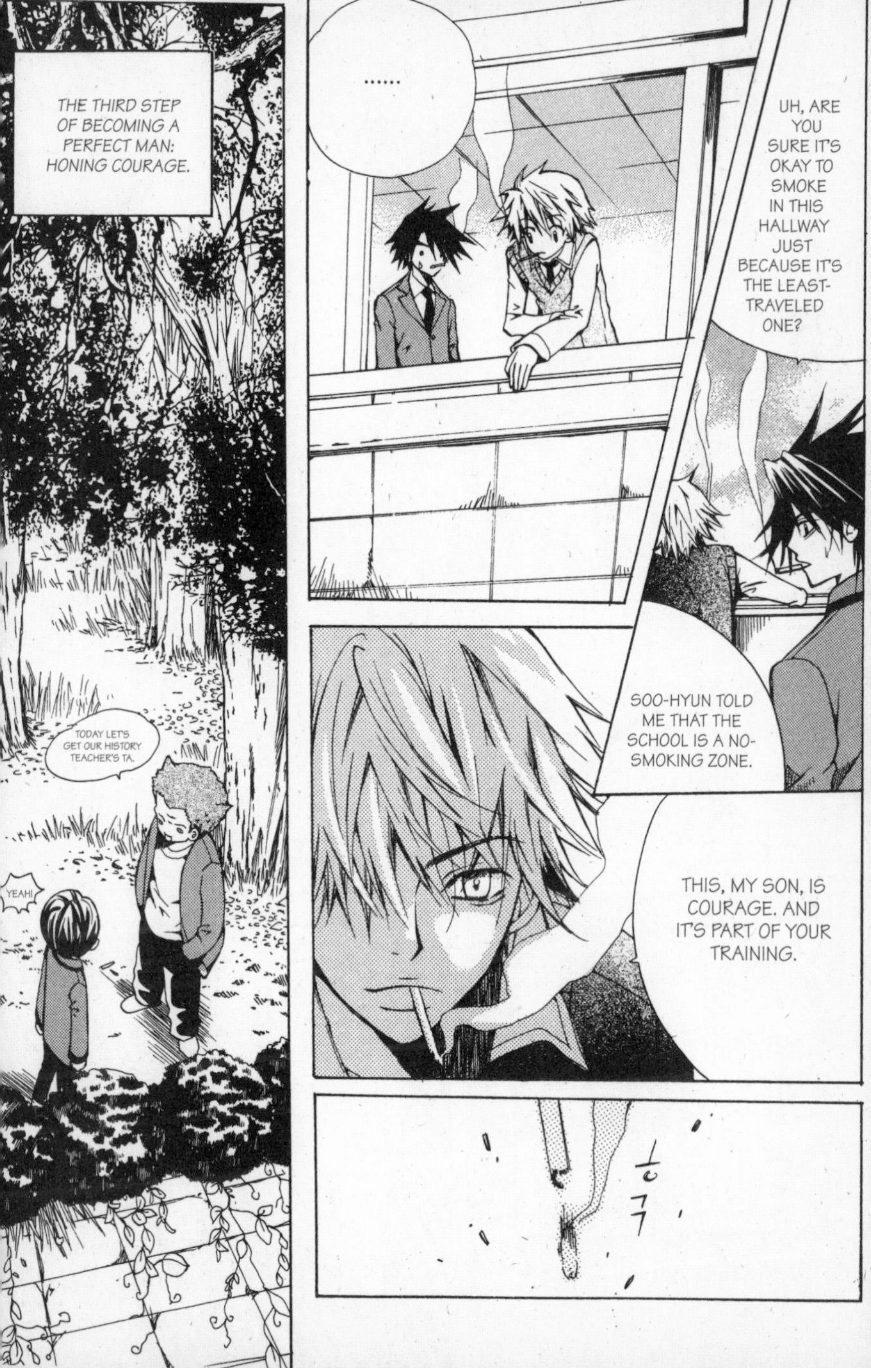
THE THIRD STEP OF BECOMING A PERFECT MAN: HONING COURAGE.
TODAY LET'S GET OUR HISTORY TEACHER'S TA.
YEAH!
......
UH, ARE YOU SURE IT'S OKAY TO SMOKE IN THIS HALLWAY JUST BECAUSE IT'S THE LEAST-TRAVELED ONE?
SOO-HYUN TOLD ME THAT THE SCHOOL IS A NO-SMOKING ZONE.
THIS, MY SON, IS COURAGE. AND IT'S PART OF YOUR TRAINING.

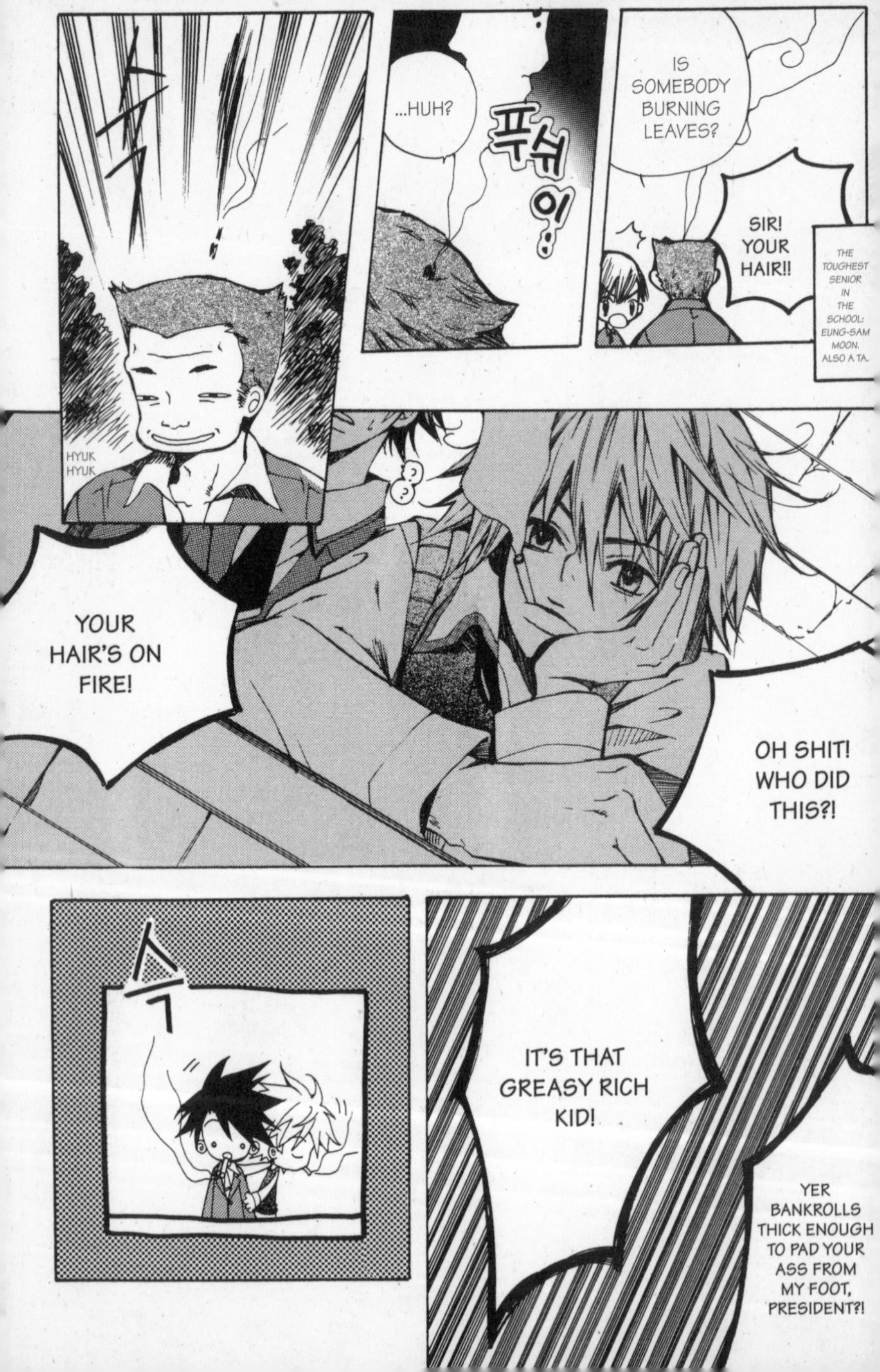
HYUK HYUK
...HUH?
푸쉬이
IS SOMEBODY BURNING LEAVES?
SIR! YOUR HAIR!!
THE TOUGHEST SENIOR IN THE SCHOOL: EUNG-SAM MOON. ALSO A TA.
YOUR HAIR'S ON FIRE!
OH SHIT! WHO DID THIS?!
IT'S THAT GREASY RICH KID!
YER BANKROLLS THICK ENOUGH TO PAD YOUR ASS FROM MY FOOT, PRESIDENT?!

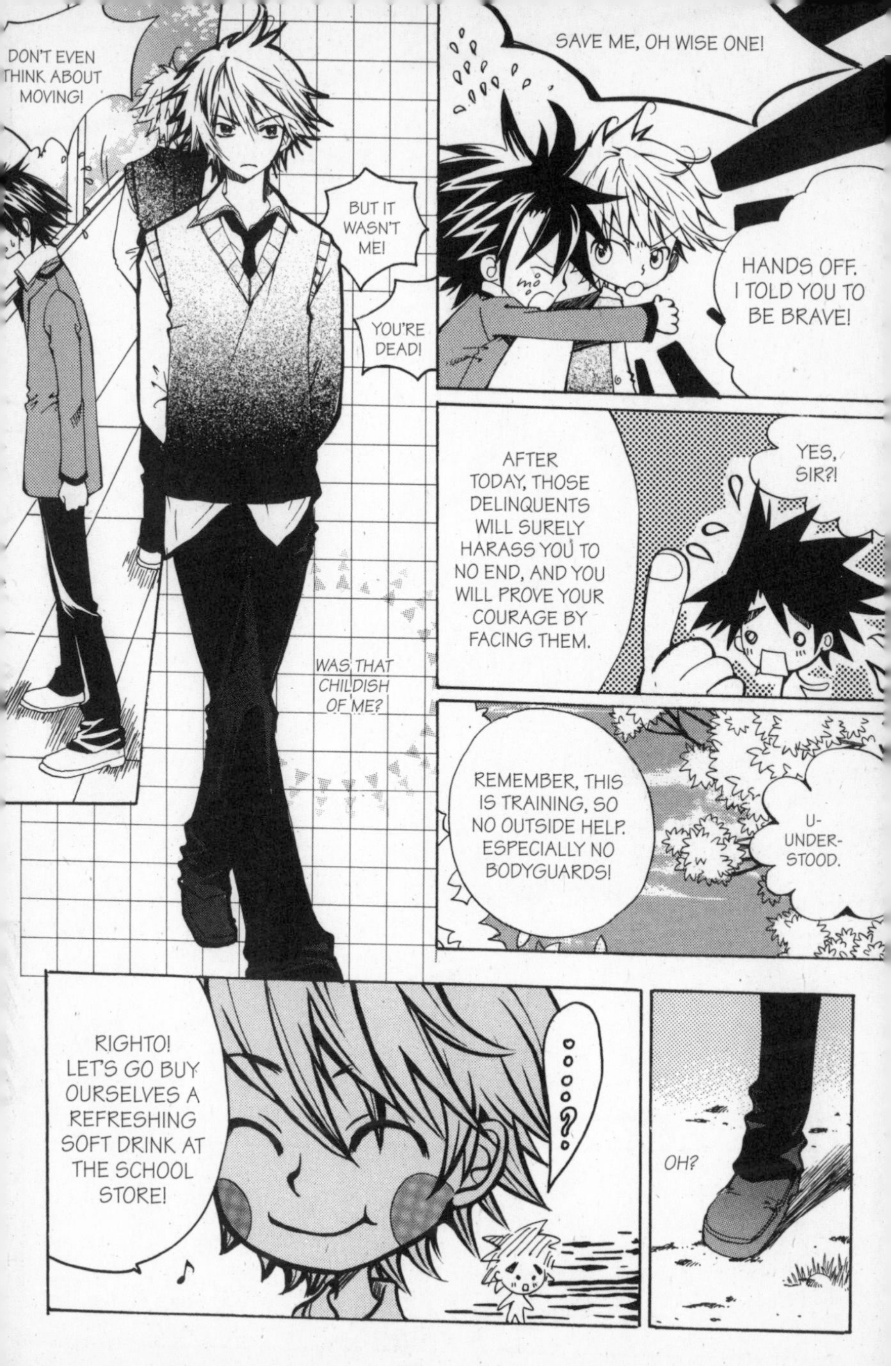
DON'T EVEN THINK ABOUT MOVING!
BUT IT WASN'T ME!
YOU'RE DEAD!
WAS THAT CHILDISH OF ME?
SAVE ME, OH WISE ONE!
HANDS OFF. I TOLD YOU TO BE BRAVE!
AFTER TODAY, THOSE DELINQUENTS WILL SURELY HARASS YOU TO NO END, AND YOU WILL PROVE YOUR COURAGE BY FACING THEM.
YES, SIR?!
REMEMBER, THIS IS TRAINING, SO NO OUTSIDE HELP. ESPECIALLY NO BODYGUARDS!
U-UNDERSTOOD.
RIGHTO! LET'S GO BUY OURSELVES A REFRESHING SOFT DRINK AT THE SCHOOL STORE!
....?
OH?

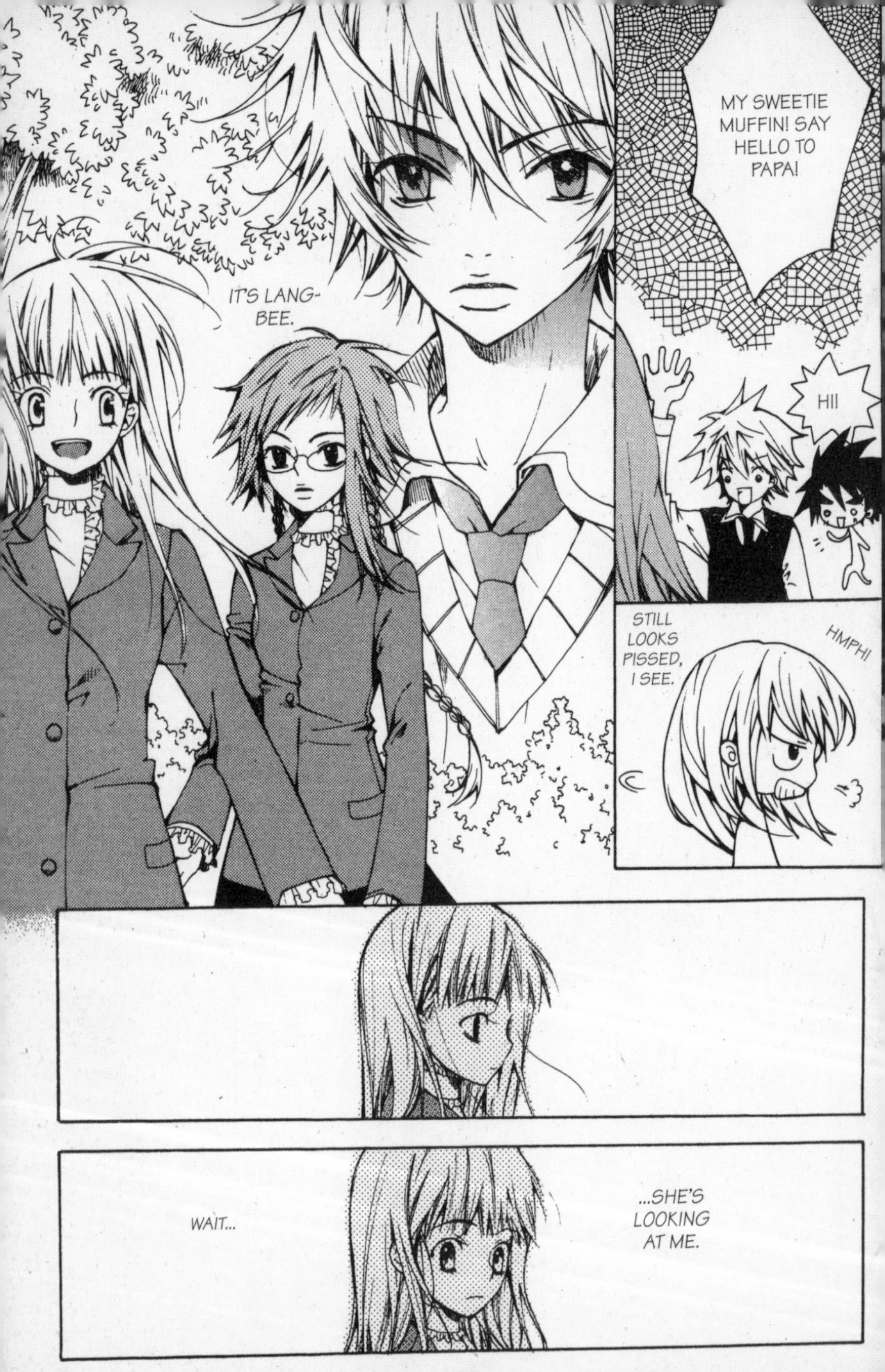
IT'S LANG-BEE.
MY SWEETIE MUFFIN! SAY HELLO TO PAPA!
HI!
STILL LOOKS PISSED, I SEE.
HMPH!
WAIT...
...SHE'S LOOKING AT ME.

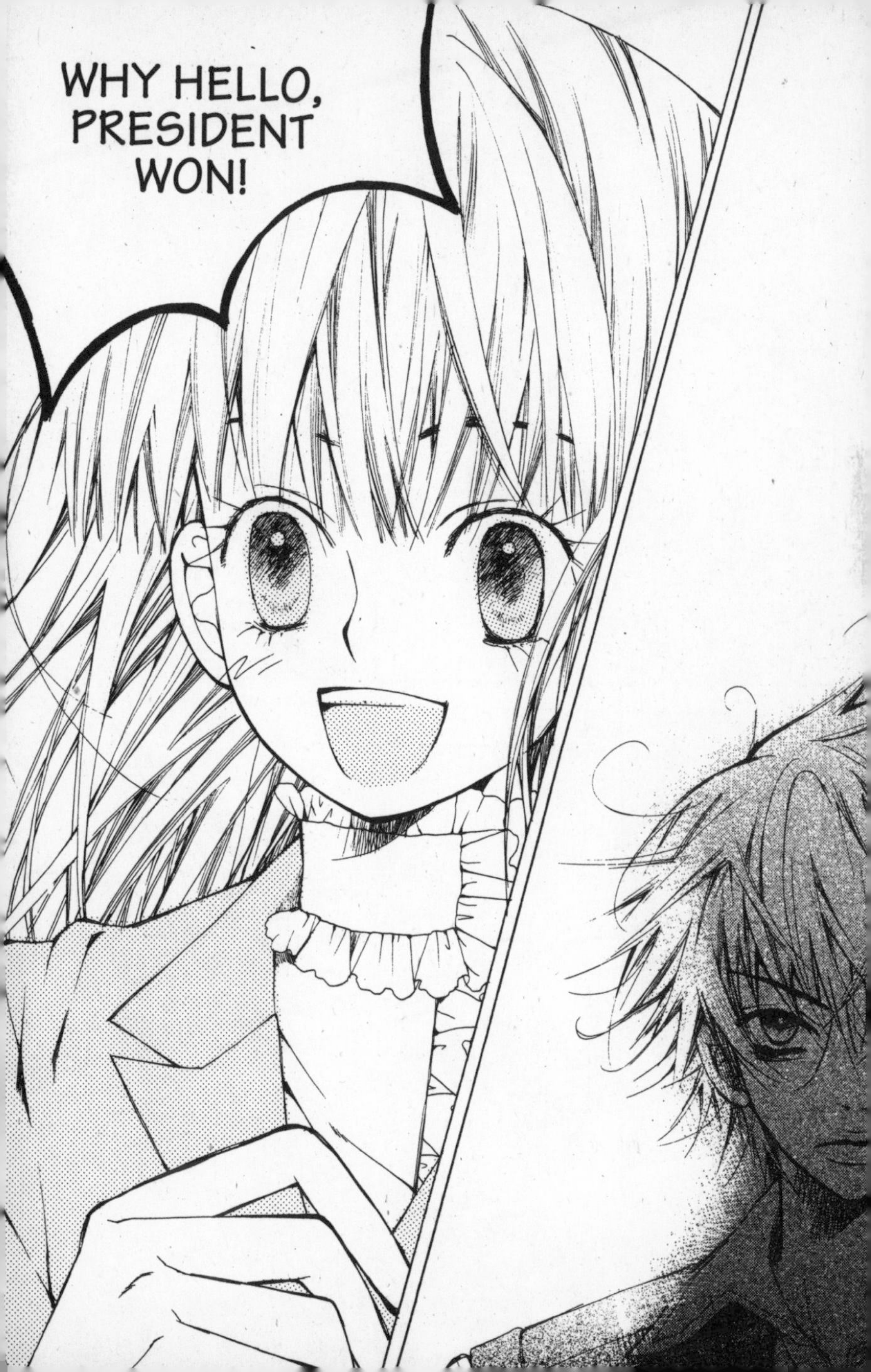
WHY HELLO, PRESIDENT WON!

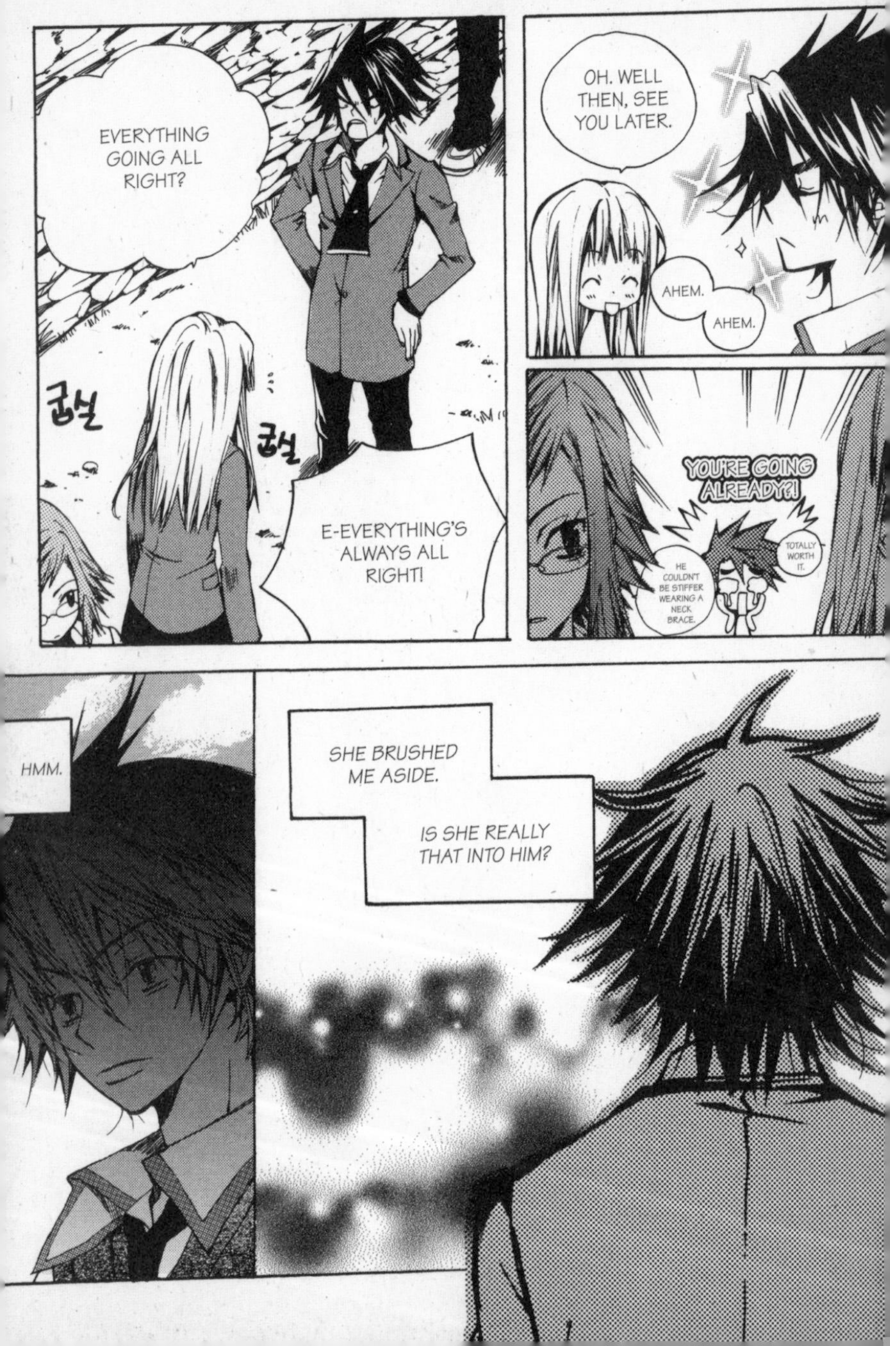
EVERYTHING GOING ALL RIGHT?
굽실
굽실
E-EVERYTHING'S ALWAYS ALL RIGHT!
OH. WELL THEN, SEE YOU LATER.
AHEM.
AHEM.
YOU'RE GOING ALREADY?!
HE COULDN'T BE STIFFER WEARING A NECK BRACE.
TOTALLY WORTH IT.
HMM.
SHE BRUSHED ME ASIDE.
IS SHE REALLY THAT INTO HIM?

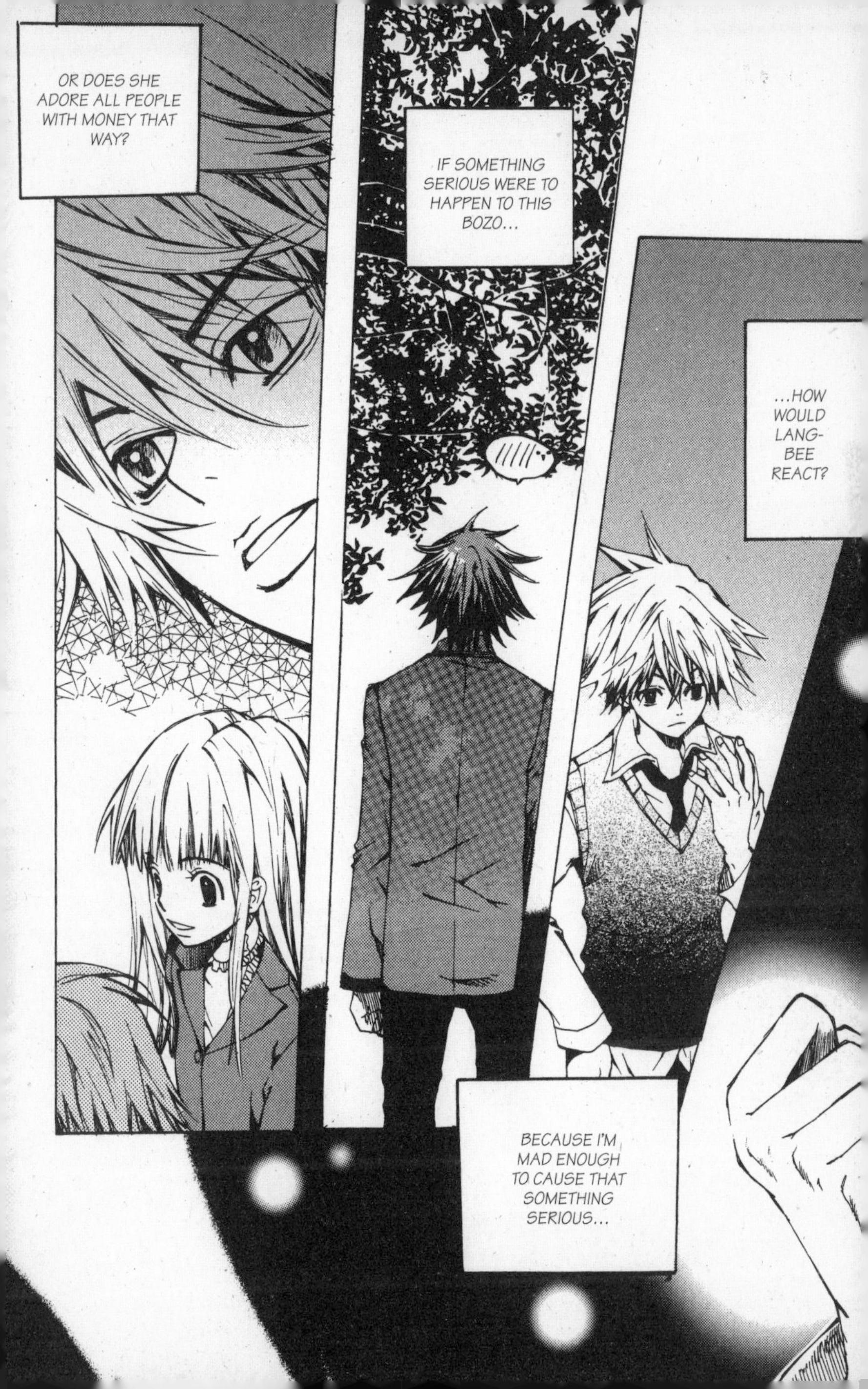
OR DOES SHE ADORE ALL PEOPLE WITH MONEY THAT WAY?
IF SOMETHING SERIOUS WERE TO HAPPEN TO THIS BOZO...
...HOW WOULD LANG-BEE REACT?
BECAUSE I'M MAD ENOUGH TO CAUSE THAT SOMETHING SERIOUS...

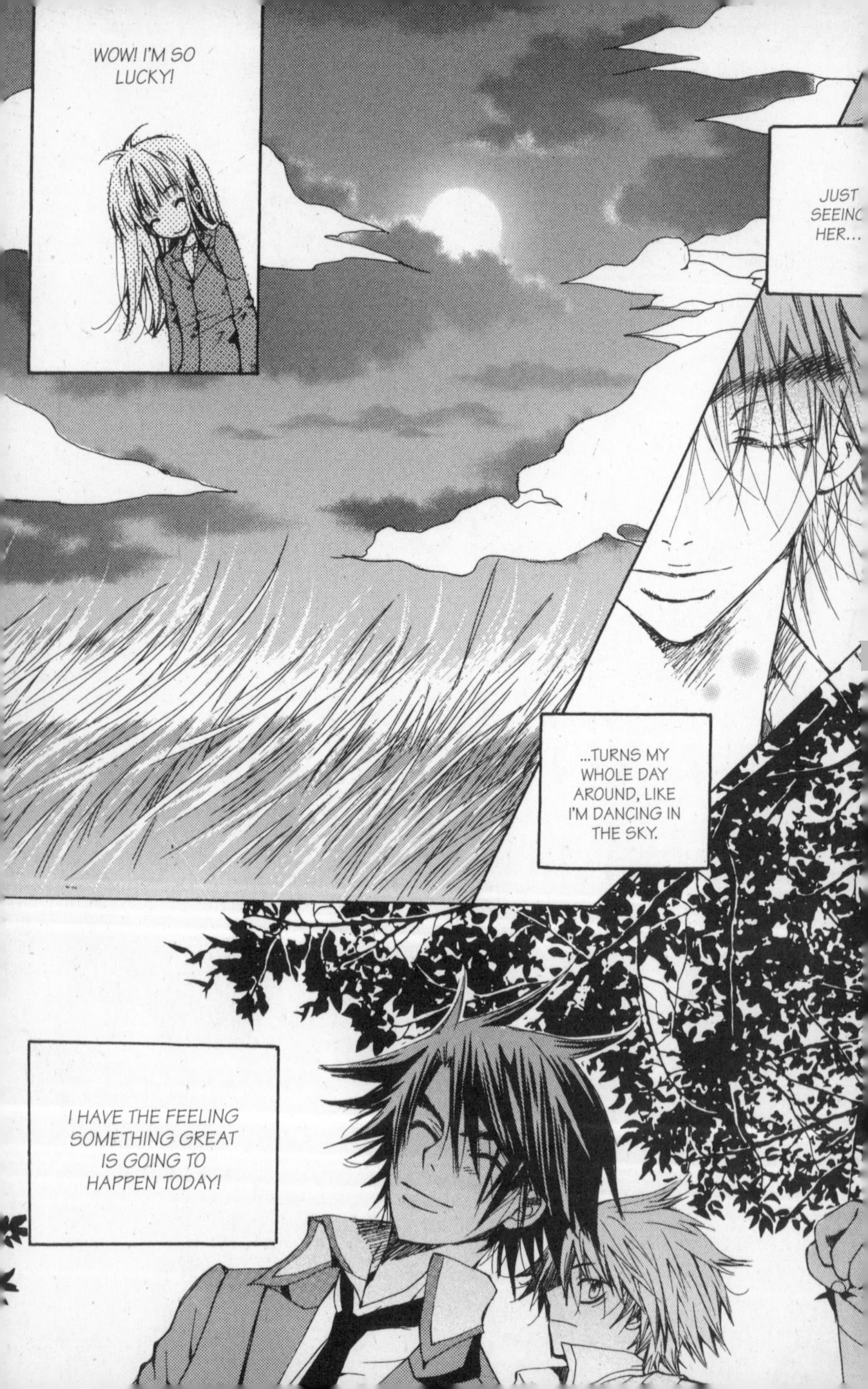
WOW! I'M SO LUCKY!
JUST SEEING HER...
...TURNS MY WHOLE DAY AROUND, LIKE I'M DANCING IN THE SKY.
I HAVE THE FEELING SOMETHING GREAT IS GOING TO HAPPEN TODAY!

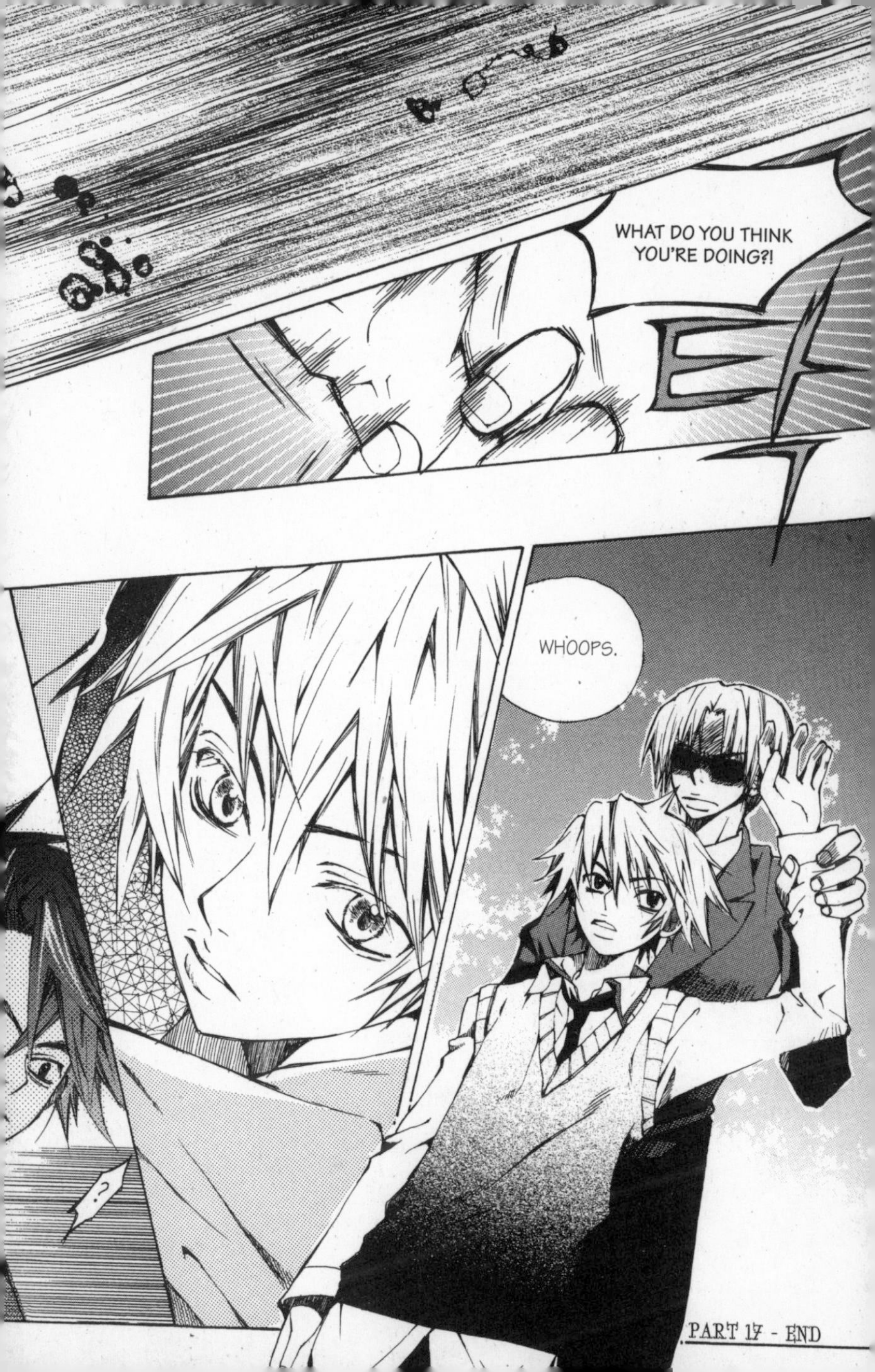
WHAT DO YOU THINK YOU'RE DOING?!
탁
WHOOPS.
?

PART 17 - END

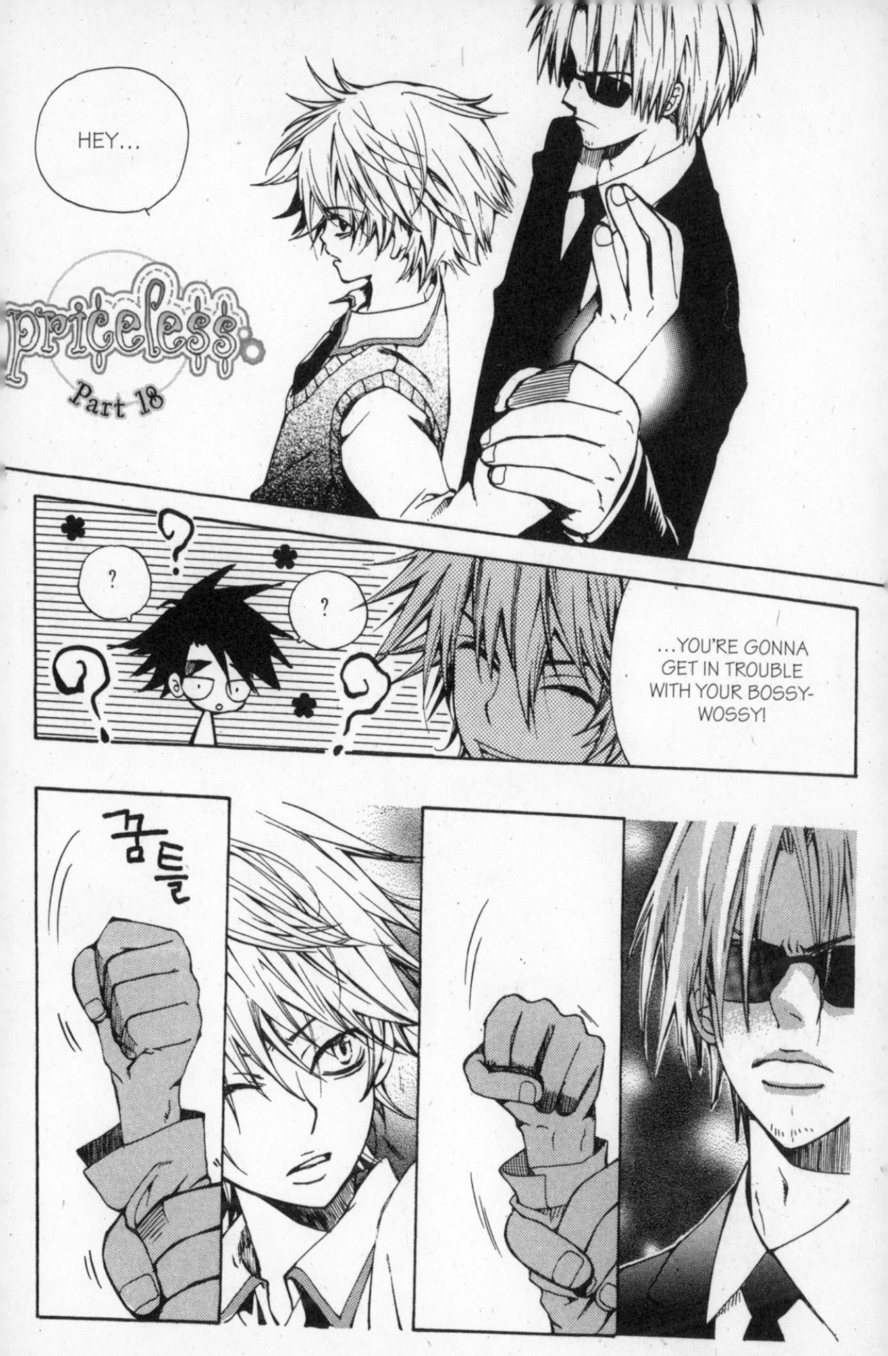
HEY...
priceless
Part 18
?
?
...YOU'RE GONNA GET IN TROUBLE WITH YOUR BOSSY-WOSSY!
꿈틀

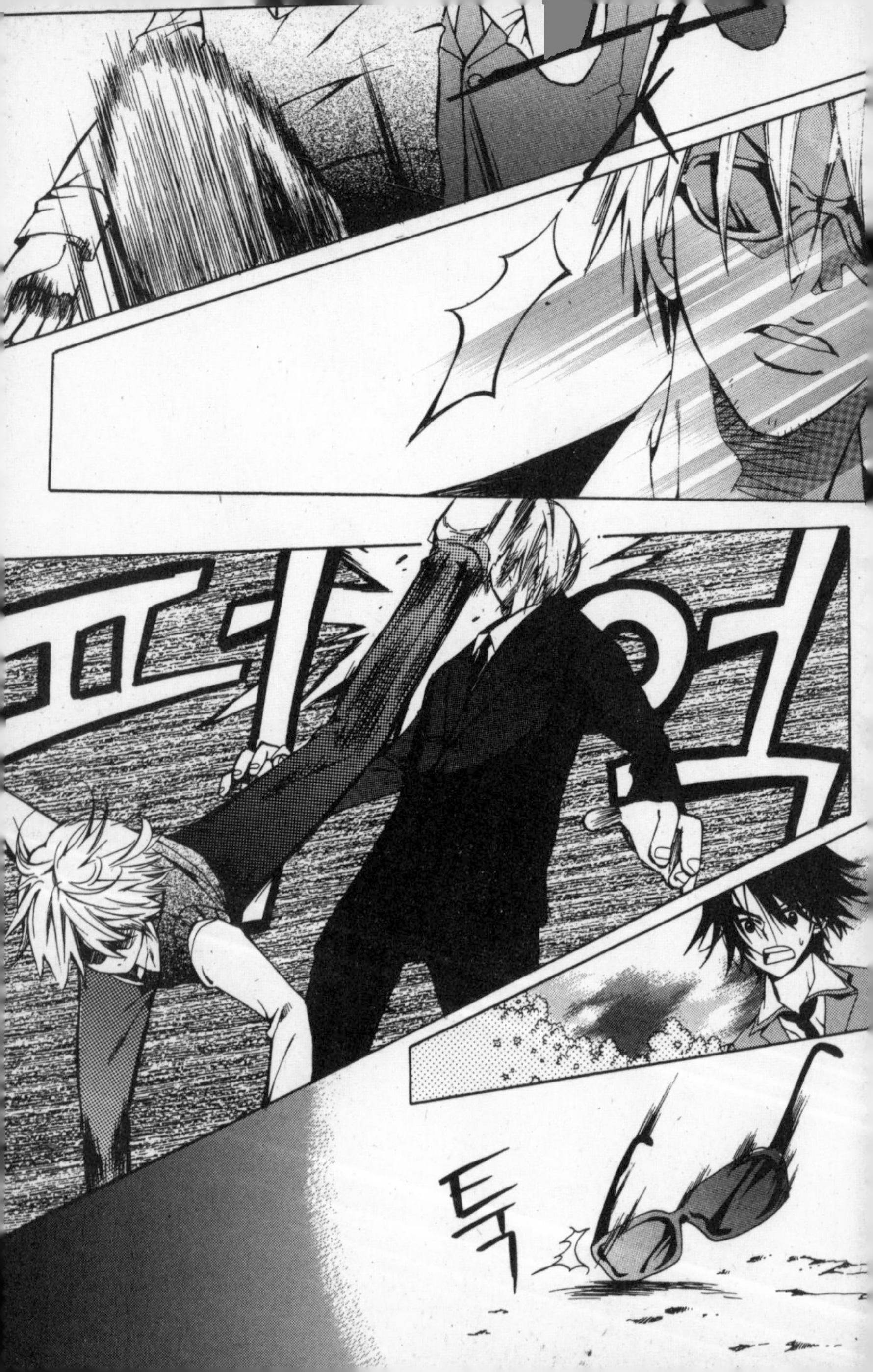
퍼억
툭

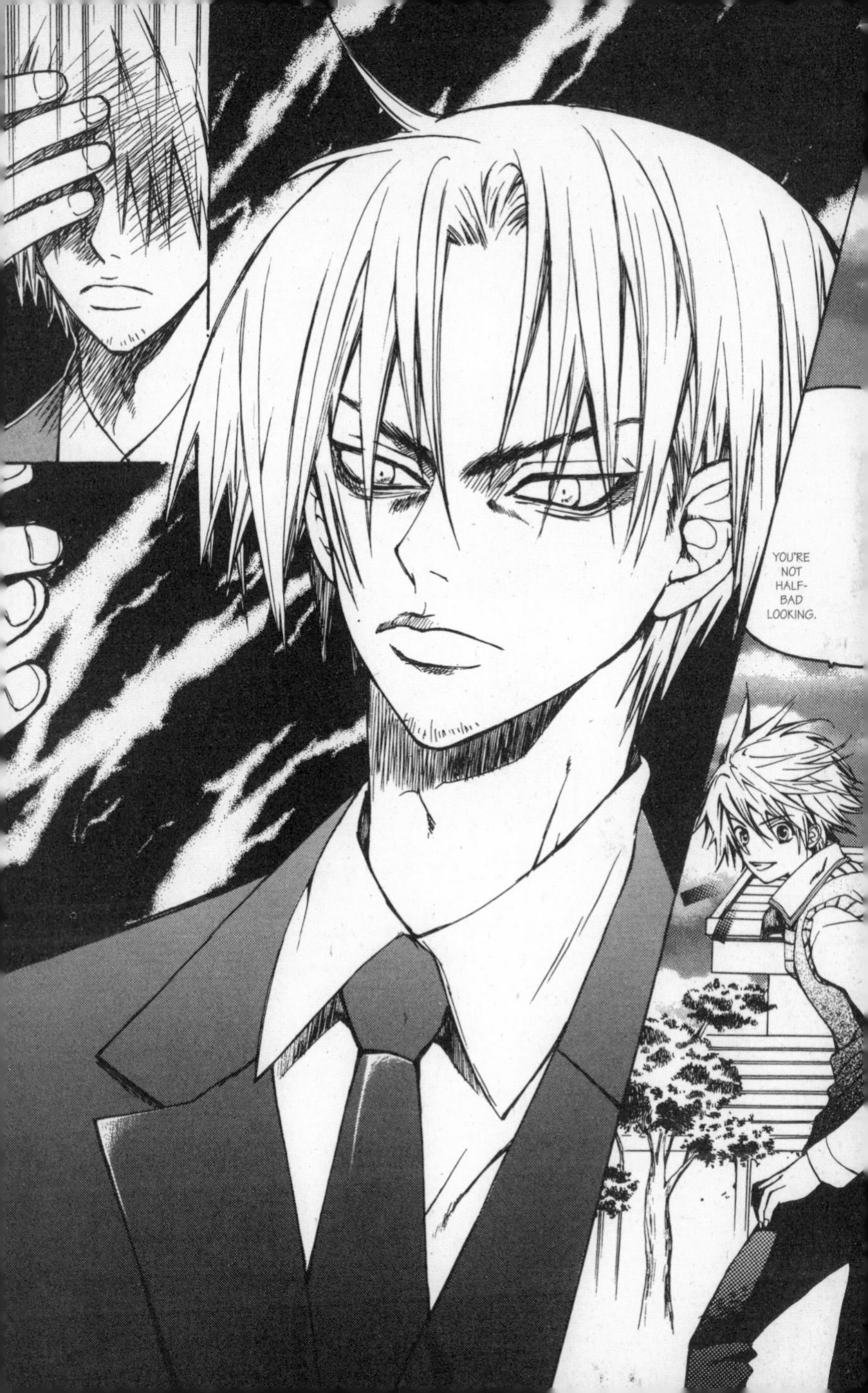
YOU'RE NOT HALF-BAD LOOKING.

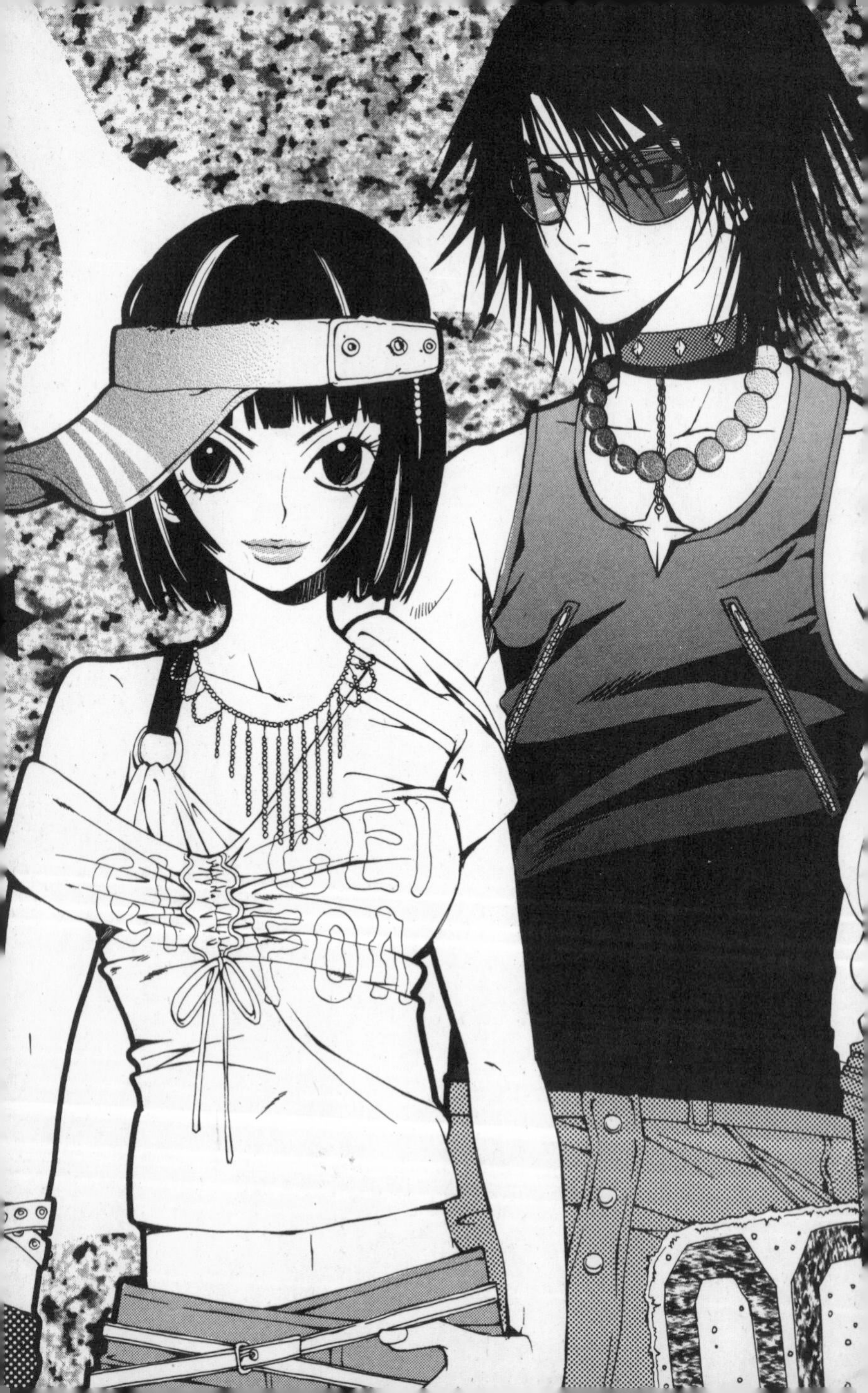

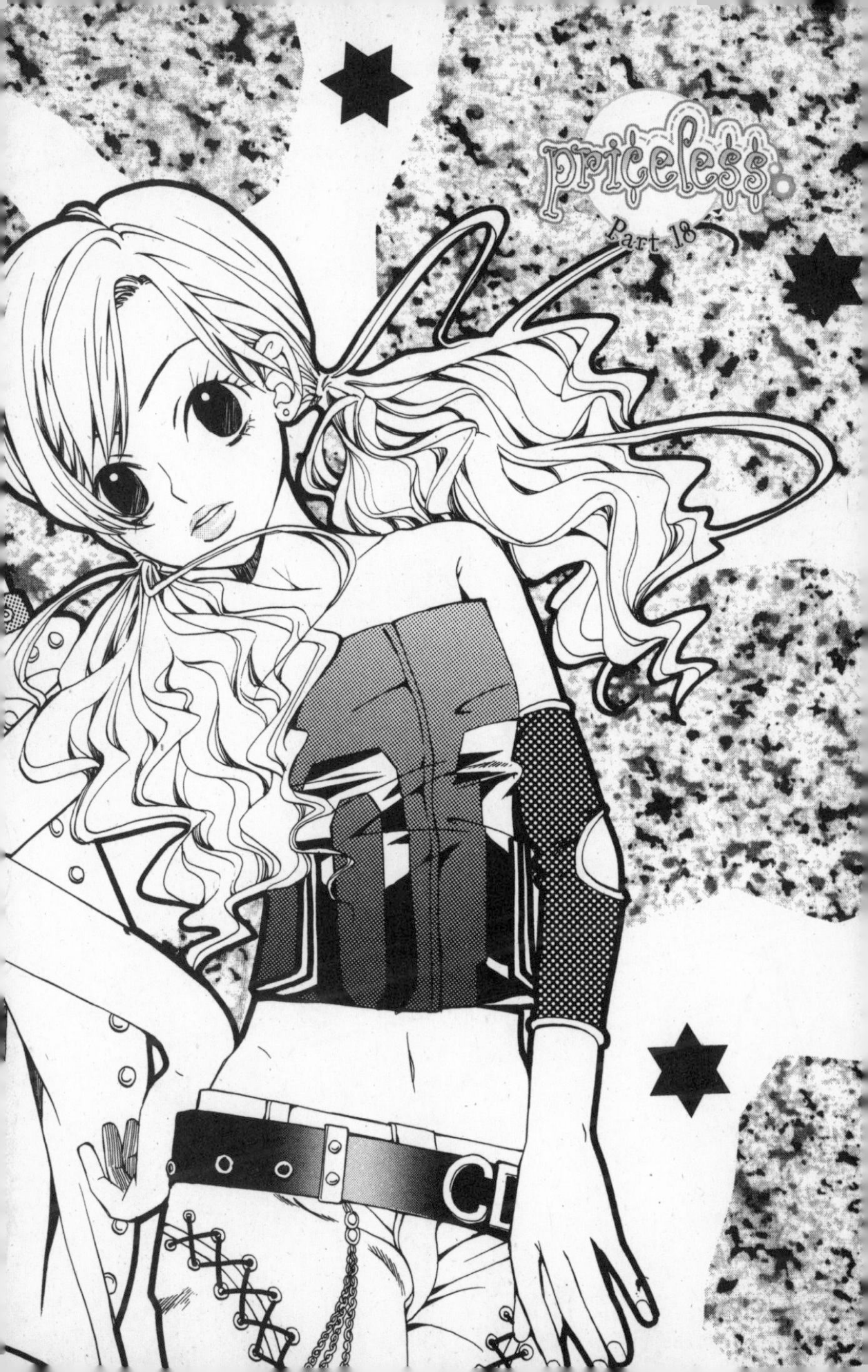
priceless
Part 18
CD

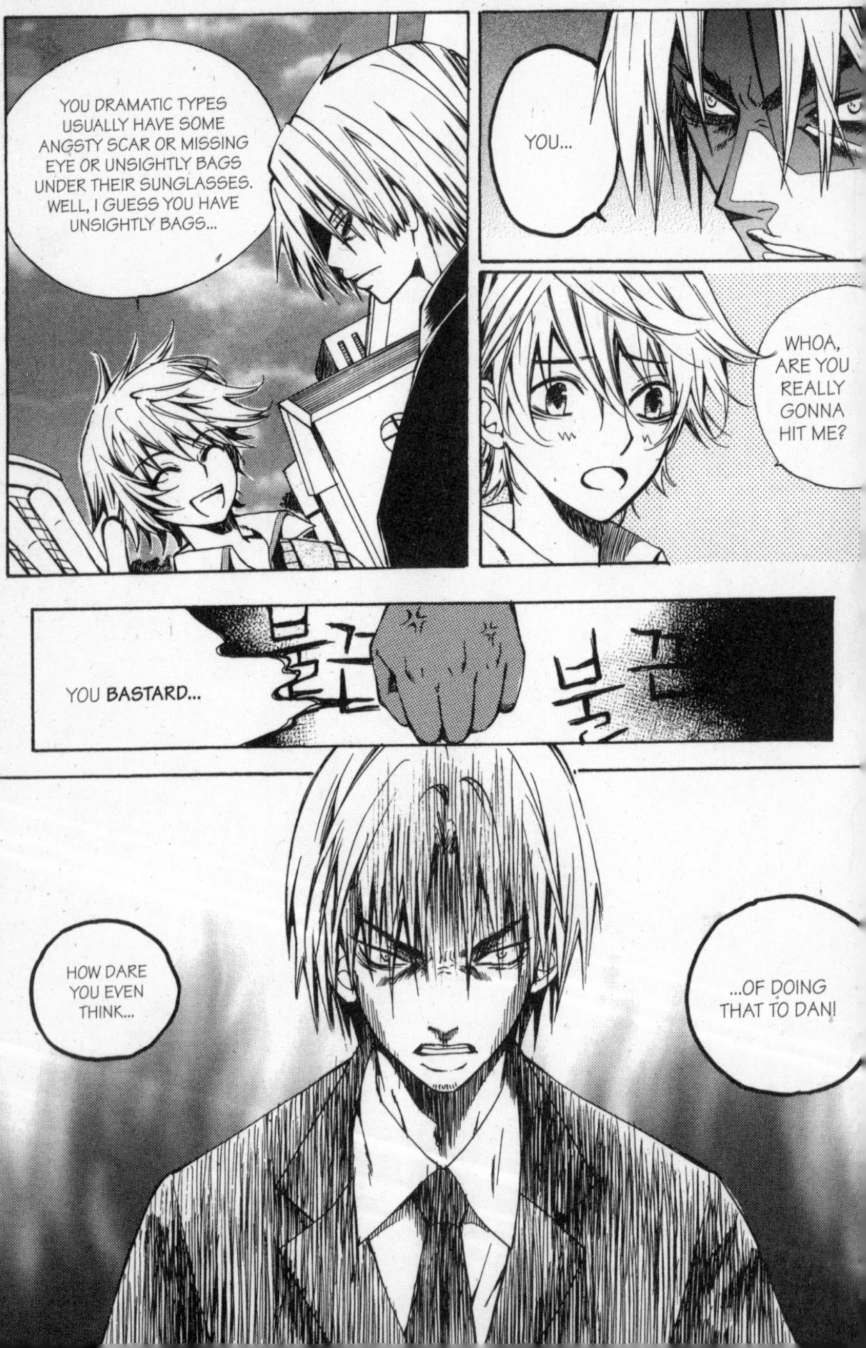
YOU DRAMATIC TYPES USUALLY HAVE SOME ANGSTY SCAR OR MISSING EYE OR UNSIGHTLY BAGS UNDER THEIR SUNGLASSES. WELL, I GUESS YOU HAVE UNSIGHTLY BAGS...
YOU...
WHOA, ARE YOU REALLY GONNA HIT ME?
YOU **BASTARD...**
HOW DARE YOU EVEN THINK...
...OF DOING THAT TO DAN!

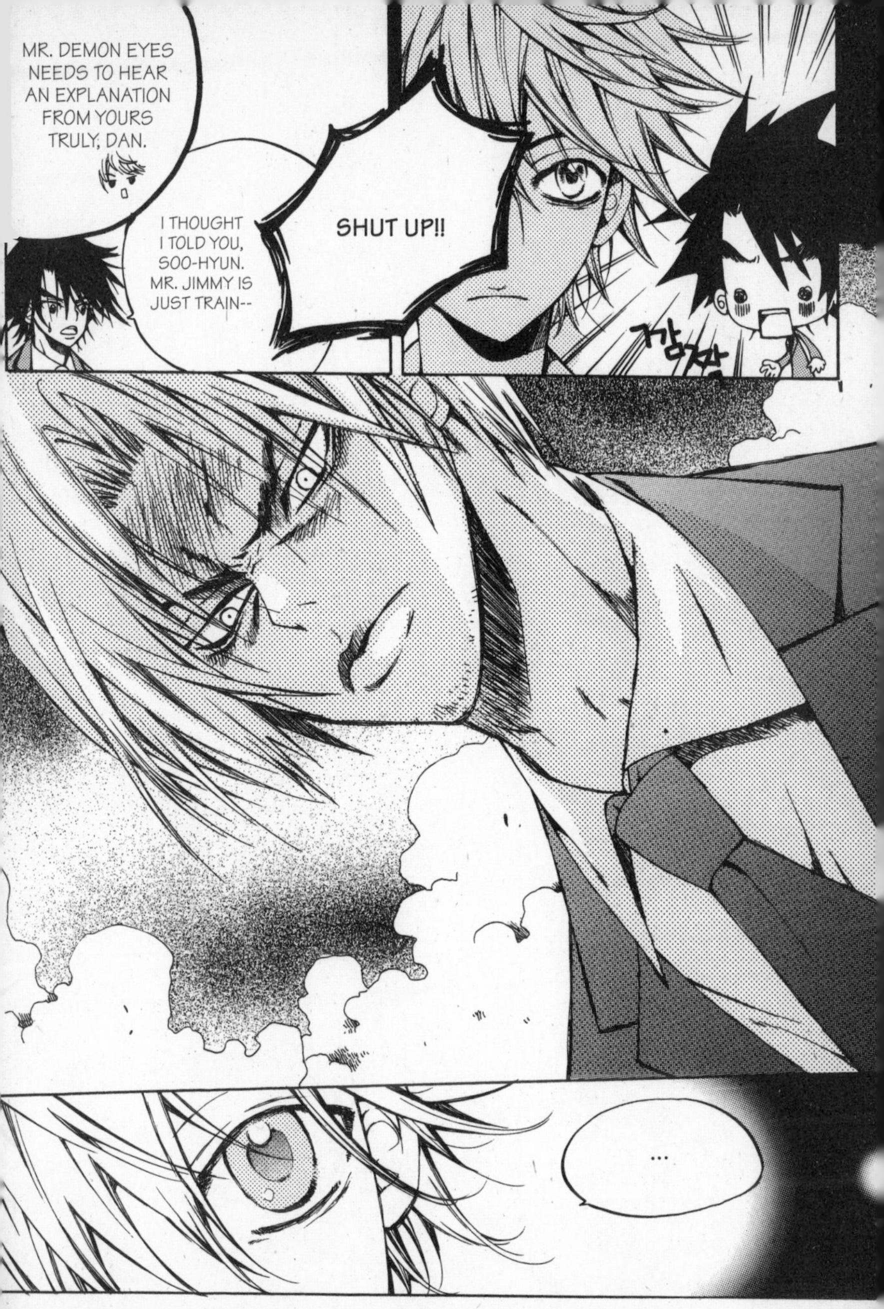
MR. DEMON EYES NEEDS TO HEAR AN EXPLANATION FROM YOURS TRULY, DAN.
I THOUGHT I TOLD YOU, SOO-HYUN. MR. JIMMY IS JUST TRAIN--
SHUT UP!!
...

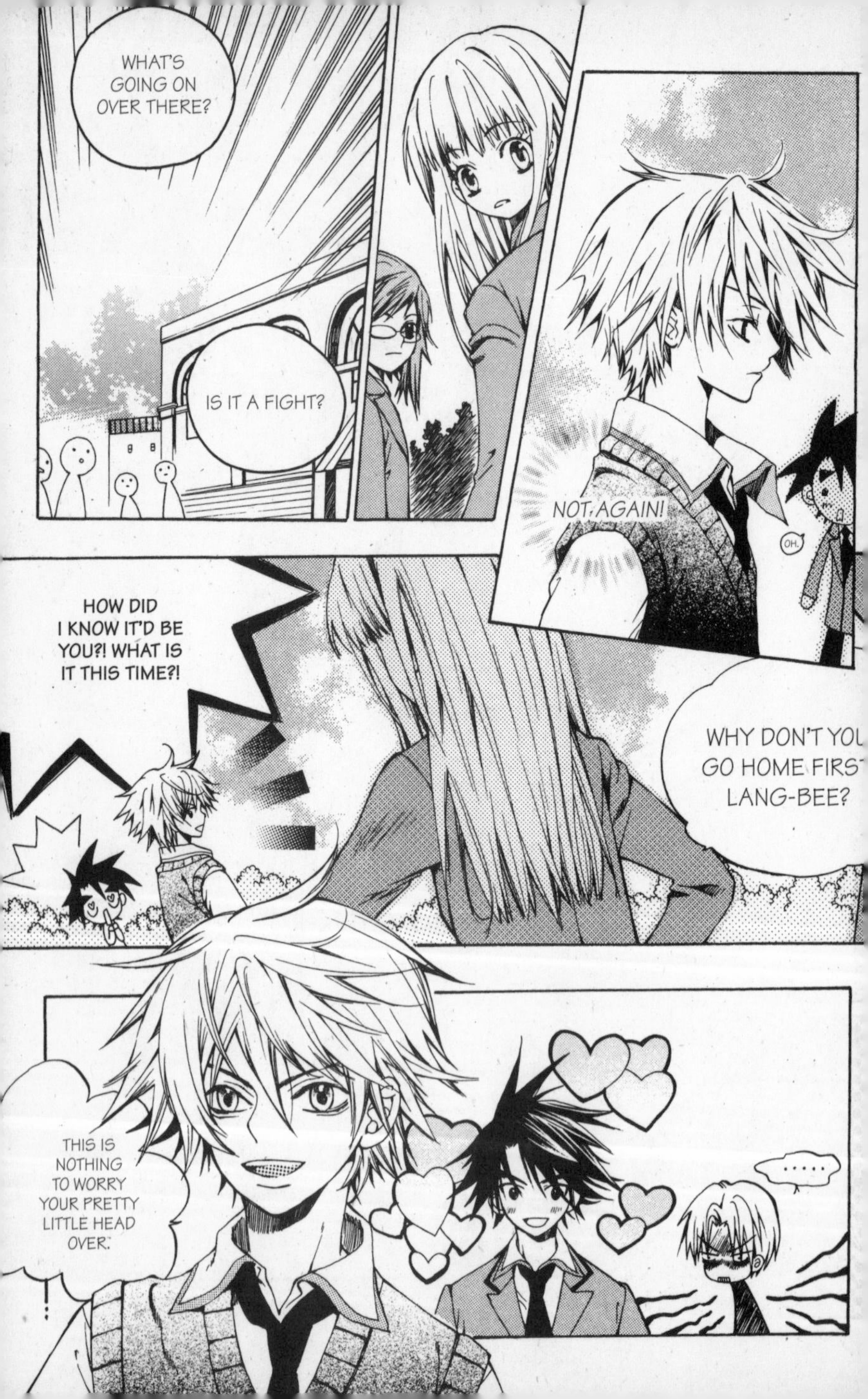
WHAT'S GOING ON OVER THERE?
IS IT A FIGHT?
NOT AGAIN!
OH.
HOW DID I KNOW IT'D BE YOU?! WHAT IS IT THIS TIME?!
WHY DON'T YOU GO HOME FIRST LANG-BEE?
THIS IS NOTHING TO WORRY YOUR PRETTY LITTLE HEAD OVER.
!
.....

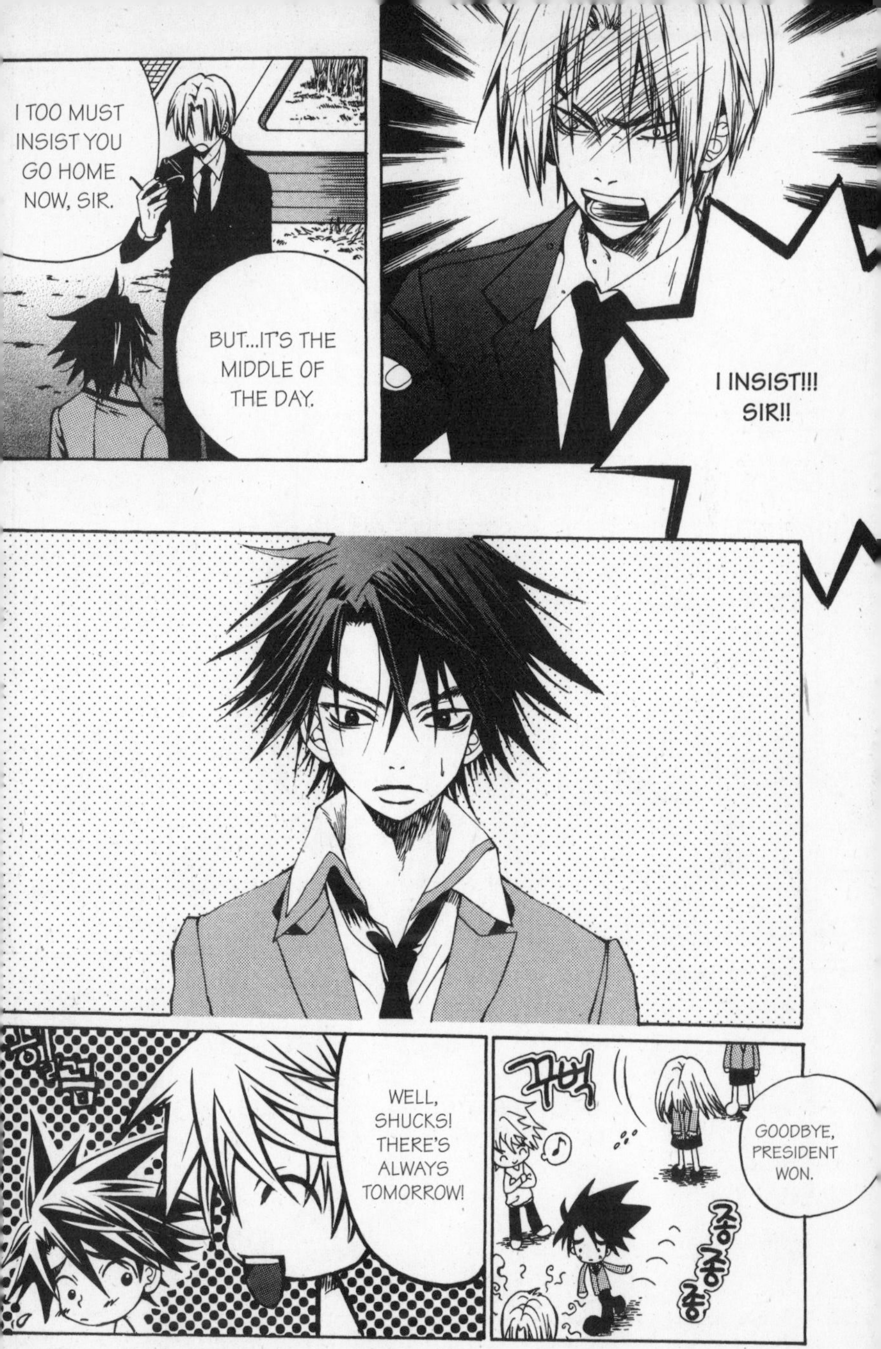
I TOO MUST INSIST YOU GO HOME NOW, SIR.
BUT...IT'S THE MIDDLE OF THE DAY.
I INSIST!!! SIR!!
WELL, SHUCKS! THERE'S ALWAYS TOMORROW!
꾸벅
GOODBYE, PRESIDENT WON.
종종종

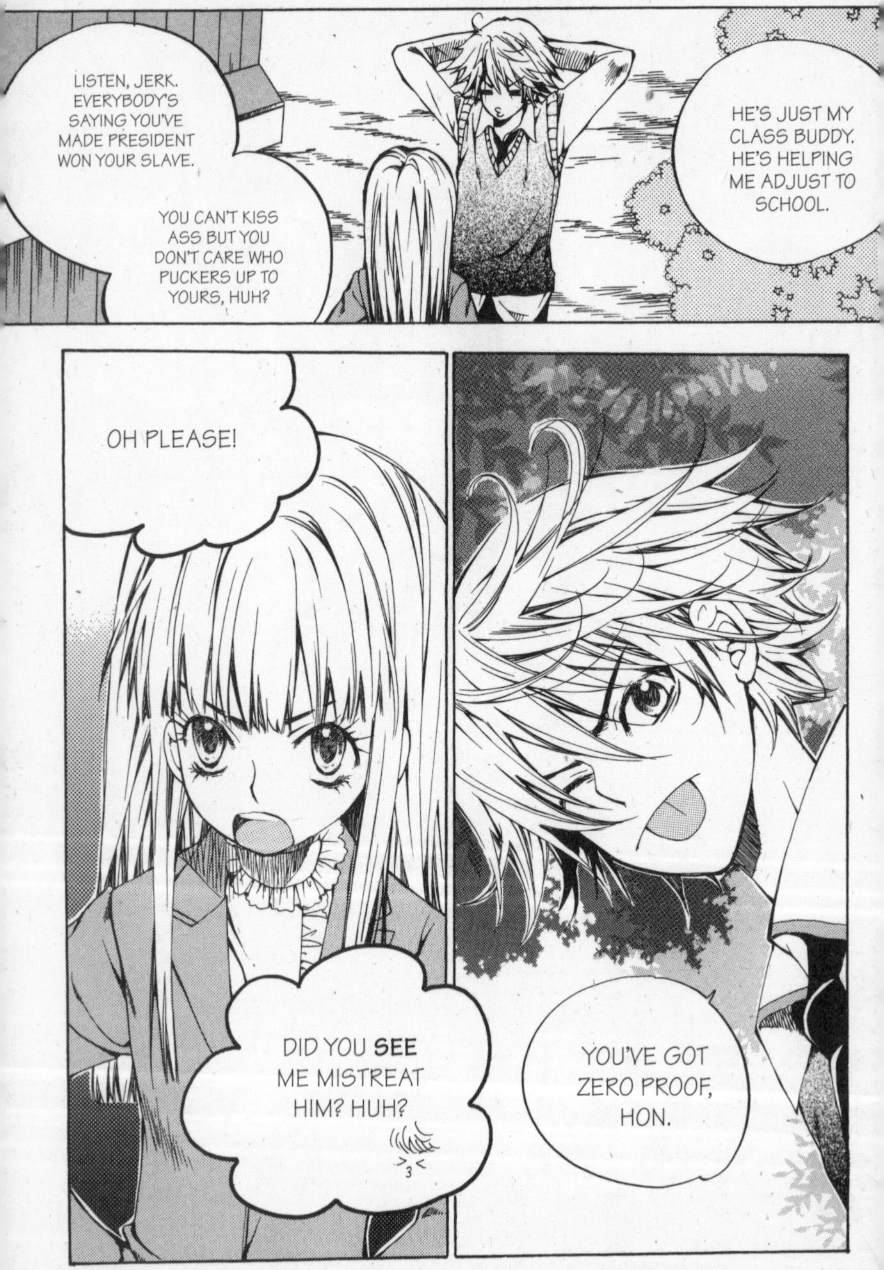
LISTEN, JERK. EVERYBODY'S SAYING YOU'VE MADE PRESIDENT WON YOUR SLAVE.
YOU CAN'T KISS ASS BUT YOU DON'T CARE WHO PUCKERS UP TO YOURS, HUH?
HE'S JUST MY CLASS BUDDY. HE'S HELPING ME ADJUST TO SCHOOL.
OH PLEASE!
DID YOU **SEE** ME MISTREAT HIM? HUH?
YOU'VE GOT ZERO PROOF, HON.

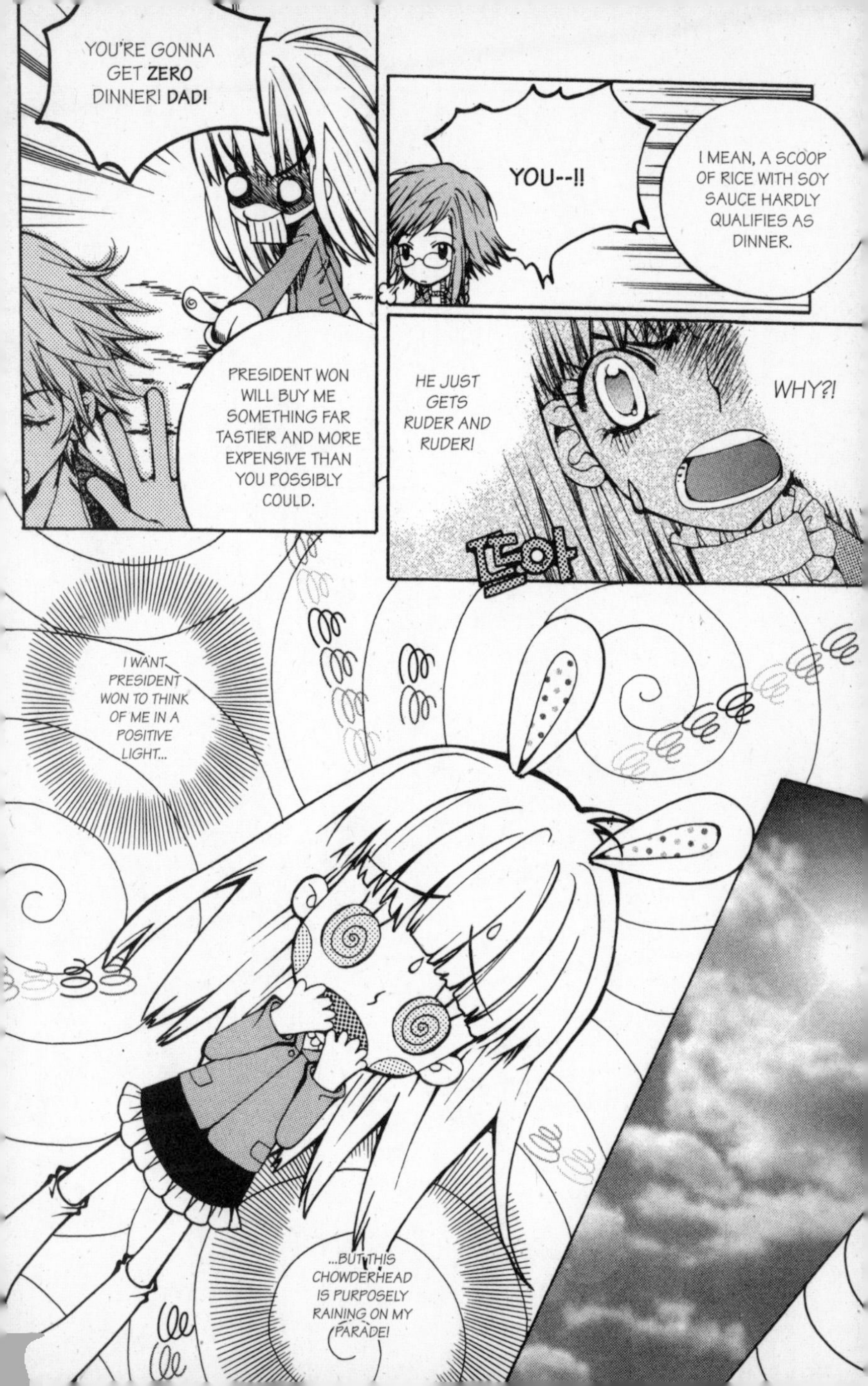
YOU'RE GONNA GET **ZERO** DINNER! **DAD!**
PRESIDENT WON WILL BUY ME SOMETHING FAR TASTIER AND MORE EXPENSIVE THAN YOU POSSIBLY COULD.
YOU--!!
I MEAN, A SCOOP OF RICE WITH SOY SAUCE HARDLY QUALIFIES AS DINNER.
HE JUST GETS RUDER AND RUDER!
WHY?!
I WANT PRESIDENT WON TO THINK OF ME IN A POSITIVE LIGHT...
...BUT THIS CHOWDERHEAD IS PURPOSELY RAINING ON MY PARADE!

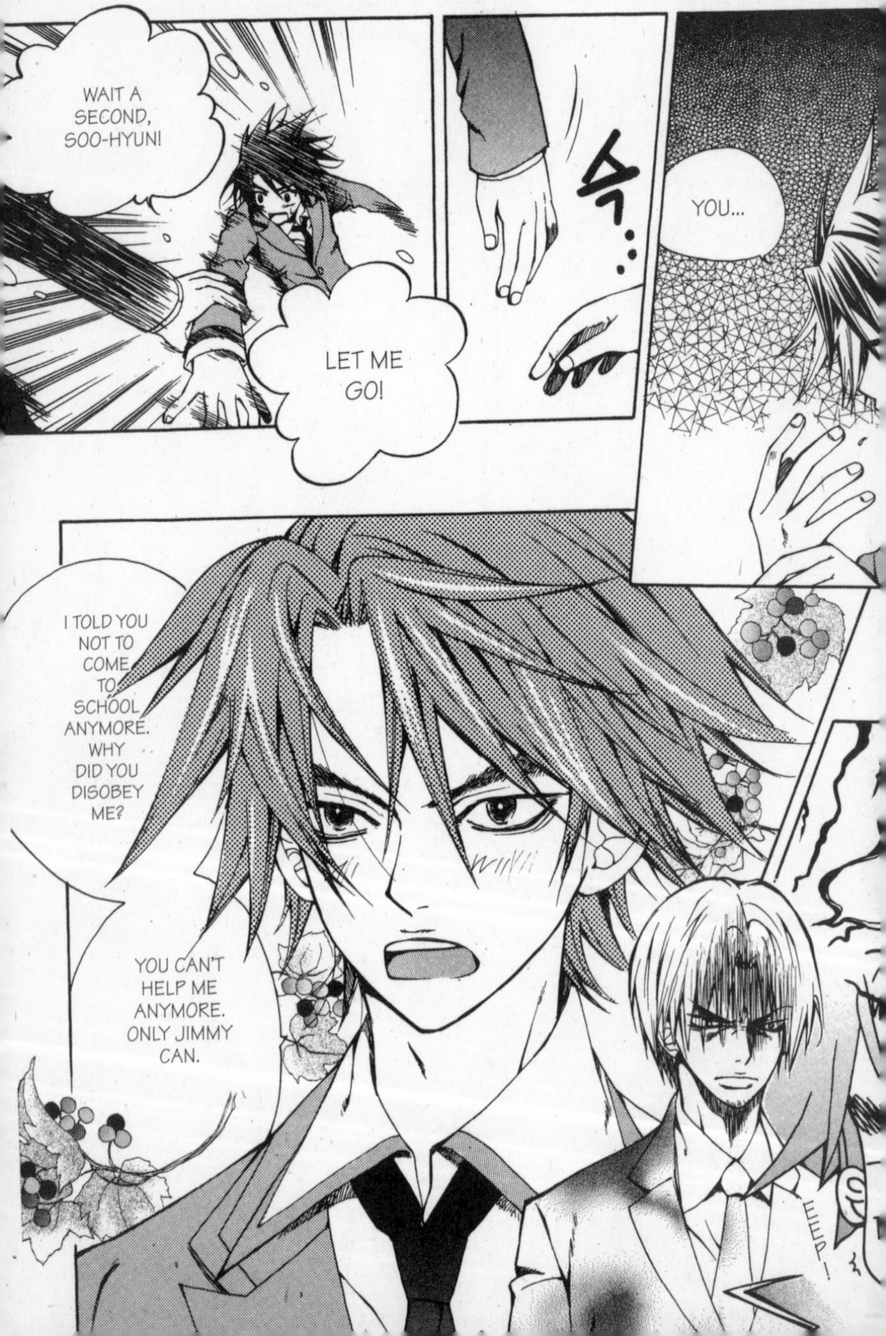
WAIT A SECOND, SOO-HYUN!
LET ME GO!
슥...
YOU...
I TOLD YOU NOT TO COME TO SCHOOL ANYMORE. WHY DID YOU DISOBEY ME?
YOU CAN'T HELP ME ANYMORE. ONLY JIMMY CAN.
EEP!

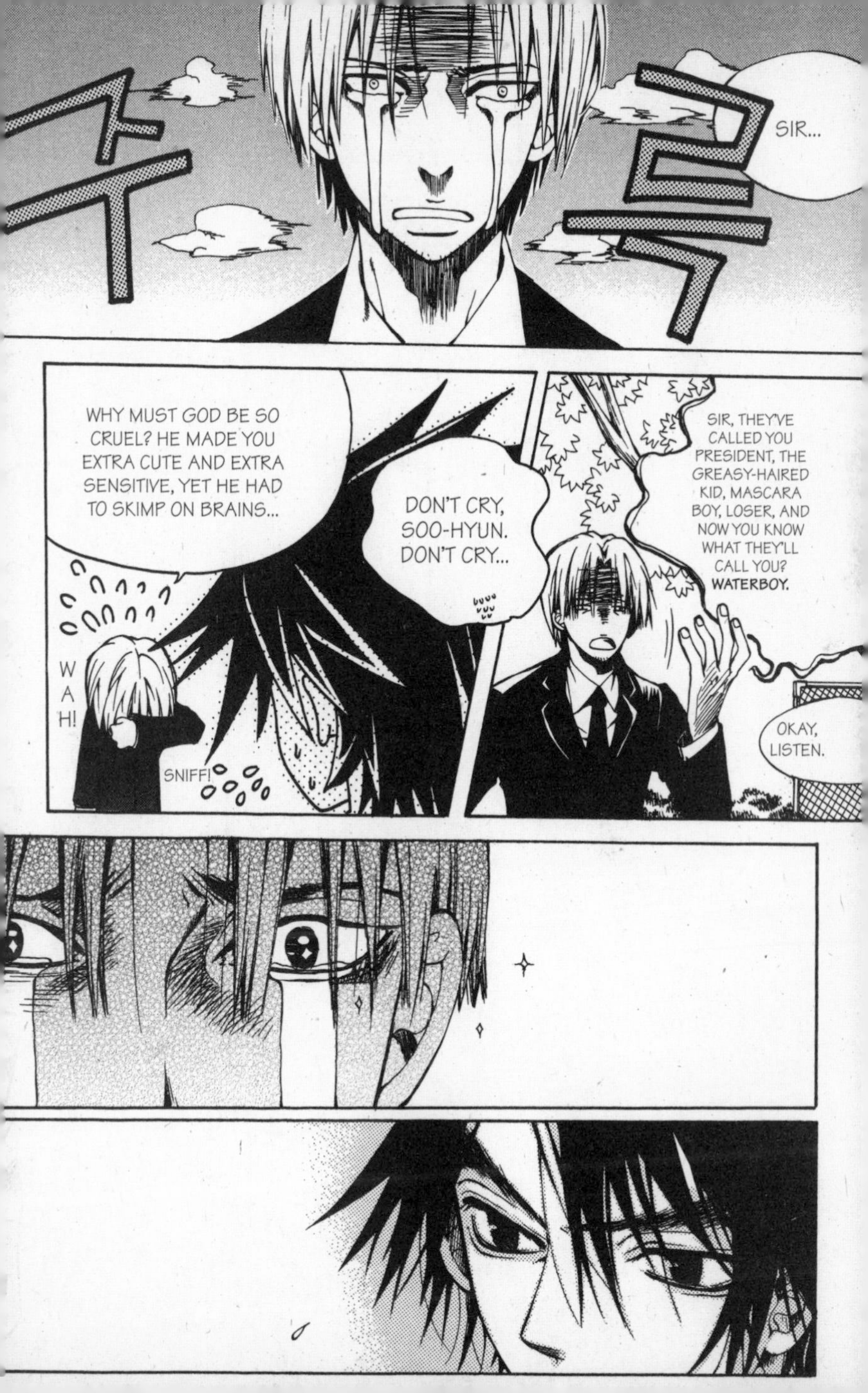
SIR...
WHY MUST GOD BE SO CRUEL? HE MADE YOU EXTRA CUTE AND EXTRA SENSITIVE, YET HE HAD TO SKIMP ON BRAINS...
WAH!
SNIFF!
DON'T CRY, SOO-HYUN. DON'T CRY...
SIR, THEY'VE CALLED YOU PRESIDENT, THE GREASY-HAIRED KID, MASCARA BOY, LOSER, AND NOW YOU KNOW WHAT THEY'LL CALL YOU? **WATERBOY.**
OKAY, LISTEN.

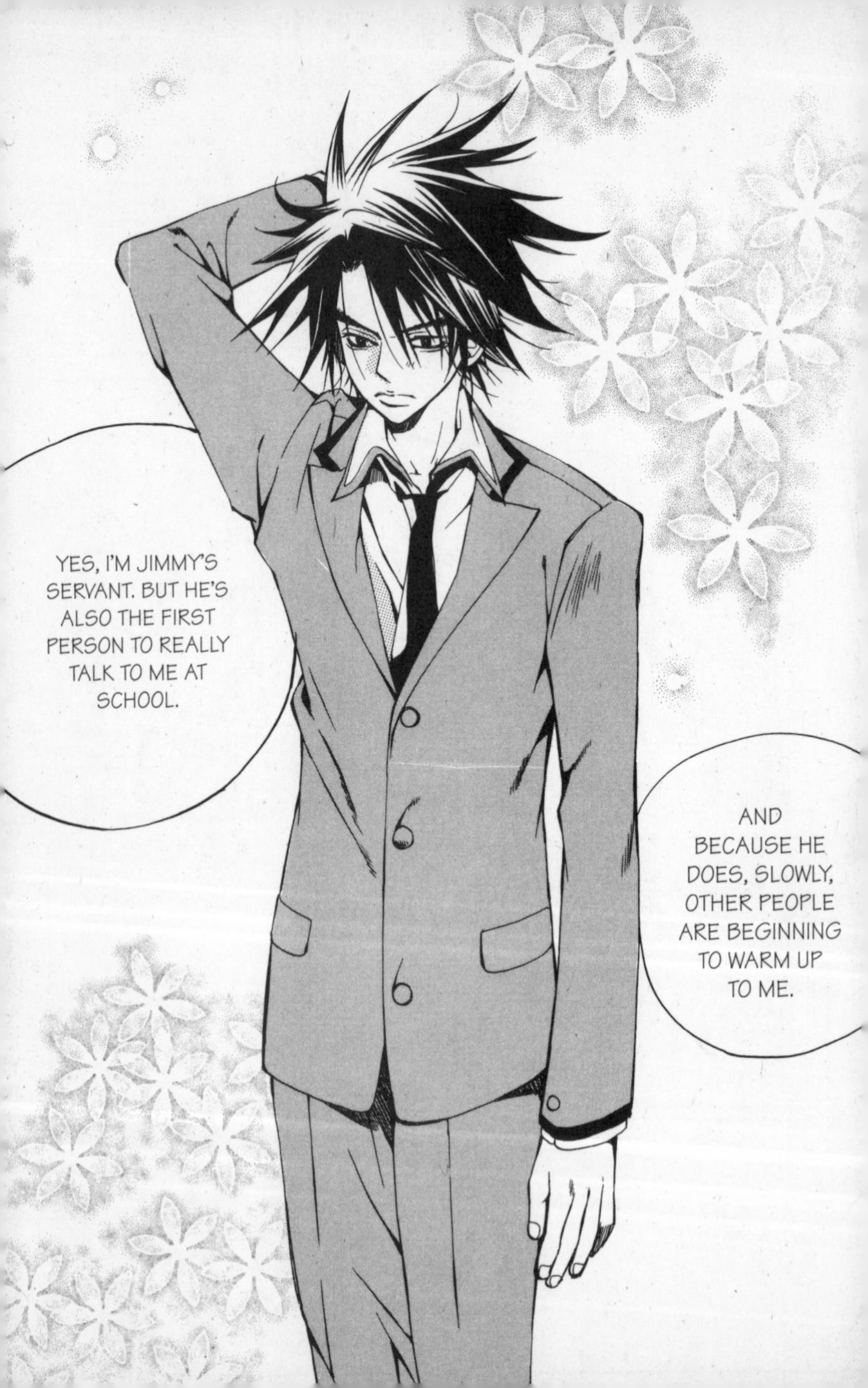
YES, I'M JIMMY'S SERVANT. BUT HE'S ALSO THE FIRST PERSON TO REALLY TALK TO ME AT SCHOOL.
AND BECAUSE HE DOES, SLOWLY, OTHER PEOPLE ARE BEGINNING TO WARM UP TO ME.

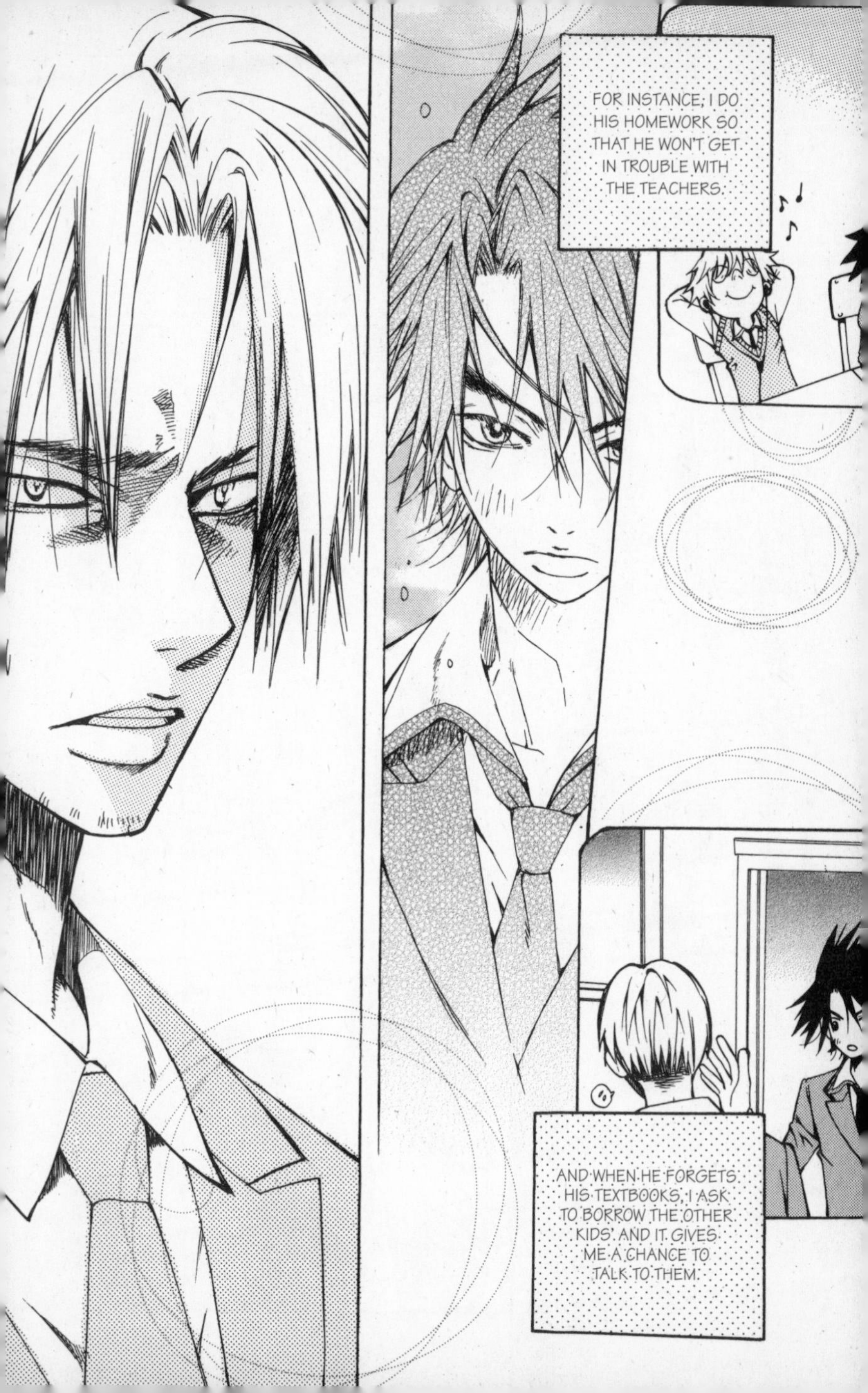
FOR INSTANCE, I DO HIS HOMEWORK SO THAT HE WON'T GET IN TROUBLE WITH THE TEACHERS.
AND WHEN HE FORGETS HIS TEXTBOOKS, I ASK TO BORROW THE OTHER KIDS' AND IT GIVES ME A CHANCE TO TALK TO THEM.

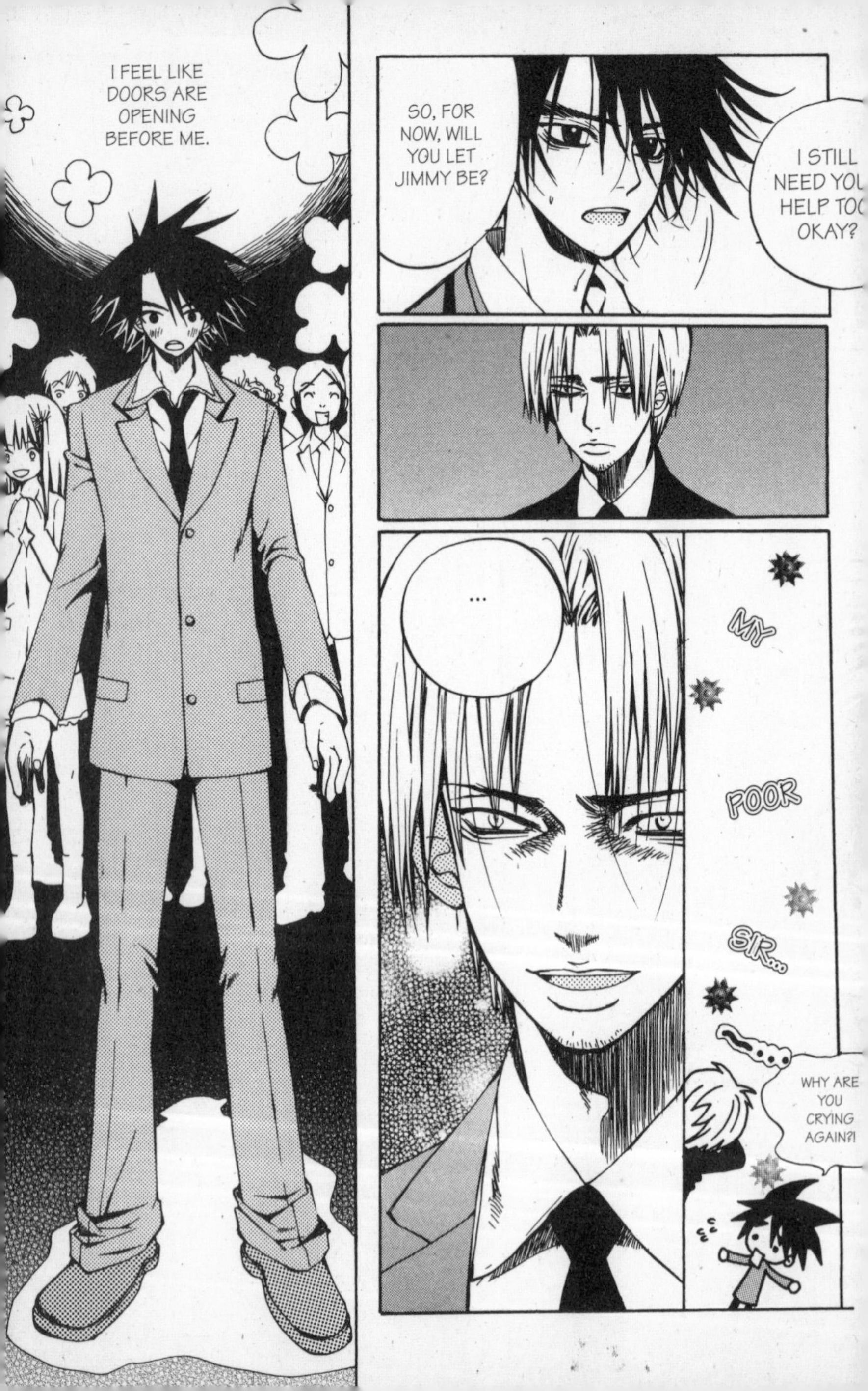
I FEEL LIKE DOORS ARE OPENING BEFORE ME.
SO, FOR NOW, WILL YOU LET JIMMY BE?
I STILL NEED YOU HELP TOO OKAY?
...
MY POOR SIR...
...
WHY ARE YOU CRYING AGAIN?!

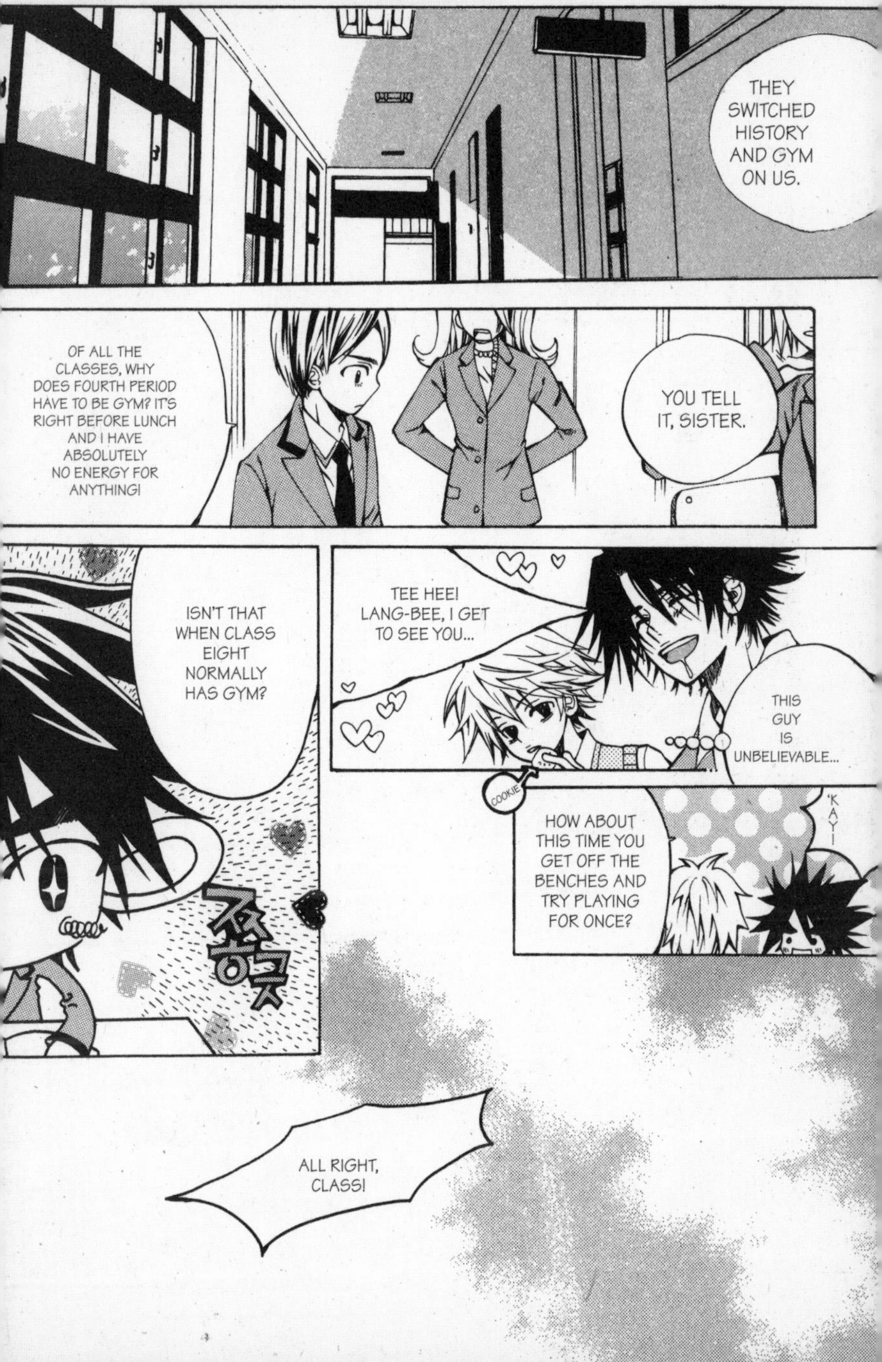
THEY SWITCHED HISTORY AND GYM ON US.
OF ALL THE CLASSES, WHY DOES FOURTH PERIOD HAVE TO BE GYM? IT'S RIGHT BEFORE LUNCH AND I HAVE ABSOLUTELY NO ENERGY FOR ANYTHING!
YOU TELL IT, SISTER.
ISN'T THAT WHEN CLASS EIGHT NORMALLY HAS GYM?
쫑긋
TEE HEE! LANG-BEE, I GET TO SEE YOU...
THIS GUY IS UNBELIEVABLE...
COOKIE
HOW ABOUT THIS TIME YOU GET OFF THE BENCHES AND TRY PLAYING FOR ONCE?
'KAYI
ALL RIGHT, CLASS!

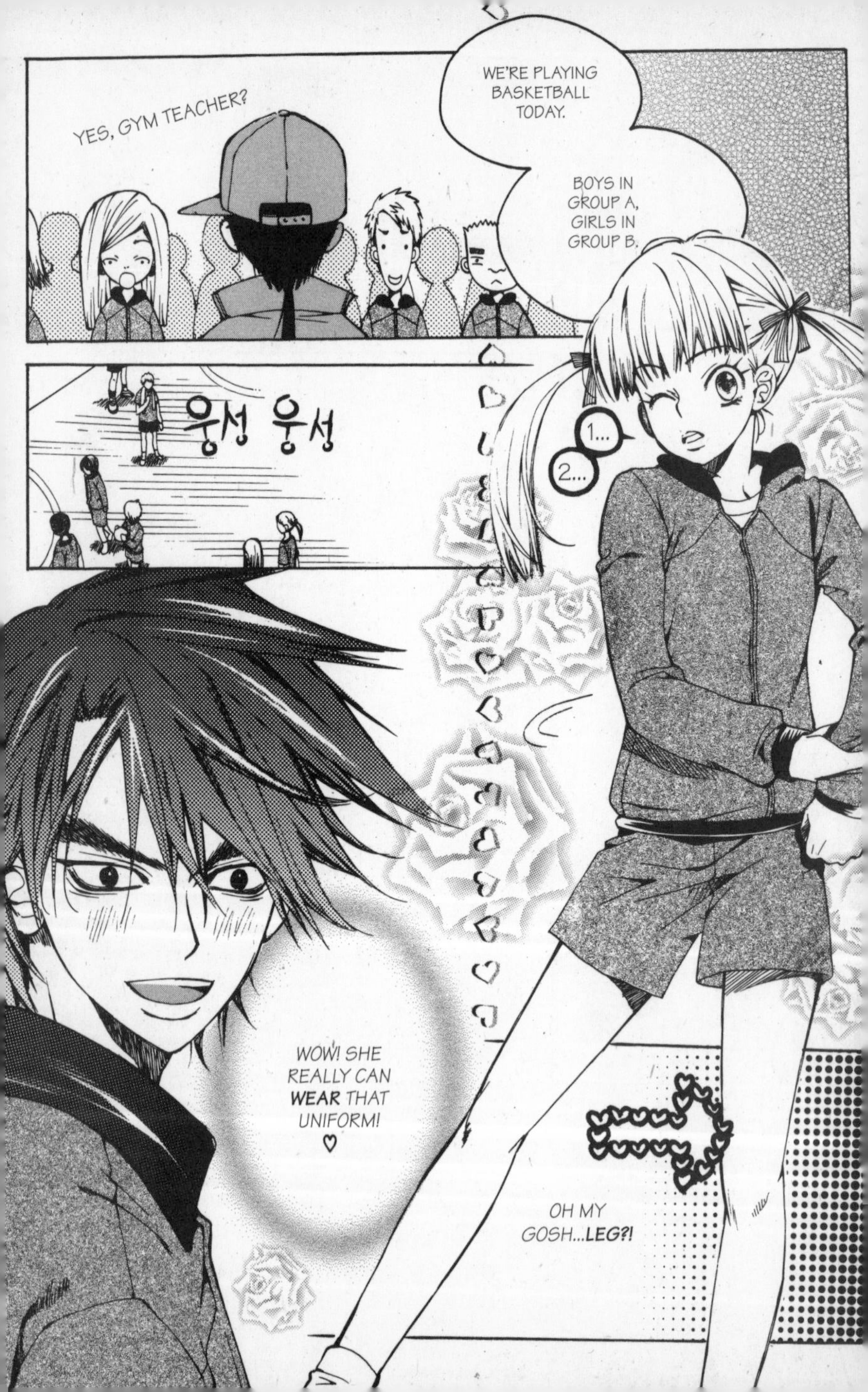
YES, GYM TEACHER?
WE'RE PLAYING BASKETBALL TODAY.
BOYS IN GROUP A, GIRLS IN GROUP B.
웅성 웅성
1...
2...
WOW! SHE REALLY CAN **WEAR** THAT UNIFORM! ♡
OH MY GOSH...**LEG?!**

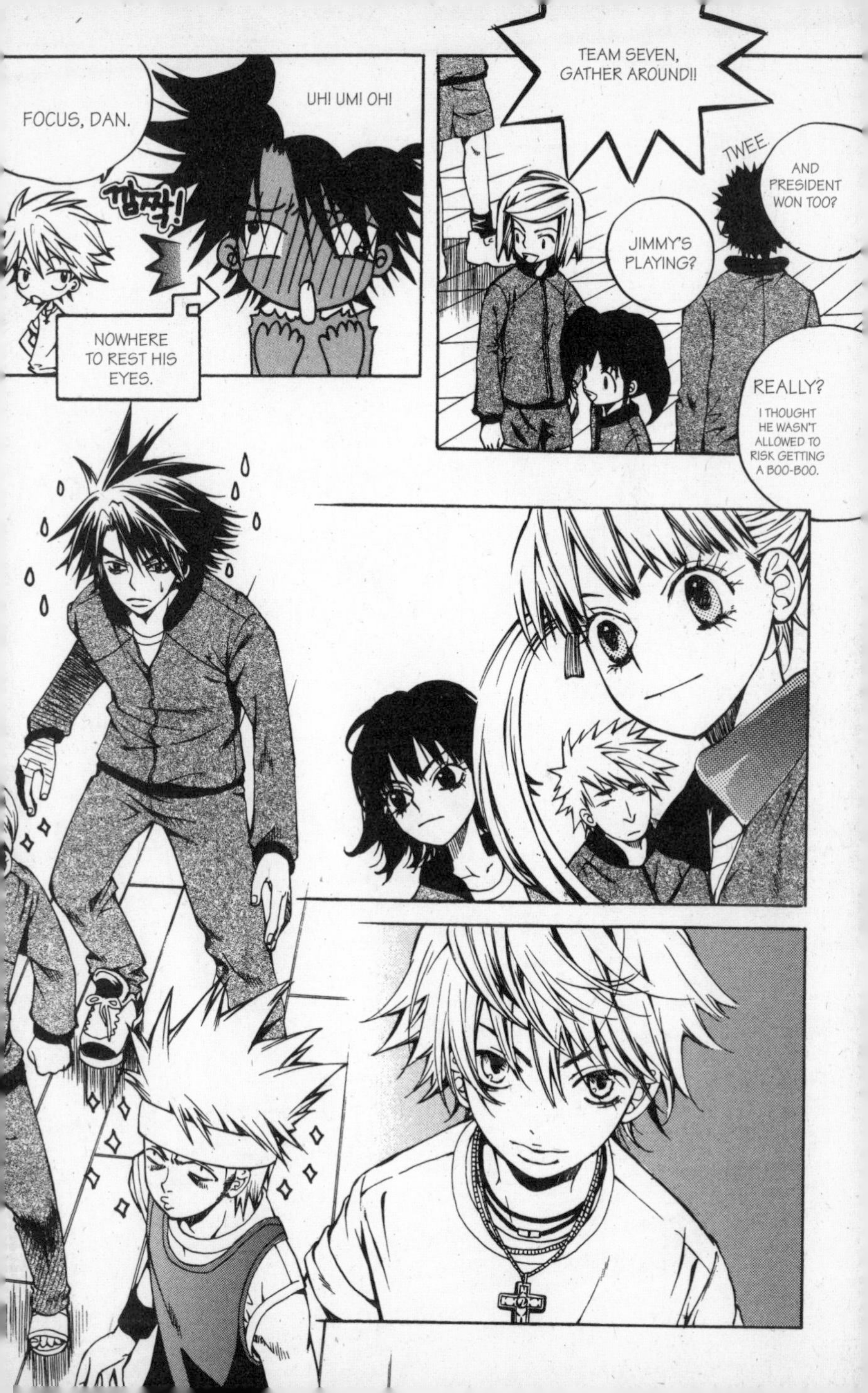
FOCUS, DAN.
UH! UM! OH!
깜짝!
NOWHERE TO REST HIS EYES.
TEAM SEVEN, GATHER AROUND!!
JIMMY'S PLAYING?
TWEE.
AND PRESIDENT WON TOO?
REALLY?
I THOUGHT HE WASN'T ALLOWED TO RISK GETTING A BOO-BOO.

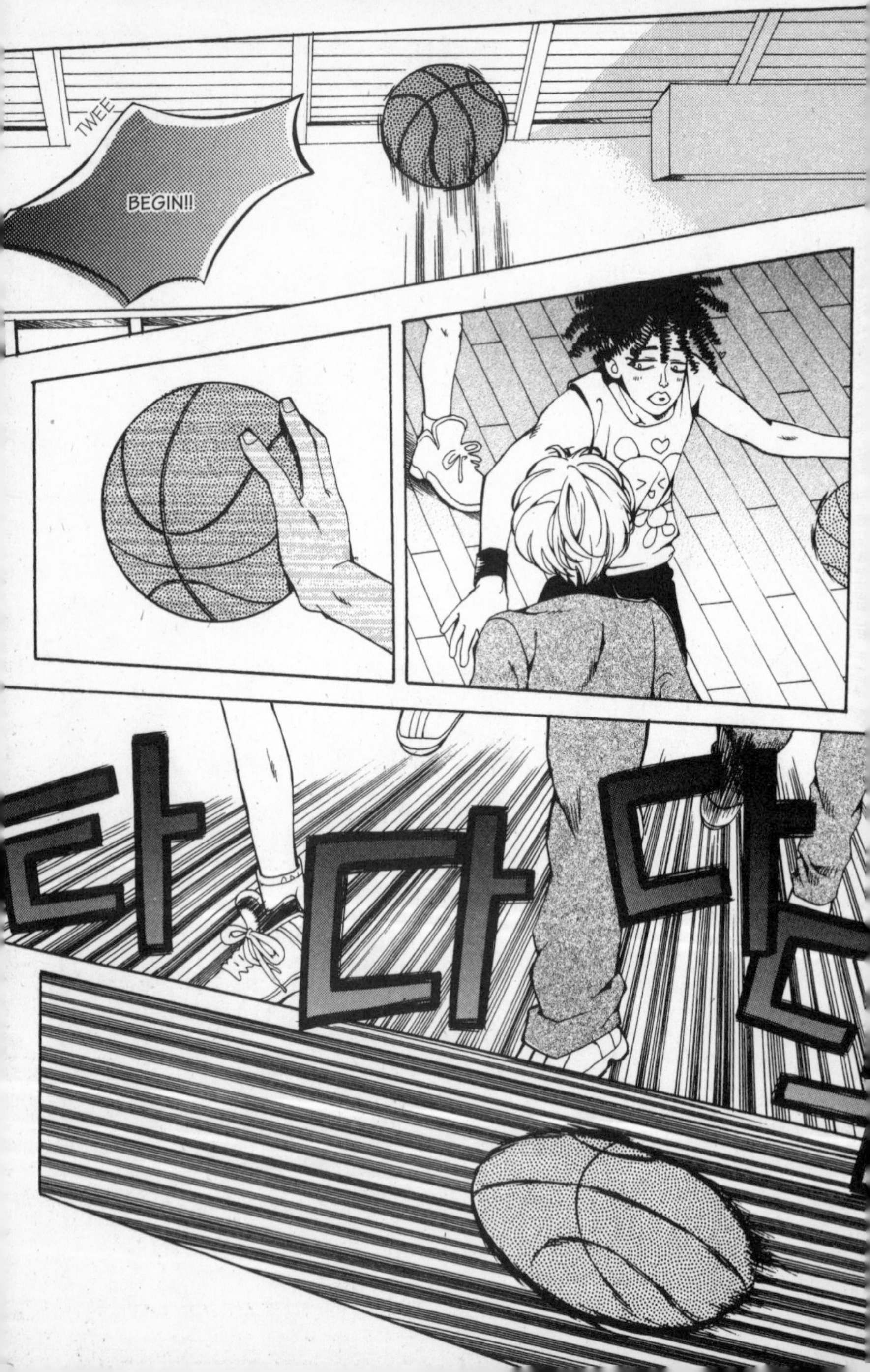
TWEE
BEGIN!!
다다다다

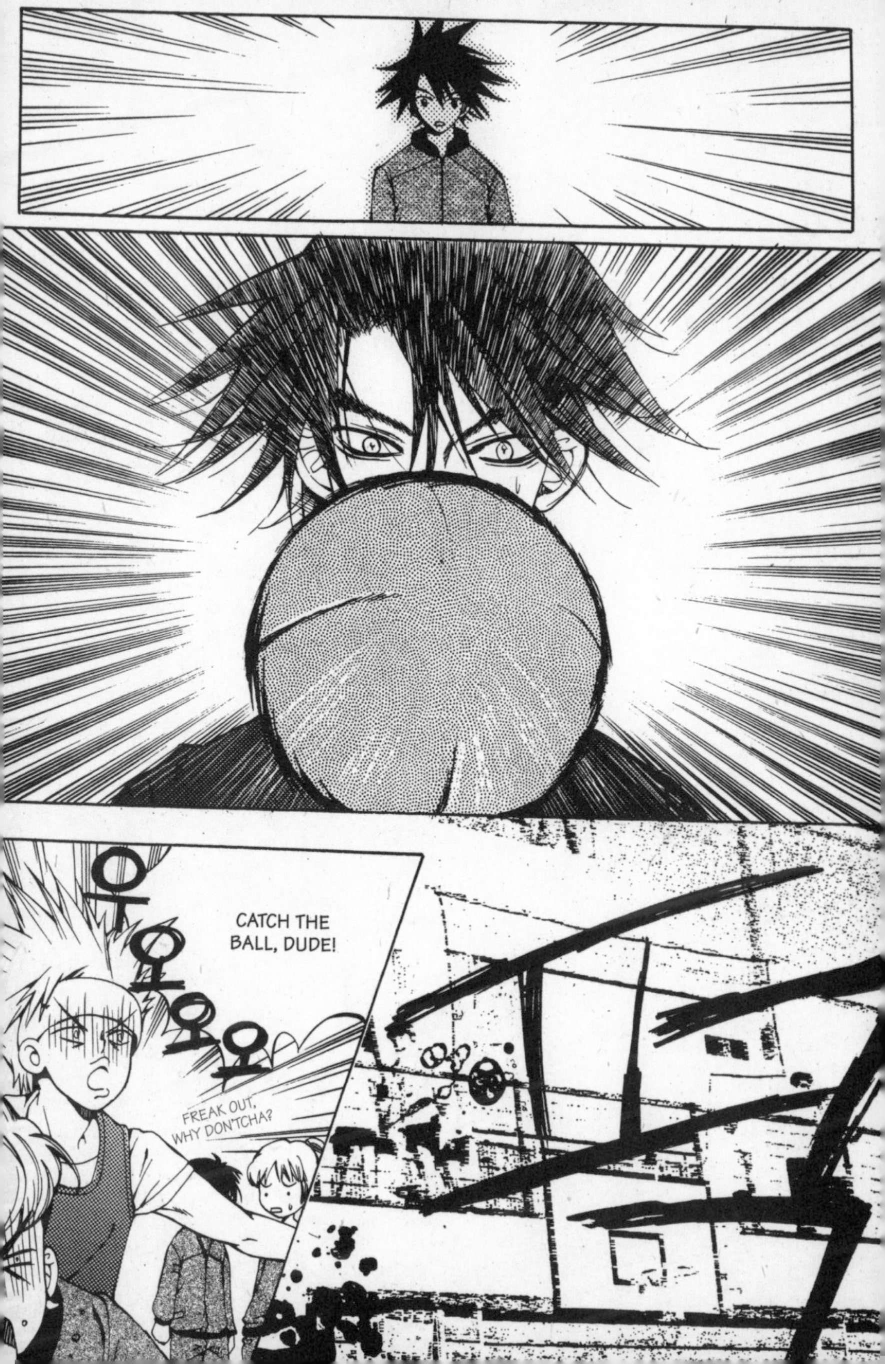
CATCH THE BALL, DUDE!
FREAK OUT, WHY DON'TCHA?

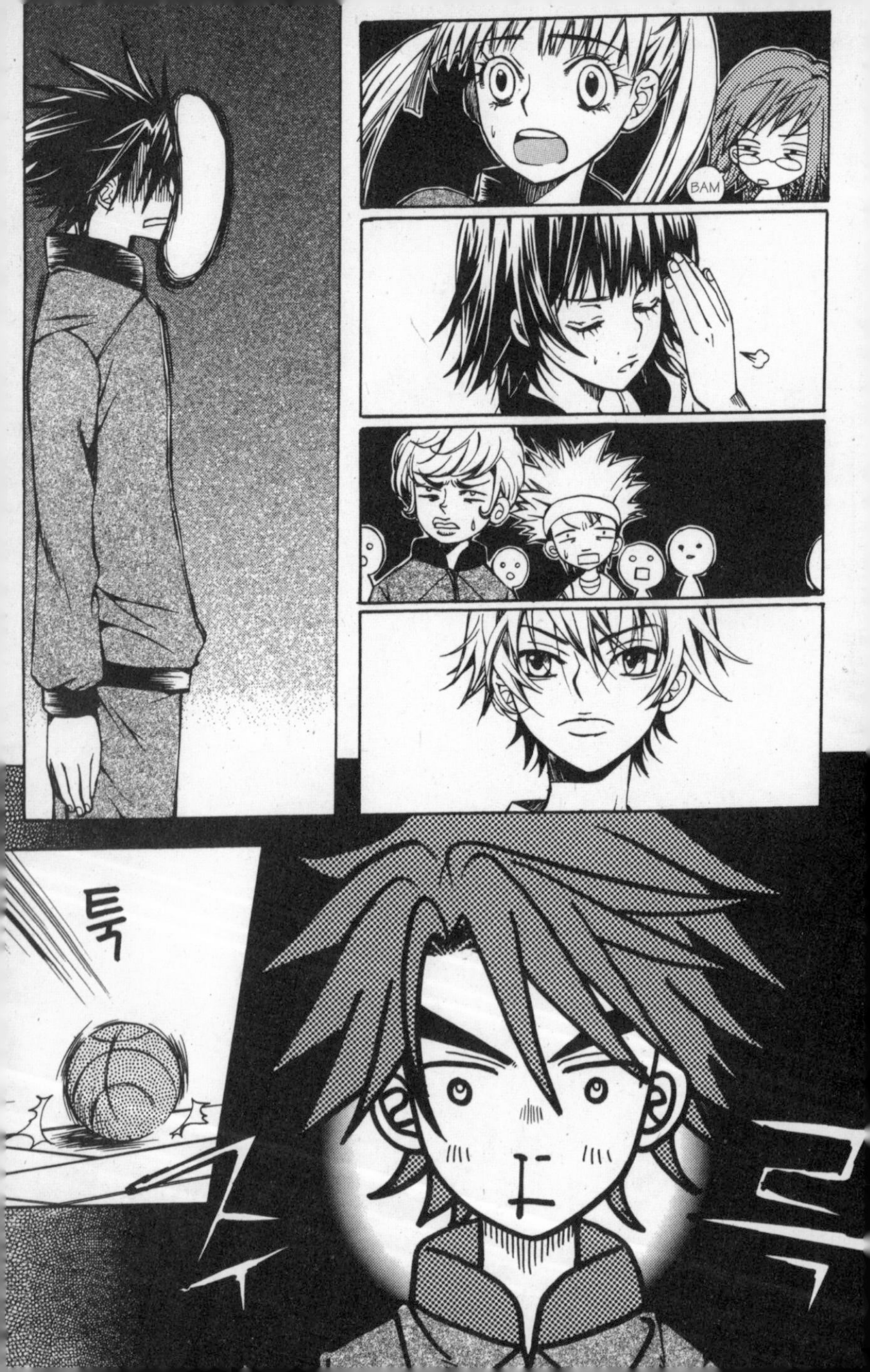

BAM
툭

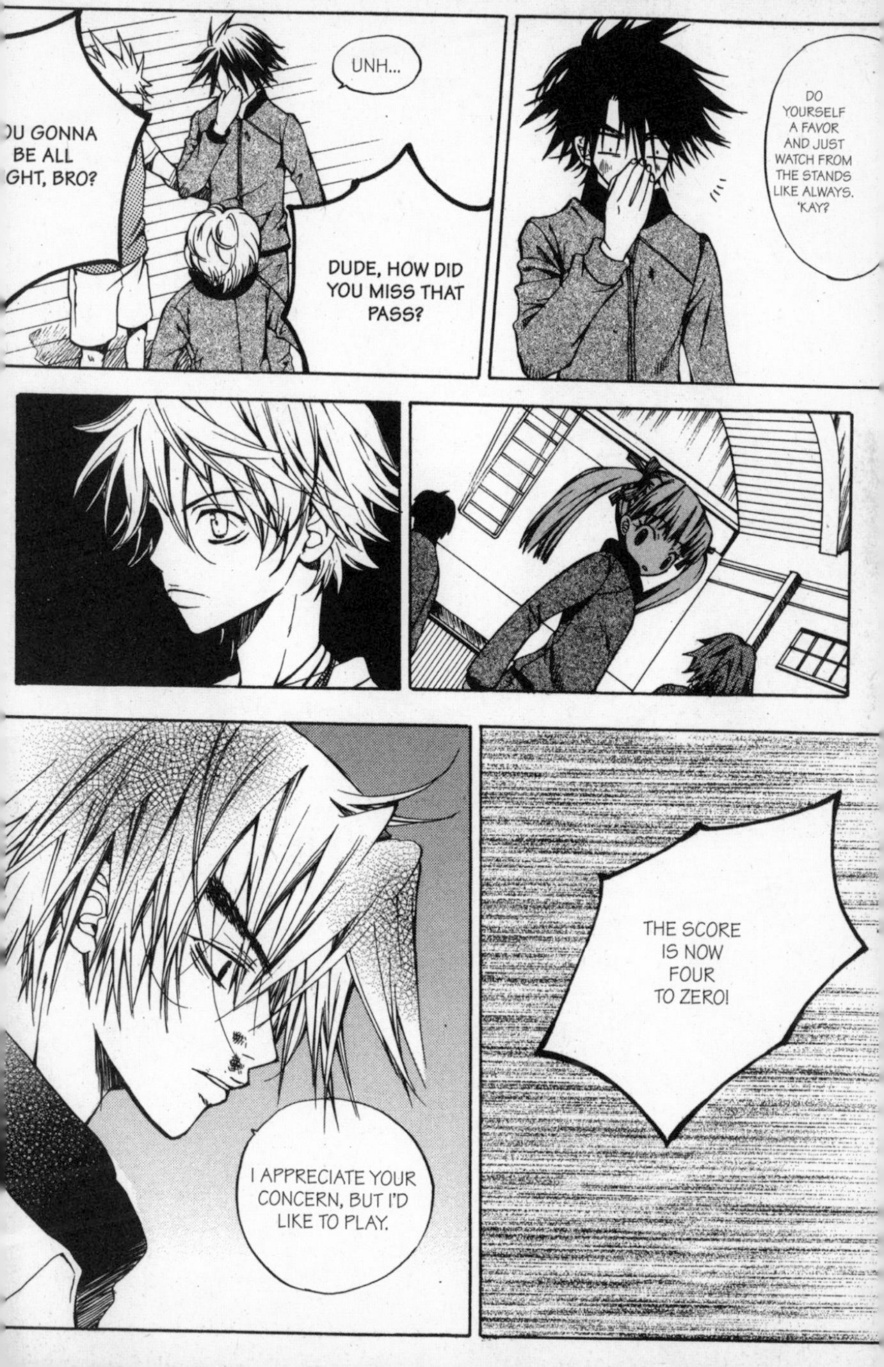

OU GONNA BE ALL GHT, BRO?
UNH...
DUDE, HOW DID YOU MISS THAT PASS?
DO YOURSELF A FAVOR AND JUST WATCH FROM THE STANDS LIKE ALWAYS. 'KAY?
I APPRECIATE YOUR CONCERN, BUT I'D LIKE TO PLAY.
THE SCORE IS NOW FOUR TO ZERO!

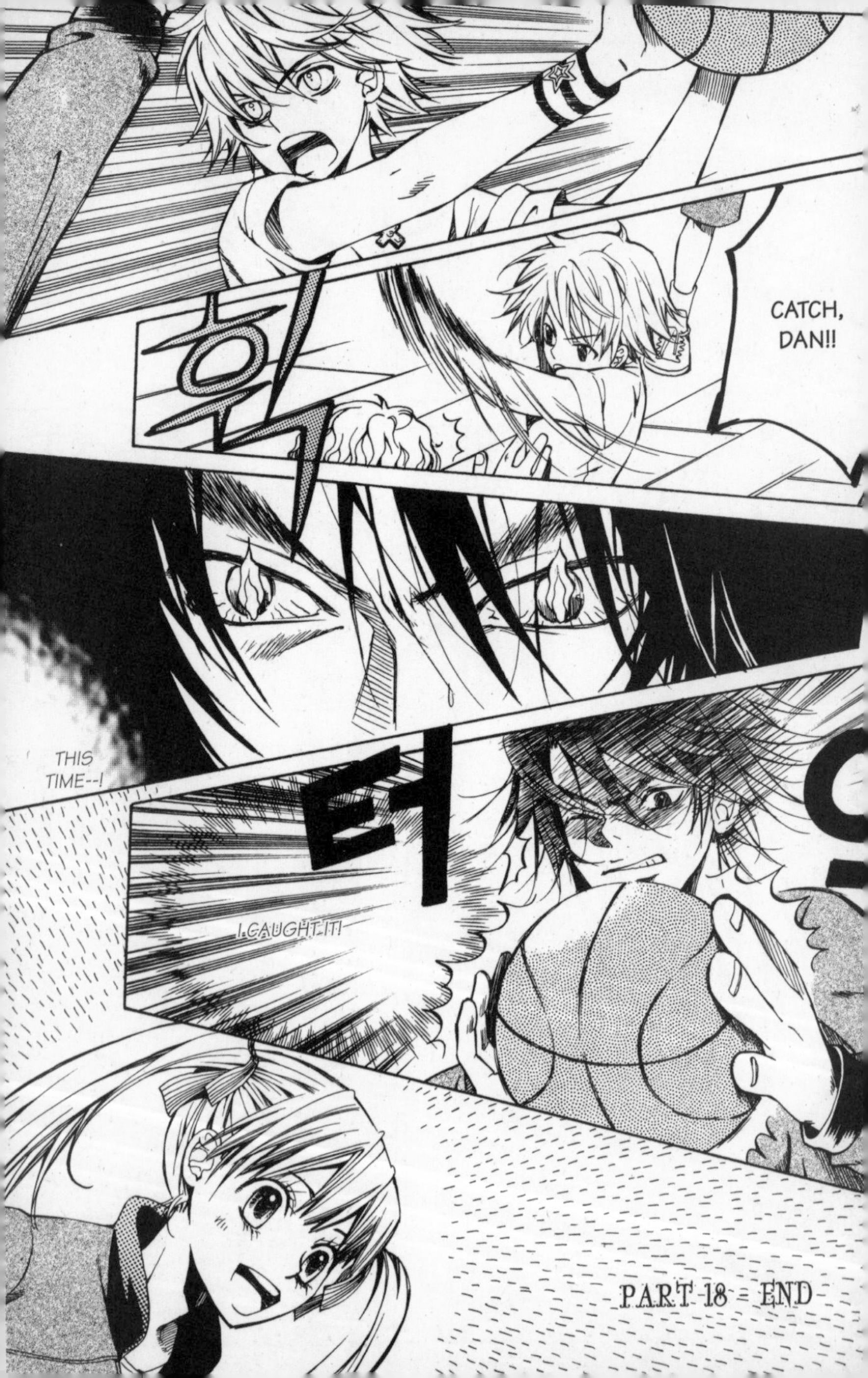
CATCH, DAN!!
THIS TIME--!
I CAUGHT IT!
PART 18 - END

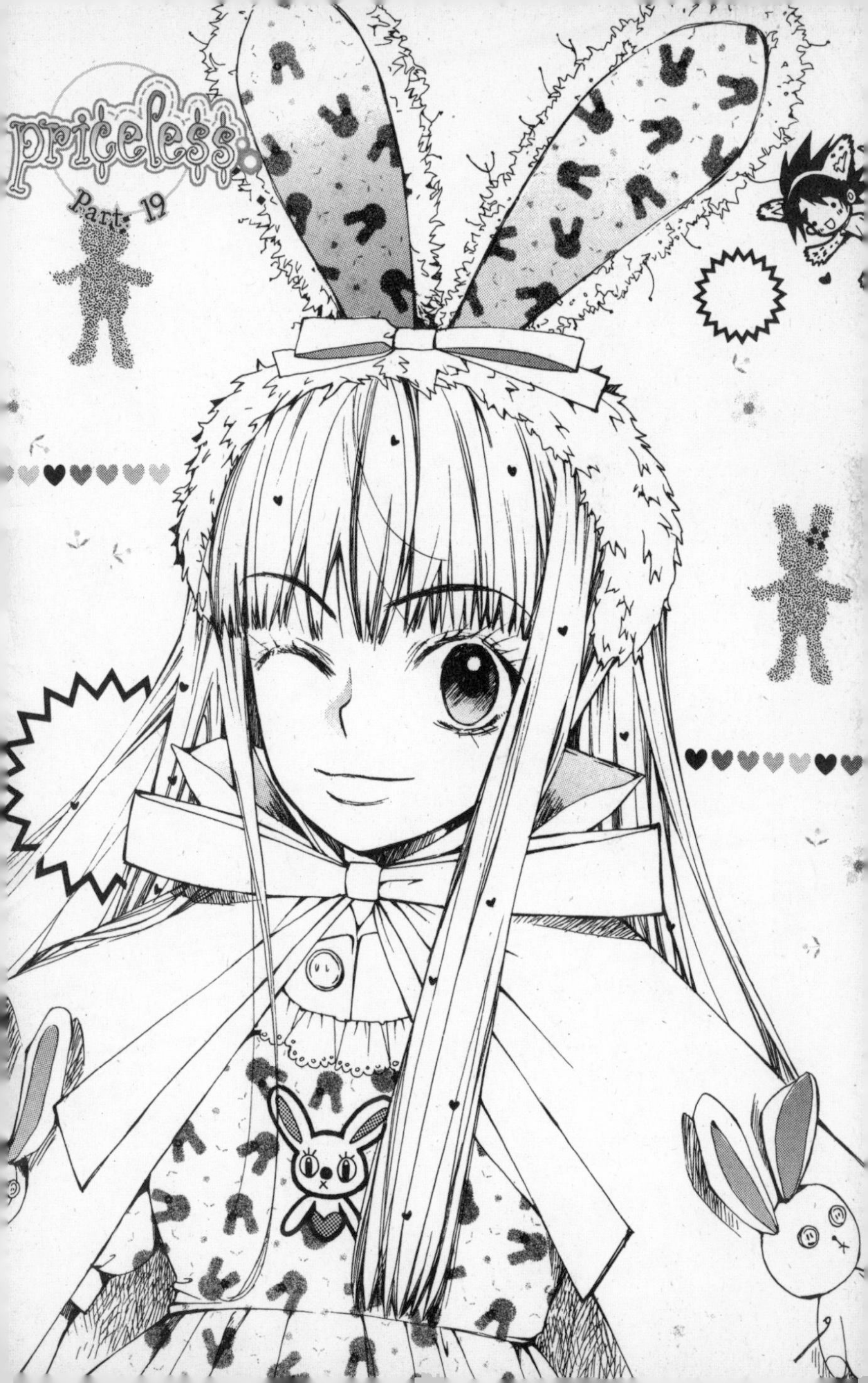
priceless
Part. 19

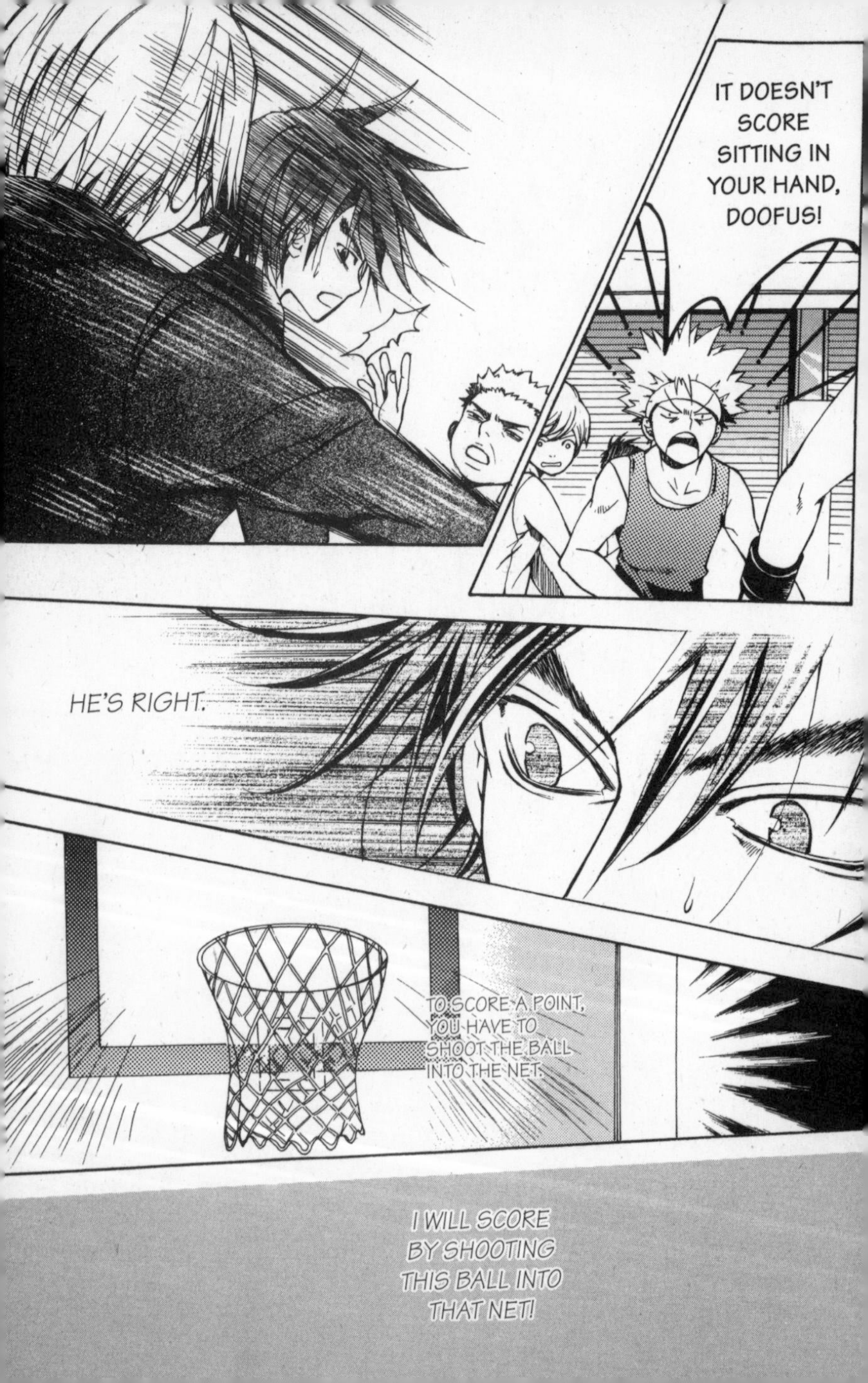
IT DOESN'T SCORE SITTING IN YOUR HAND, DOOFUS!
HE'S RIGHT.
TO SCORE A POINT, YOU HAVE TO SHOOT THE BALL INTO THE NET.
I WILL SCORE BY SHOOTING THIS BALL INTO THAT NET!

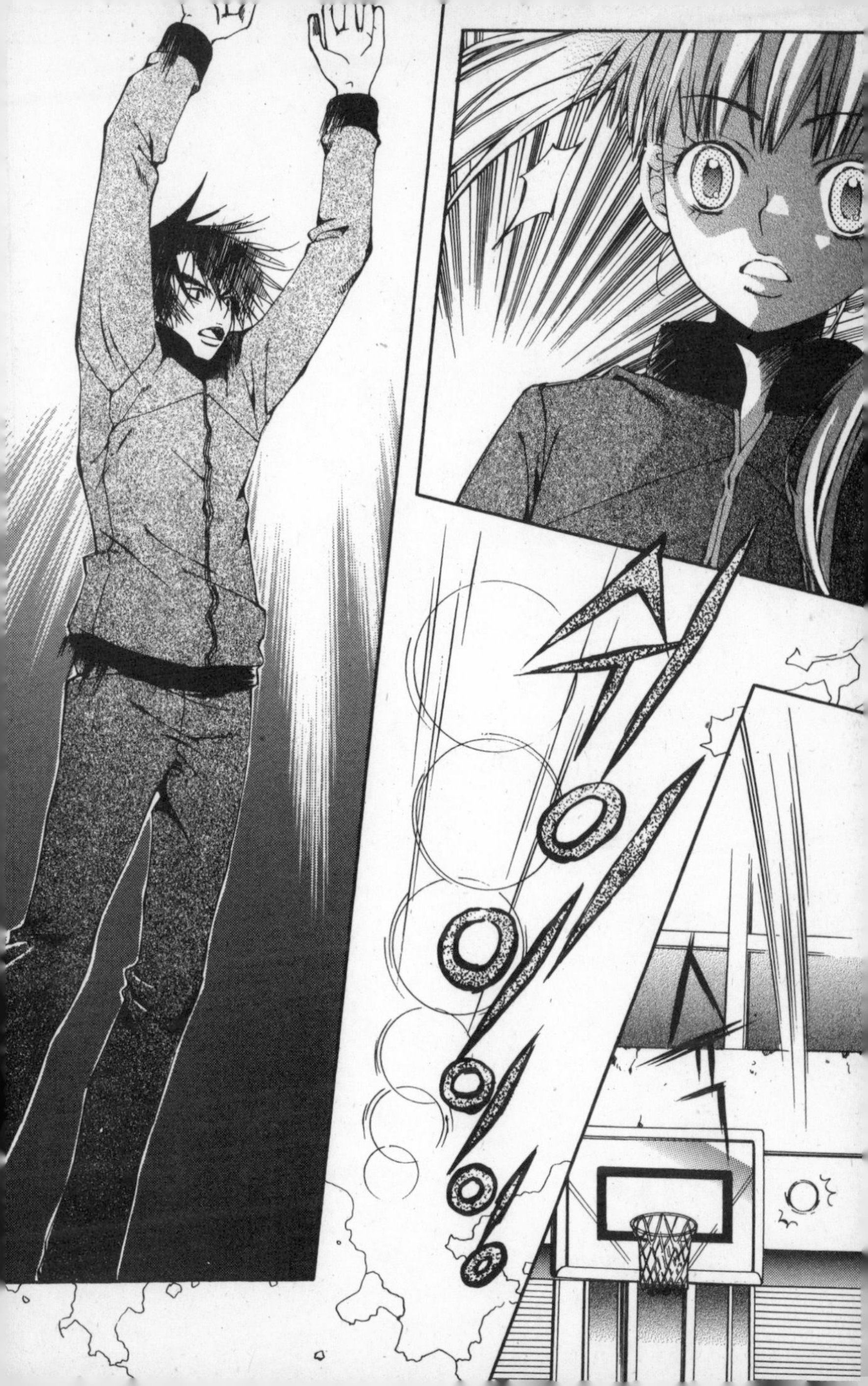

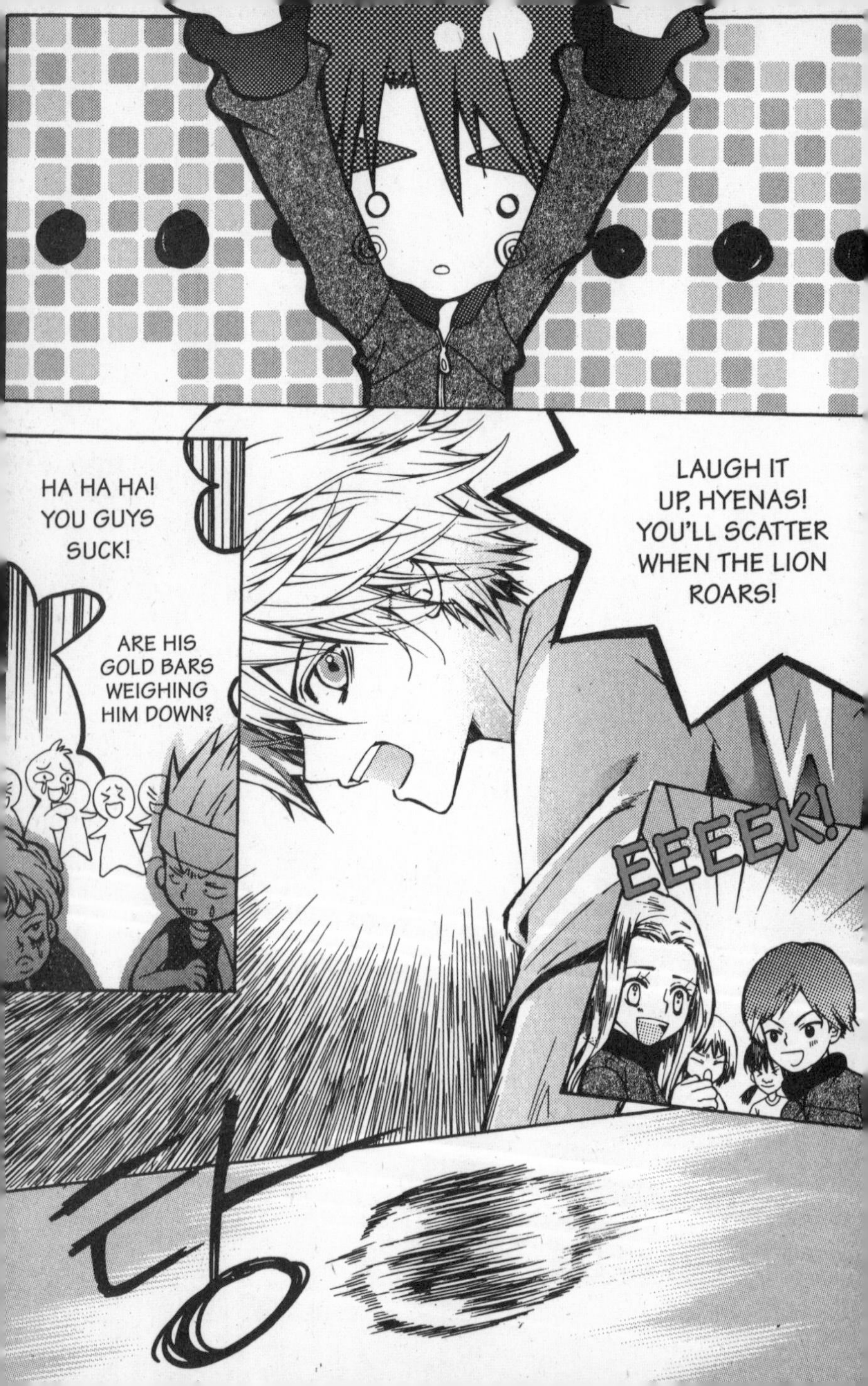
HA HA HA! YOU GUYS SUCK!
ARE HIS GOLD BARS WEIGHING HIM DOWN?
LAUGH IT UP, HYENAS! YOU'LL SCATTER WHEN THE LION ROARS!
EEEEK!

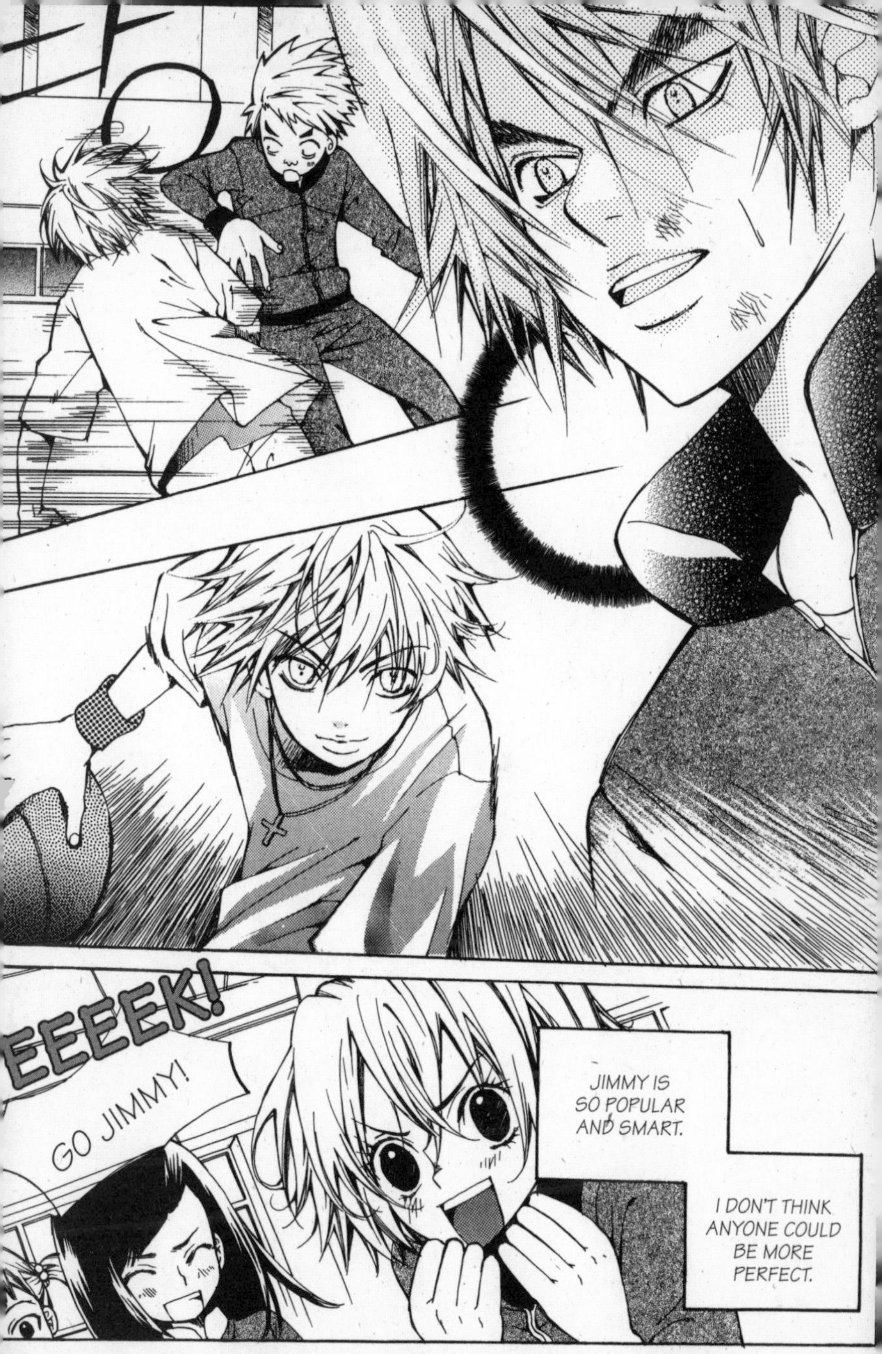
EEEEK!
GO JIMMY!
JIMMY IS SO POPULAR AND SMART.
I DON'T THINK ANYONE COULD BE MORE PERFECT.

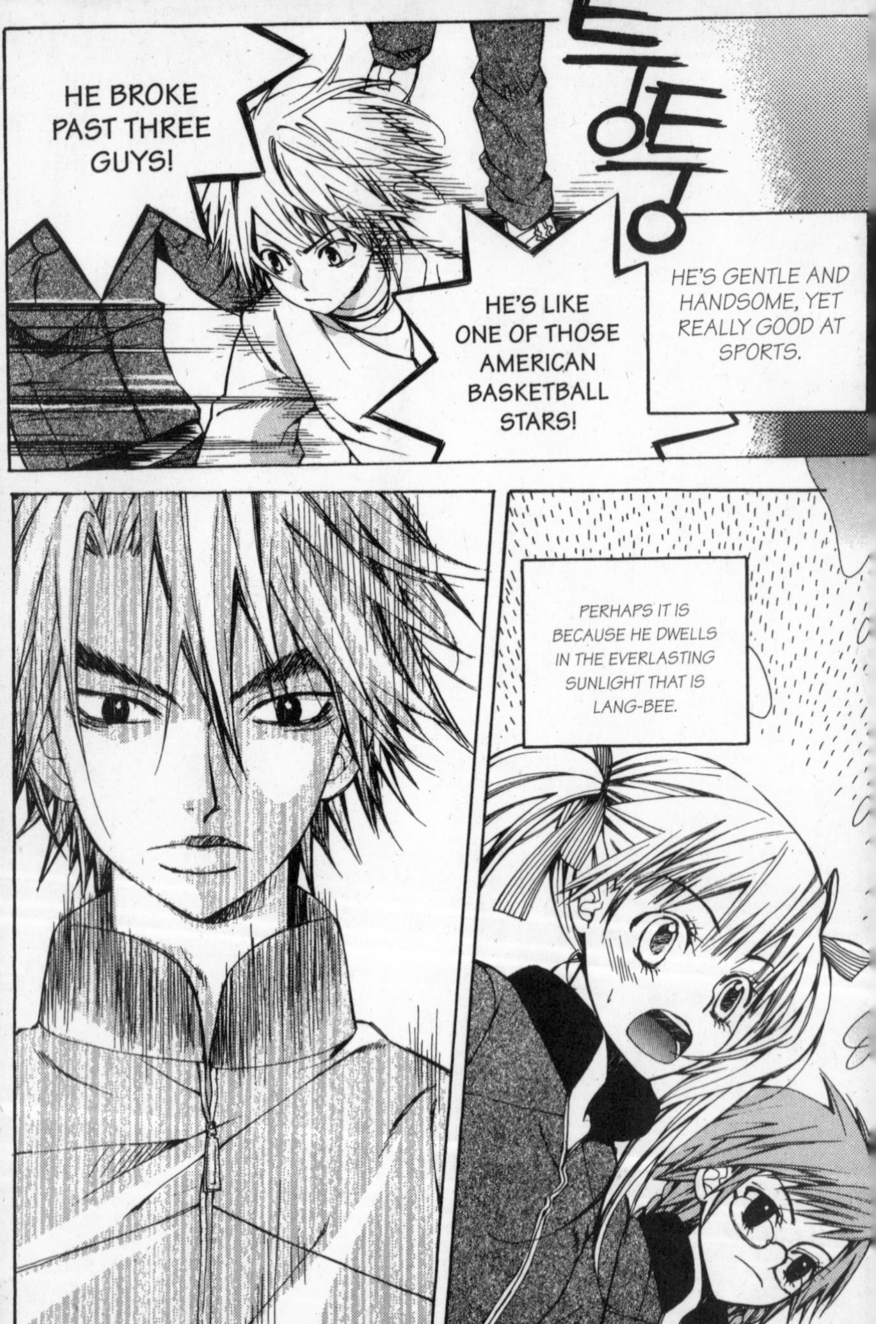
HE BROKE PAST THREE GUYS!
HE'S LIKE ONE OF THOSE AMERICAN BASKETBALL STARS!
HE'S GENTLE AND HANDSOME, YET REALLY GOOD AT SPORTS.
PERHAPS IT IS BECAUSE HE DWELLS IN THE EVERLASTING SUNLIGHT THAT IS LANG-BEE.

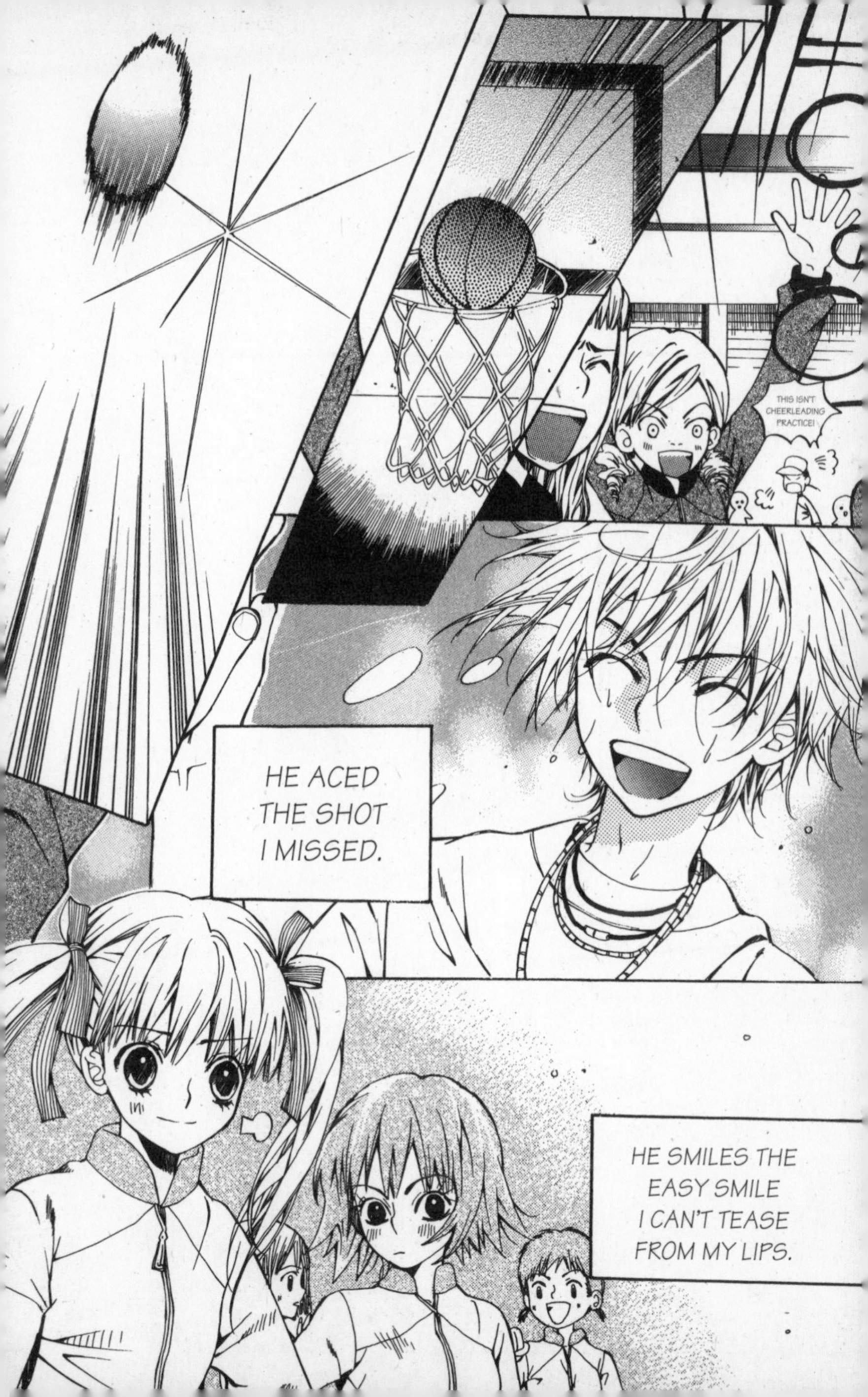
THIS ISN'T CHEERLEADING PRACTICE!
HE ACED THE SHOT I MISSED.
HE SMILES THE EASY SMILE I CAN'T TEASE FROM MY LIPS.

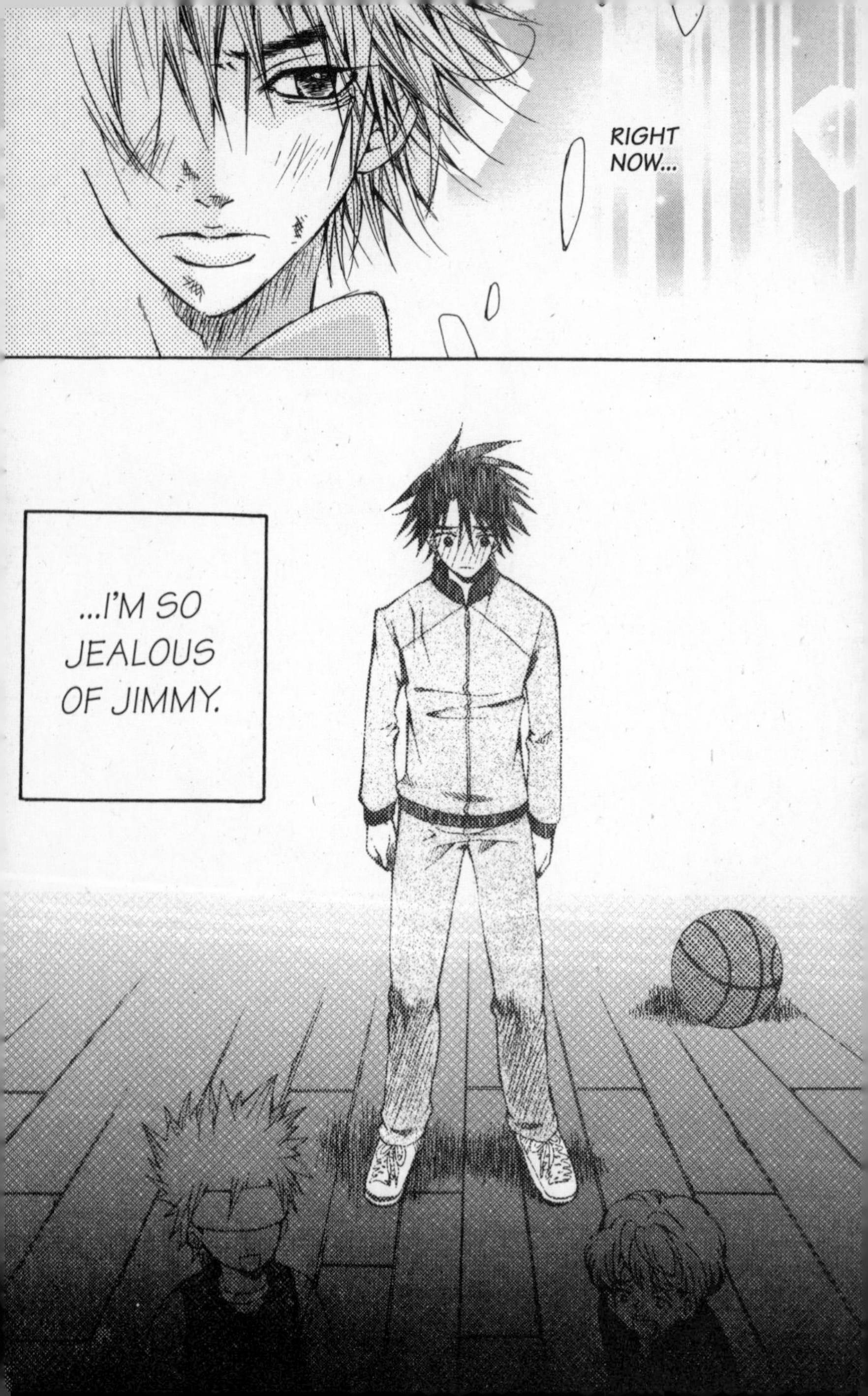
RIGHT NOW...
...I'M SO JEALOUS OF JIMMY.

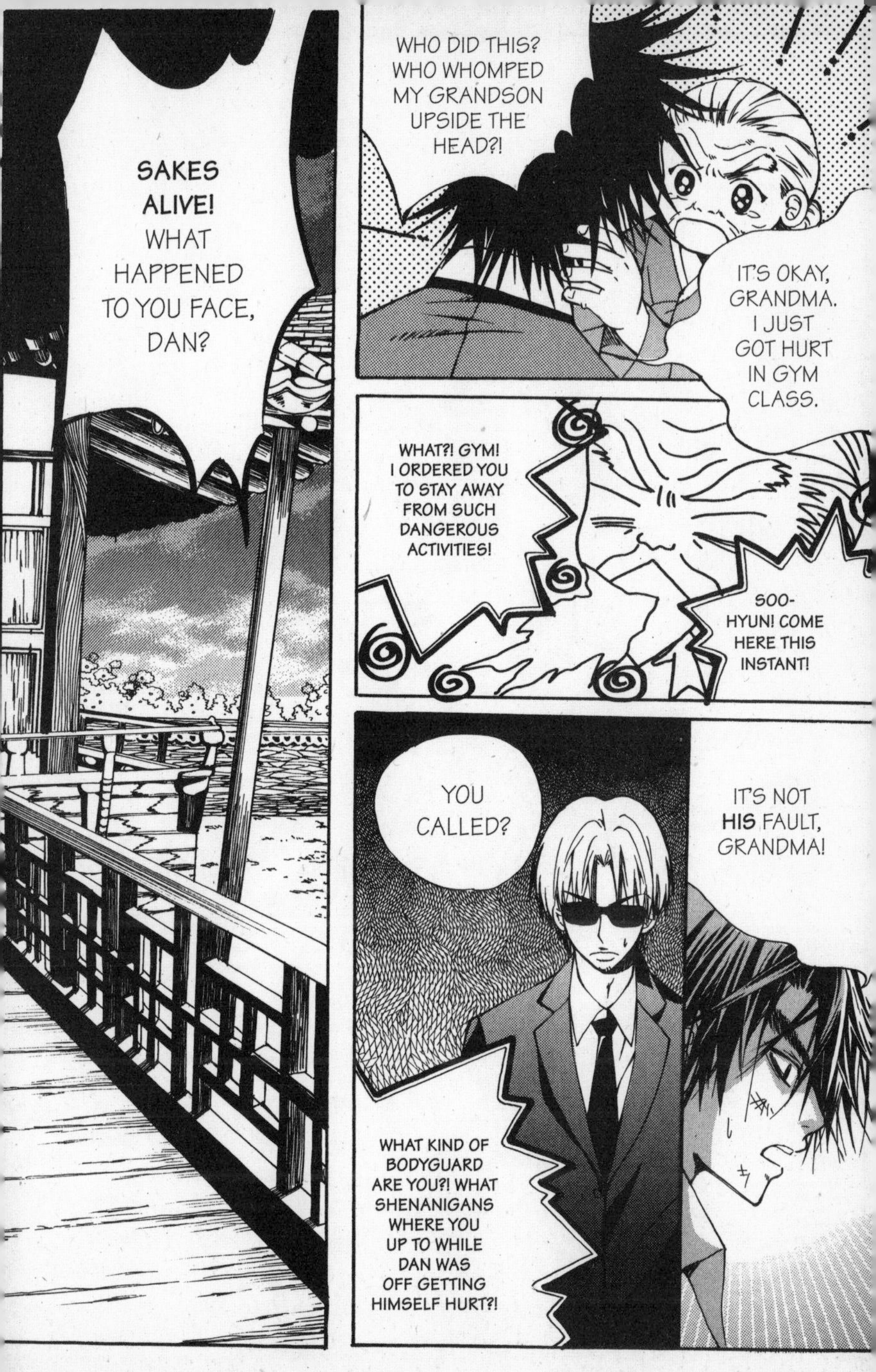
SAKES ALIVE! WHAT HAPPENED TO YOU FACE, DAN?
WHO DID THIS? WHO WHOMPED MY GRANDSON UPSIDE THE HEAD?!
IT'S OKAY, GRANDMA. I JUST GOT HURT IN GYM CLASS.
WHAT?! GYM! I ORDERED YOU TO STAY AWAY FROM SUCH DANGEROUS ACTIVITIES!
SOO-HYUN! COME HERE THIS INSTANT!
YOU CALLED?
IT'S NOT HIS FAULT, GRANDMA!
WHAT KIND OF BODYGUARD ARE YOU?! WHAT SHENANIGANS WHERE YOU UP TO WHILE DAN WAS OFF GETTING HIMSELF HURT?!

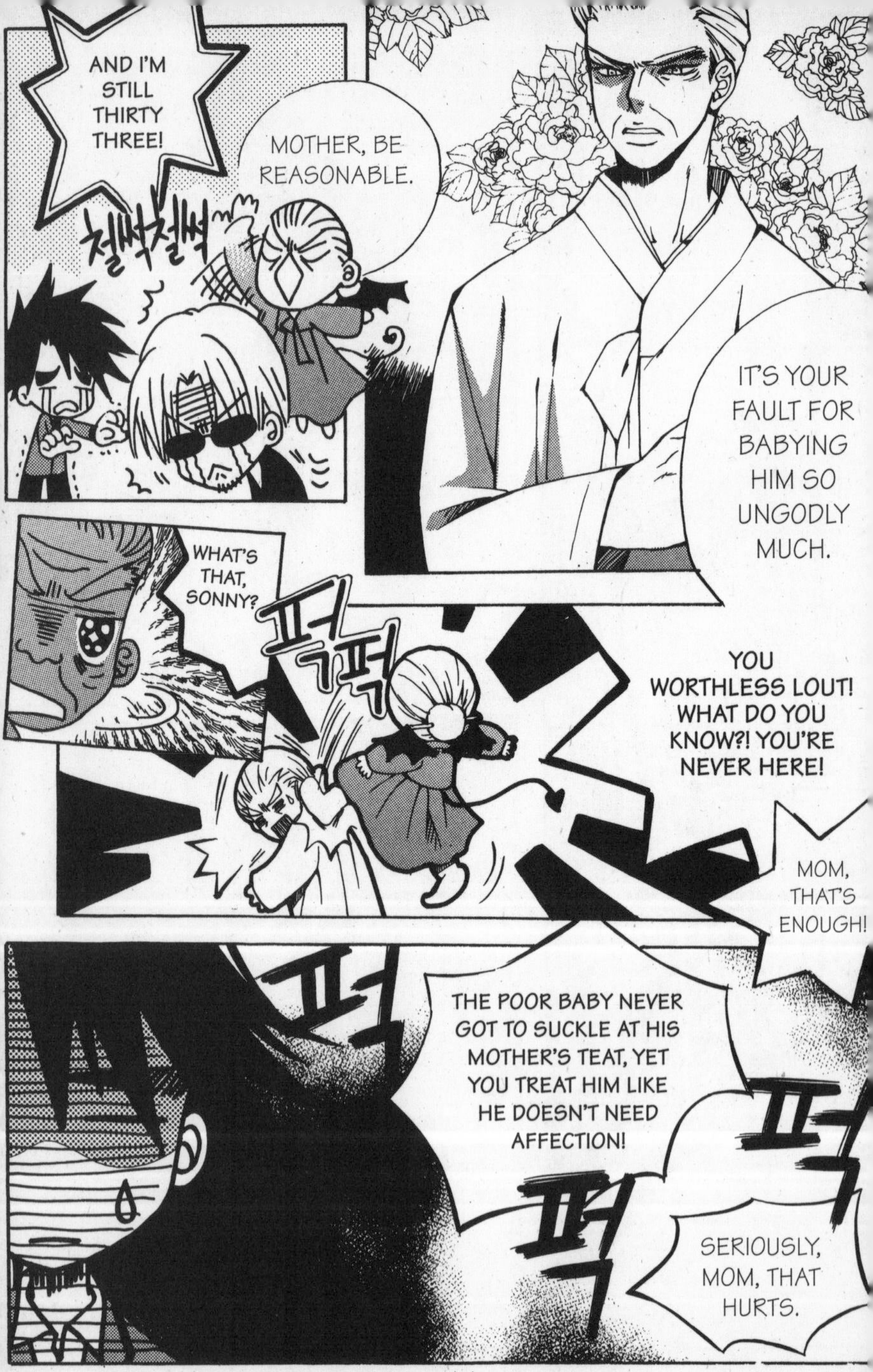

AND I'M STILL THIRTY THREE!
철썩철썩
MOTHER, BE REASONABLE.
IT'S YOUR FAULT FOR BABYING HIM SO UNGODLY MUCH.
WHAT'S THAT, SONNY?
YOU WORTHLESS LOUT! WHAT DO YOU KNOW?! YOU'RE NEVER HERE!
MOM, THAT'S ENOUGH!
THE POOR BABY NEVER GOT TO SUCKLE AT HIS MOTHER'S TEAT, YET YOU TREAT HIM LIKE HE DOESN'T NEED AFFECTION!
SERIOUSLY, MOM, THAT HURTS.

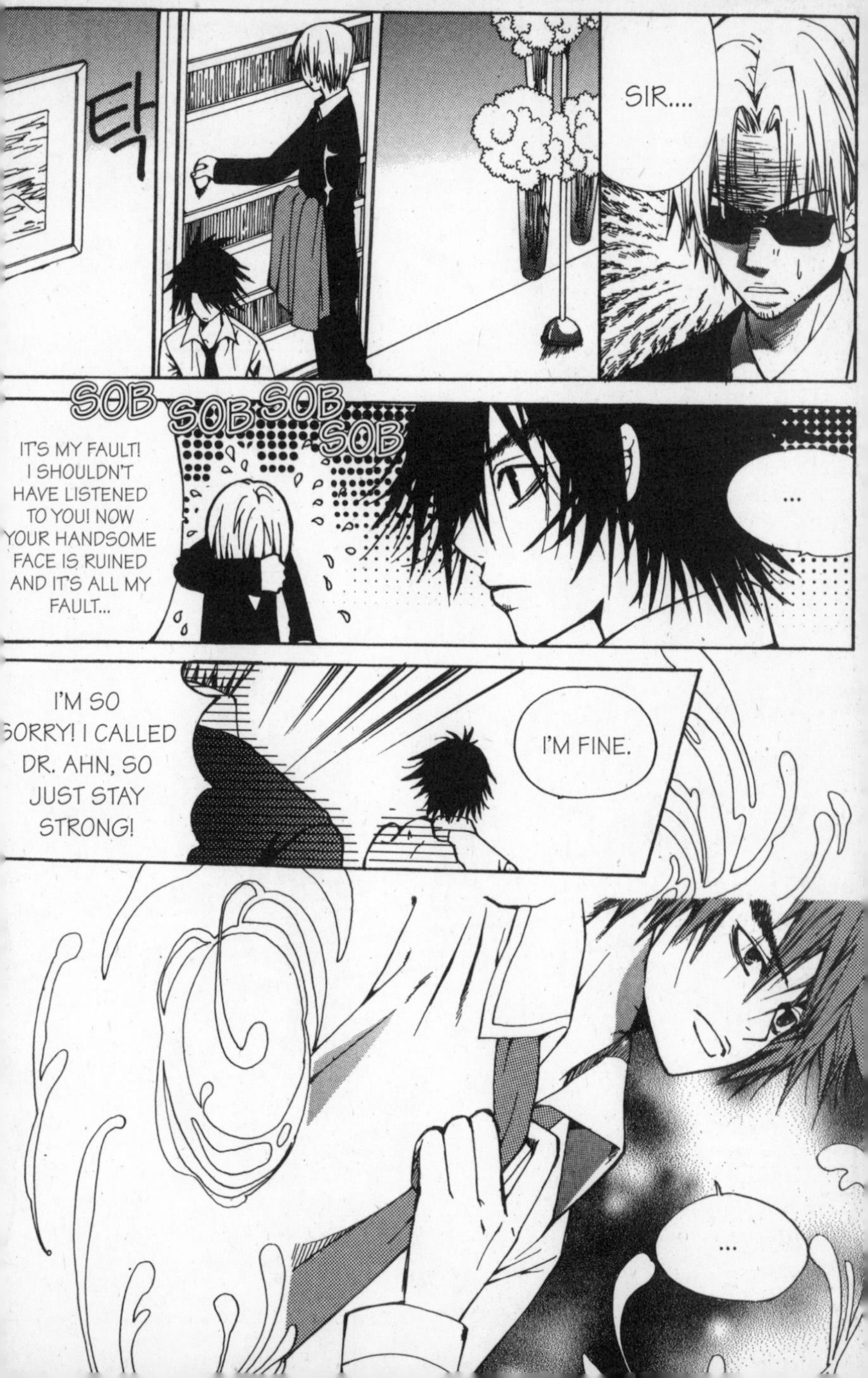

탁
SIR....
SOB SOB SOB SOB
IT'S MY FAULT! I SHOULDN'T HAVE LISTENED TO YOU! NOW YOUR HANDSOME FACE IS RUINED AND IT'S ALL MY FAULT...
...
I'M SO SORRY! I CALLED DR. AHN, SO JUST STAY STRONG!
I'M FINE.
...

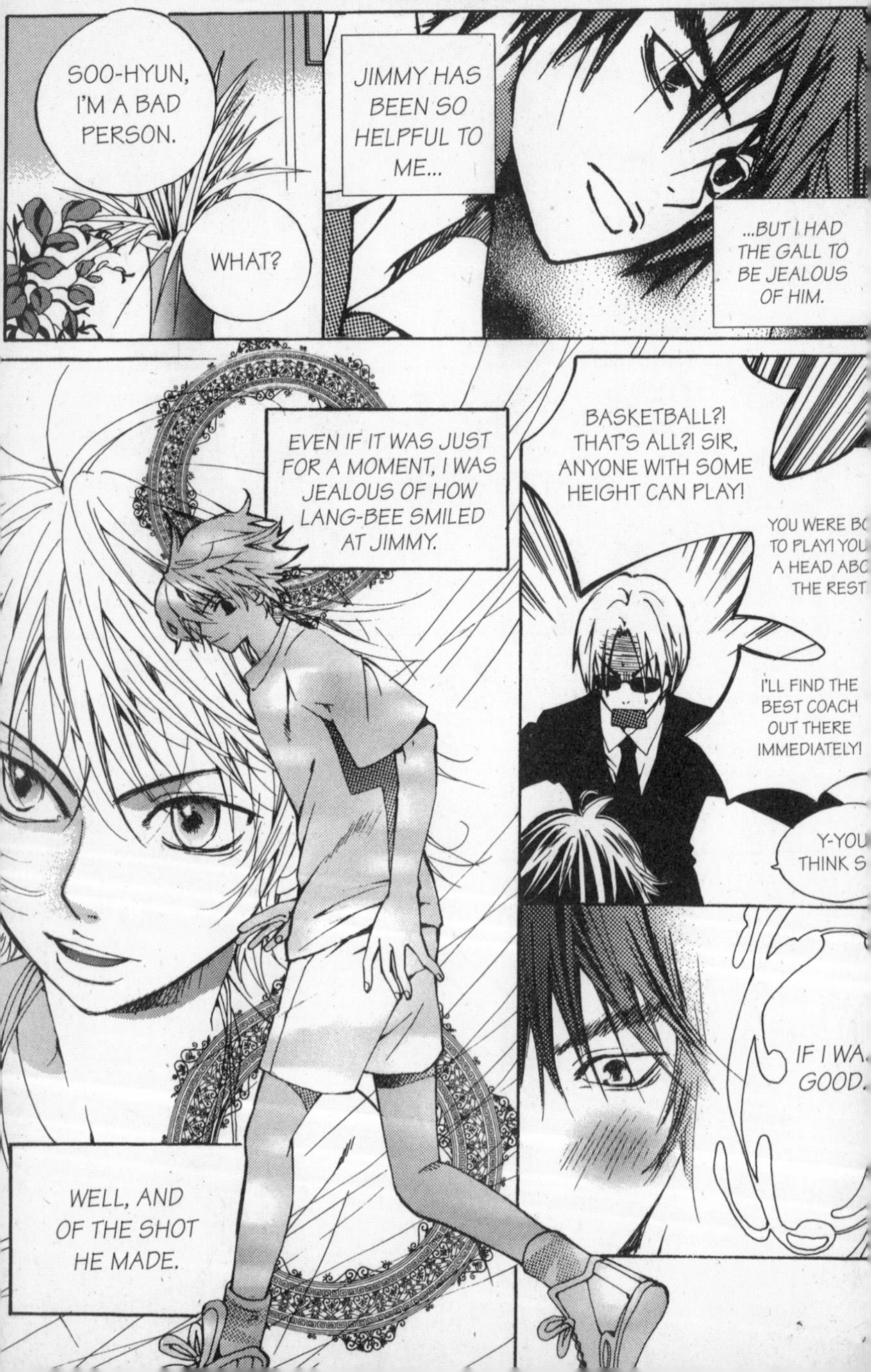
SOO-HYUN, I'M A BAD PERSON.
WHAT?
JIMMY HAS BEEN SO HELPFUL TO ME...
...BUT I HAD THE GALL TO BE JEALOUS OF HIM.
EVEN IF IT WAS JUST FOR A MOMENT, I WAS JEALOUS OF HOW LANG-BEE SMILED AT JIMMY.
WELL, AND OF THE SHOT HE MADE.
BASKETBALL?! THAT'S ALL?! SIR, ANYONE WITH SOME HEIGHT CAN PLAY!
YOU WERE B
TO PLAY! YOU
A HEAD ABO
THE REST
I'LL FIND THE BEST COACH OUT THERE IMMEDIATELY!
Y-YOU THINK S
IF I WA
GOOD.

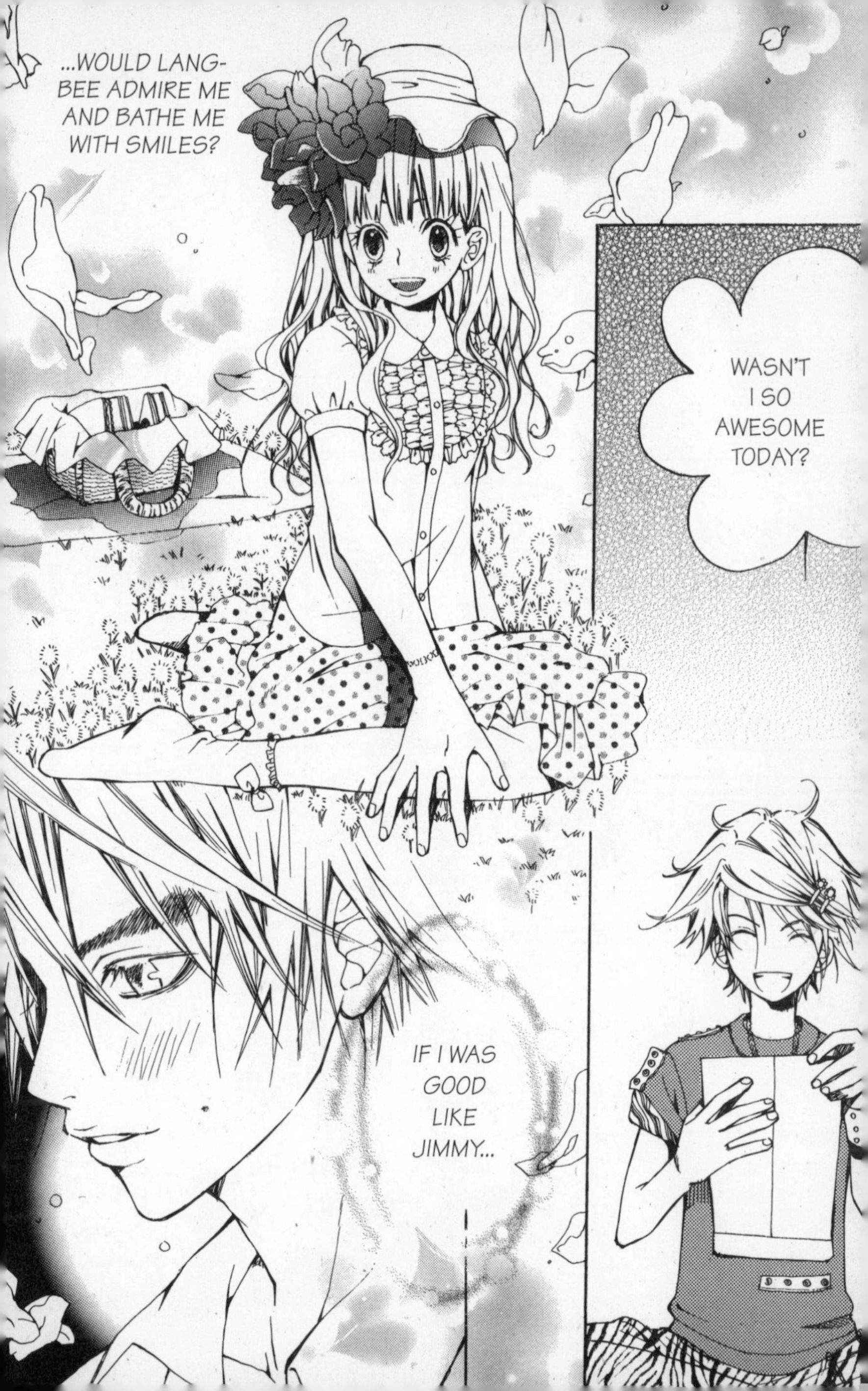
...WOULD LANG-BEE ADMIRE ME AND BATHE ME WITH SMILES?
WASN'T I SO AWESOME TODAY?
IF I WAS GOOD LIKE JIMMY...

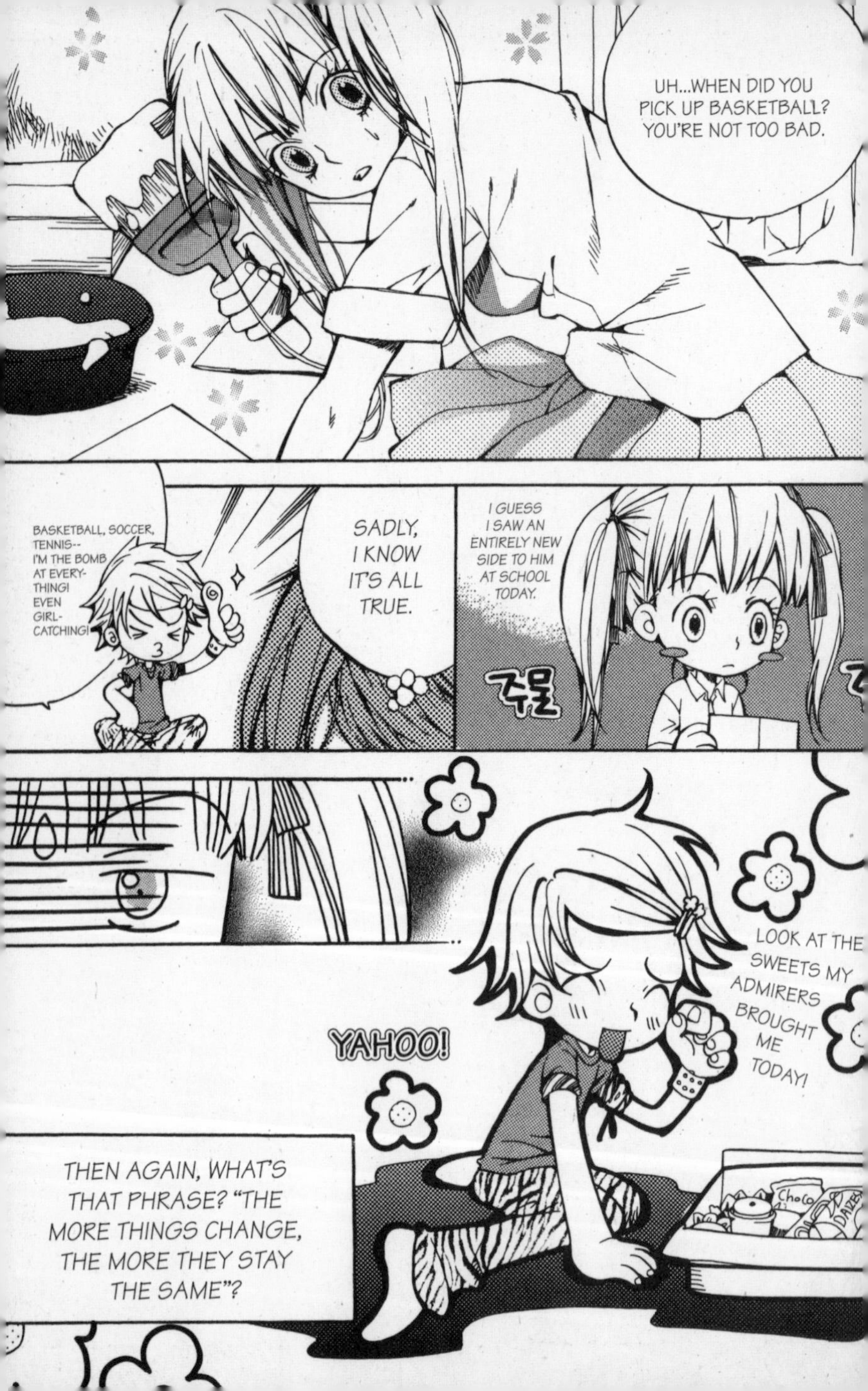
UH...WHEN DID YOU PICK UP BASKETBALL? YOU'RE NOT TOO BAD.
BASKETBALL, SOCCER, TENNIS-- I'M THE BOMB AT EVERY-THING! EVEN GIRL-CATCHING!
SADLY, I KNOW IT'S ALL TRUE.
I GUESS I SAW AN ENTIRELY NEW SIDE TO HIM AT SCHOOL TODAY.
주물
YAHOO!
LOOK AT THE SWEETS MY ADMIRERS BROUGHT ME TODAY!
THEN AGAIN, WHAT'S THAT PHRASE? "THE MORE THINGS CHANGE, THE MORE THEY STAY THE SAME"?
Choco

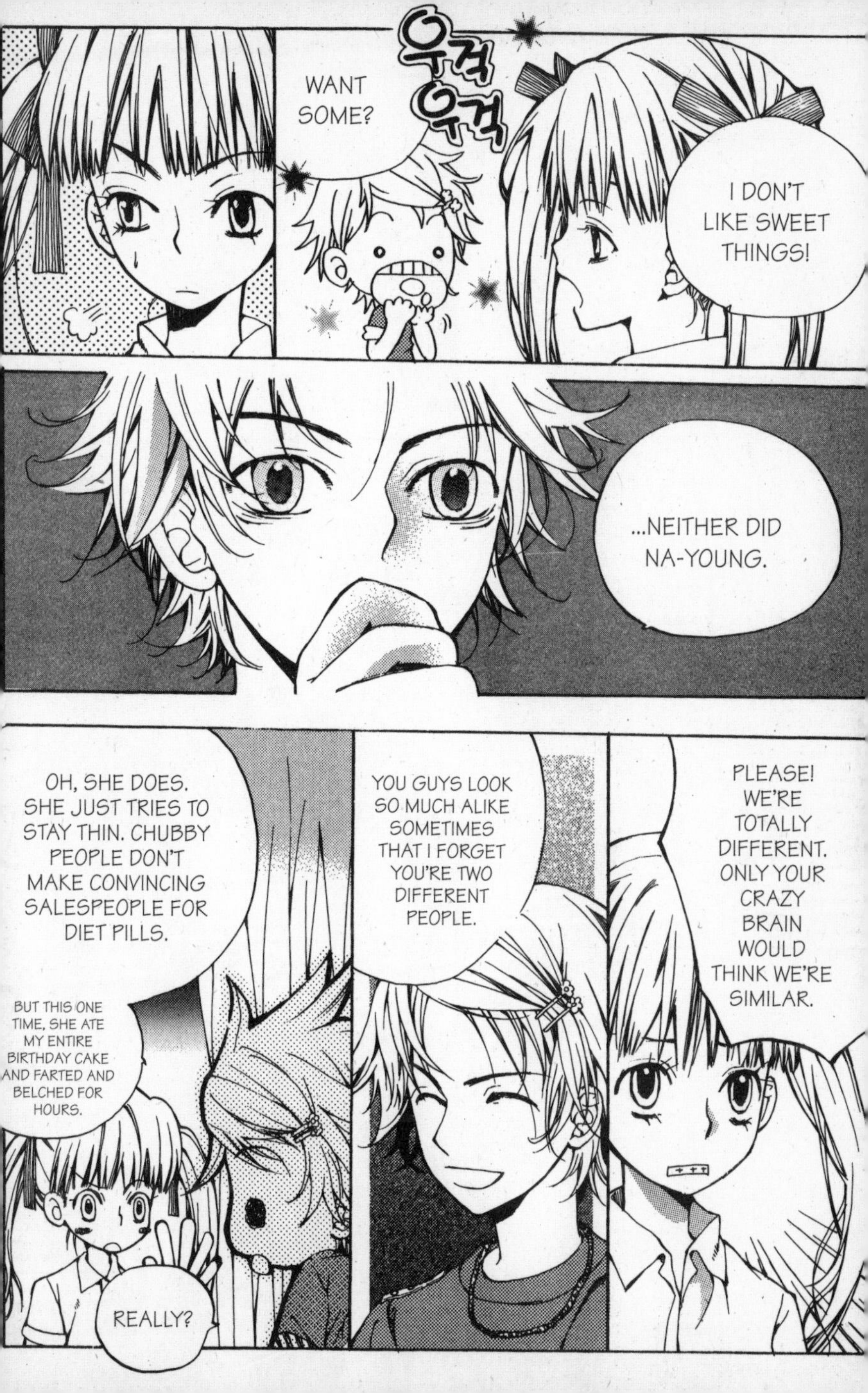
WANT SOME?
우걱 우걱
I DON'T LIKE SWEET THINGS!
...NEITHER DID NA-YOUNG.
OH, SHE DOES. SHE JUST TRIES TO STAY THIN. CHUBBY PEOPLE DON'T MAKE CONVINCING SALESPEOPLE FOR DIET PILLS.
BUT THIS ONE TIME, SHE ATE MY ENTIRE BIRTHDAY CAKE AND FARTED AND BELCHED FOR HOURS.
REALLY?
YOU GUYS LOOK SO MUCH ALIKE SOMETIMES THAT I FORGET YOU'RE TWO DIFFERENT PEOPLE.
PLEASE! WE'RE TOTALLY DIFFERENT. ONLY YOUR CRAZY BRAIN WOULD THINK WE'RE SIMILAR.

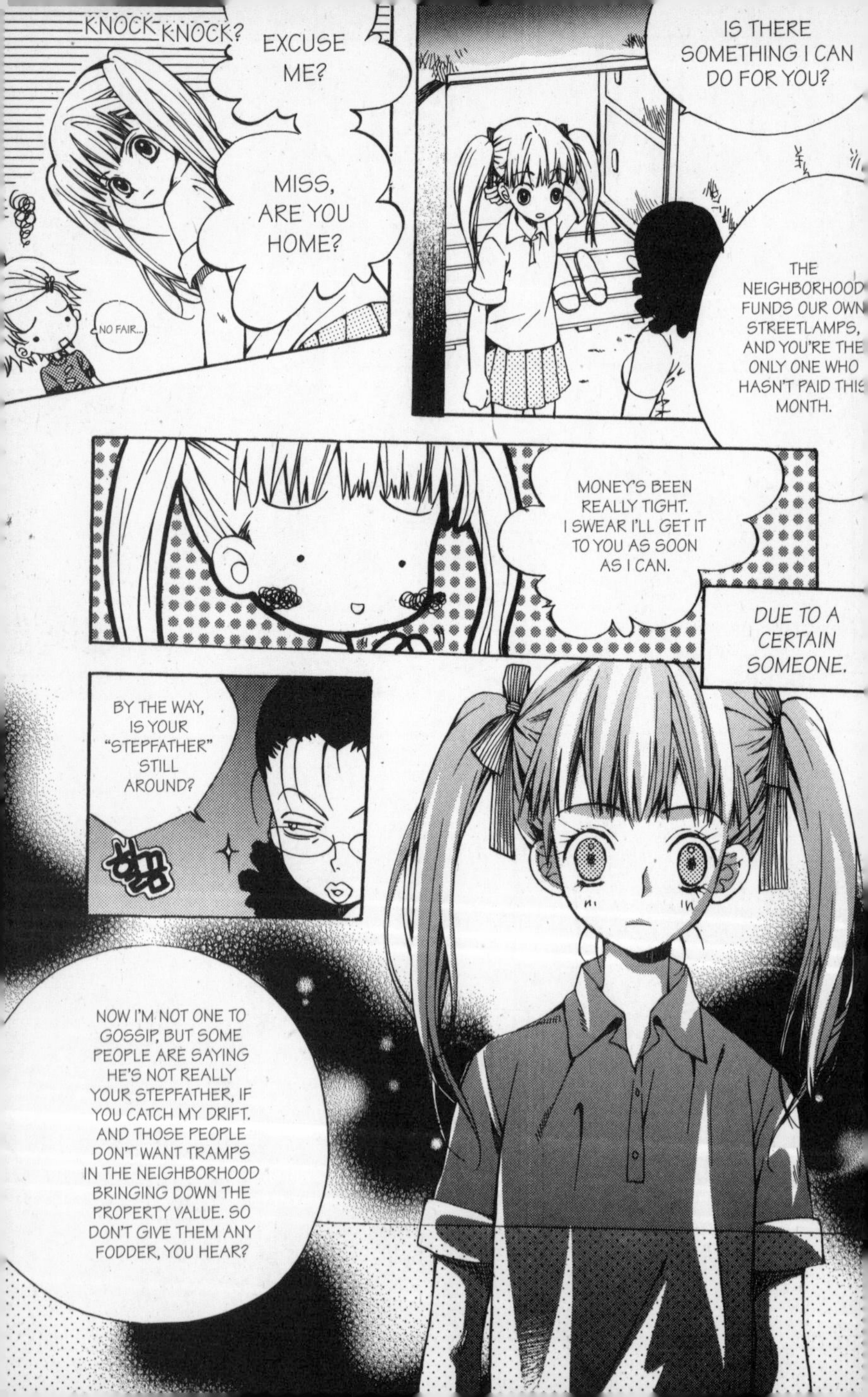
KNOCK KNOCK?
EXCUSE ME?
MISS, ARE YOU HOME?
NO FAIR...
IS THERE SOMETHING I CAN DO FOR YOU?
THE NEIGHBORHOOD FUNDS OUR OWN STREETLAMPS, AND YOU'RE THE ONLY ONE WHO HASN'T PAID THIS MONTH.
MONEY'S BEEN REALLY TIGHT. I SWEAR I'LL GET IT TO YOU AS SOON AS I CAN.
DUE TO A CERTAIN SOMEONE.
BY THE WAY, IS YOUR "STEPFATHER" STILL AROUND?
NOW I'M NOT ONE TO GOSSIP, BUT SOME PEOPLE ARE SAYING HE'S NOT REALLY YOUR STEPFATHER, IF YOU CATCH MY DRIFT. AND THOSE PEOPLE DON'T WANT TRAMPS IN THE NEIGHBORHOOD BRINGING DOWN THE PROPERTY VALUE. SO DON'T GIVE THEM ANY FODDER, YOU HEAR?

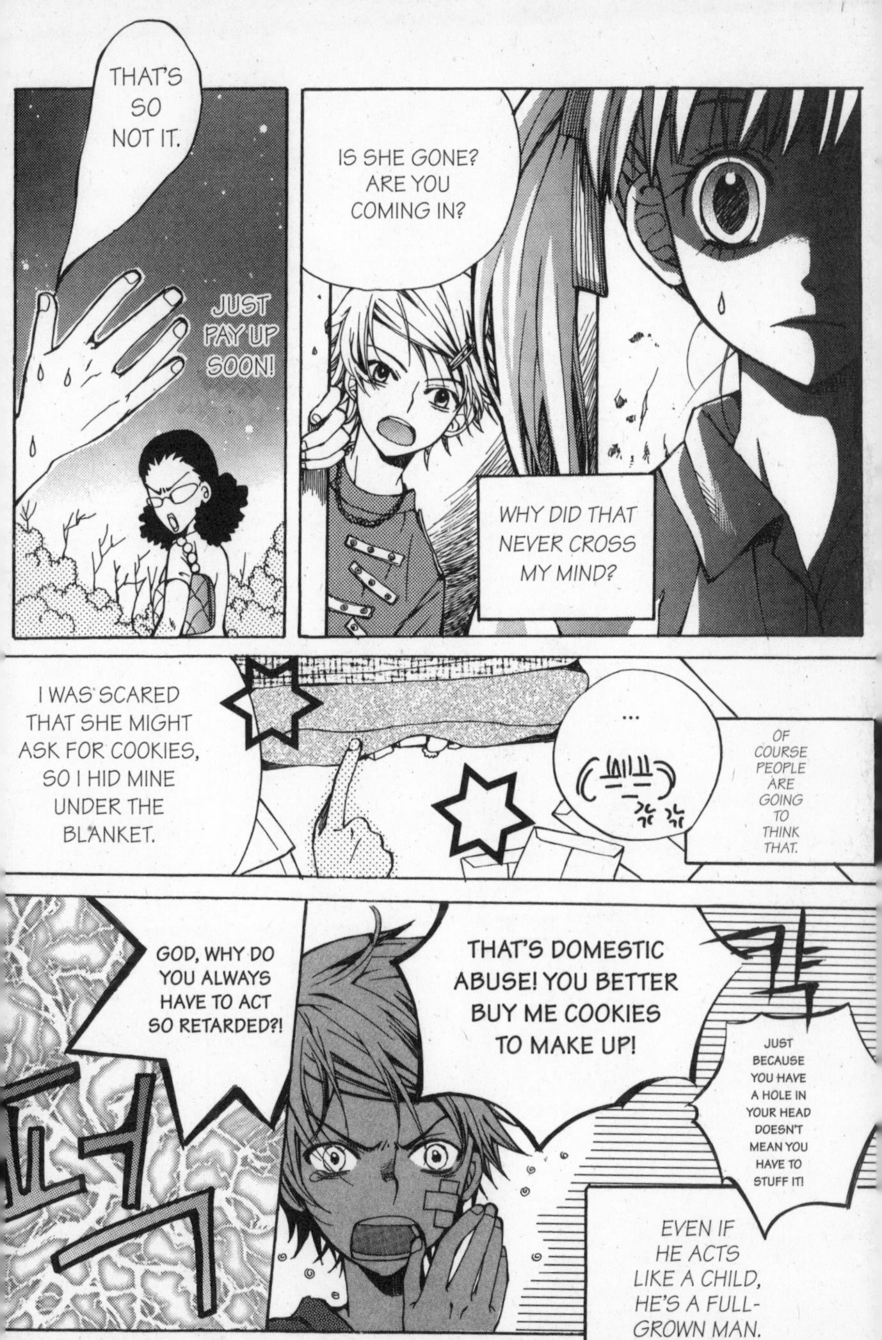
THAT'S SO NOT IT.
JUST PAY UP SOON!
IS SHE GONE? ARE YOU COMING IN?
WHY DID THAT NEVER CROSS MY MIND?
I WAS SCARED THAT SHE MIGHT ASK FOR COOKIES, SO I HID MINE UNDER THE BLANKET.
...
OF COURSE PEOPLE ARE GOING TO THINK THAT.
GOD, WHY DO YOU ALWAYS HAVE TO ACT SO RETARDED?!
THAT'S DOMESTIC ABUSE! YOU BETTER BUY ME COOKIES TO MAKE UP!
JUST BECAUSE YOU HAVE A HOLE IN YOUR HEAD DOESN'T MEAN YOU HAVE TO STUFF IT!
EVEN IF HE ACTS LIKE A CHILD, HE'S A FULL-GROWN MAN.

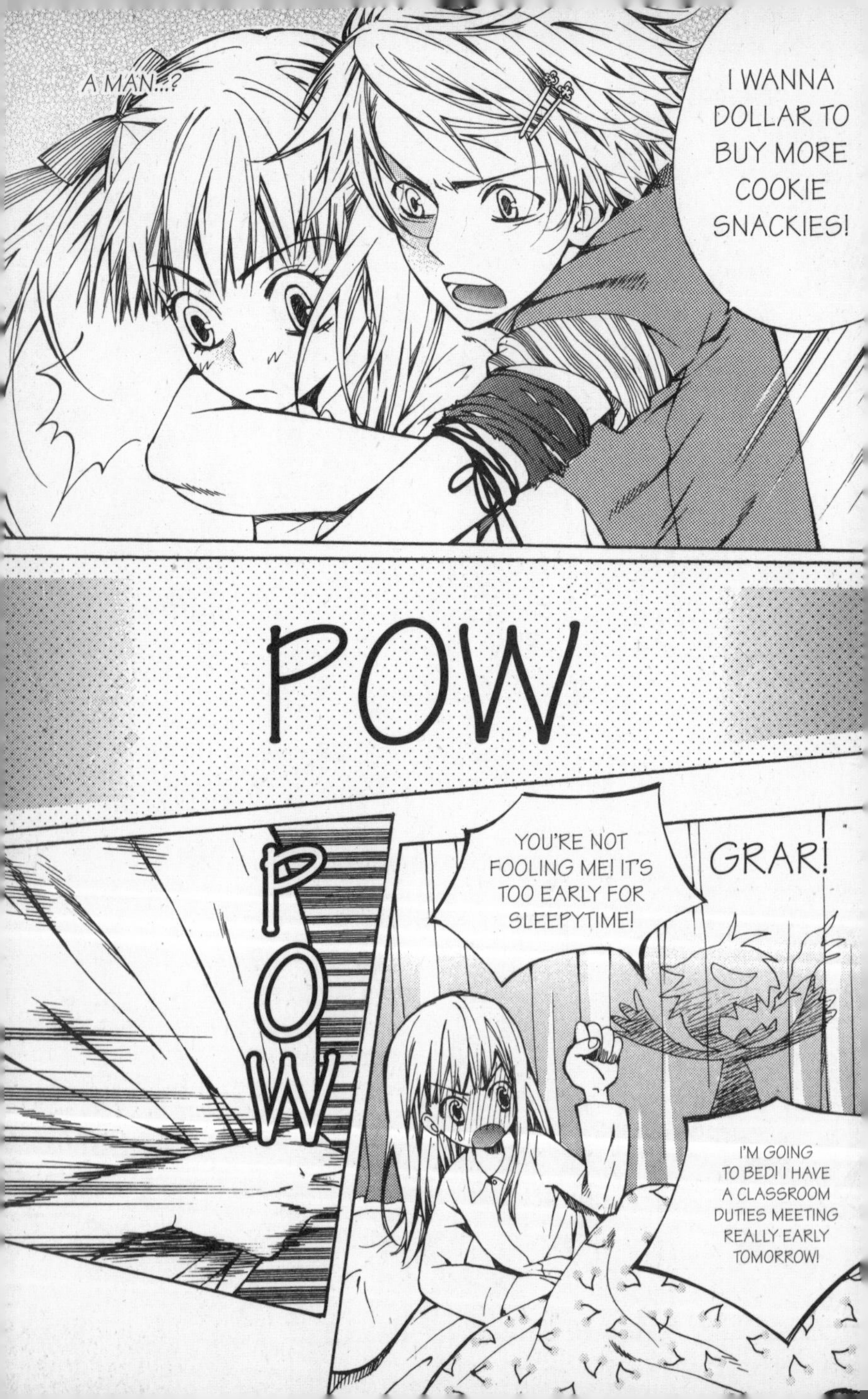

A MAN...?
I WANNA DOLLAR TO BUY MORE COOKIE SNACKIES!
POW
POW
YOU'RE NOT FOOLING ME! IT'S TOO EARLY FOR SLEEPYTIME!
GRAR!
I'M GOING TO BED! I HAVE A CLASSROOM DUTIES MEETING REALLY EARLY TOMORROW!

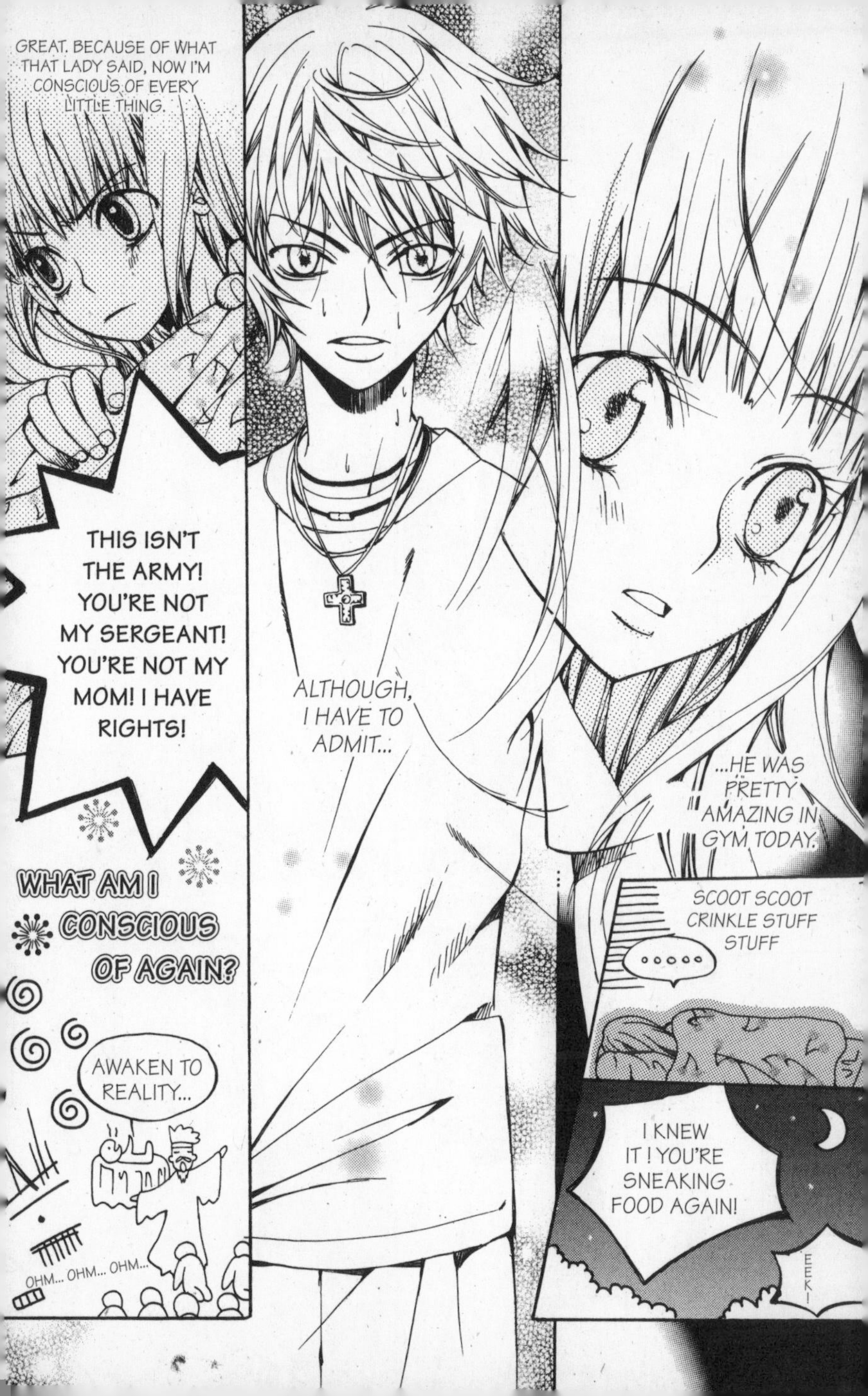
GREAT. BECAUSE OF WHAT THAT LADY SAID, NOW I'M CONSCIOUS OF EVERY LITTLE THING.
THIS ISN'T THE ARMY! YOU'RE NOT MY SERGEANT! YOU'RE NOT MY MOM! I HAVE RIGHTS!
WHAT AM I CONSCIOUS OF AGAIN?
AWAKEN TO REALITY...
OHM... OHM... OHM...
ALTHOUGH, I HAVE TO ADMIT...
...HE WAS PRETTY AMAZING IN GYM TODAY.
SCOOT SCOOT CRINKLE STUFF STUFF
.....
I KNEW IT! YOU'RE SNEAKING FOOD AGAIN!
EEK!

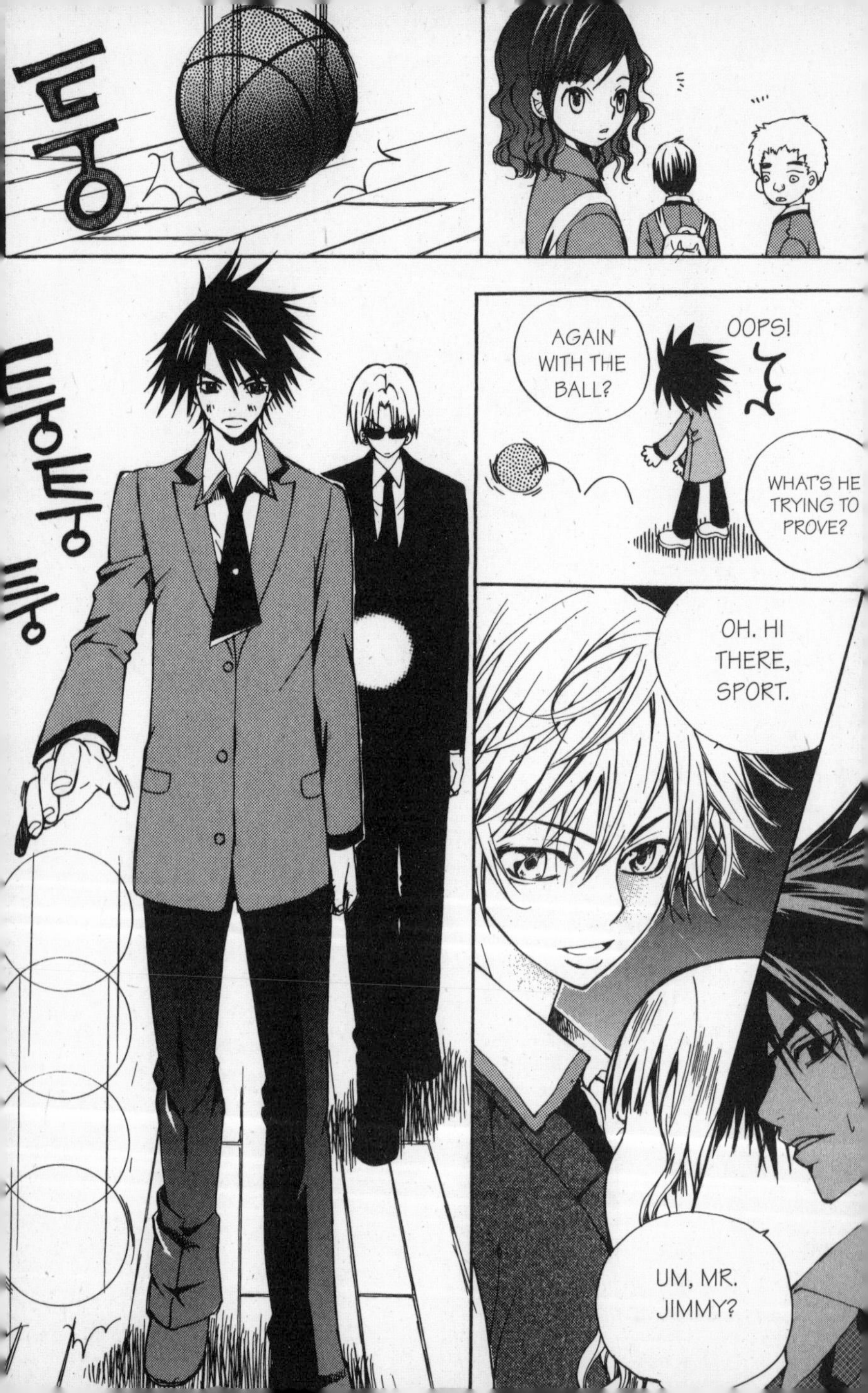

둥
퉁퉁
퉁
AGAIN WITH THE BALL?
OOPS!
WHAT'S HE TRYING TO PROVE?
OH. HI THERE, SPORT.
UM, MR. JIMMY?

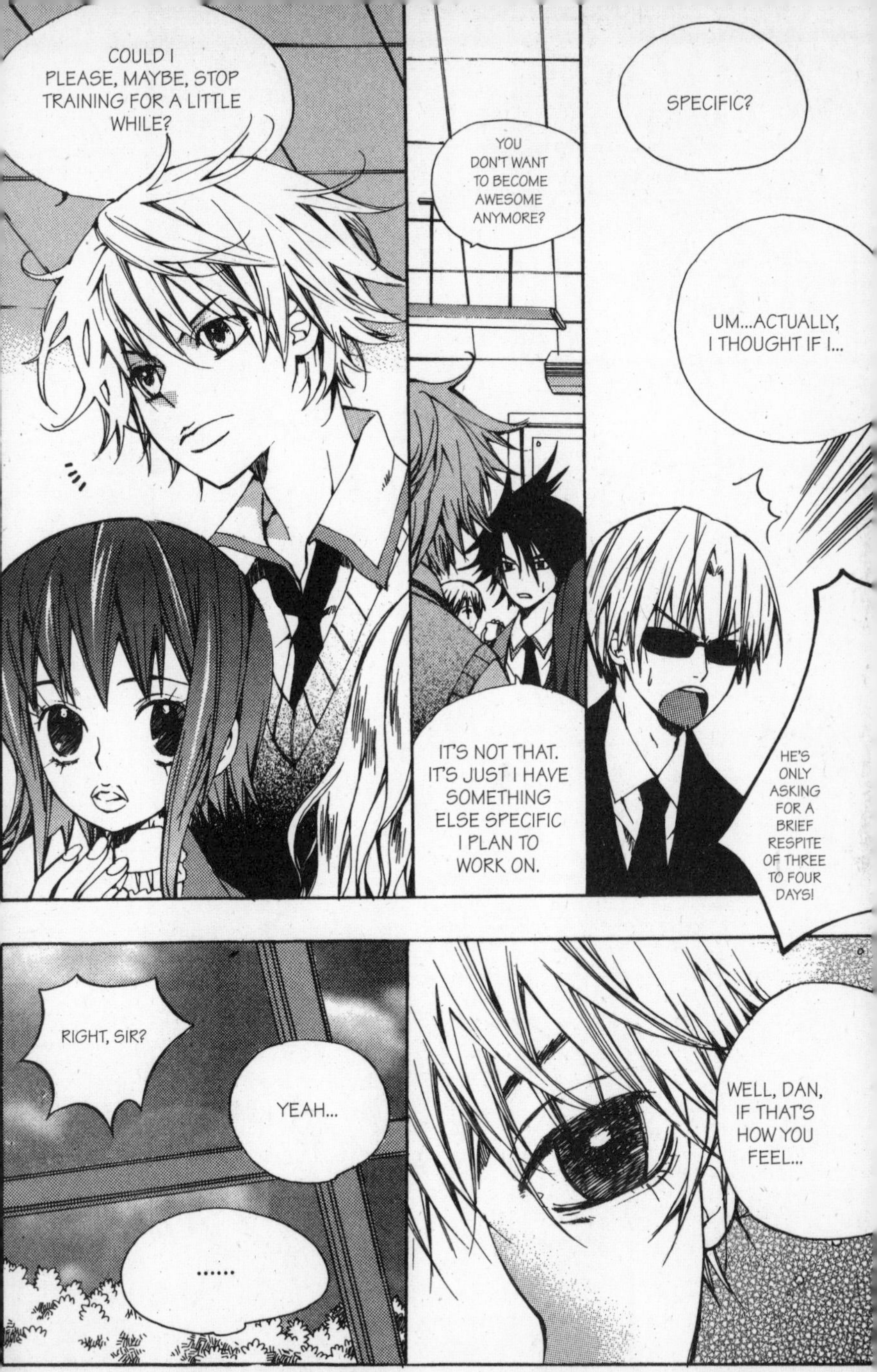
COULD I PLEASE, MAYBE, STOP TRAINING FOR A LITTLE WHILE?
YOU DON'T WANT TO BECOME AWESOME ANYMORE?
IT'S NOT THAT. IT'S JUST I HAVE SOMETHING ELSE SPECIFIC I PLAN TO WORK ON.
SPECIFIC?
UM...ACTUALLY, I THOUGHT IF I...
HE'S ONLY ASKING FOR A BRIEF RESPITE OF THREE TO FOUR DAYS!
RIGHT, SIR?
YEAH...
......
WELL, DAN, IF THAT'S HOW YOU FEEL...

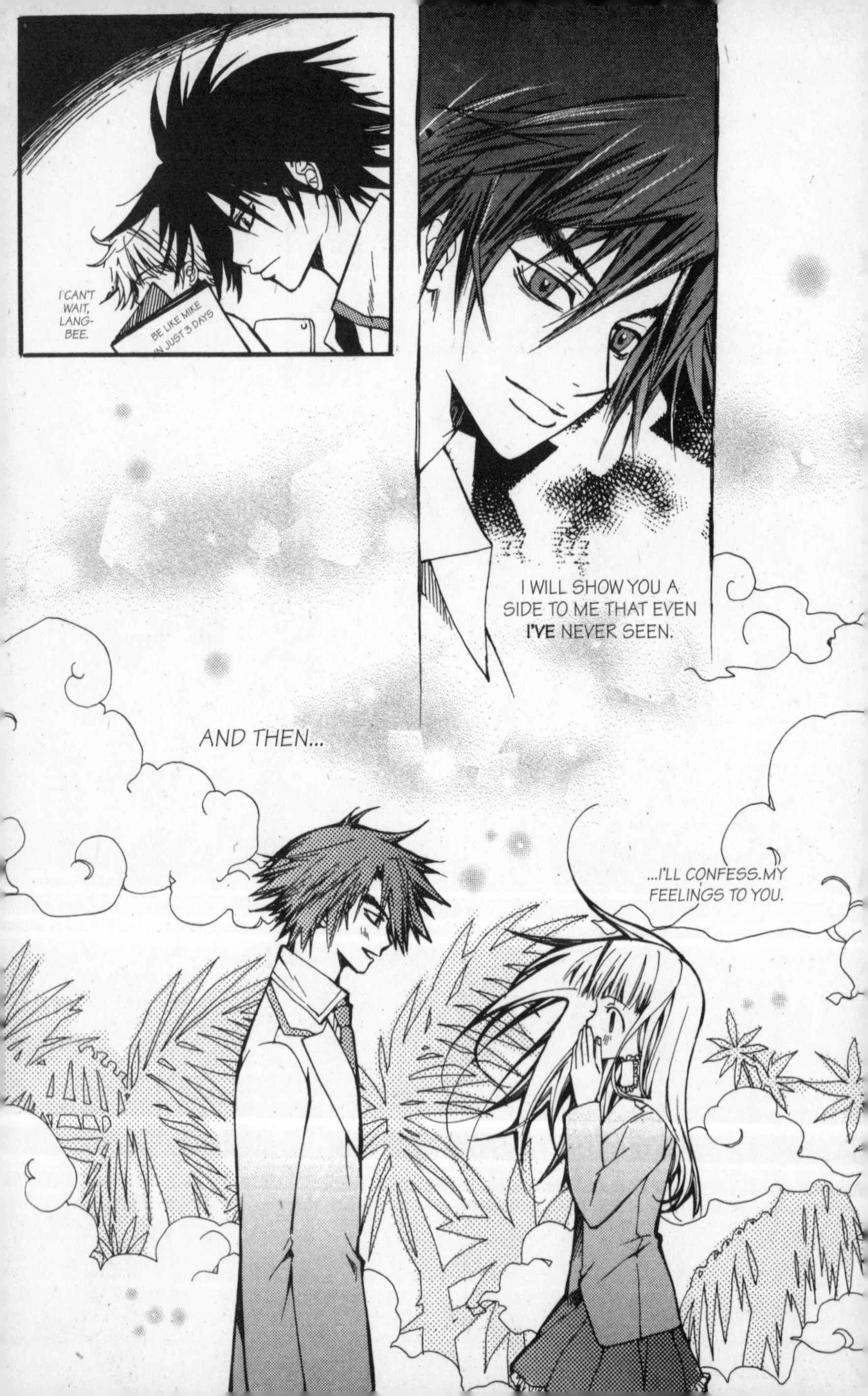
I CAN'T WAIT, LANG-BEE.
BE LIKE MIKE IN JUST 3 DAYS
I WILL SHOW YOU A SIDE TO ME THAT EVEN **I'VE** NEVER SEEN.
AND THEN...
...I'LL CONFESS MY FEELINGS TO YOU.

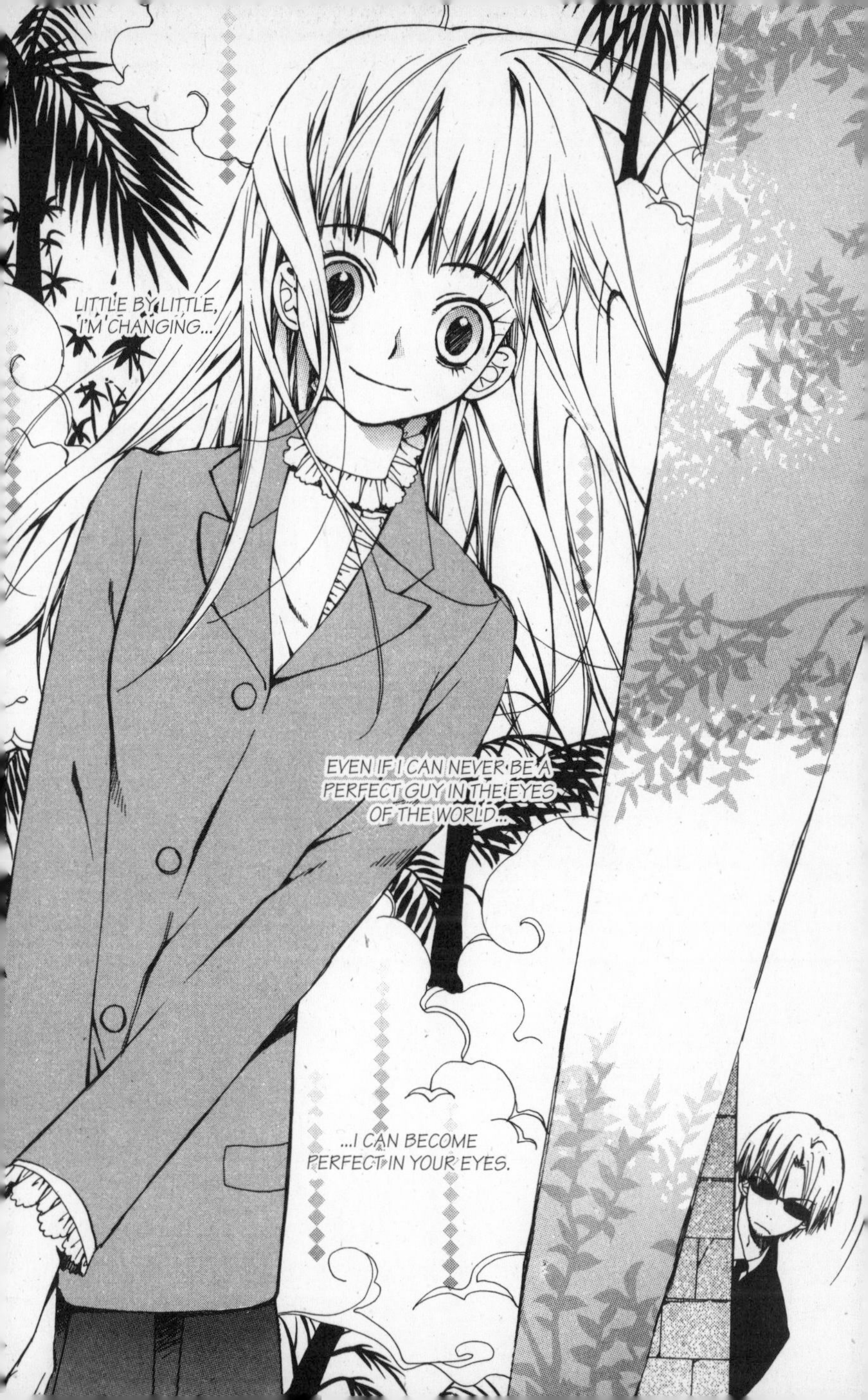
LITTLE BY LITTLE, I'M CHANGING...
EVEN IF I CAN NEVER BE A PERFECT GUY IN THE EYES OF THE WORLD...
...I CAN BECOME PERFECT IN YOUR EYES.

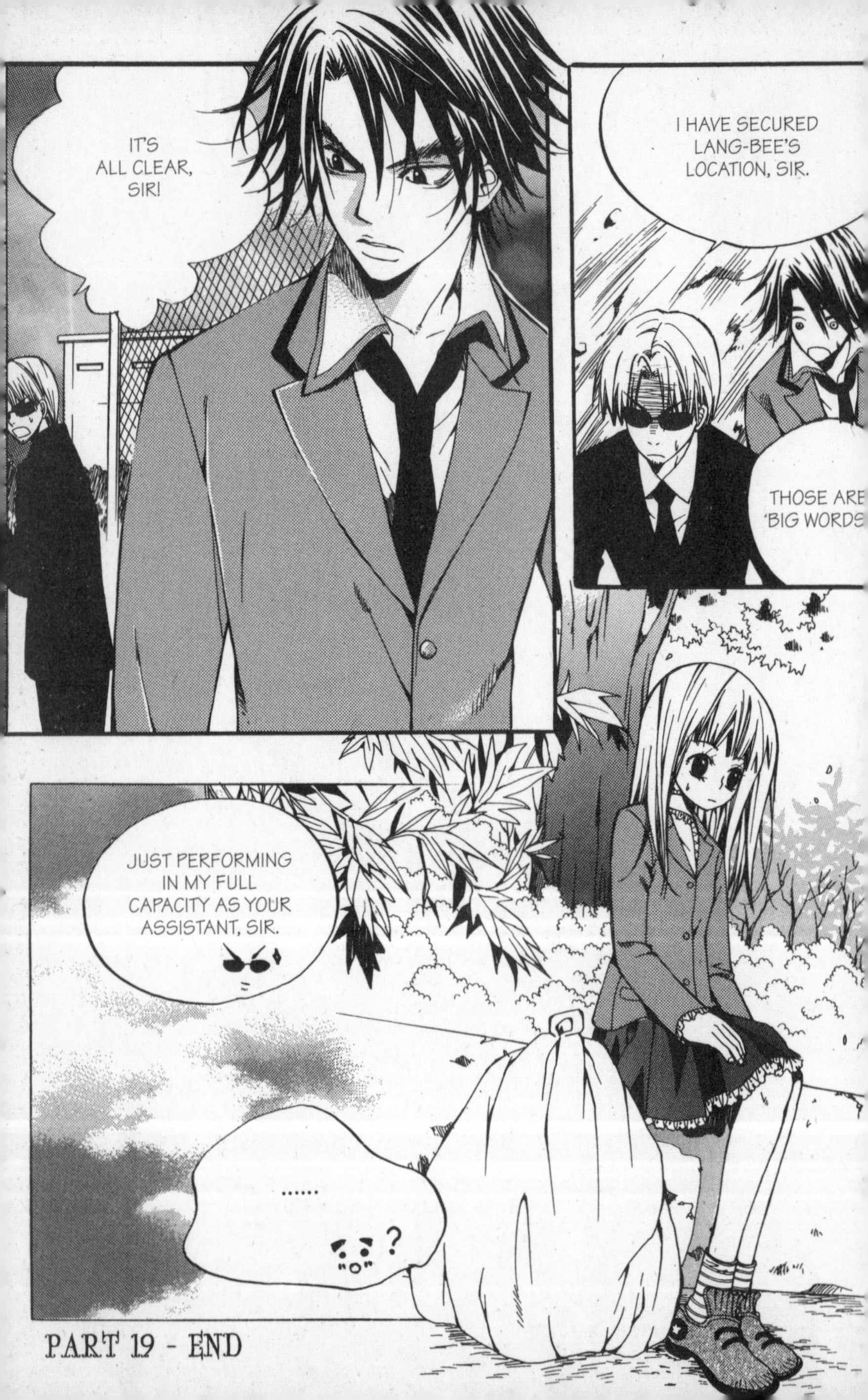
IT'S ALL CLEAR, SIR!
I HAVE SECURED LANG-BEE'S LOCATION, SIR.
THOSE ARE BIG WORDS
JUST PERFORMING IN MY FULL CAPACITY AS YOUR ASSISTANT, SIR.
......
?
PART 19 - END

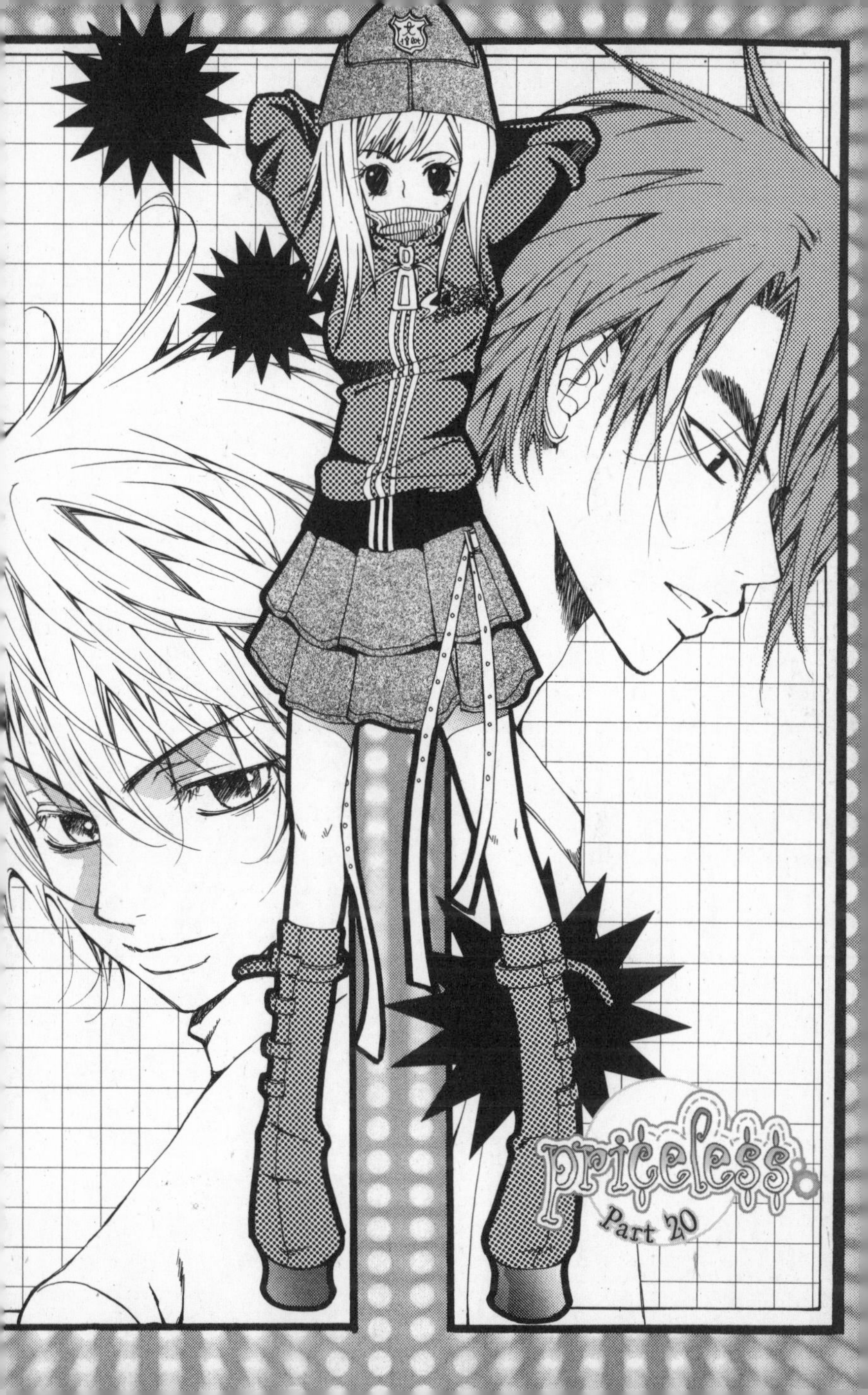
priceless
Part 20

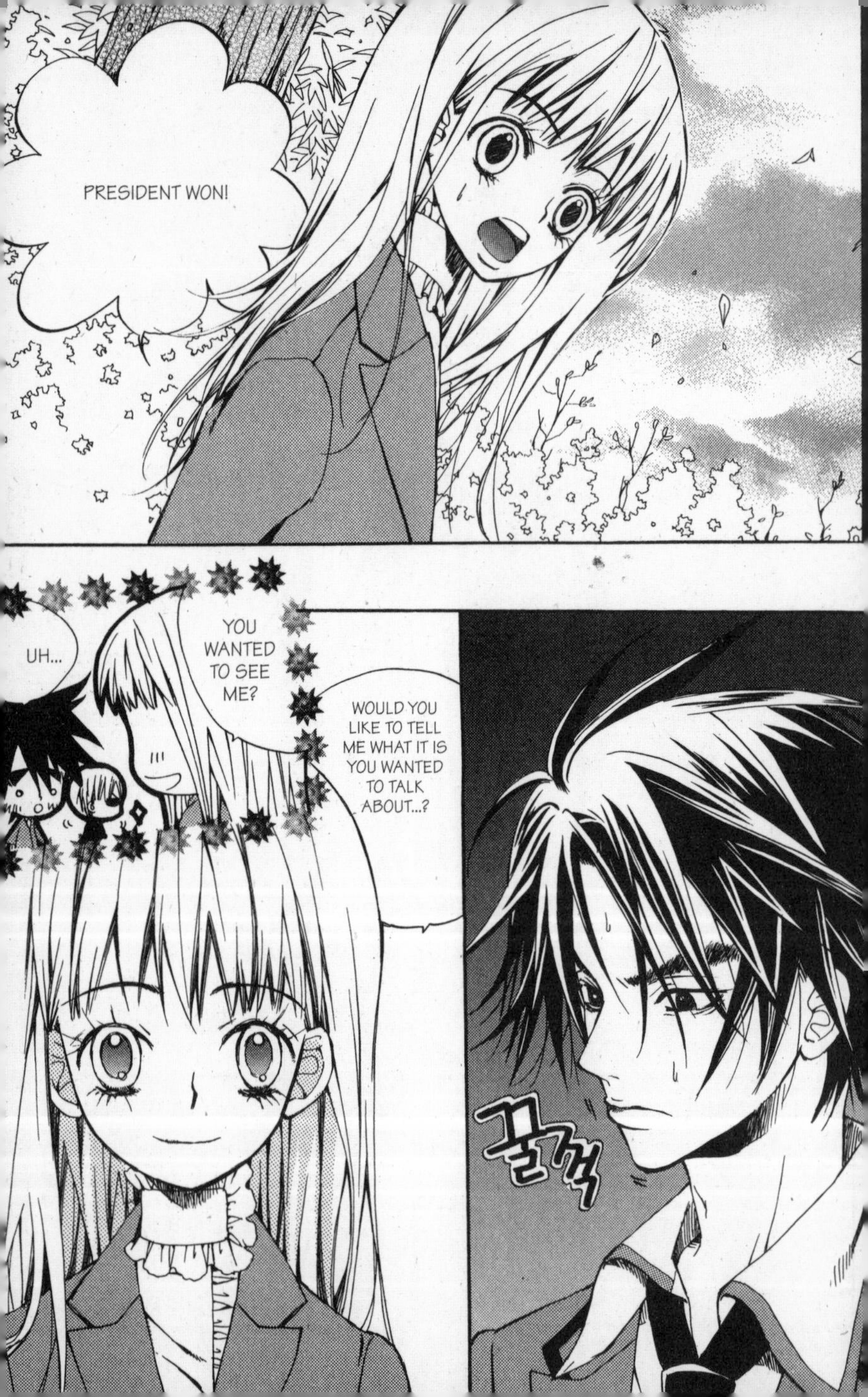
PRESIDENT WON!
UH...
YOU WANTED TO SEE ME?
WOULD YOU LIKE TO TELL ME WHAT IT IS YOU WANTED TO TALK ABOUT...?
꿀꺽

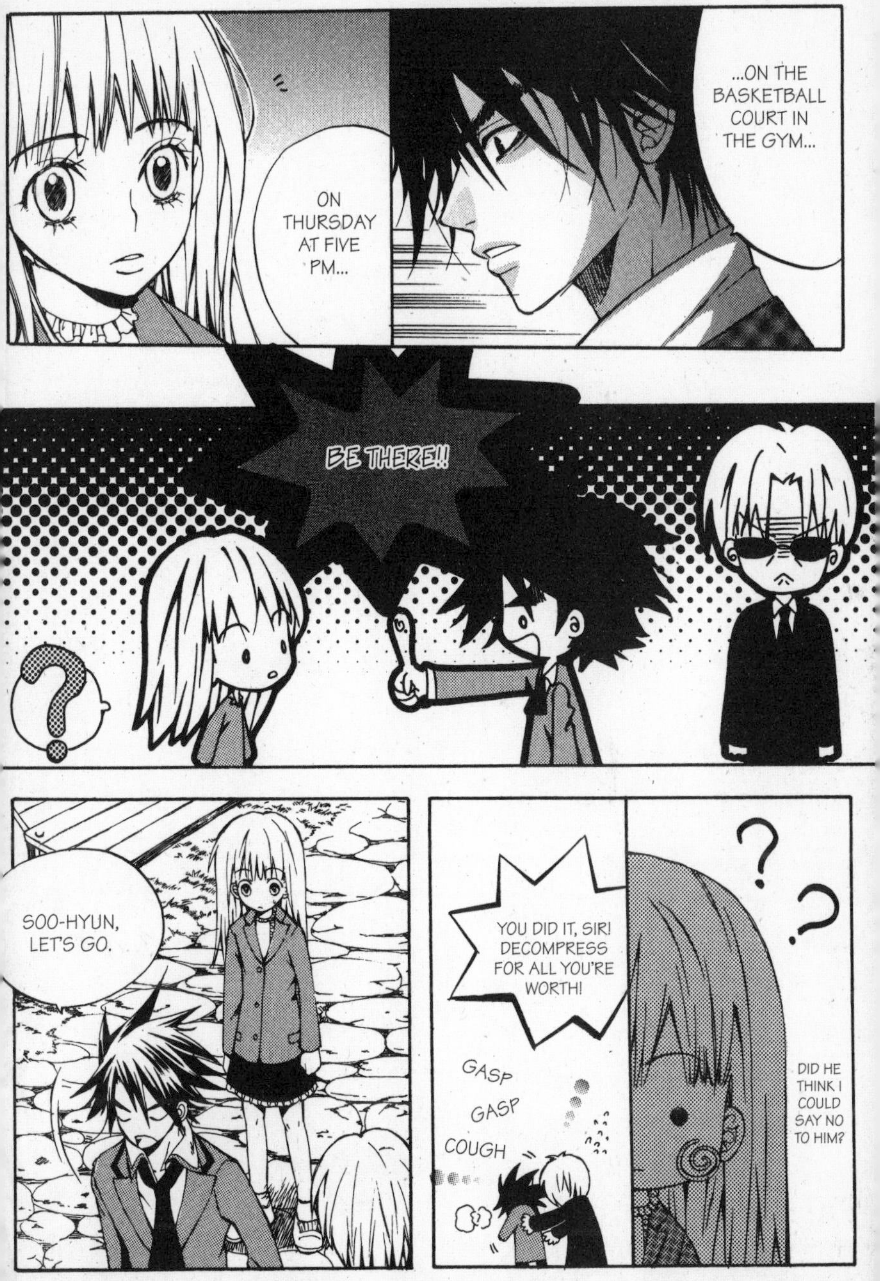
ON THURSDAY AT FIVE PM...
...ON THE BASKETBALL COURT IN THE GYM...
BE THERE!!
SOO-HYUN, LET'S GO.
YOU DID IT, SIR! DECOMPRESS FOR ALL YOU'RE WORTH!
GASP
GASP
COUGH
DID HE THINK I COULD SAY NO TO HIM?

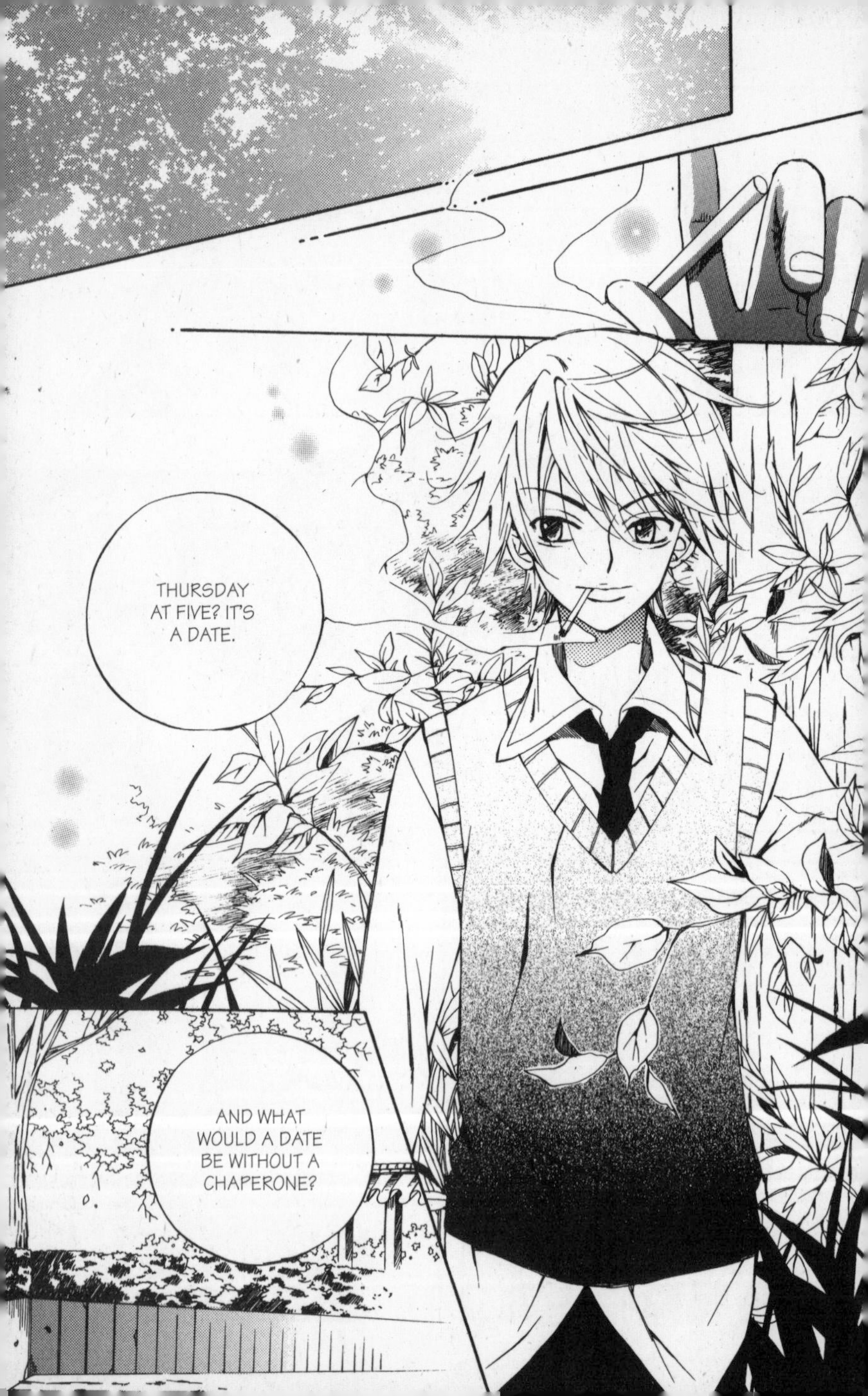
THURSDAY AT FIVE? IT'S A DATE.
AND WHAT WOULD A DATE BE WITHOUT A CHAPERONE?

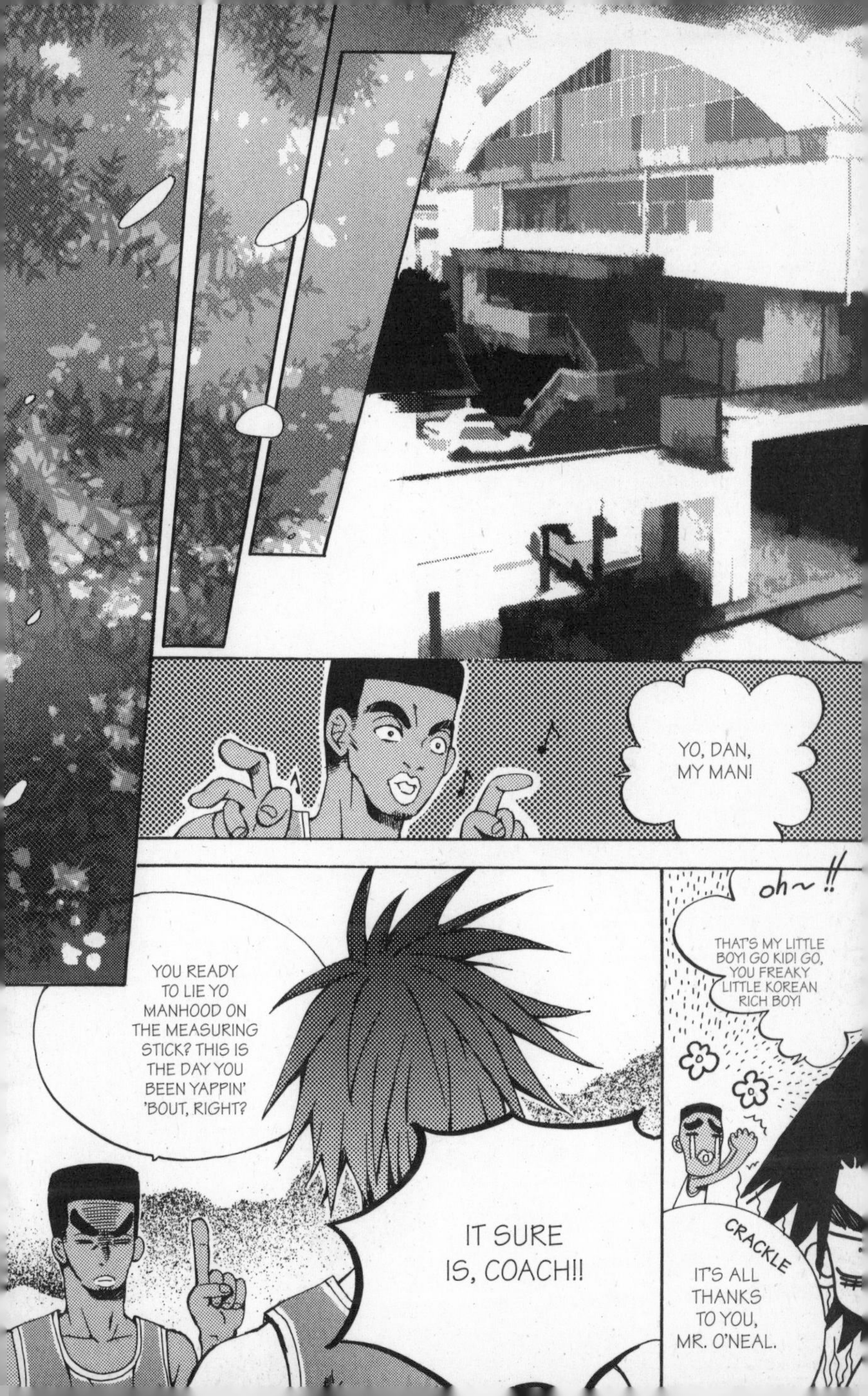
YO, DAN, MY MAN!
YOU READY TO LIE YO MANHOOD ON THE MEASURING STICK? THIS IS THE DAY YOU BEEN YAPPIN' 'BOUT, RIGHT?
IT SURE IS, COACH!!
oh~ !!
THAT'S MY LITTLE BOY! GO KID! GO, YOU FREAKY LITTLE KOREAN RICH BOY!
CRACKLE
IT'S ALL THANKS TO YOU, MR. O'NEAL.

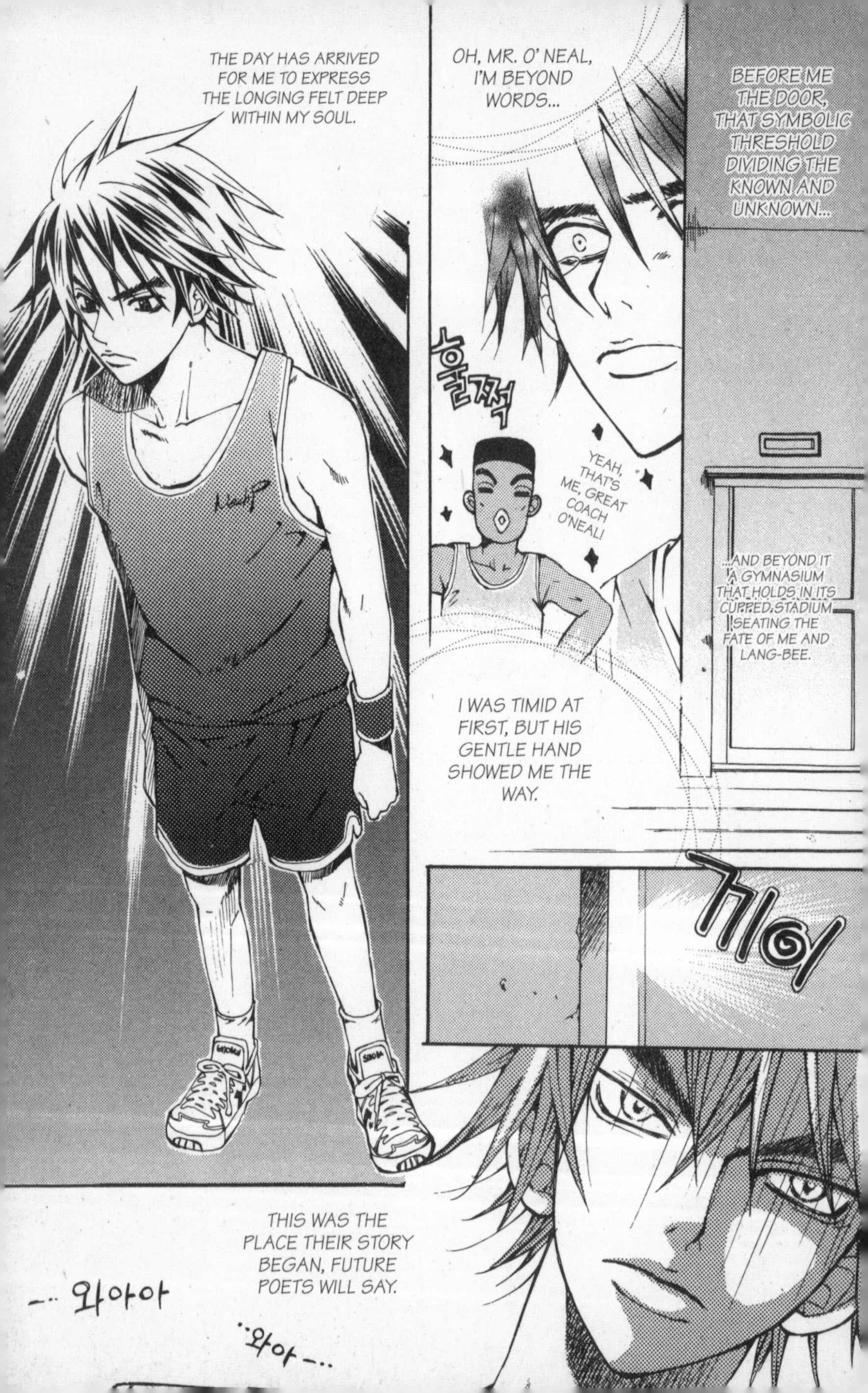
THE DAY HAS ARRIVED FOR ME TO EXPRESS THE LONGING FELT DEEP WITHIN MY SOUL.
OH, MR. O' NEAL, I'M BEYOND WORDS...
훌쩍
YEAH, THAT'S ME, GREAT COACH O'NEAL!
I WAS TIMID AT FIRST, BUT HIS GENTLE HAND SHOWED ME THE WAY.
BEFORE ME THE DOOR, THAT SYMBOLIC THRESHOLD DIVIDING THE KNOWN AND UNKNOWN...
...AND BEYOND IT A GYMNASIUM THAT HOLDS IN ITS CUPPED STADIUM SEATING THE FATE OF ME AND LANG-BEE.
끼익
THIS WAS THE PLACE THEIR STORY BEGAN, FUTURE POETS WILL SAY.
-.. 와아아
..와아-..

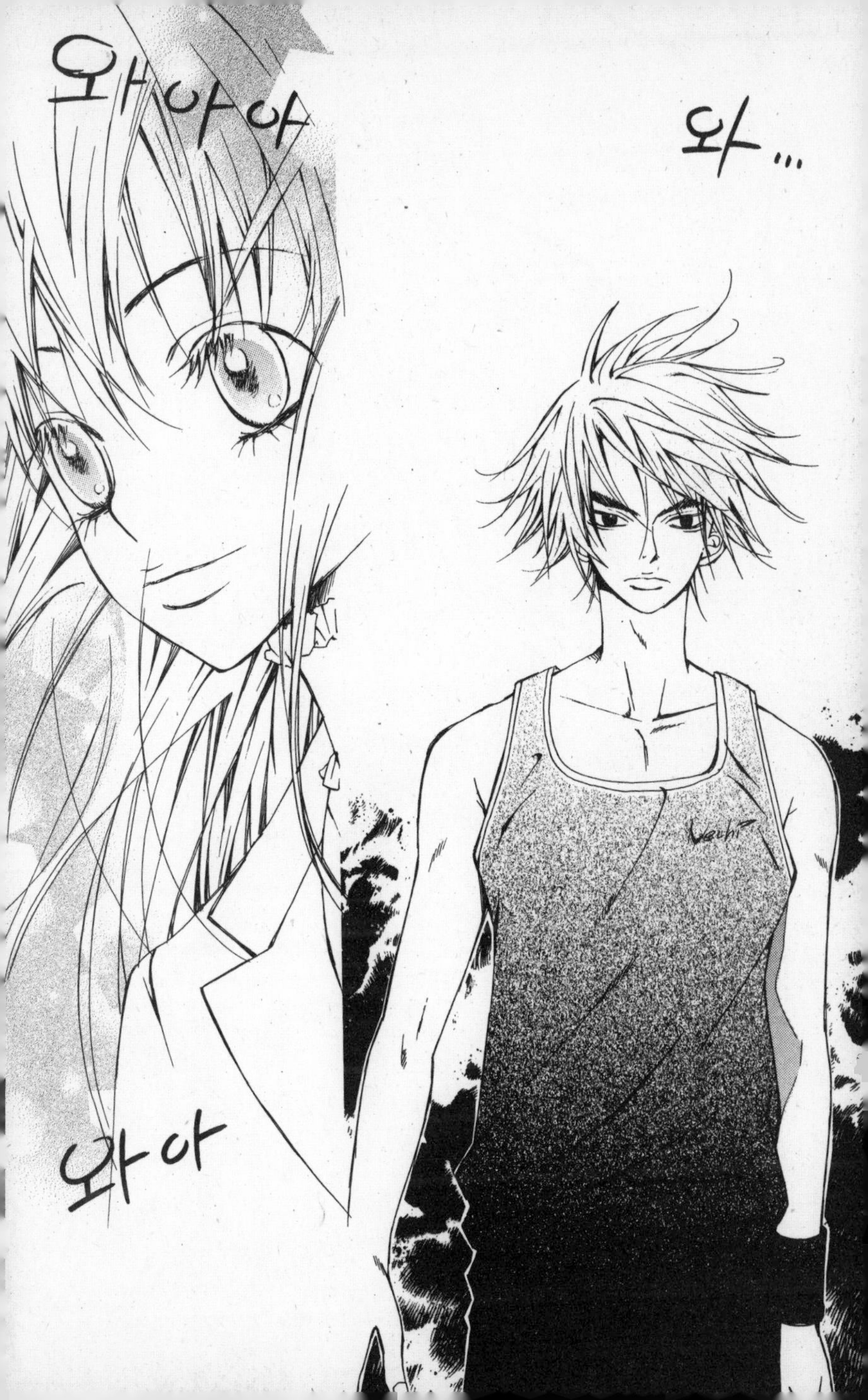
와아아
와...
와아

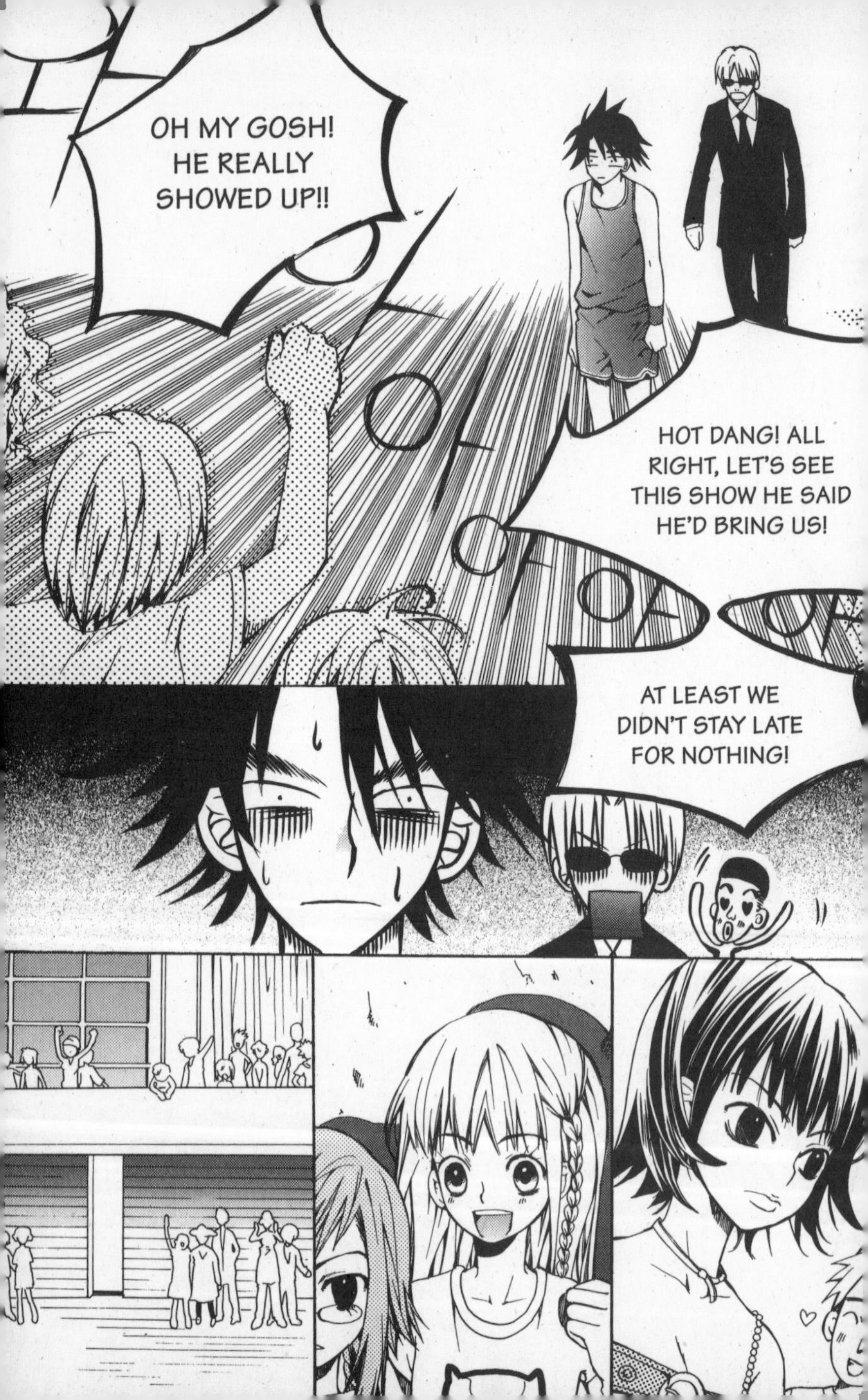
OH MY GOSH! HE REALLY SHOWED UP!!
HOT DANG! ALL RIGHT, LET'S SEE THIS SHOW HE SAID HE'D BRING US!
AT LEAST WE DIDN'T STAY LATE FOR NOTHING!

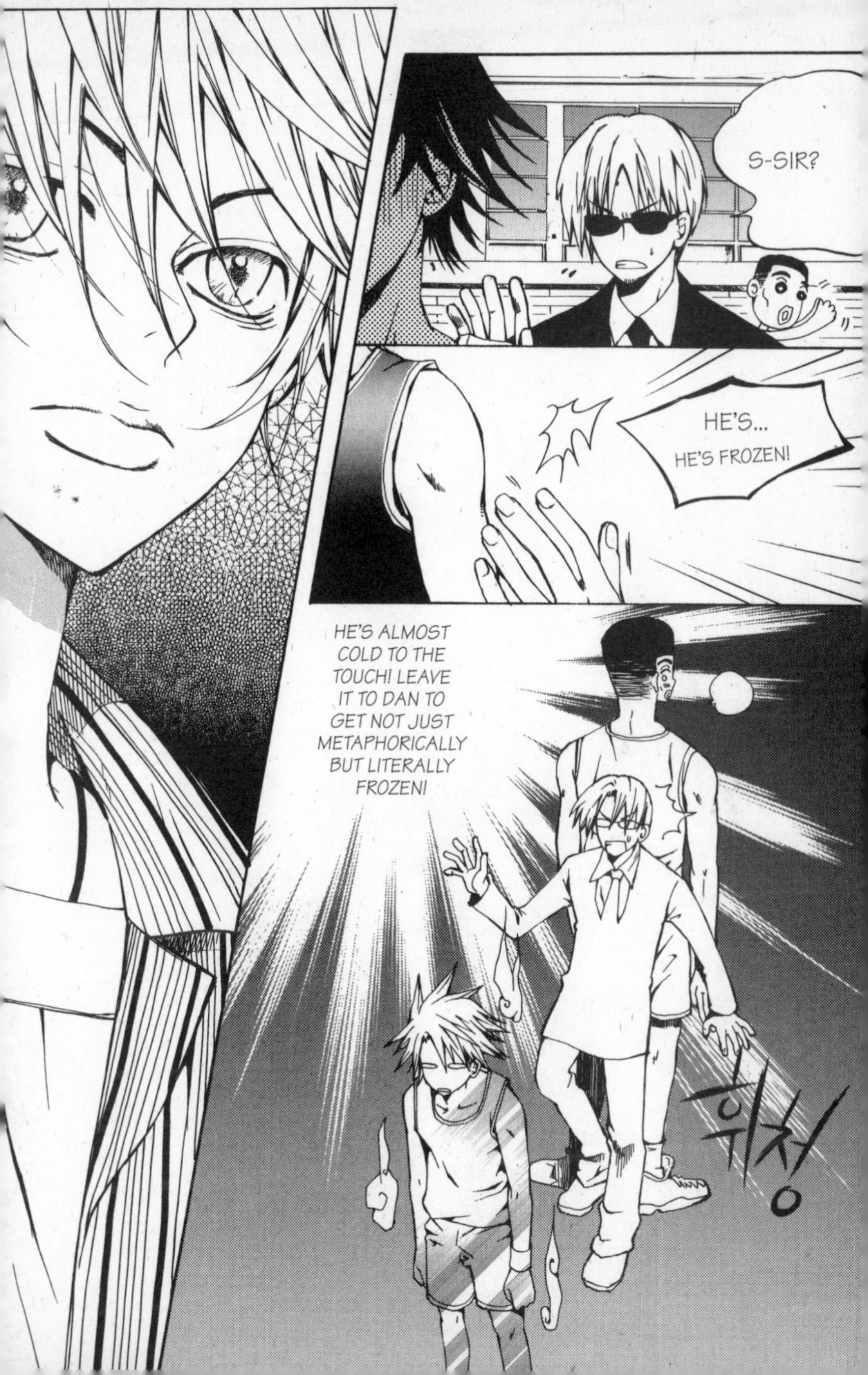
S-SIR?
HE'S... HE'S FROZEN!
HE'S ALMOST COLD TO THE TOUCH! LEAVE IT TO DAN TO GET NOT JUST METAPHORICALLY BUT LITERALLY FROZEN!

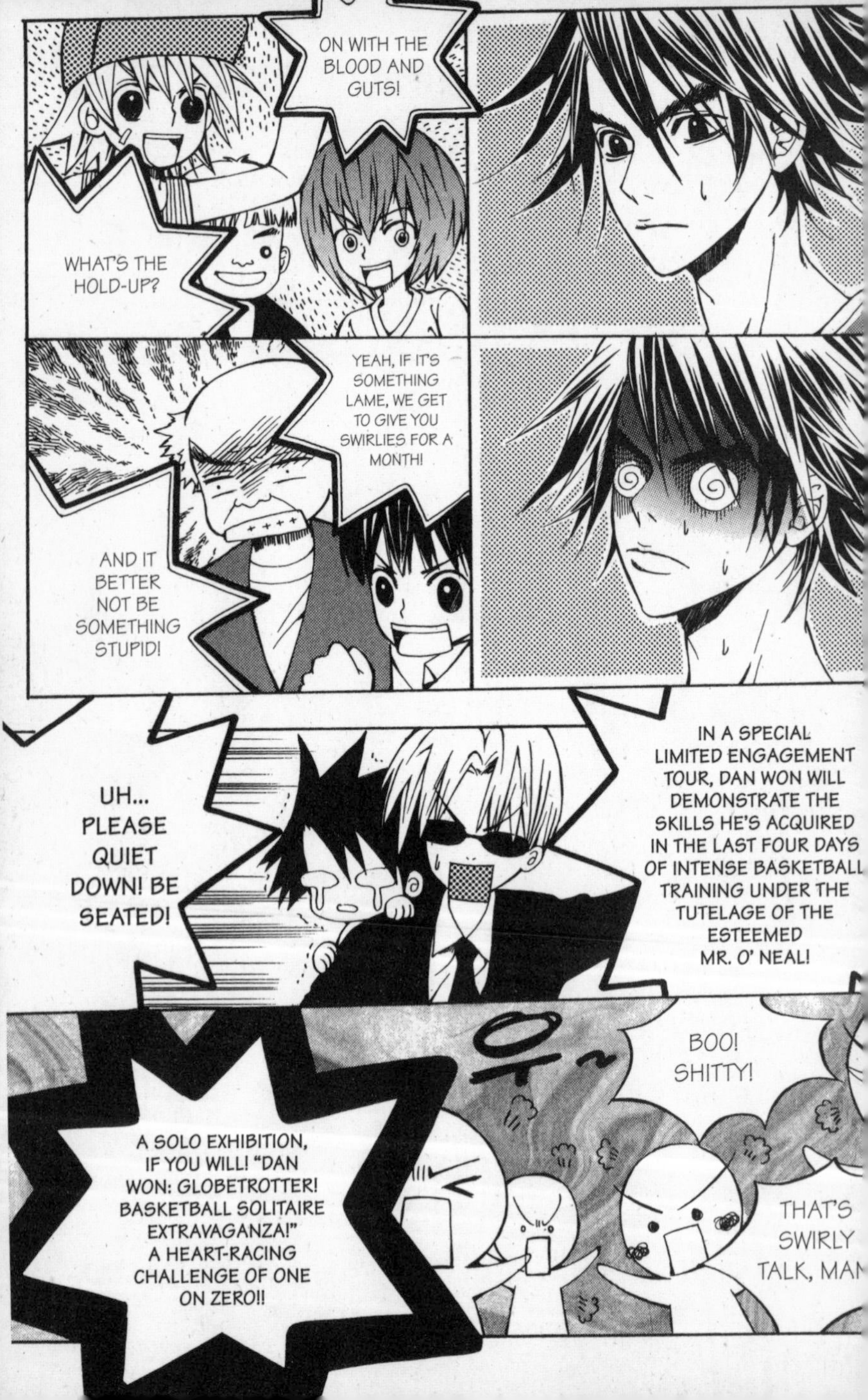
ON WITH THE BLOOD AND GUTS!
WHAT'S THE HOLD-UP?
YEAH, IF IT'S SOMETHING LAME, WE GET TO GIVE YOU SWIRLIES FOR A MONTH!
AND IT BETTER NOT BE SOMETHING STUPID!
UH... PLEASE QUIET DOWN! BE SEATED!
IN A SPECIAL LIMITED ENGAGEMENT TOUR, DAN WON WILL DEMONSTRATE THE SKILLS HE'S ACQUIRED IN THE LAST FOUR DAYS OF INTENSE BASKETBALL TRAINING UNDER THE TUTELAGE OF THE ESTEEMED MR. O' NEAL!
A SOLO EXHIBITION, IF YOU WILL! "DAN WON: GLOBETROTTER! BASKETBALL SOLITAIRE EXTRAVAGANZA!" A HEART-RACING CHALLENGE OF ONE ON ZERO!!
BOO! SHITTY!
THAT'S SWIRLY TALK, MAN

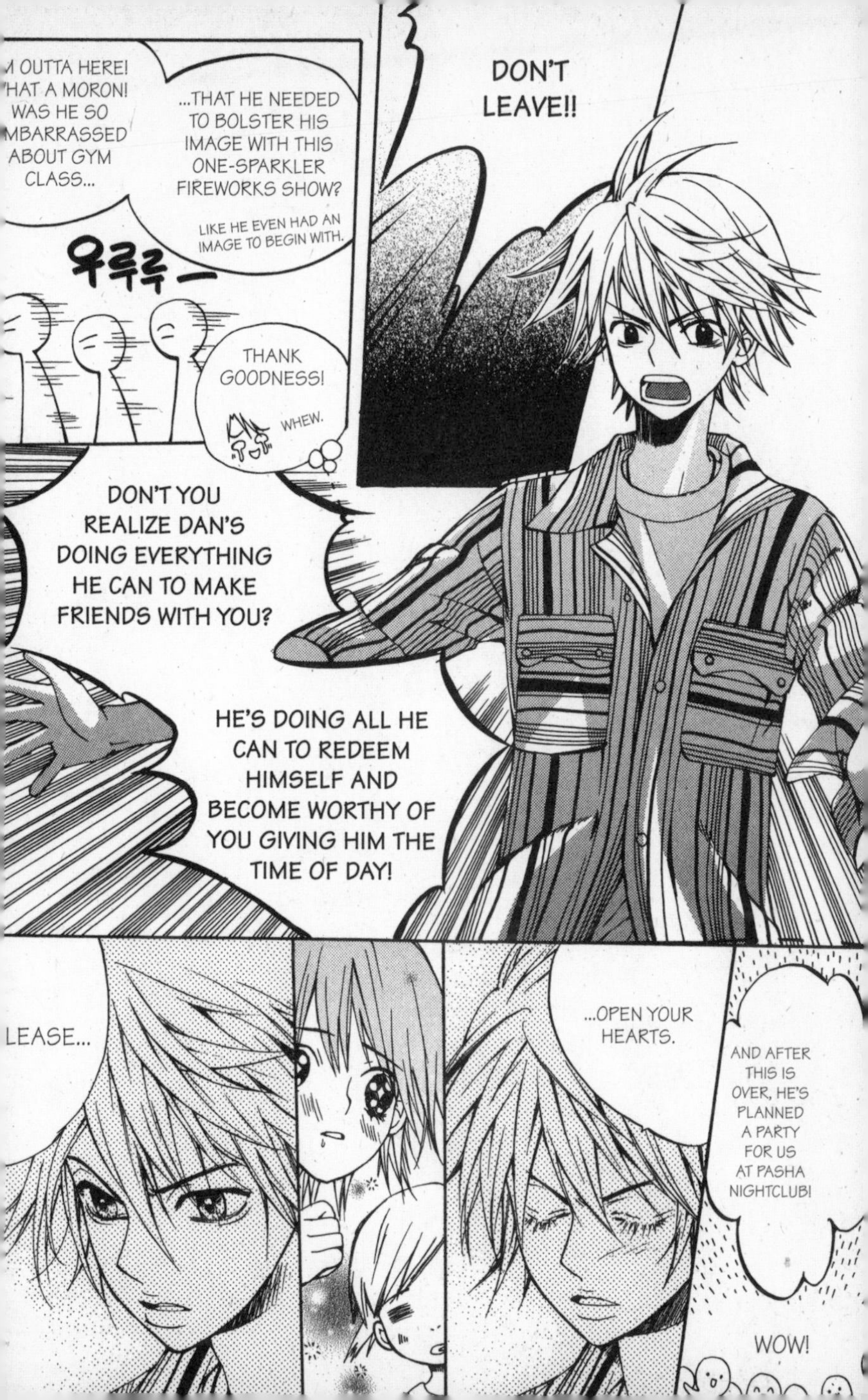

M OUTTA HERE! HAT A MORON! WAS HE SO MBARRASSED ABOUT GYM CLASS...
...THAT HE NEEDED TO BOLSTER HIS IMAGE WITH THIS ONE-SPARKLER FIREWORKS SHOW?
LIKE HE EVEN HAD AN IMAGE TO BEGIN WITH.
우루루—
THANK GOODNESS!
WHEW.
DON'T LEAVE!!
DON'T YOU REALIZE DAN'S DOING EVERYTHING HE CAN TO MAKE FRIENDS WITH YOU?
HE'S DOING ALL HE CAN TO REDEEM HIMSELF AND BECOME WORTHY OF YOU GIVING HIM THE TIME OF DAY!
LEASE...
...OPEN YOUR HEARTS.
AND AFTER THIS IS OVER, HE'S PLANNED A PARTY FOR US AT PASHA NIGHTCLUB!
WOW!

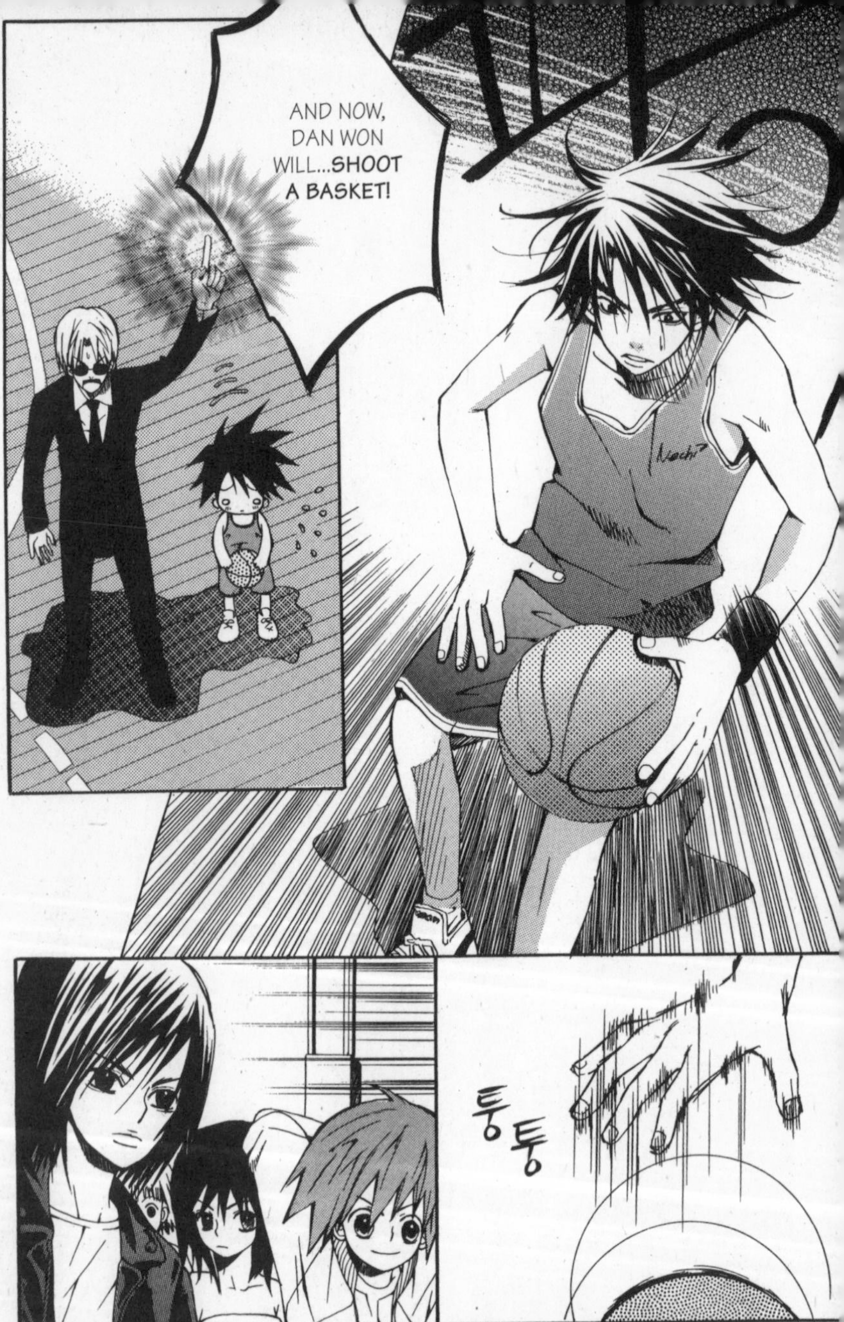
AND NOW, DAN WON WILL...**SHOOT A BASKET!**
퉁
퉁

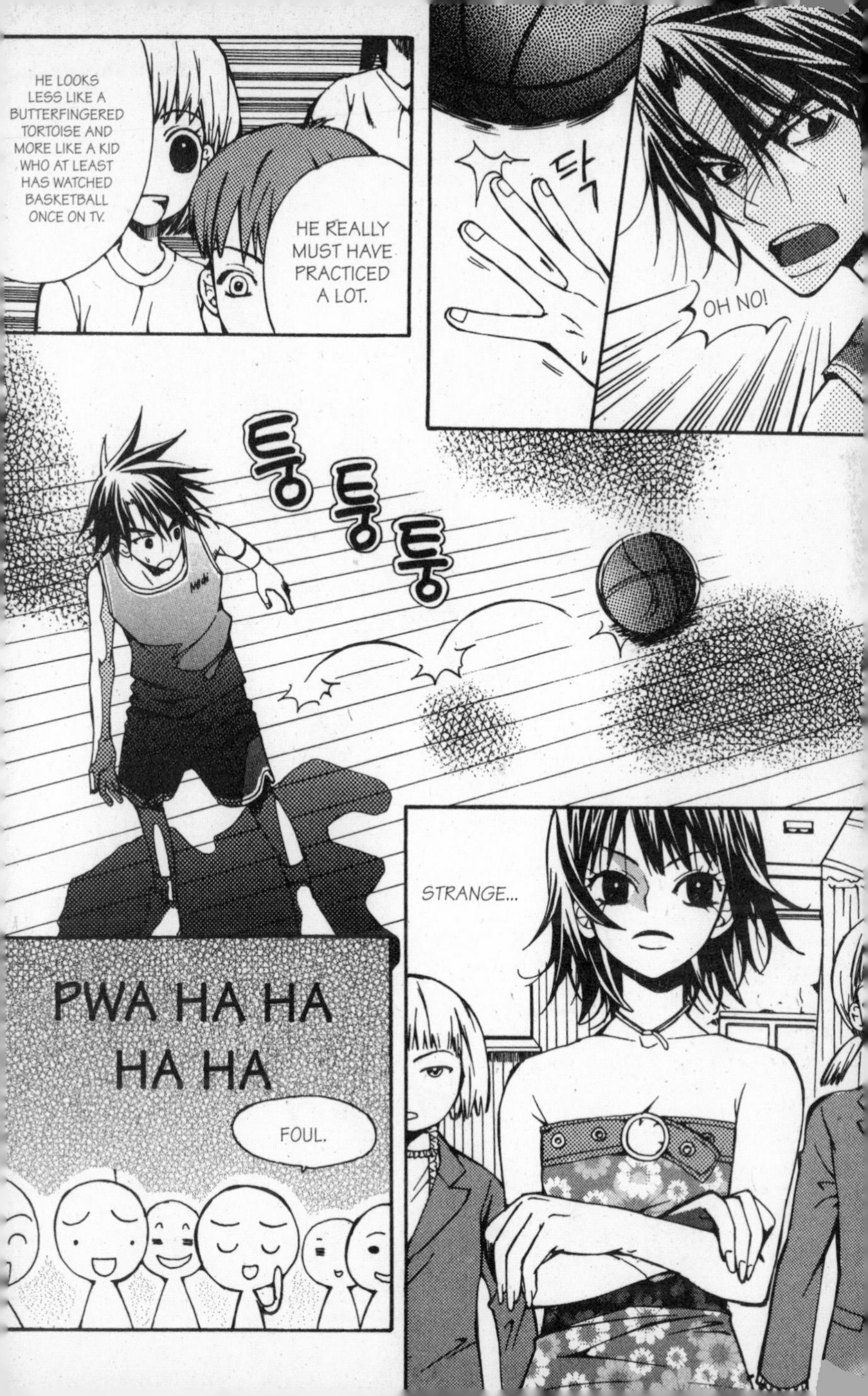
HE LOOKS LESS LIKE A BUTTERFINGERED TORTOISE AND MORE LIKE A KID WHO AT LEAST HAS WATCHED BASKETBALL ONCE ON TV.
HE REALLY MUST HAVE PRACTICED A LOT.
딱
OH NO!
퉁
퉁
퉁
PWA HA HA HA HA HA
FOUL.
STRANGE...

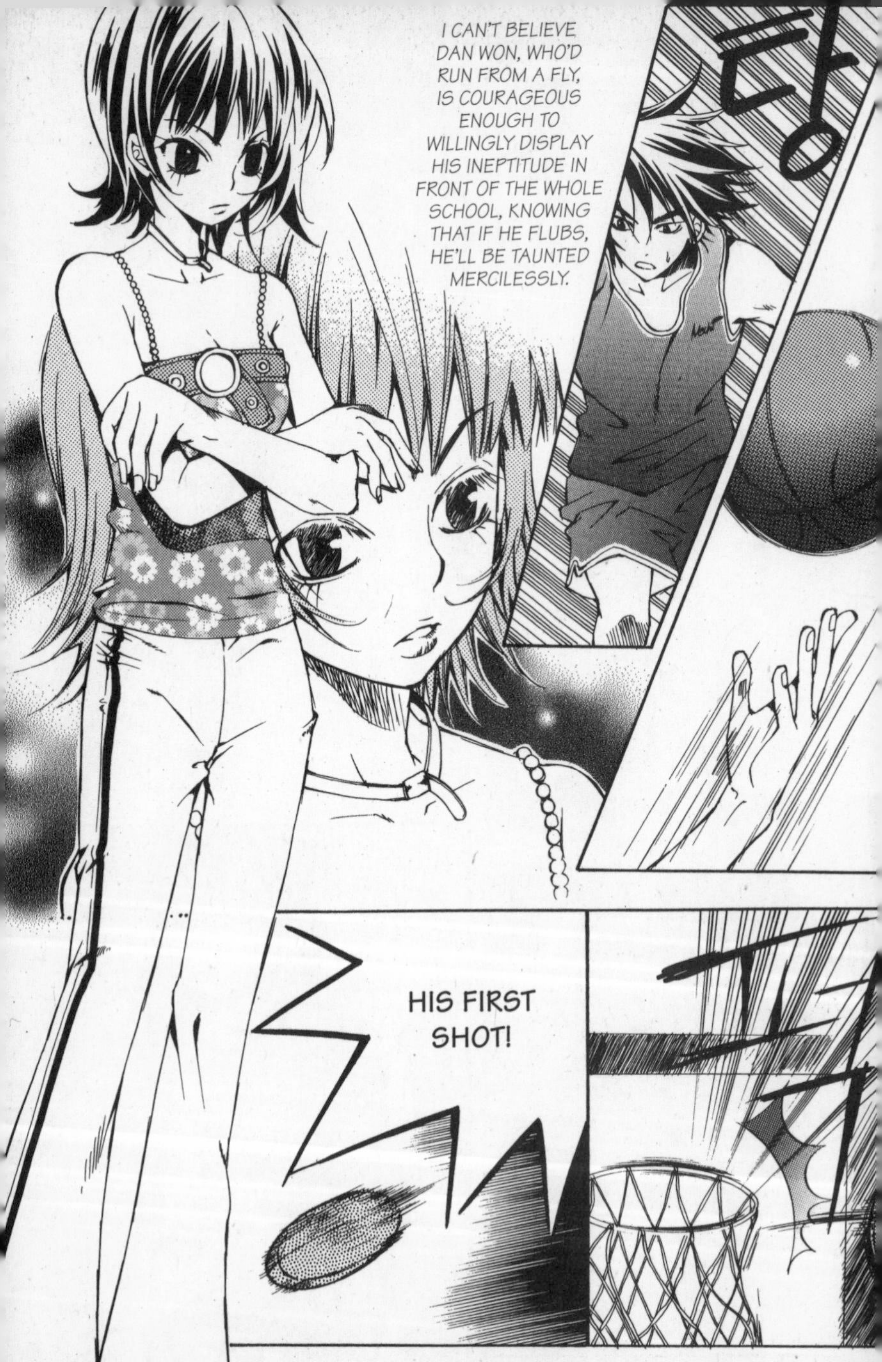
I CAN'T BELIEVE DAN WON, WHO'D RUN FROM A FLY, IS COURAGEOUS ENOUGH TO WILLINGLY DISPLAY HIS INEPTITUDE IN FRONT OF THE WHOLE SCHOOL, KNOWING THAT IF HE FLUBS, HE'LL BE TAUNTED MERCILESSLY.
HIS FIRST SHOT!

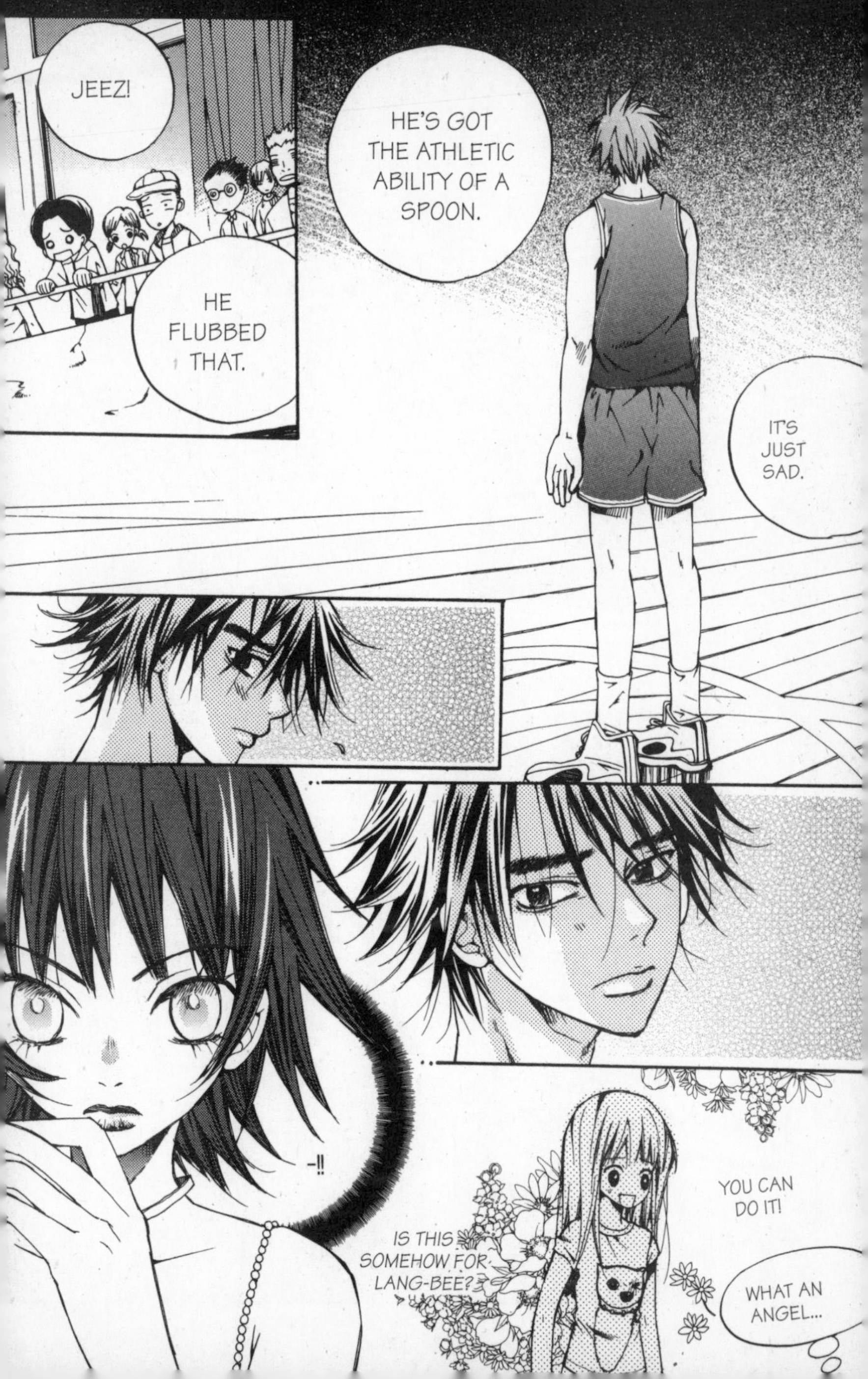
JEEZ!
HE FLUBBED THAT.
HE'S GOT THE ATHLETIC ABILITY OF A SPOON.
IT'S JUST SAD.
-!!
YOU CAN DO IT!
IS THIS SOMEHOW FOR LANG-BEE?
WHAT AN ANGEL...

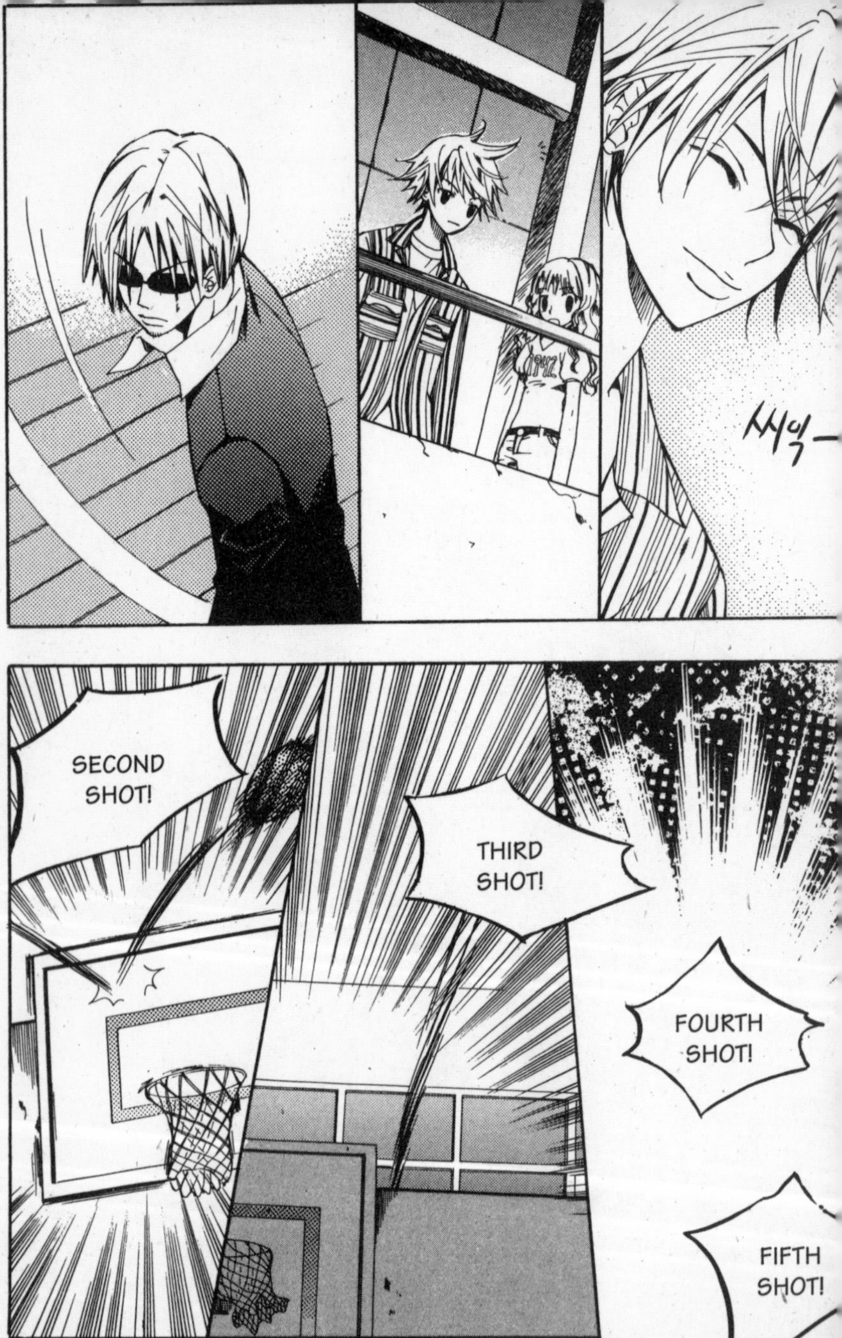

씨익ー
SECOND SHOT!
THIRD SHOT!
FOURTH SHOT!
FIFTH SHOT!

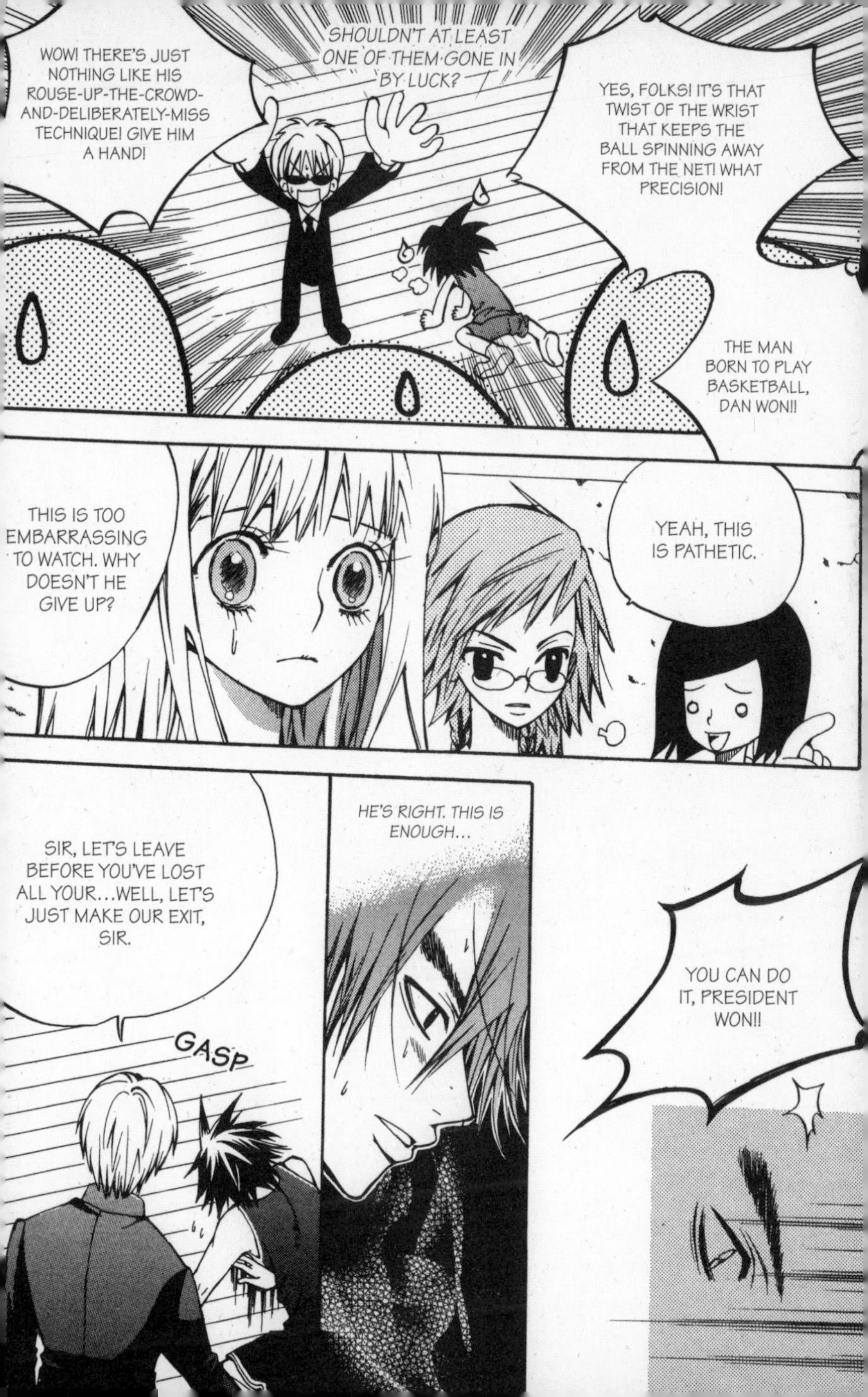
WOW! THERE'S JUST NOTHING LIKE HIS ROUSE-UP-THE-CROWD-AND-DELIBERATELY-MISS TECHNIQUE! GIVE HIM A HAND!
SHOULDN'T AT LEAST ONE OF THEM GONE IN BY LUCK?
YES, FOLKS! IT'S THAT TWIST OF THE WRIST THAT KEEPS THE BALL SPINNING AWAY FROM THE NET! WHAT PRECISION!
THE MAN BORN TO PLAY BASKETBALL, DAN WON!!
THIS IS TOO EMBARRASSING TO WATCH. WHY DOESN'T HE GIVE UP?
YEAH, THIS IS PATHETIC.
SIR, LET'S LEAVE BEFORE YOU'VE LOST ALL YOUR...WELL, LET'S JUST MAKE OUR EXIT, SIR.
GASP
HE'S RIGHT. THIS IS ENOUGH...
YOU CAN DO IT, PRESIDENT WON!!

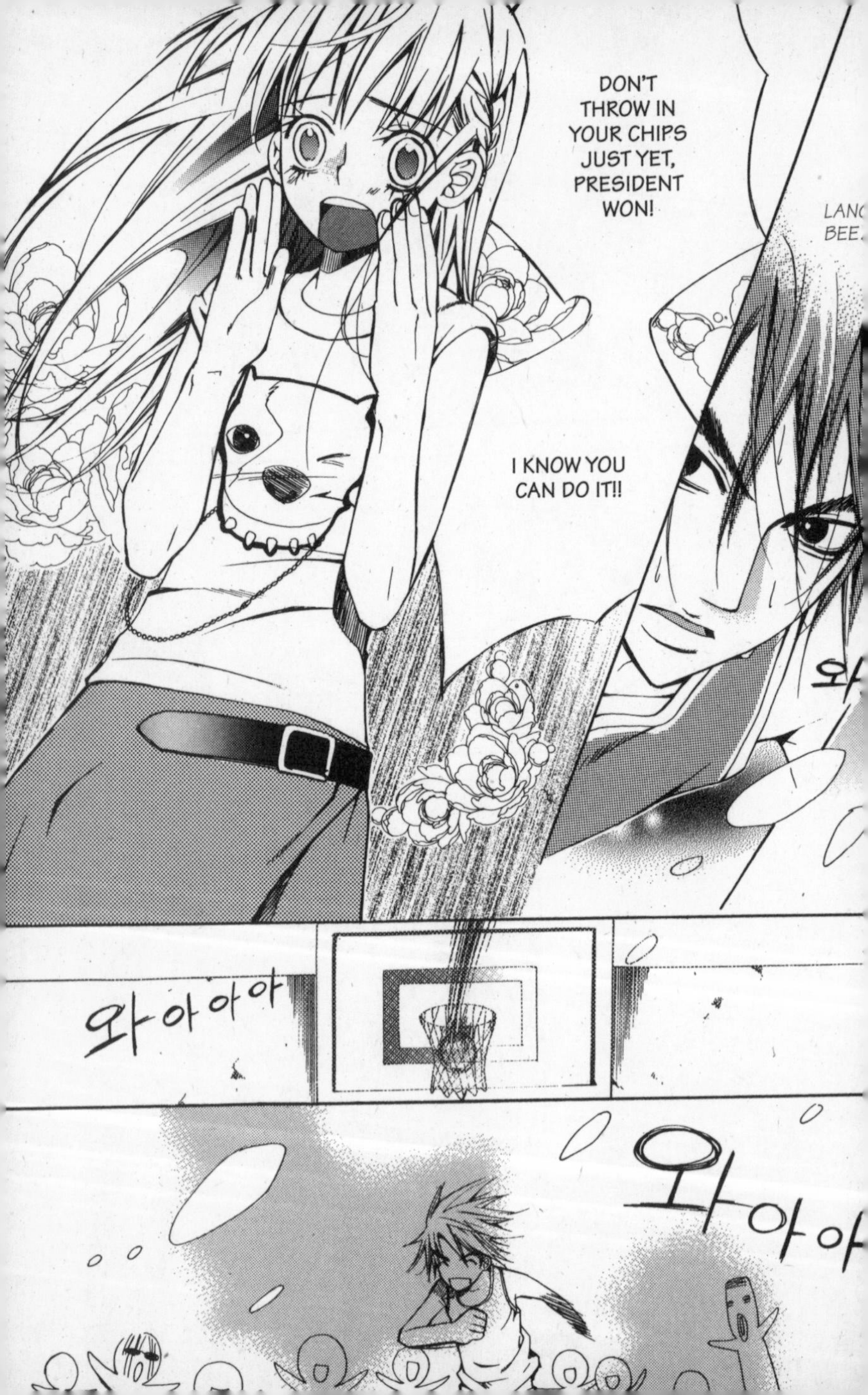
DON'T THROW IN YOUR CHIPS JUST YET, PRESIDENT WON!
I KNOW YOU CAN DO IT!!
와아아아
와아아

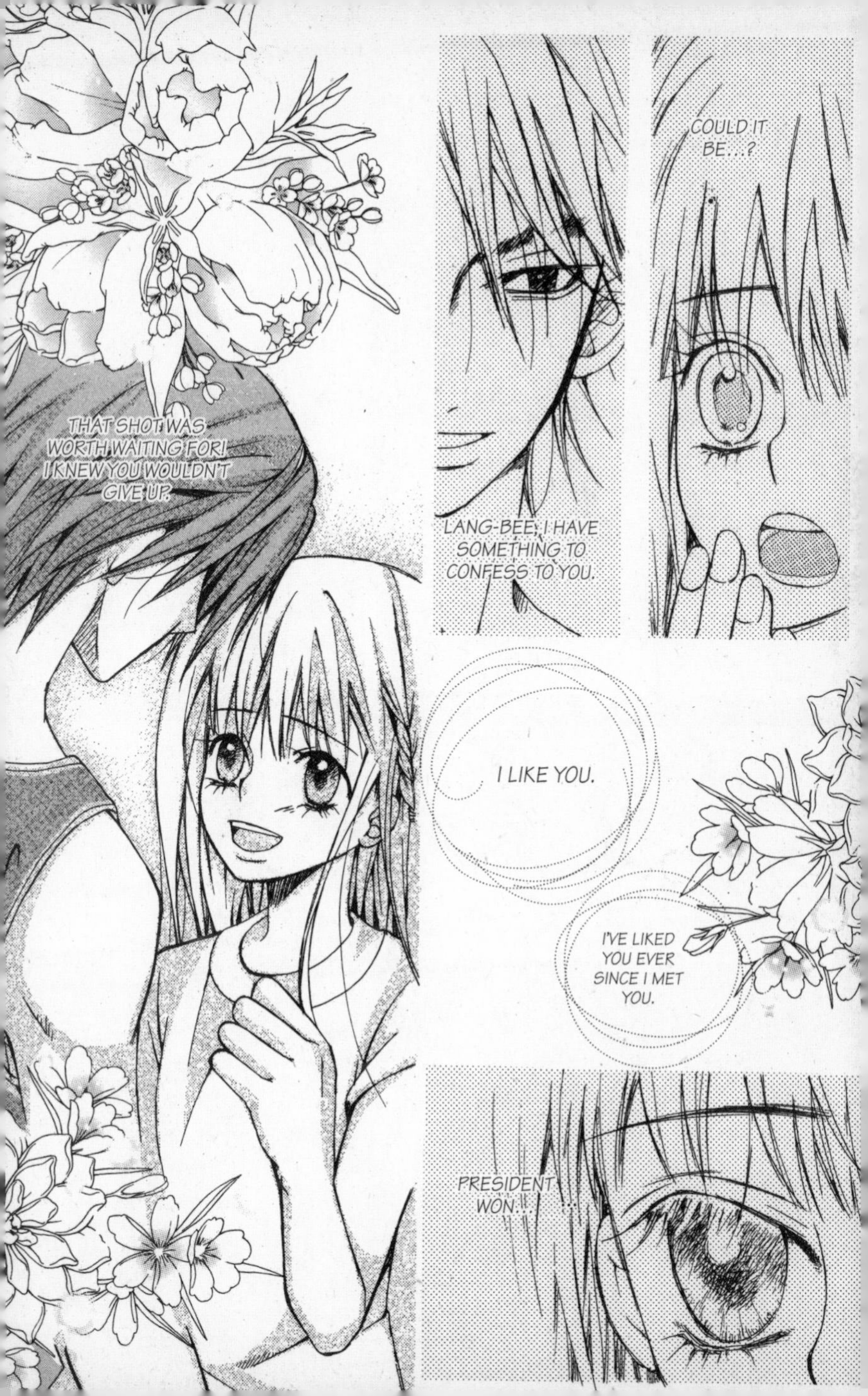
THAT SHOT WAS WORTH WAITING FOR! I KNEW YOU WOULDN'T GIVE UP.
LANG-BEE, I HAVE SOMETHING TO CONFESS TO YOU.
COULD IT BE...?
I LIKE YOU.
I'VE LIKED YOU EVER SINCE I MET YOU.
PRESIDENT WON...

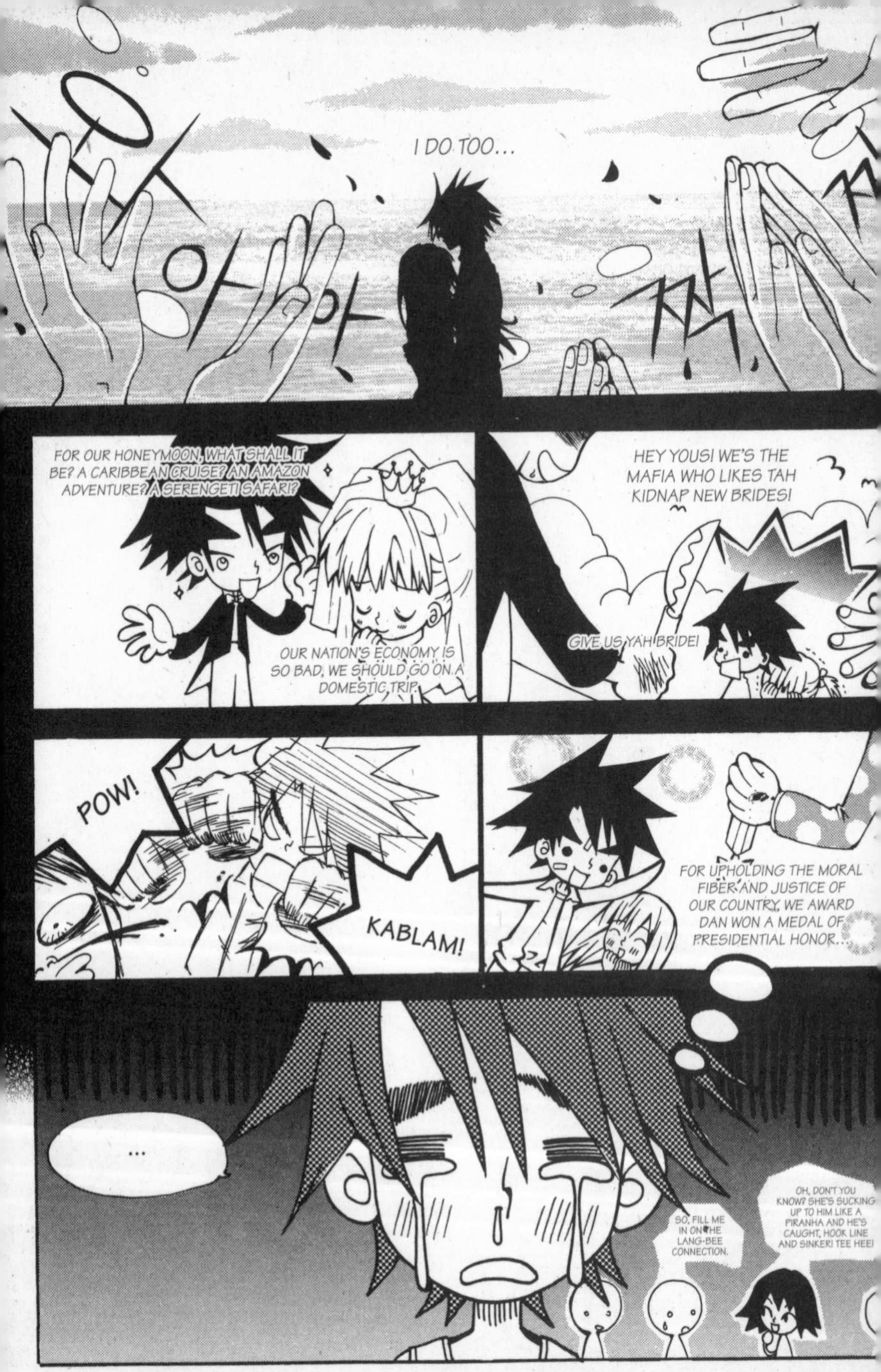

I DO TOO...
FOR OUR HONEYMOON, WHAT SHALL IT BE? A CARIBBEAN CRUISE? AN AMAZON ADVENTURE? A SERENGETI SAFARI?
OUR NATION'S ECONOMY IS SO BAD, WE SHOULD GO ON A DOMESTIC TRIP.
HEY YOUS! WE'S THE MAFIA WHO LIKES TAH KIDNAP NEW BRIDES!
GIVE US YAH BRIDE!
POW!
KABLAM!
FOR UPHOLDING THE MORAL FIBER AND JUSTICE OF OUR COUNTRY, WE AWARD DAN WON A MEDAL OF PRESIDENTIAL HONOR...
...
SO, FILL ME IN ON THE LANG-BEE CONNECTION.
OH, DON'T YOU KNOW? SHE'S SUCKING UP TO HIM LIKE A PIRANHA AND HE'S CAUGHT, HOOK LINE AND SINKER! TEE HEE!

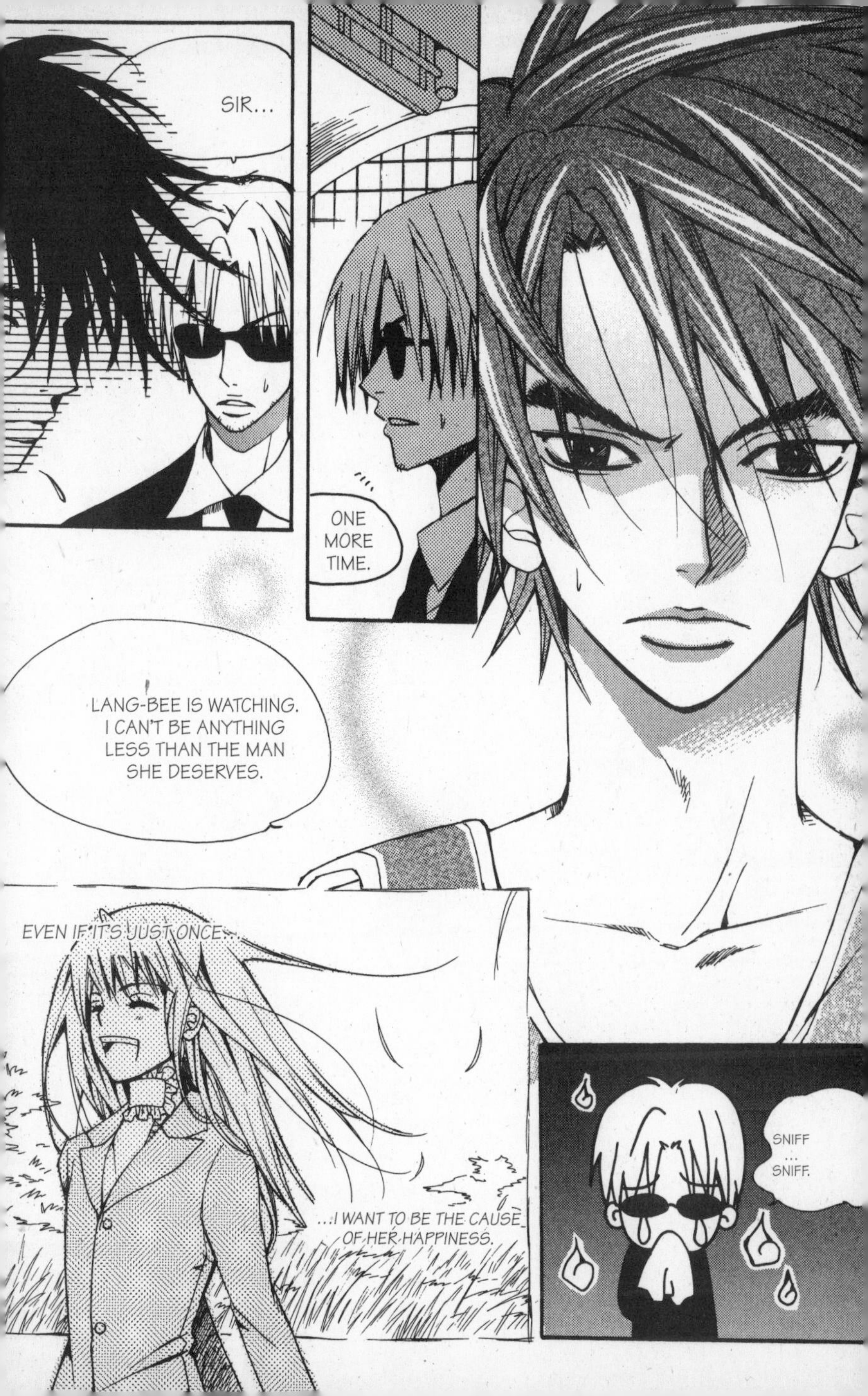
SIR...
ONE MORE TIME.
LANG-BEE IS WATCHING. I CAN'T BE ANYTHING LESS THAN THE MAN SHE DESERVES.
EVEN IF IT'S JUST ONCE...
...I WANT TO BE THE CAUSE OF HER HAPPINESS.
SNIFF ... SNIFF.

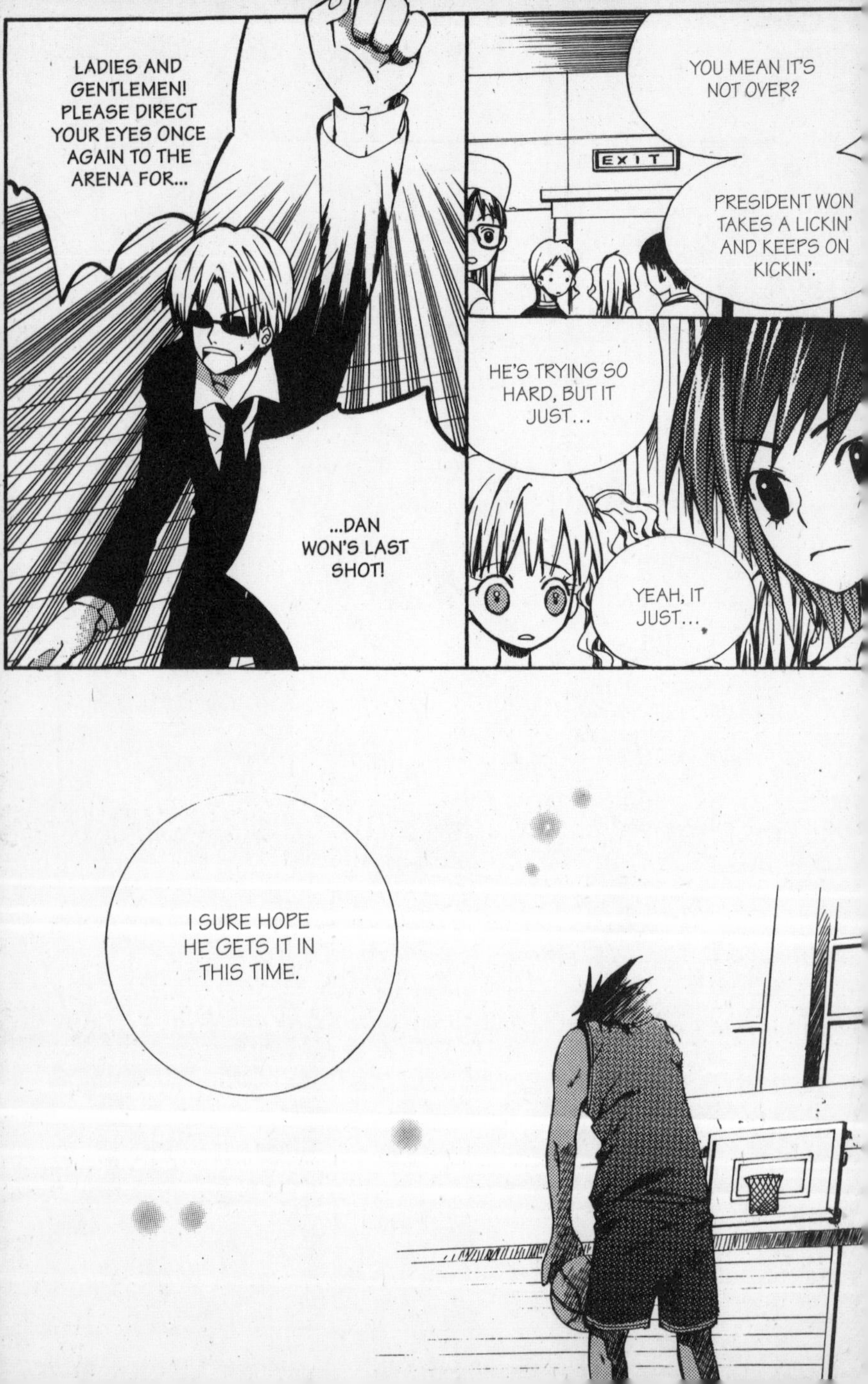
LADIES AND GENTLEMEN! PLEASE DIRECT YOUR EYES ONCE AGAIN TO THE ARENA FOR...
...DAN WON'S LAST SHOT!
YOU MEAN IT'S NOT OVER?
PRESIDENT WON TAKES A LICKIN' AND KEEPS ON KICKIN'.
EXIT
HE'S TRYING SO HARD, BUT IT JUST...
YEAH, IT JUST...
I SURE HOPE HE GETS IT IN THIS TIME.

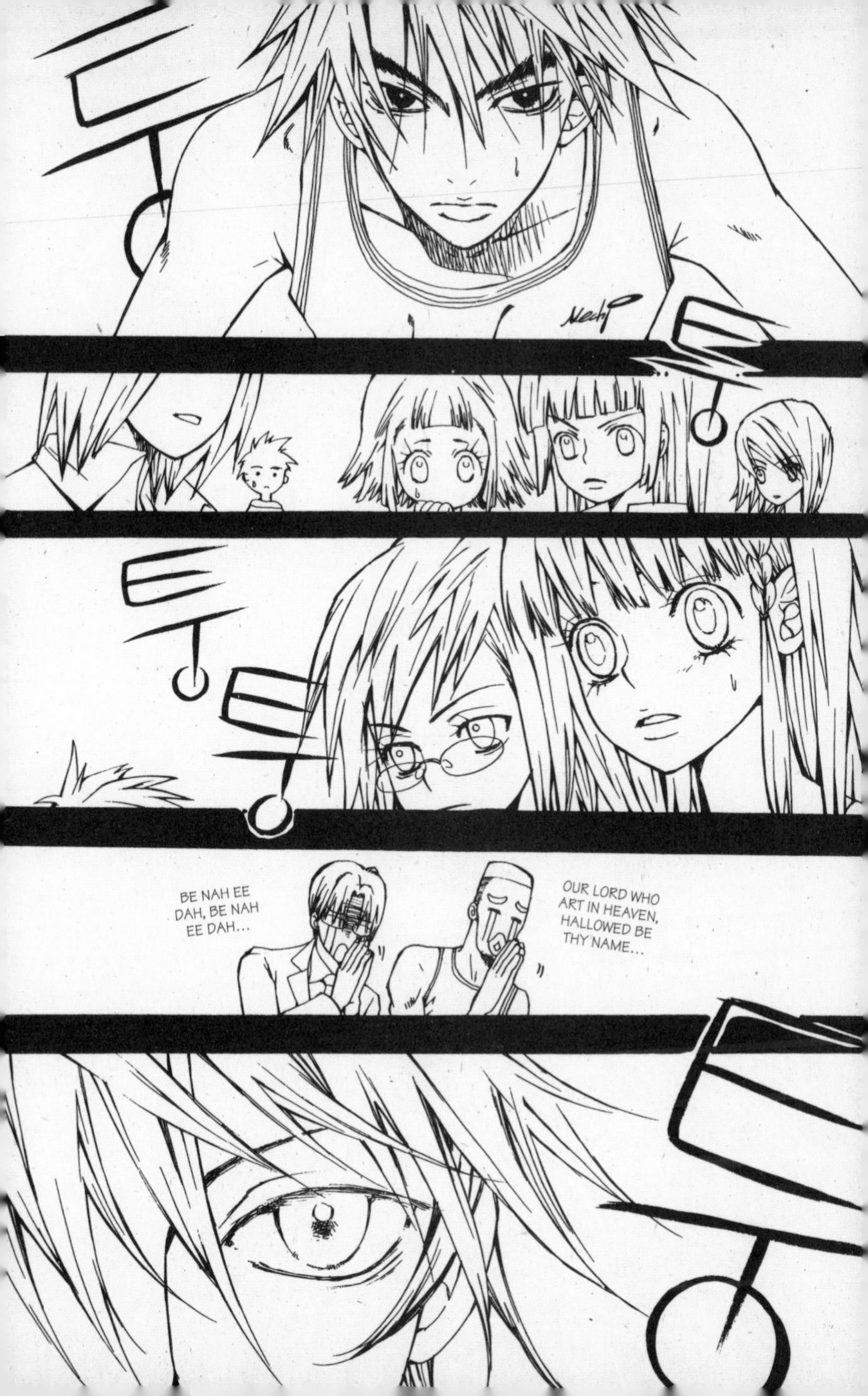
BE NAH EE DAH, BE NAH EE DAH...
OUR LORD WHO ART IN HEAVEN, HALLOWED BE THY NAME...

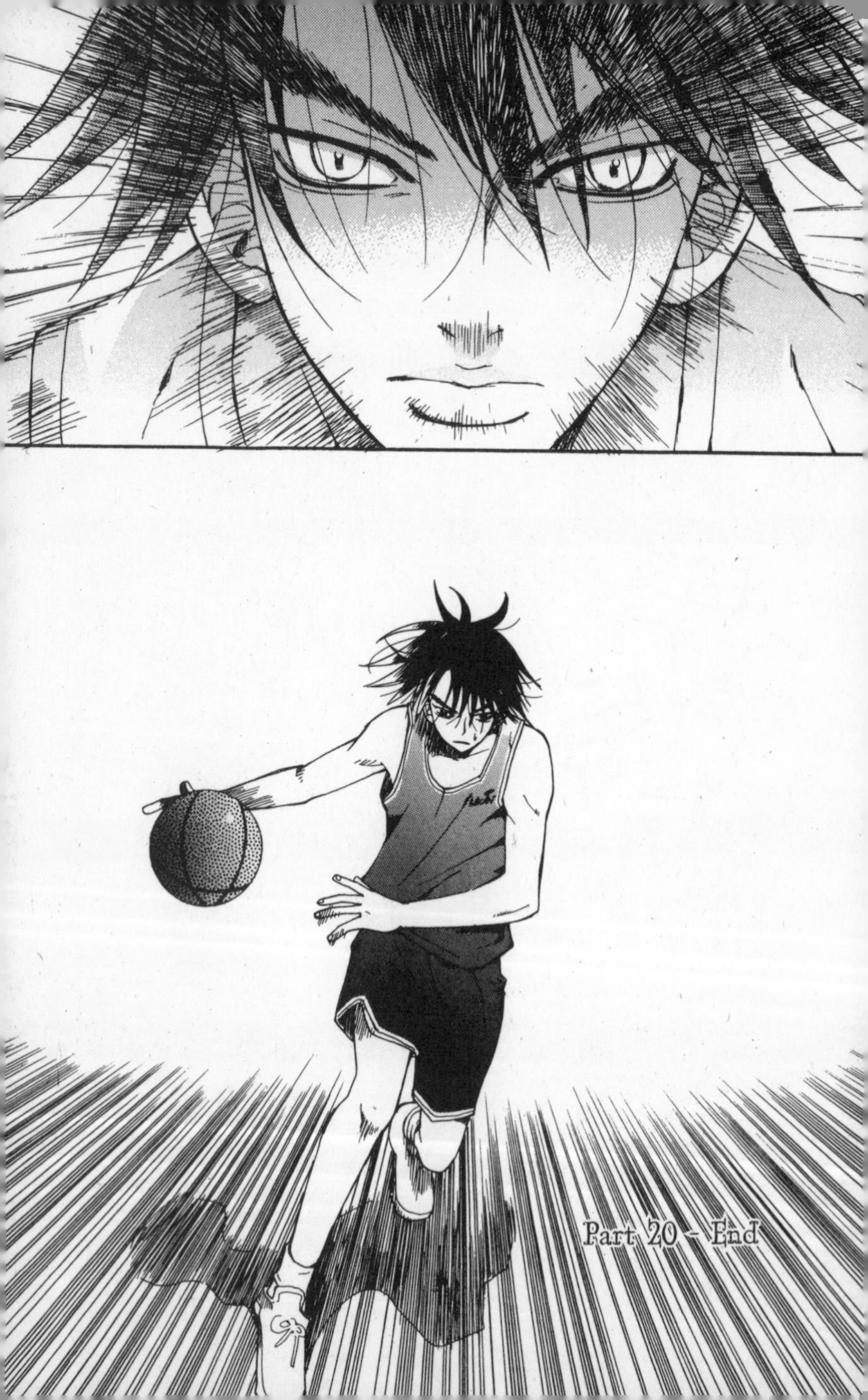
Part 20 - End

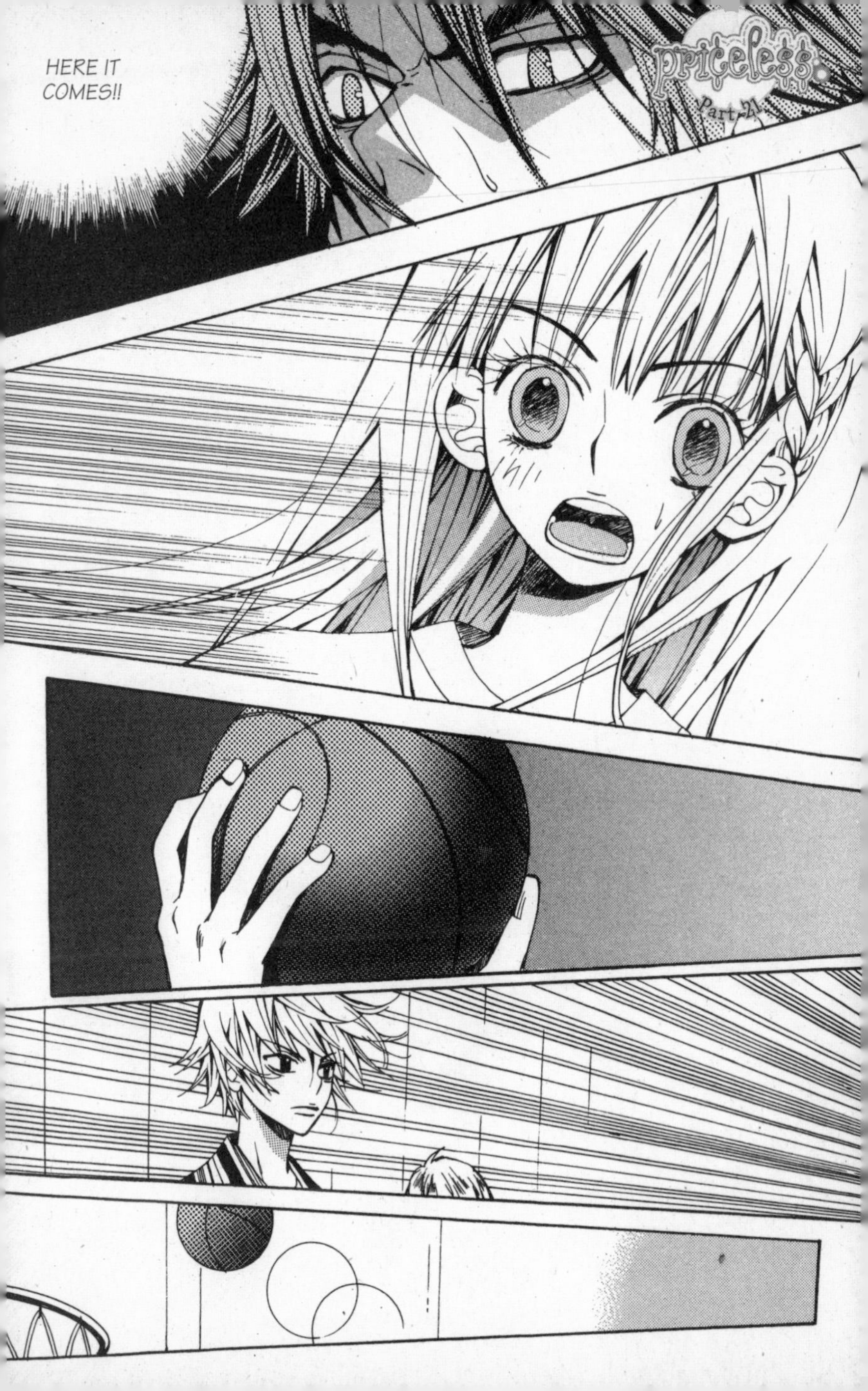
HERE IT COMES!!
priceless
Part-21

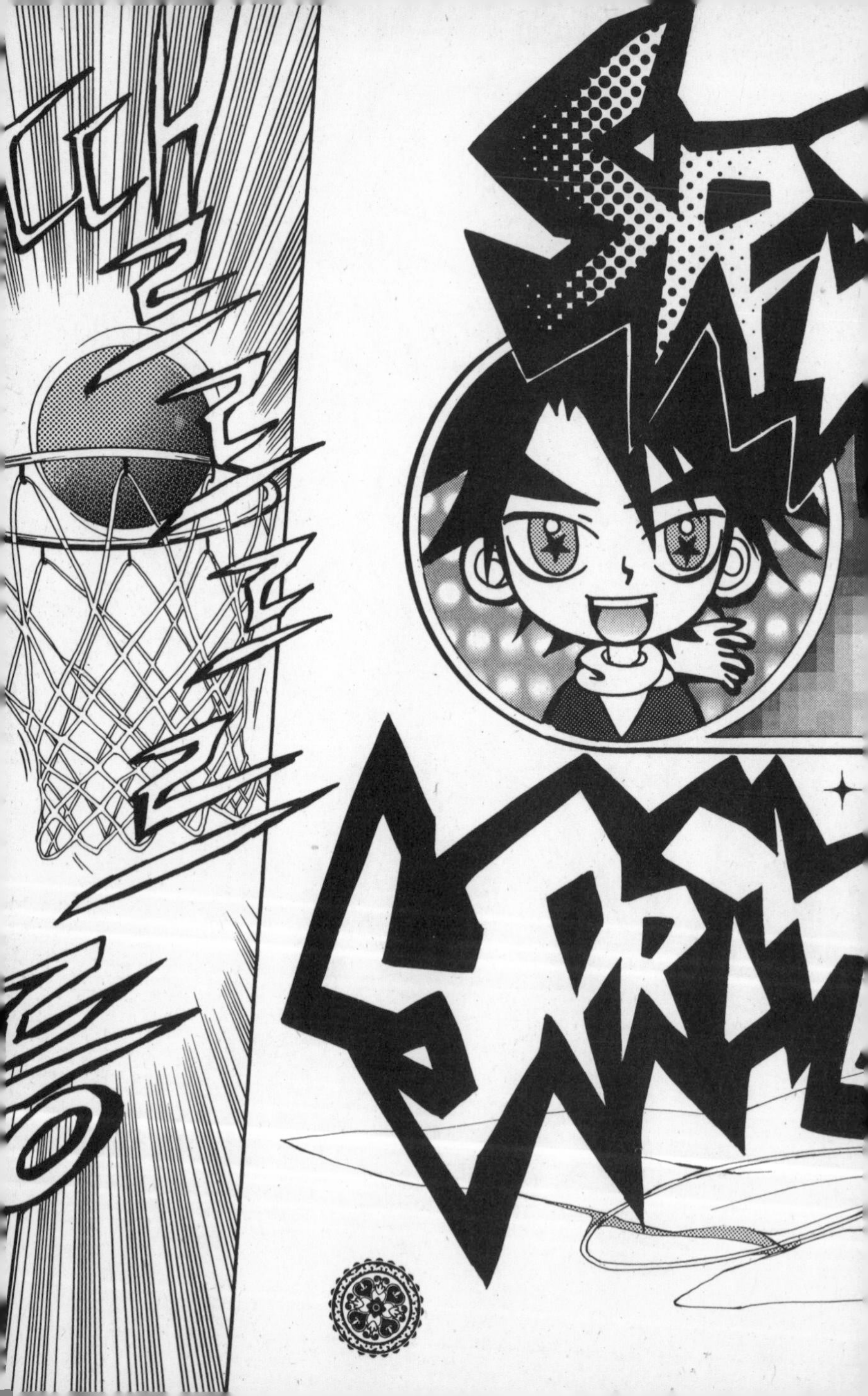

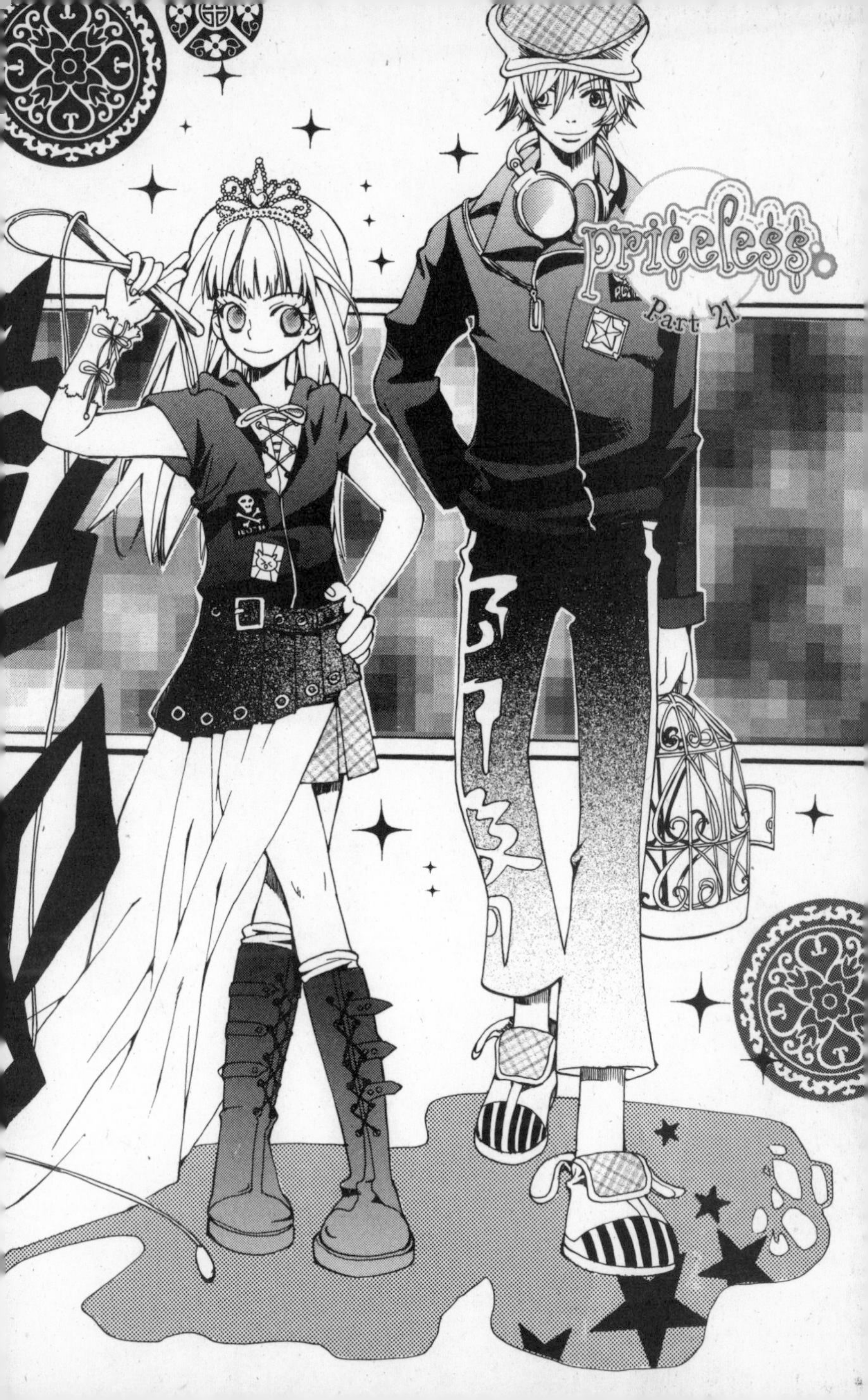
priceless
Part 21

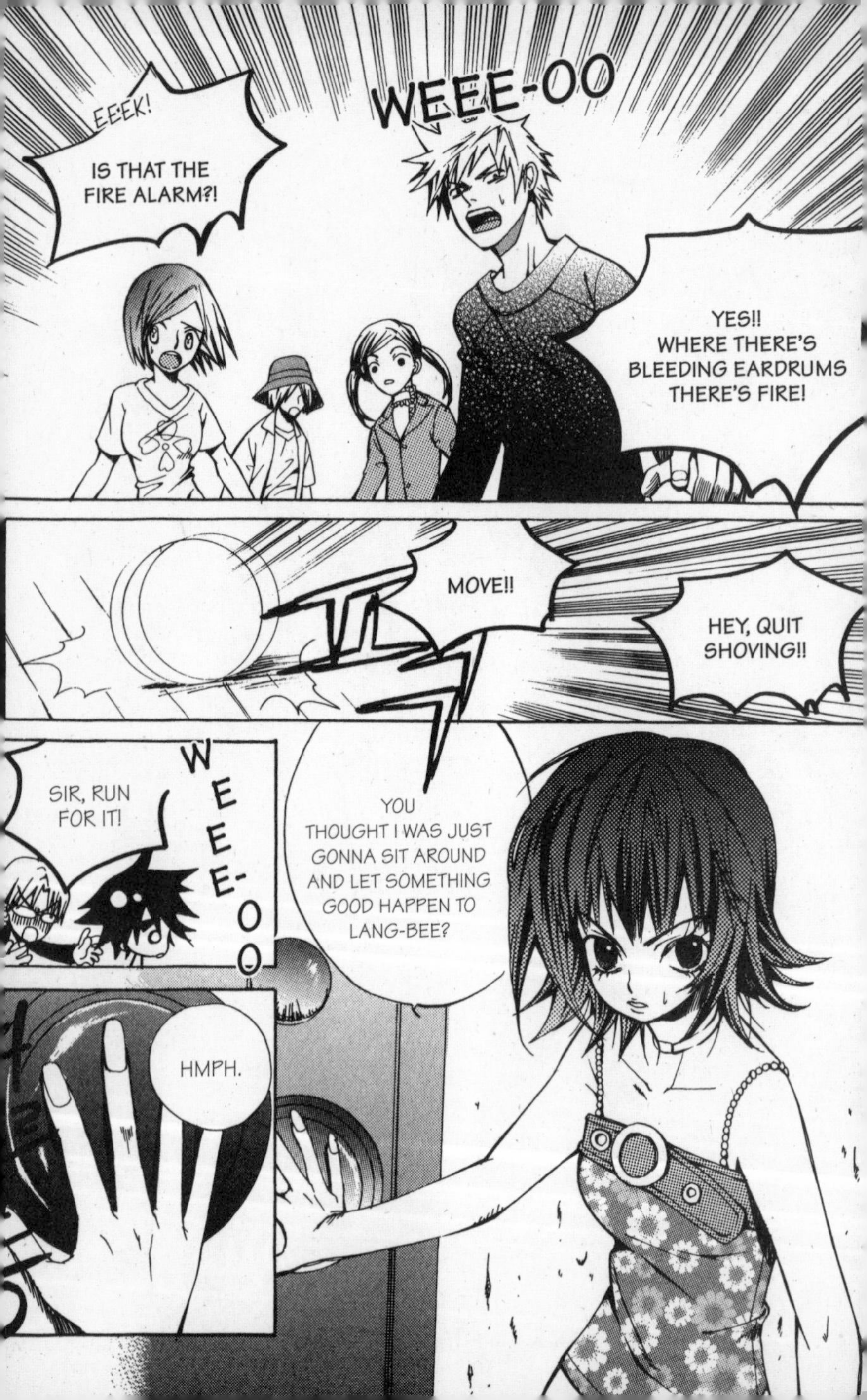
EEEK!
IS THAT THE FIRE ALARM?!
WEEE-OO
YES!! WHERE THERE'S BLEEDING EARDRUMS THERE'S FIRE!
MOVE!!
HEY, QUIT SHOVING!!
SIR, RUN FOR IT!
WEEE-OO
YOU THOUGHT I WAS JUST GONNA SIT AROUND AND LET SOMETHING GOOD HAPPEN TO LANG-BEE?
HMPH.

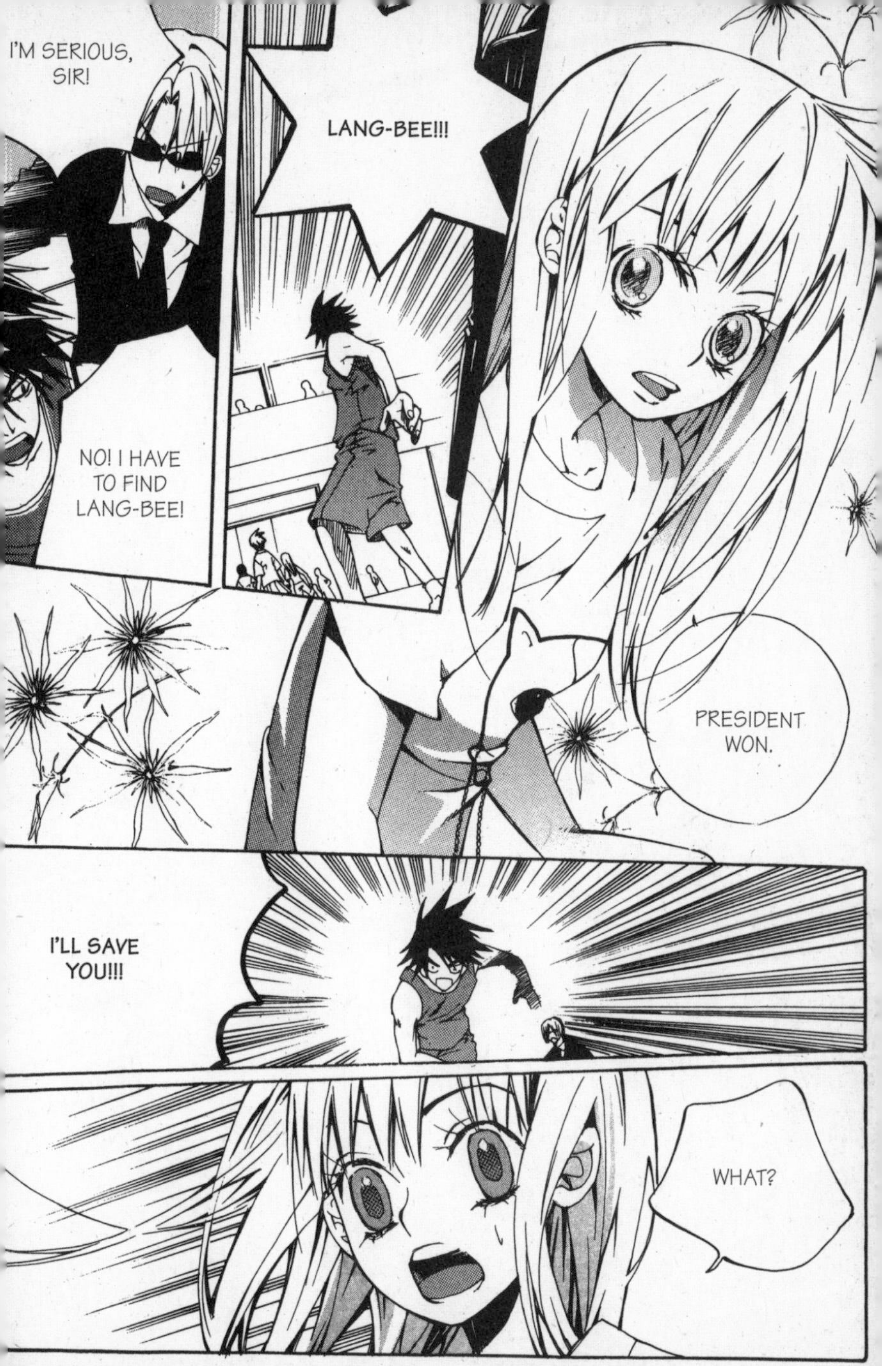
I'M SERIOUS, SIR!
LANG-BEE!!!
NO! I HAVE TO FIND LANG-BEE!
PRESIDENT WON.
I'LL SAVE YOU!!!
WHAT?

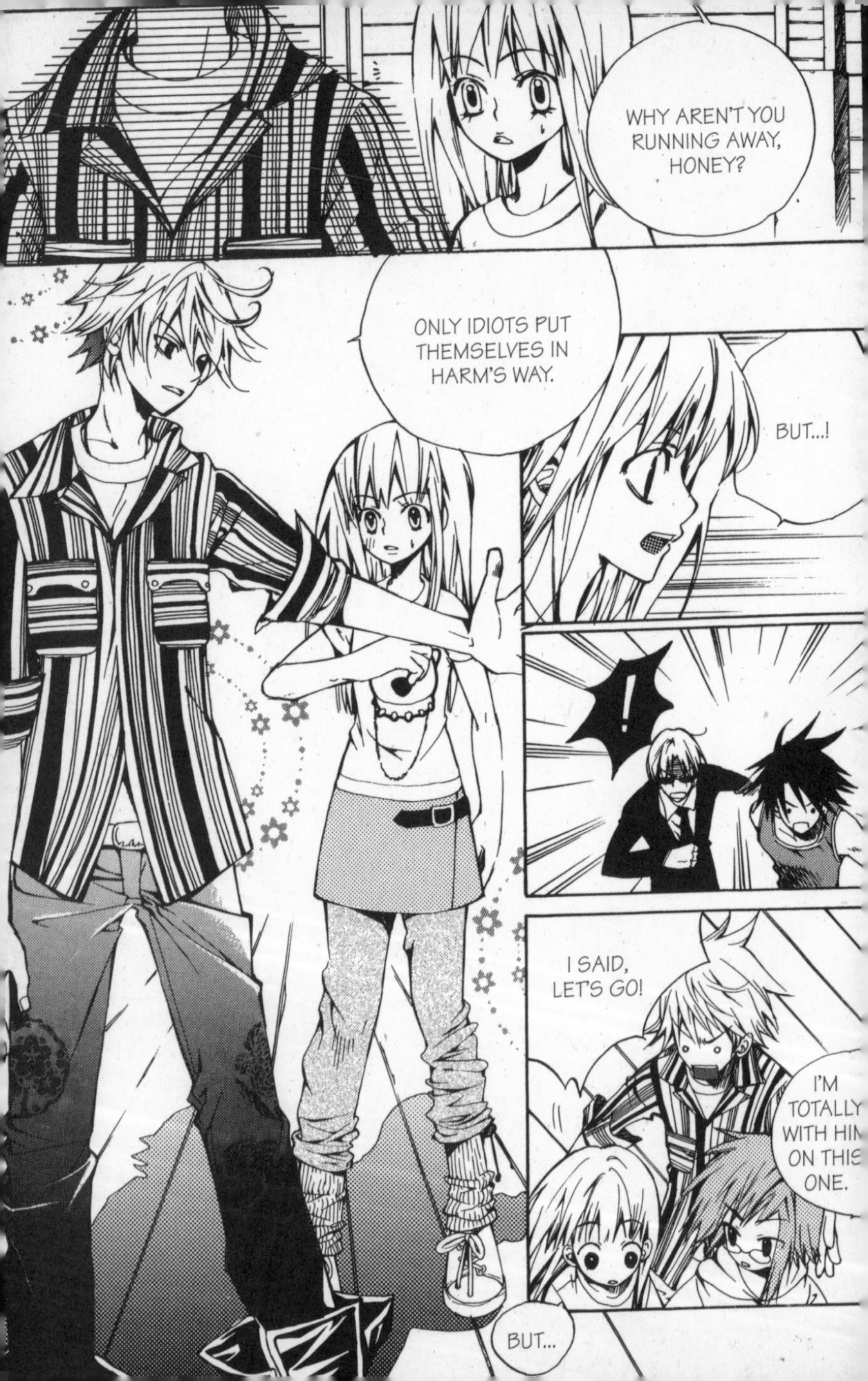
WHY AREN'T YOU RUNNING AWAY, HONEY?
ONLY IDIOTS PUT THEMSELVES IN HARM'S WAY.
BUT...
BUT...!
!
I SAID, LET'S GO!
I'M TOTALLY WITH HIM ON THIS ONE.

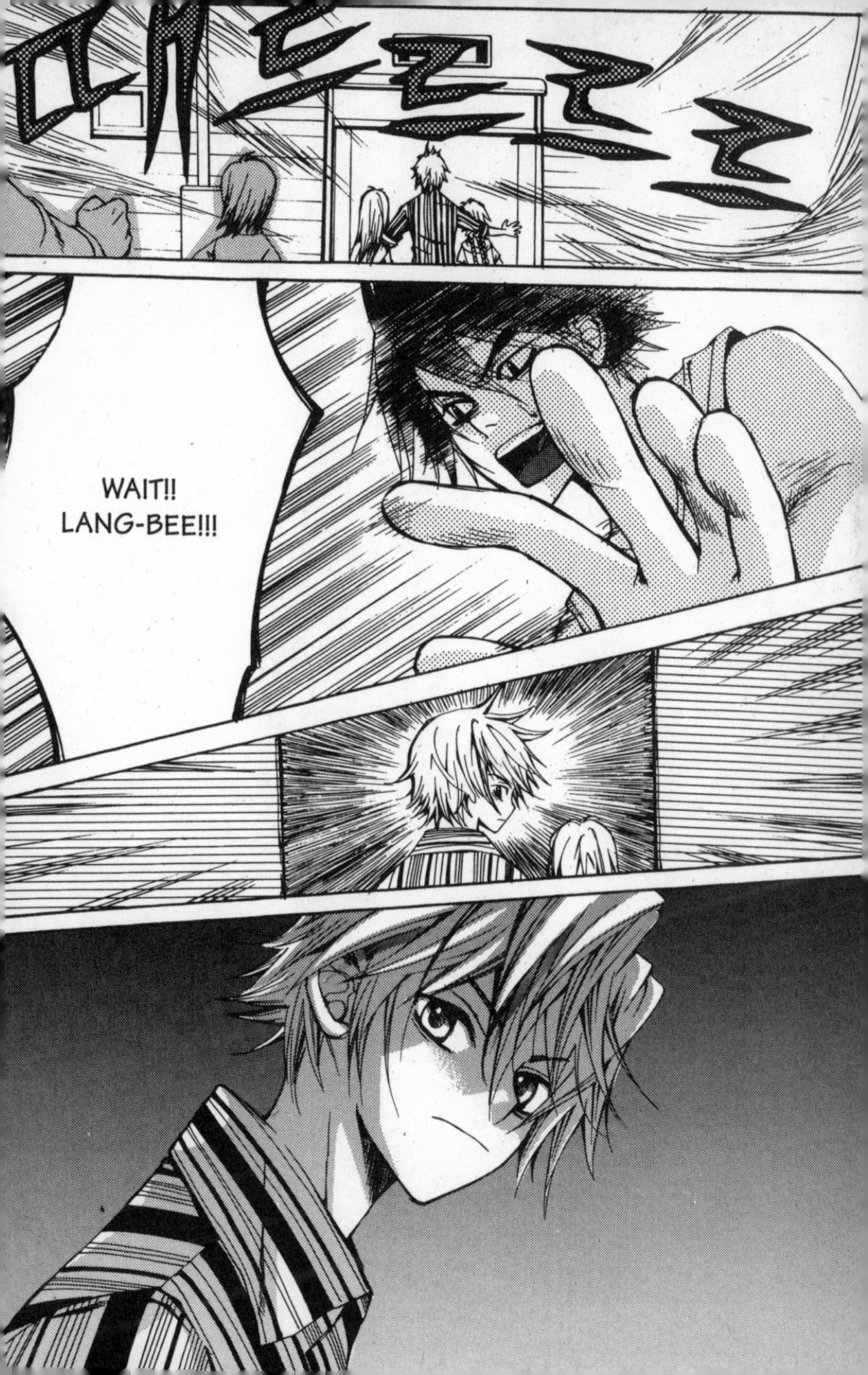
WAIT!!
LANG-BEE!!!

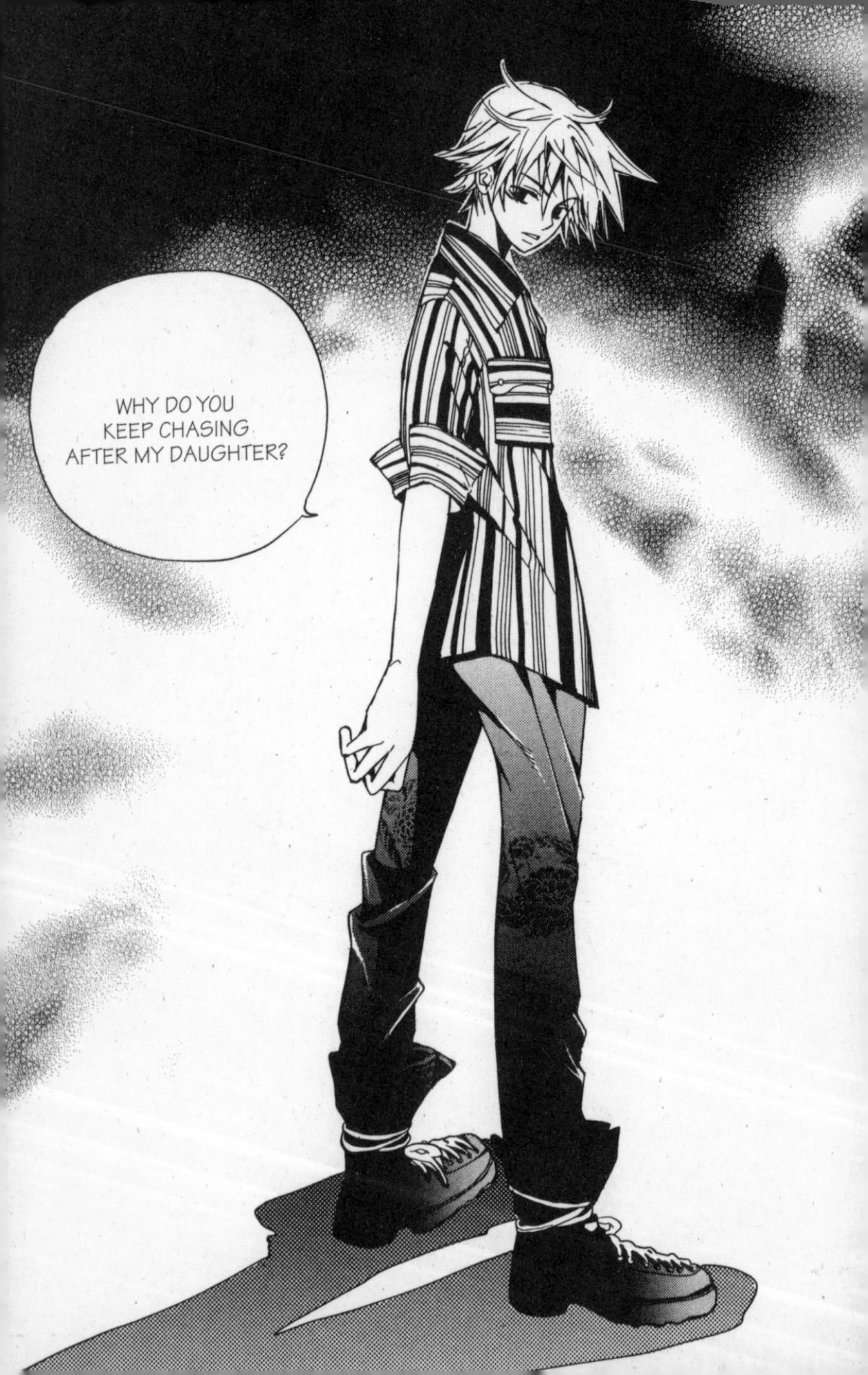
WHY DO YOU KEEP CHASING AFTER MY DAUGHTER?

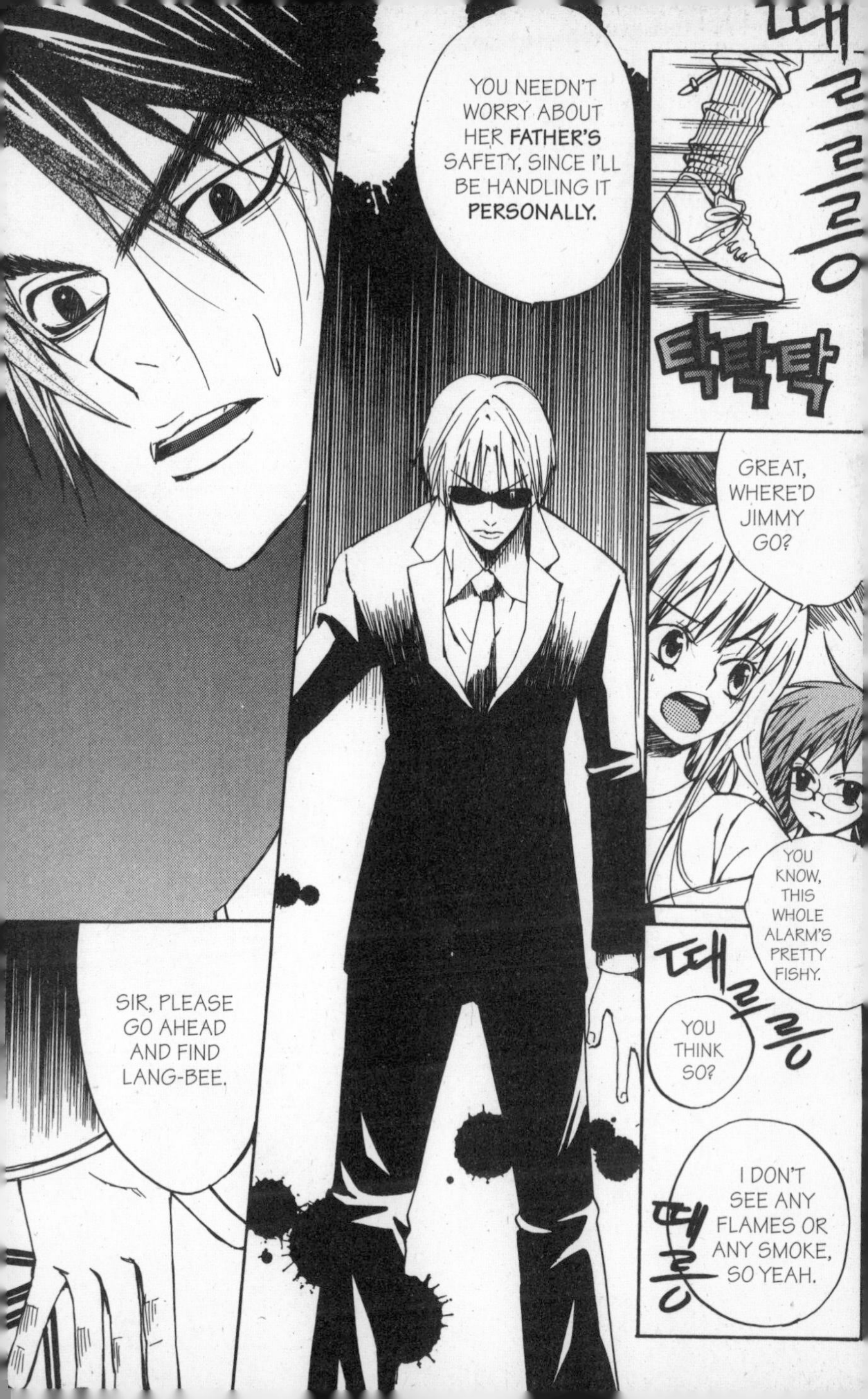
SIR, PLEASE GO AHEAD AND FIND LANG-BEE.
YOU NEEDN'T WORRY ABOUT HER **FATHER'S** SAFETY, SINCE I'LL BE HANDLING IT **PERSONALLY.**
때르르릉
탁탁탁
GREAT, WHERE'D JIMMY GO?
YOU KNOW, THIS WHOLE ALARM'S PRETTY FISHY.
때르릉
YOU THINK SO?
I DON'T SEE ANY FLAMES OR ANY SMOKE, SO YEAH.
때릉

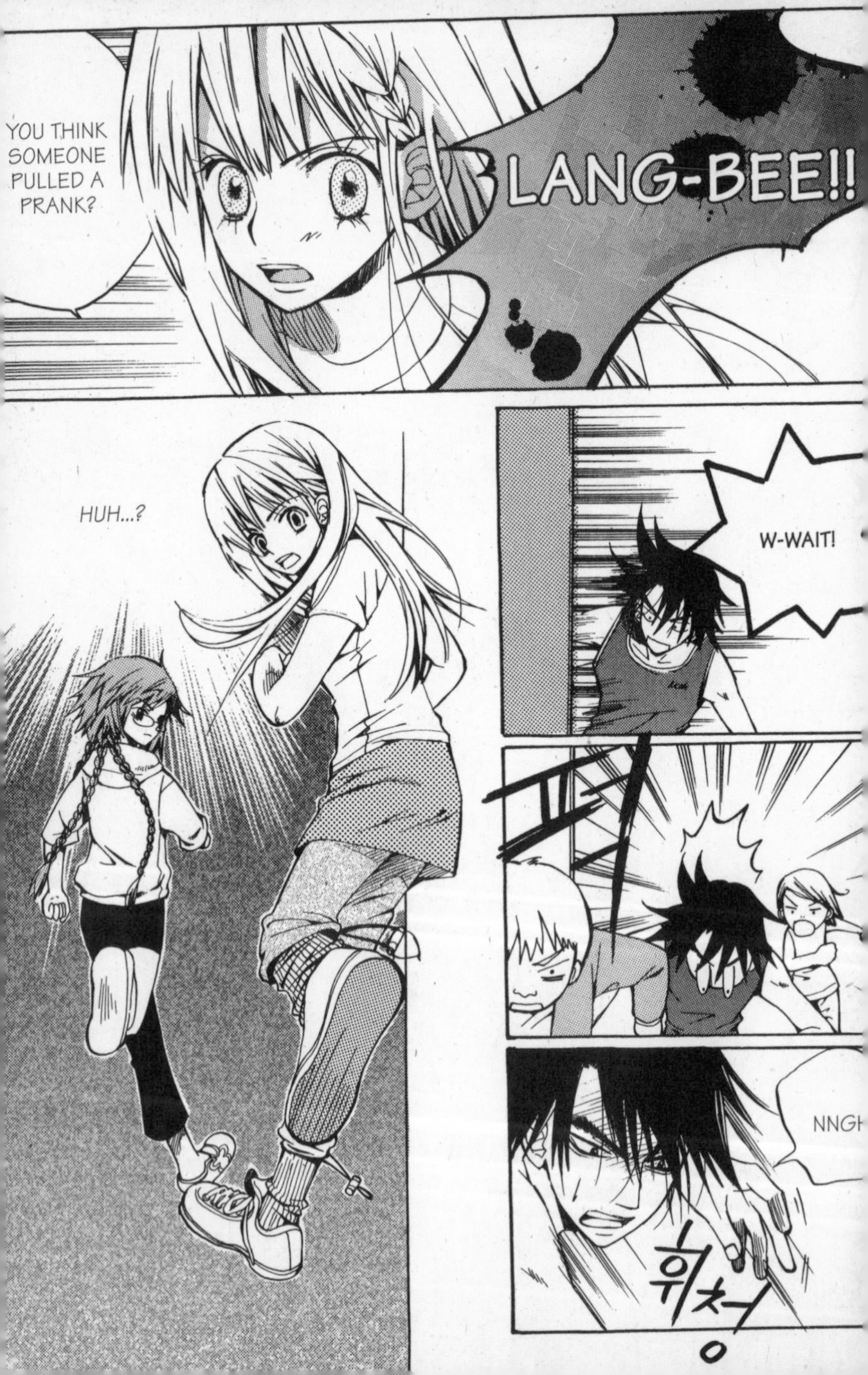
YOU THINK SOMEONE PULLED A PRANK?
LANG-BEE!!
HUH...?
W-WAIT!
NNGH
휘청

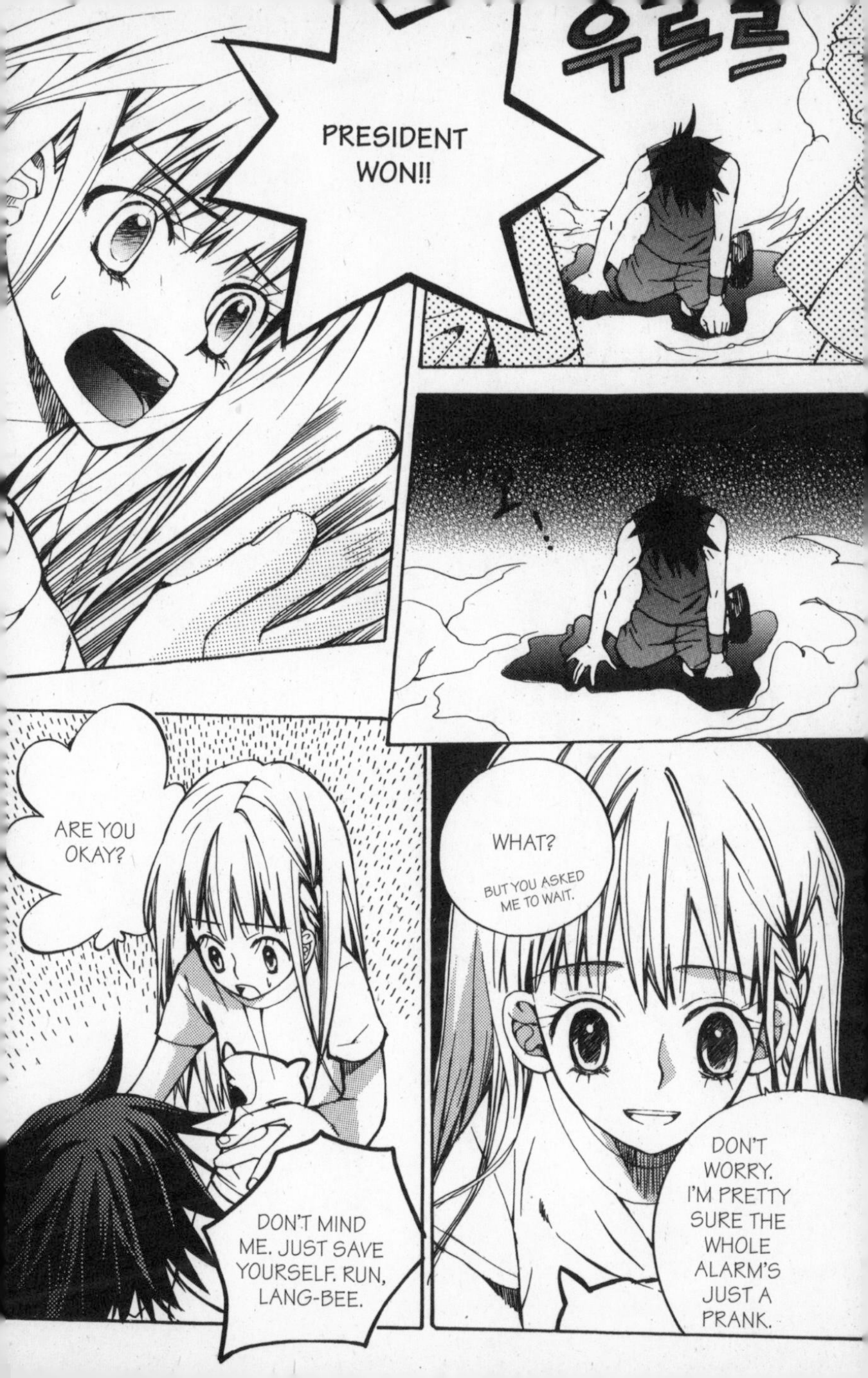
PRESIDENT WON!!
우드르
ARE YOU OKAY?
DON'T MIND ME. JUST SAVE YOURSELF. RUN, LANG-BEE.
WHAT?
BUT YOU ASKED ME TO WAIT.
DON'T WORRY. I'M PRETTY SURE THE WHOLE ALARM'S JUST A PRANK.

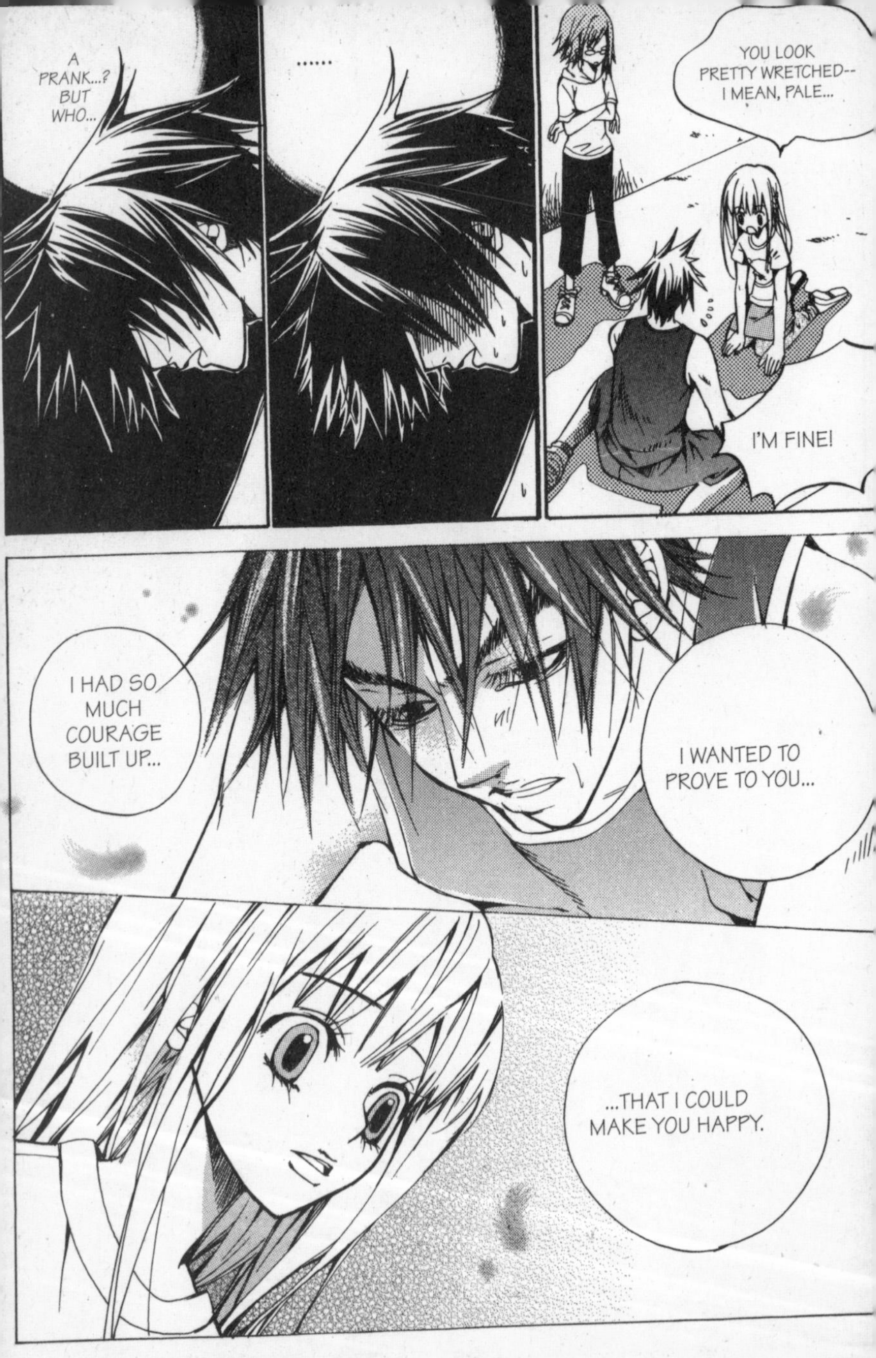
A PRANK...? BUT WHO...
......
YOU LOOK PRETTY WRETCHED-- I MEAN, PALE...
I'M FINE!
I HAD SO MUCH COURAGE BUILT UP...
I WANTED TO PROVE TO YOU...
...THAT I COULD MAKE YOU HAPPY.

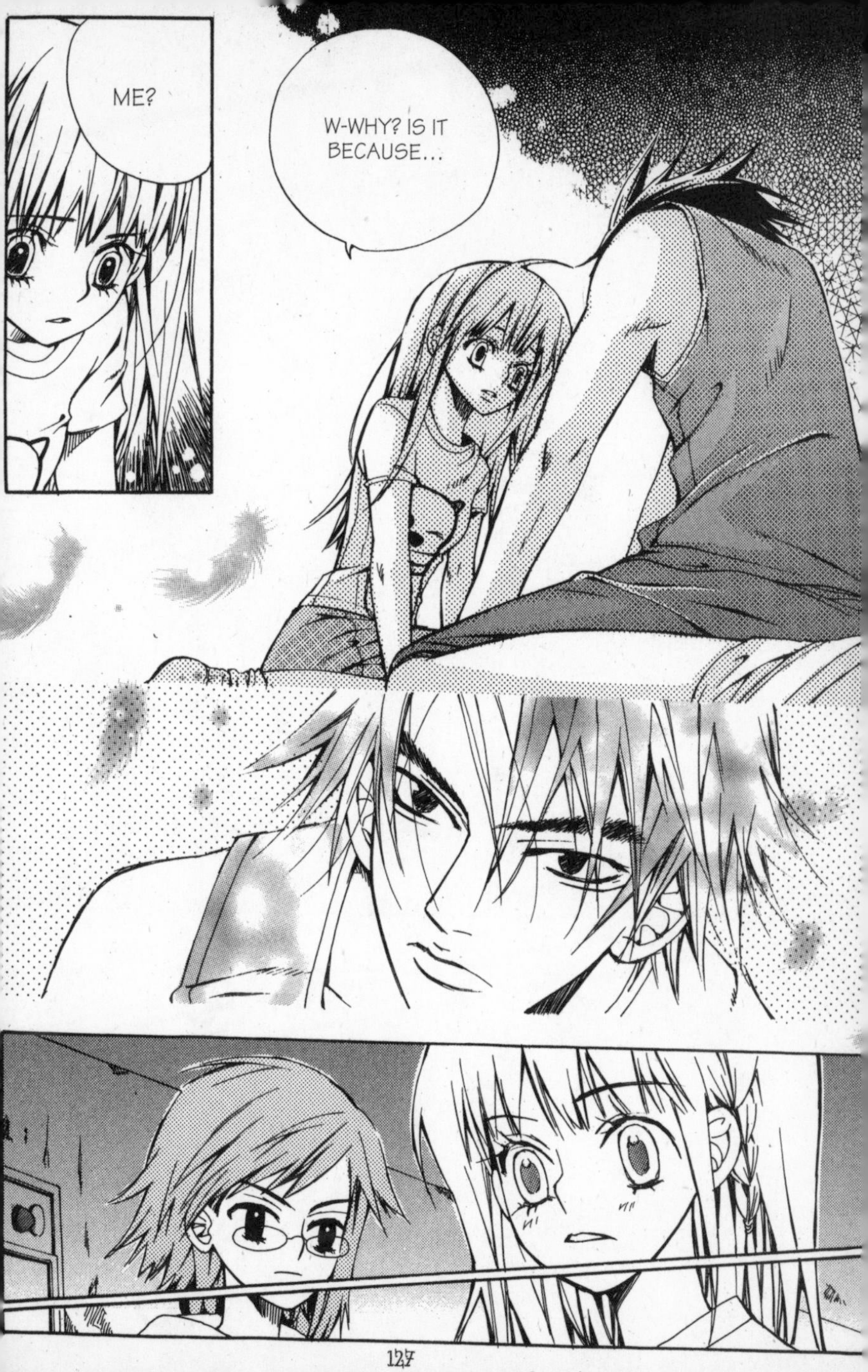
ME?
W-WHY? IS IT BECAUSE...

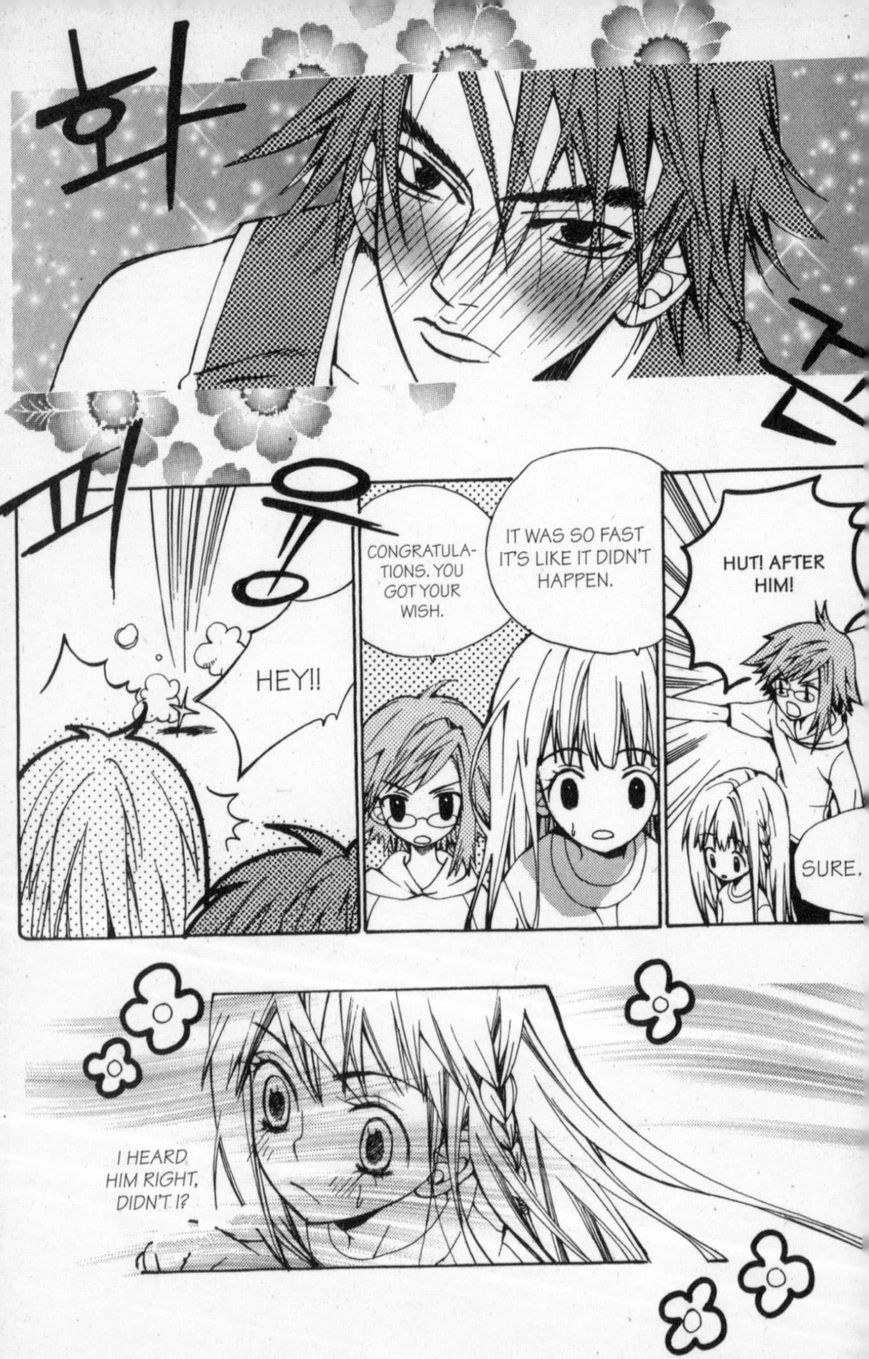
화
HEY!!
CONGRATULATIONS. YOU GOT YOUR WISH.
IT WAS SO FAST IT'S LIKE IT DIDN'T HAPPEN.
HUT! AFTER HIM!
SURE.
I HEARD HIM RIGHT, DIDN'T I?

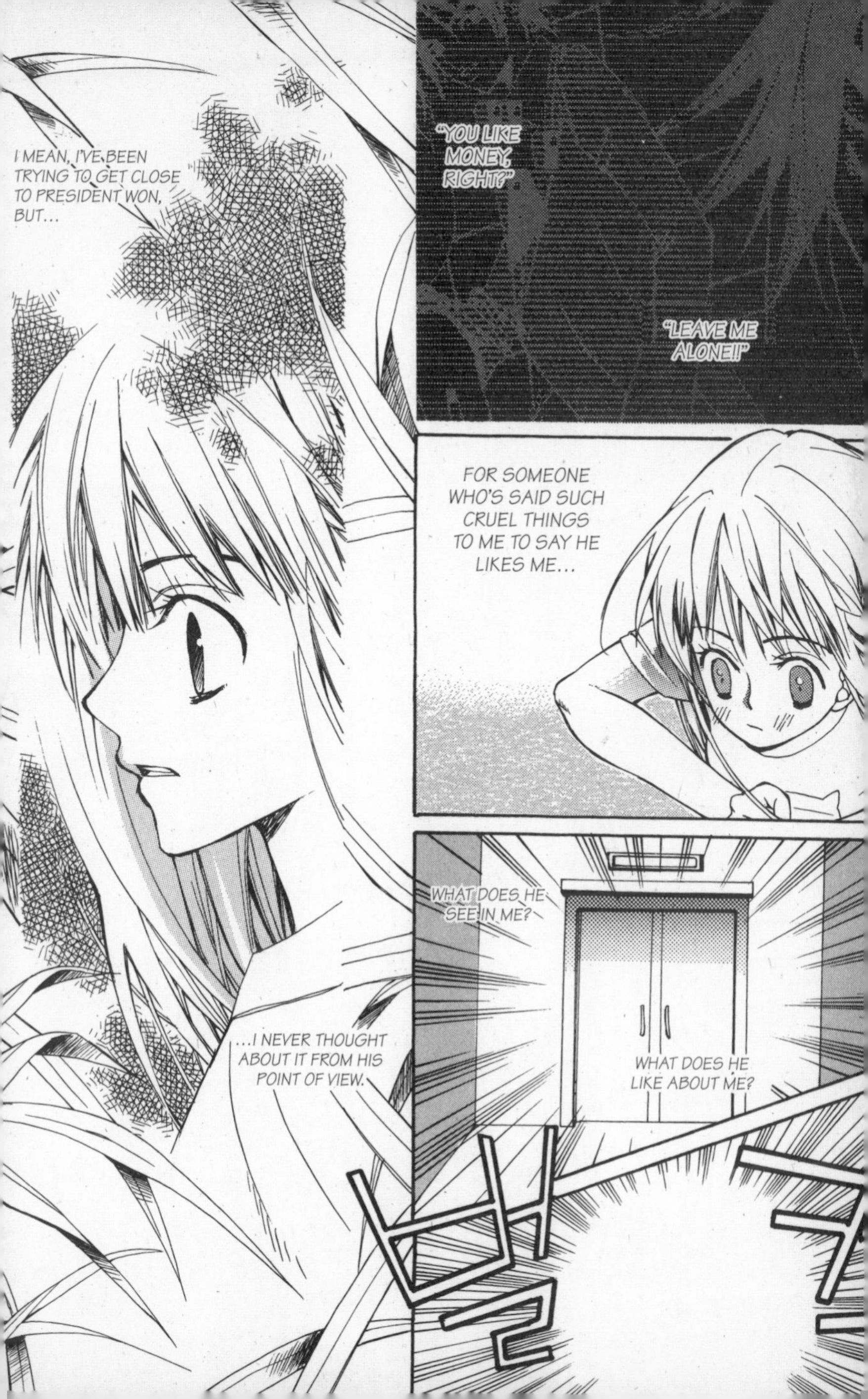
I MEAN, I'VE BEEN TRYING TO GET CLOSE TO PRESIDENT WON, BUT...
...I NEVER THOUGHT ABOUT IT FROM HIS POINT OF VIEW.
"YOU LIKE MONEY, RIGHT?"
"LEAVE ME ALONE!!"
FOR SOMEONE WHO'S SAID SUCH CRUEL THINGS TO ME TO SAY HE LIKES ME...
WHAT DOES HE SEE IN ME?
WHAT DOES HE LIKE ABOUT ME?

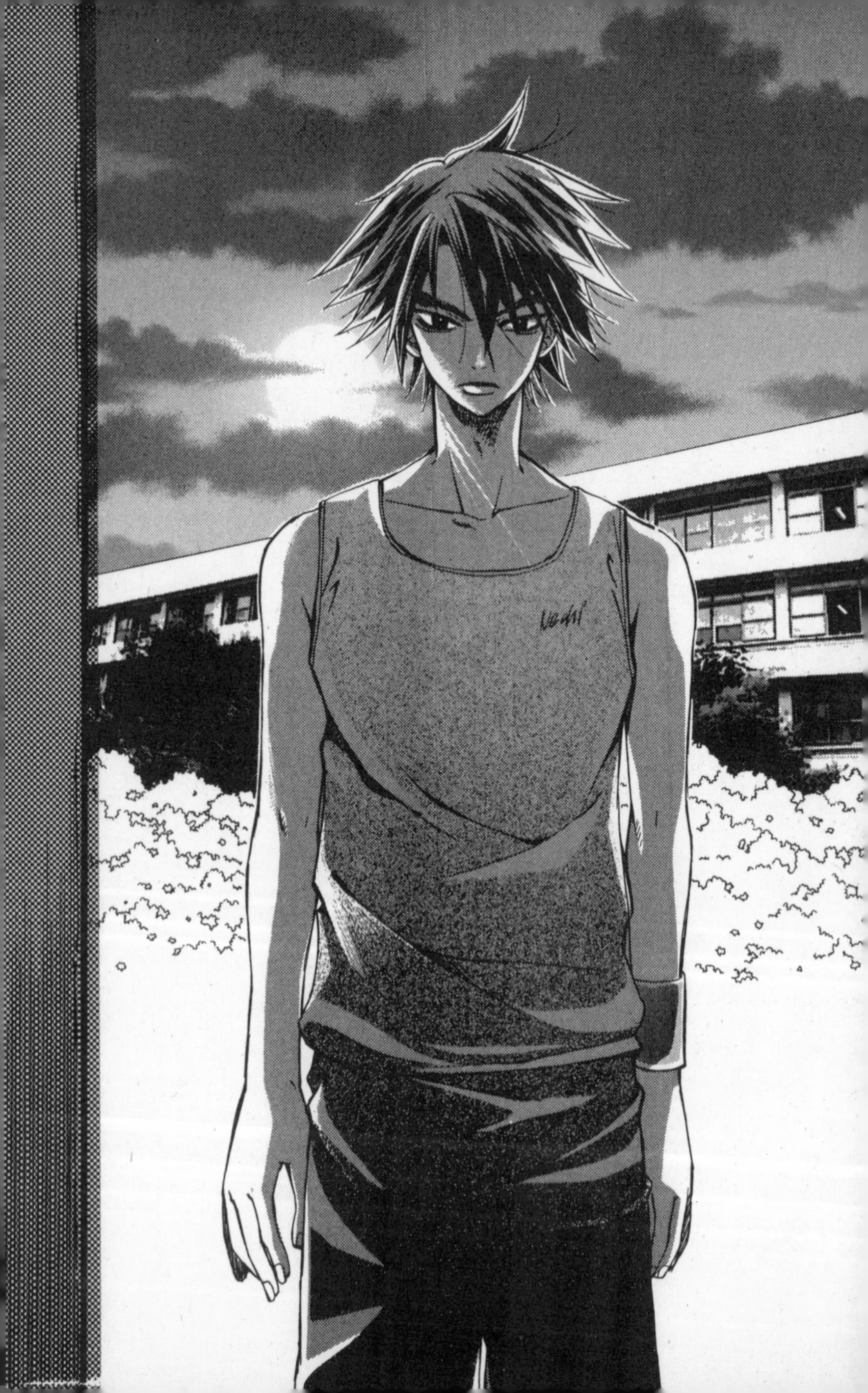

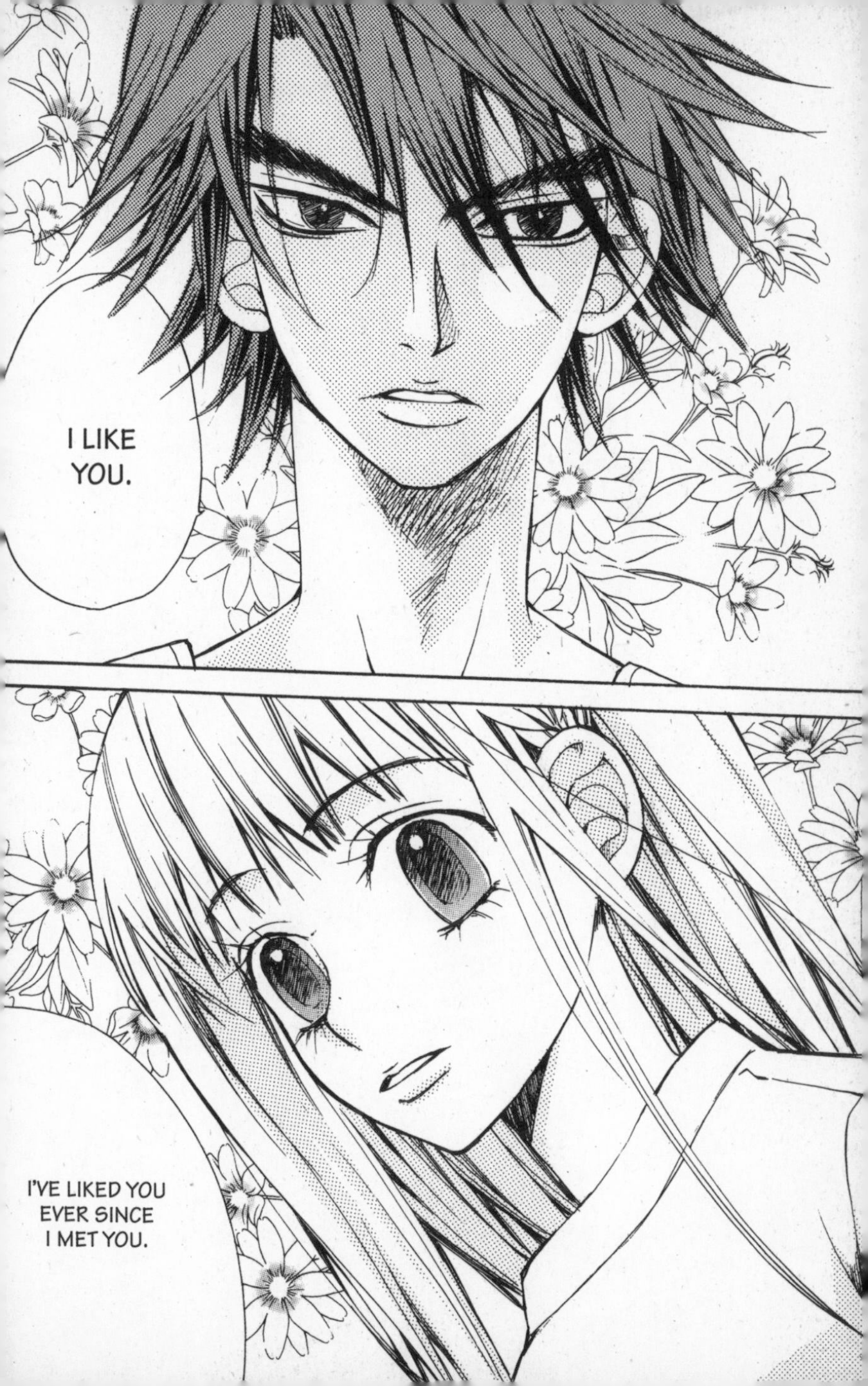
I LIKE YOU.
I'VE LIKED YOU EVER SINCE I MET YOU.

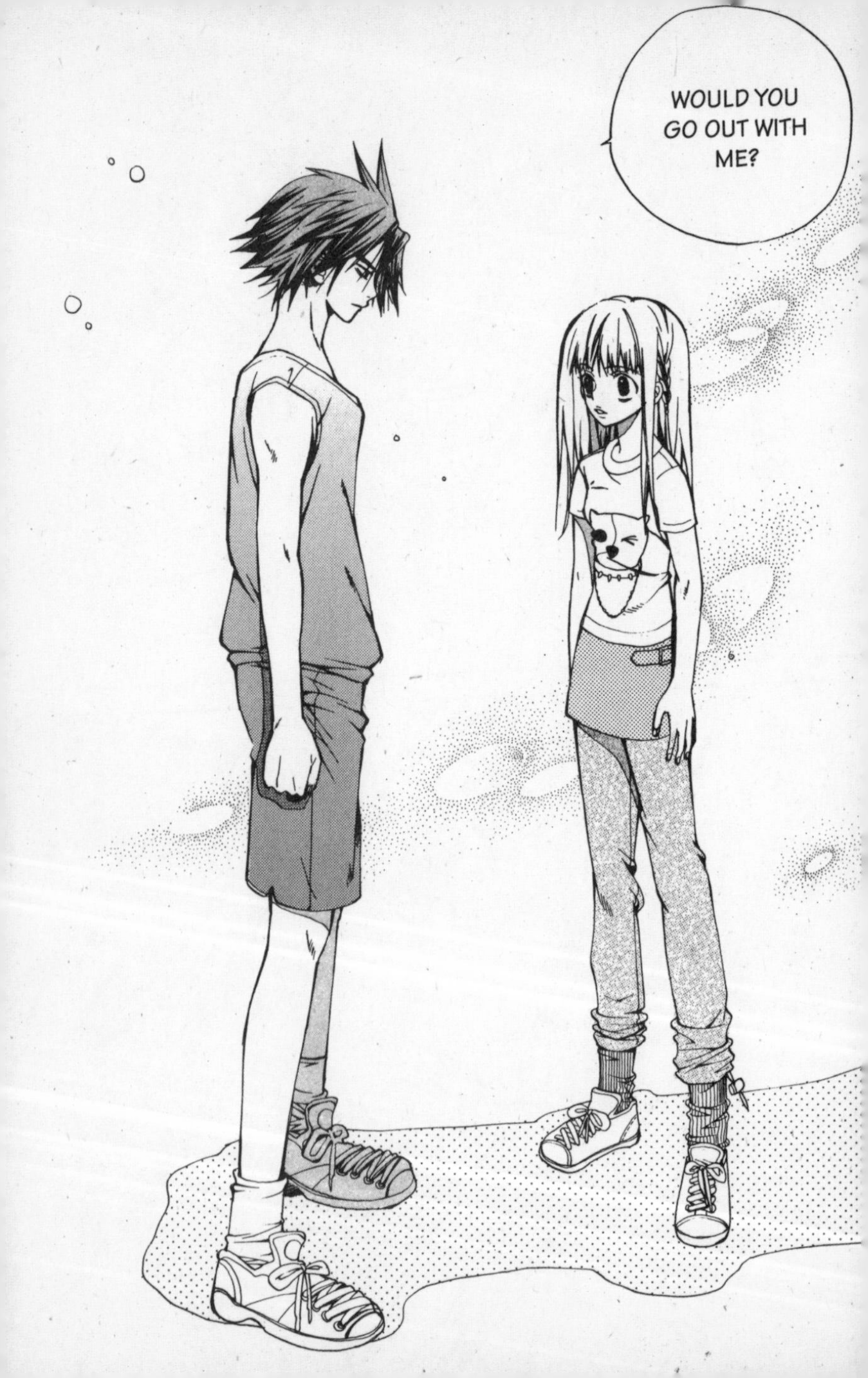
WOULD YOU GO OUT WITH ME?

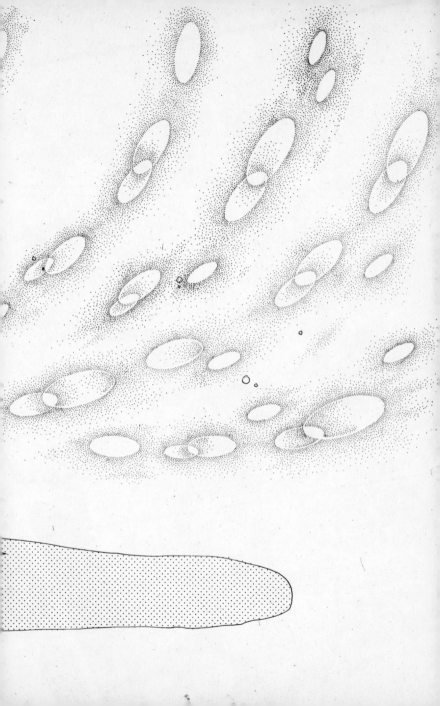

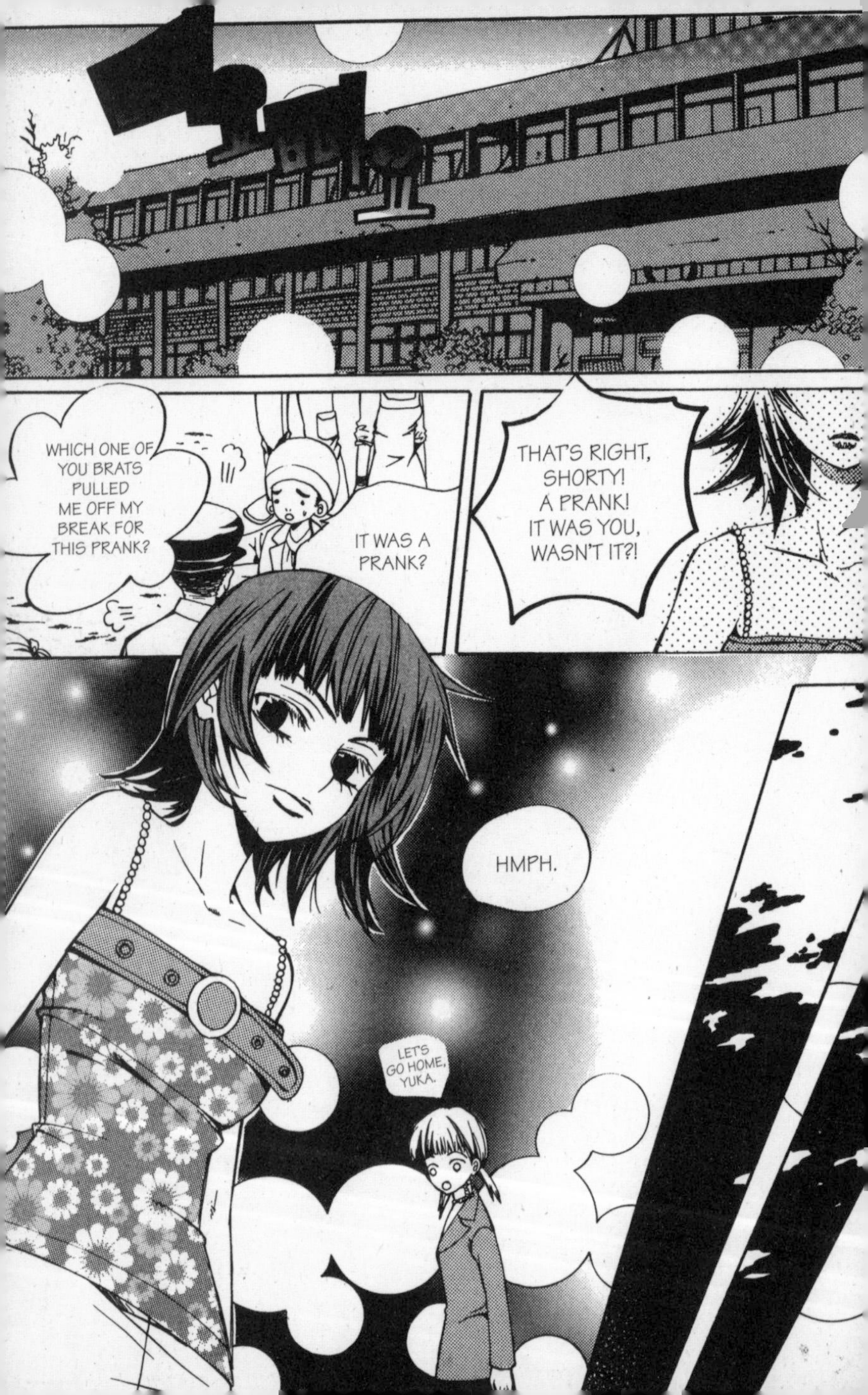
WHICH ONE OF YOU BRATS PULLED ME OFF MY BREAK FOR THIS PRANK?
IT WAS A PRANK?
THAT'S RIGHT, SHORTY! A PRANK! IT WAS YOU, WASN'T IT?!
HMPH.
LET'S GO HOME, YUKA.

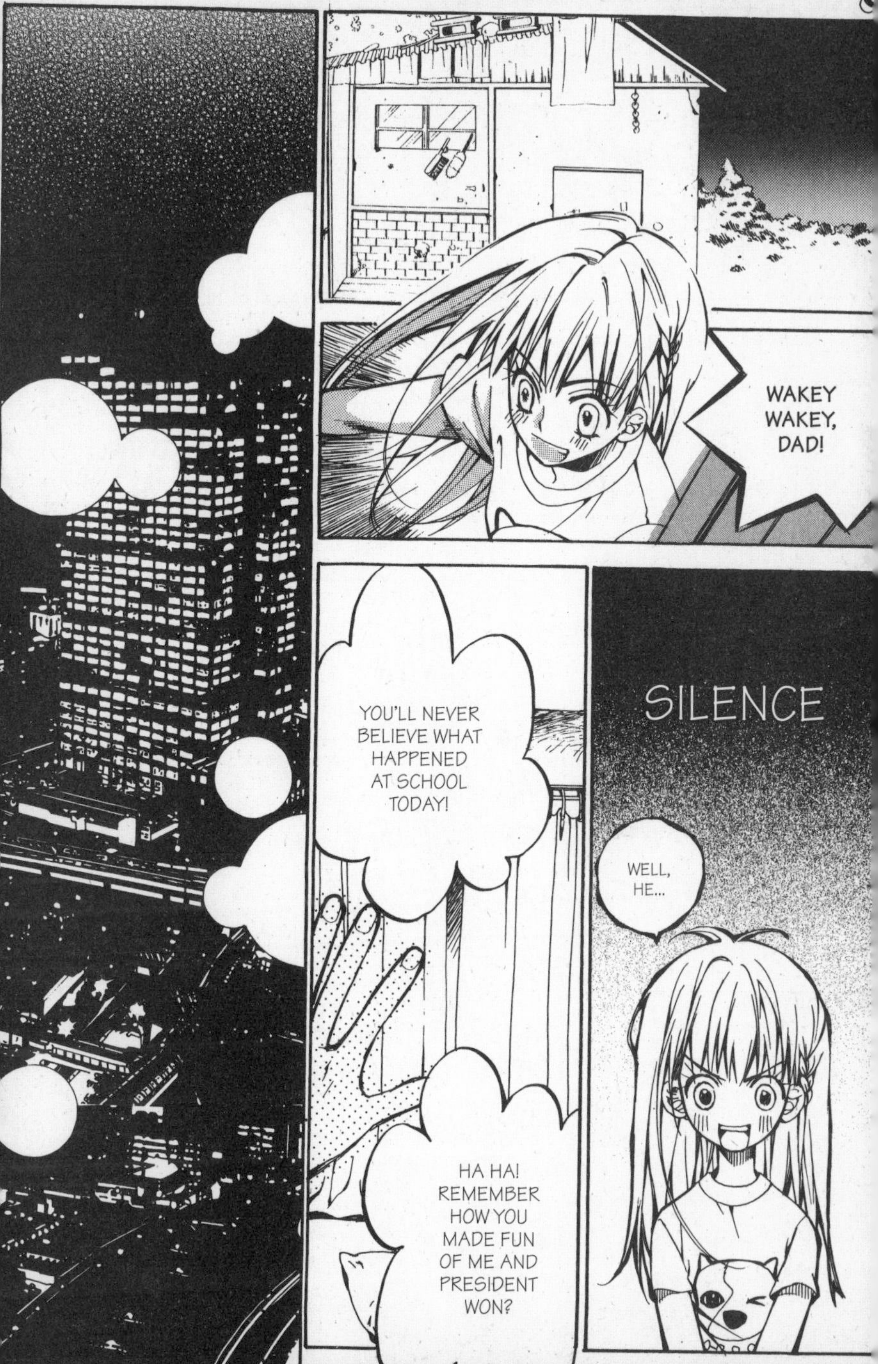
WAKEY WAKEY, DAD!
YOU'LL NEVER BELIEVE WHAT HAPPENED AT SCHOOL TODAY!
HA HA! REMEMBER HOW YOU MADE FUN OF ME AND PRESIDENT WON?
SILENCE
WELL, HE...

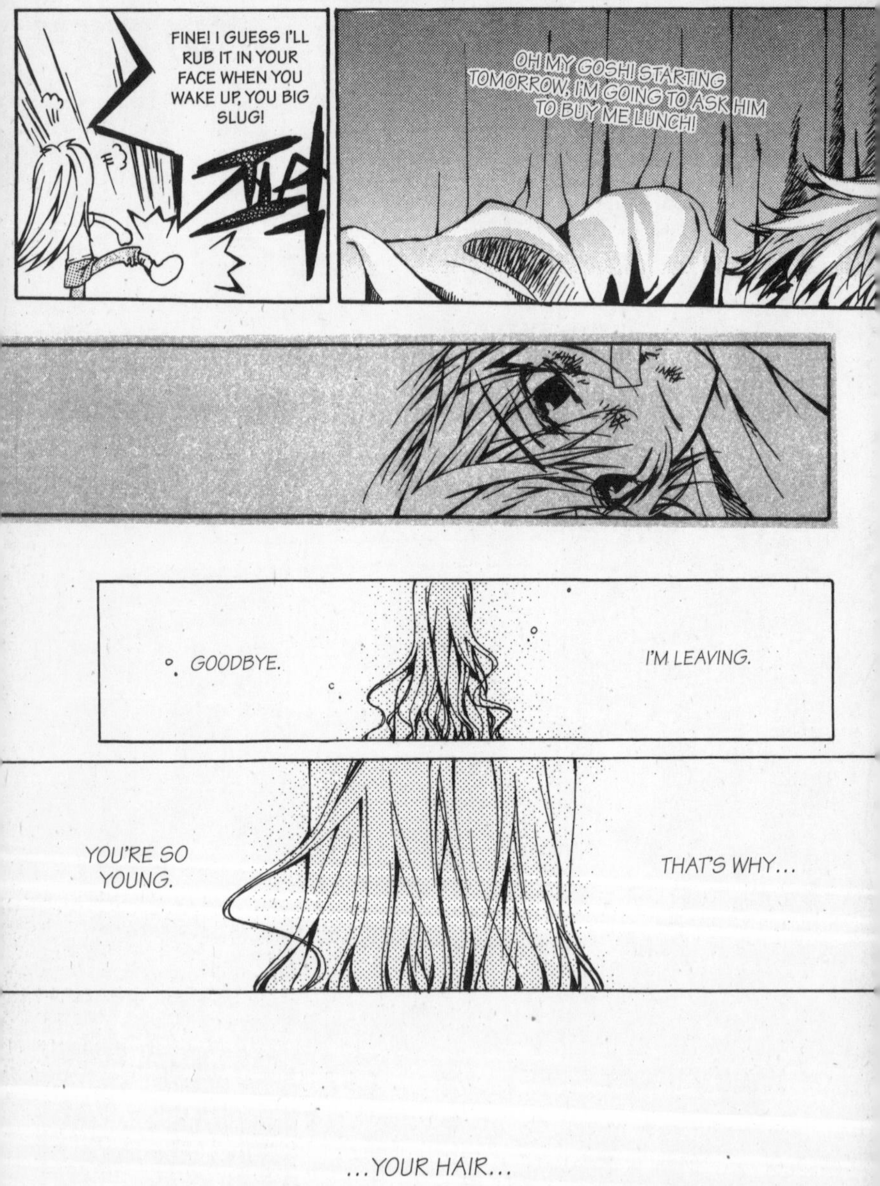
FINE! I GUESS I'LL RUB IT IN YOUR FACE WHEN YOU WAKE UP, YOU BIG SLUG!
OH MY GOSH! STARTING TOMORROW, I'M GOING TO ASK HIM TO BUY ME LUNCH!
GOODBYE.
I'M LEAVING.
YOU'RE SO YOUNG.
THAT'S WHY...
...YOUR HAIR...

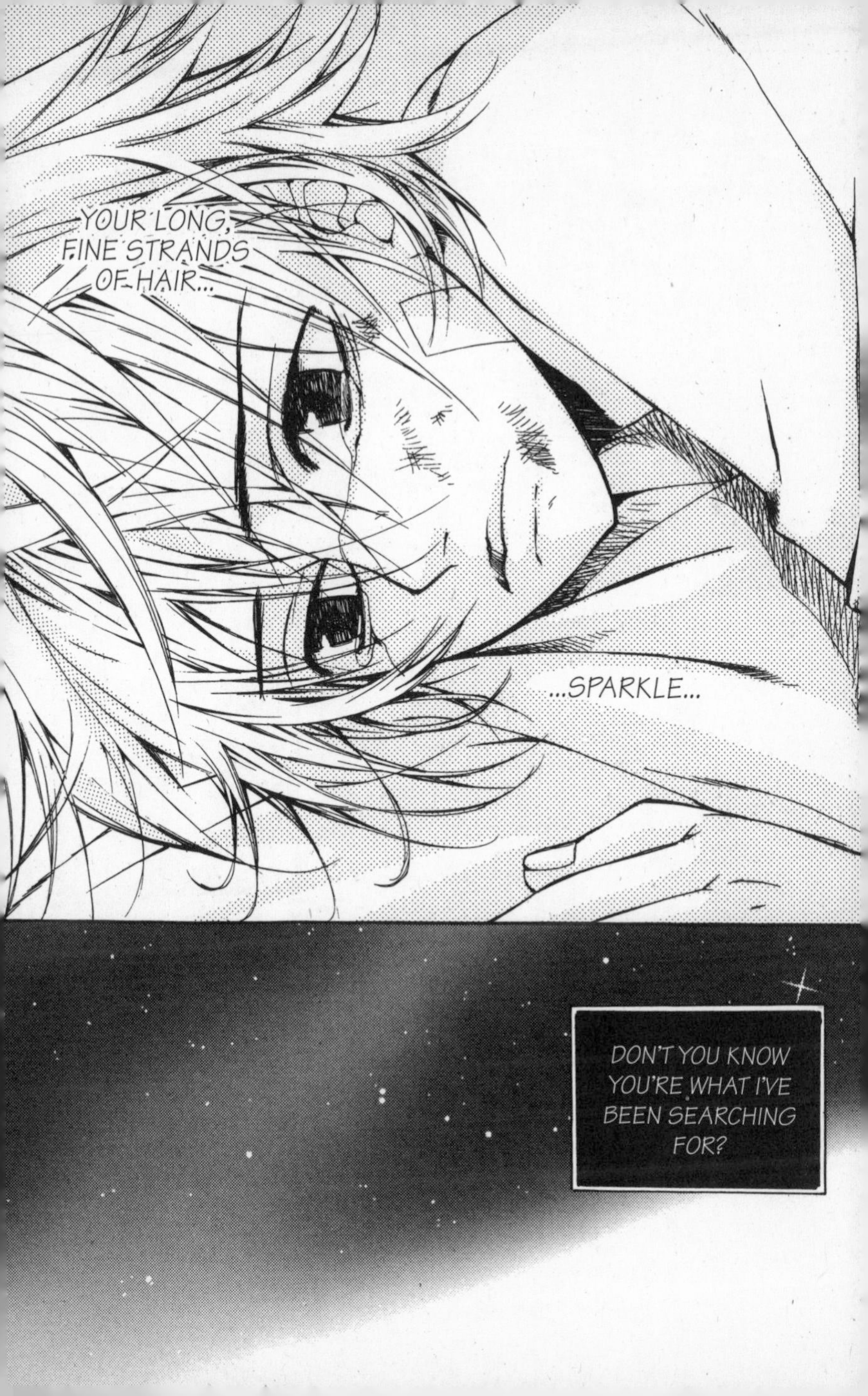
YOUR LONG, FINE STRANDS OF HAIR...
...SPARKLE...
DON'T YOU KNOW YOU'RE WHAT I'VE BEEN SEARCHING FOR?

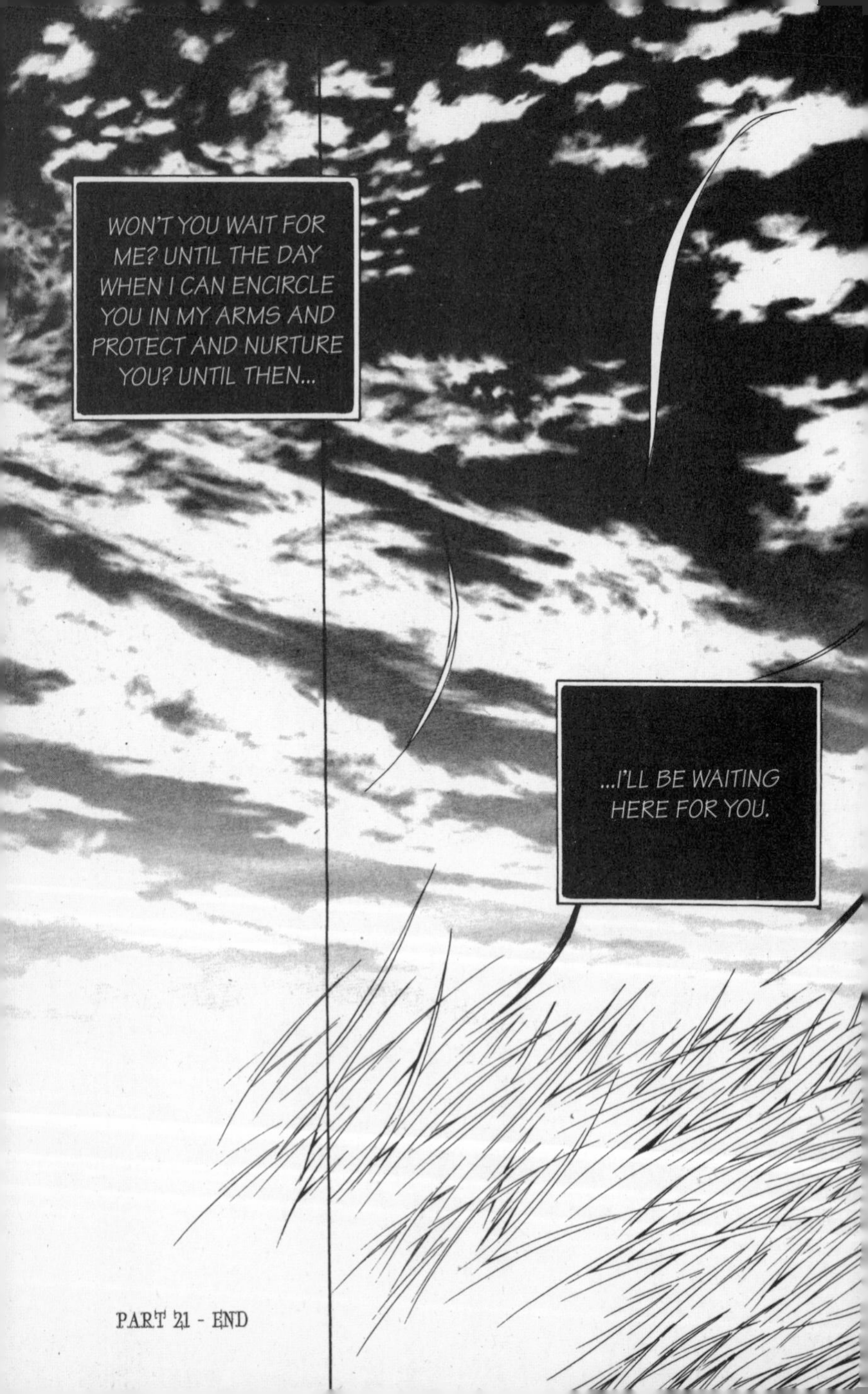
WON'T YOU WAIT FOR ME? UNTIL THE DAY WHEN I CAN ENCIRCLE YOU IN MY ARMS AND PROTECT AND NURTURE YOU? UNTIL THEN...
...I'LL BE WAITING HERE FOR YOU.
PART 21 - END

SHORT STORY

THE DEVIL'S WISH

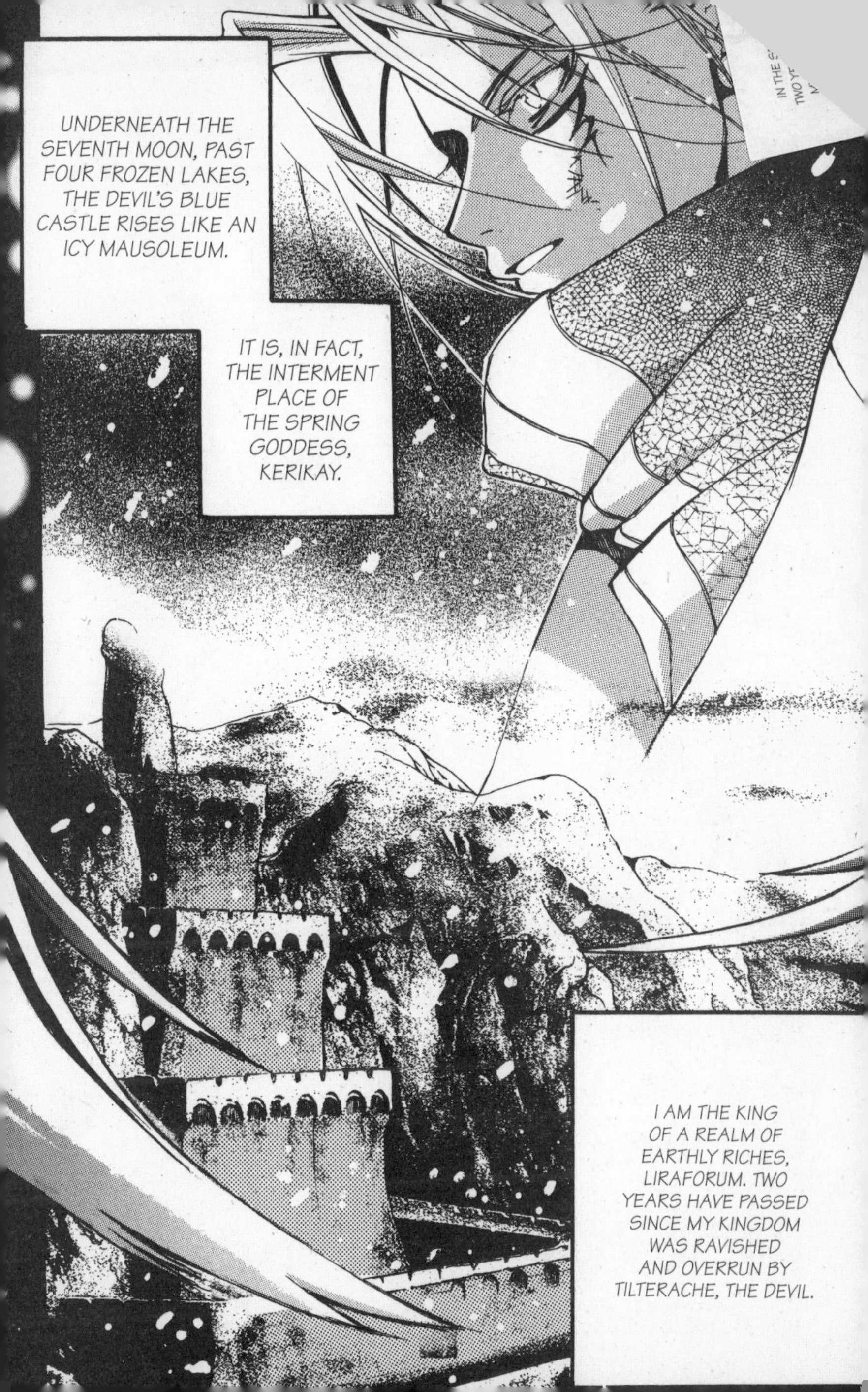
UNDERNEATH THE SEVENTH MOON, PAST FOUR FROZEN LAKES, THE DEVIL'S BLUE CASTLE RISES LIKE AN ICY MAUSOLEUM.
IT IS, IN FACT, THE INTERMENT PLACE OF THE SPRING GODDESS, KERIKAY.
I AM THE KING OF A REALM OF EARTHLY RICHES, LIRAFORUM. TWO YEARS HAVE PASSED SINCE MY KINGDOM WAS RAVISHED AND OVERRUN BY TILTERACHE, THE DEVIL.

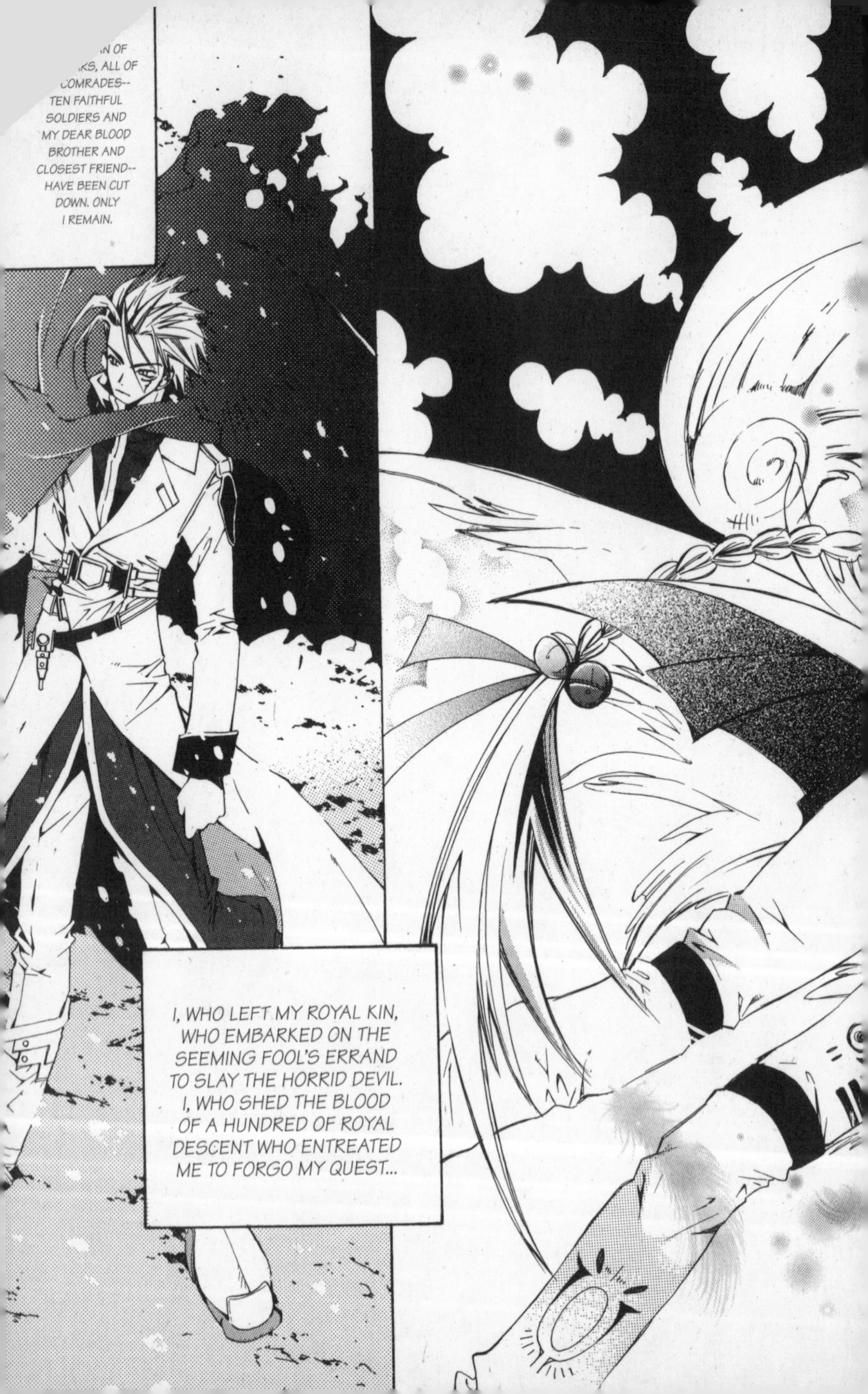
ALL OF COMRADES-- TEN FAITHFUL SOLDIERS AND MY DEAR BLOOD BROTHER AND CLOSEST FRIEND-- HAVE BEEN CUT DOWN. ONLY I REMAIN.
I, WHO LEFT MY ROYAL KIN, WHO EMBARKED ON THE SEEMING FOOL'S ERRAND TO SLAY THE HORRID DEVIL. I, WHO SHED THE BLOOD OF A HUNDRED OF ROYAL DESCENT WHO ENTREATED ME TO FORGO MY QUEST...

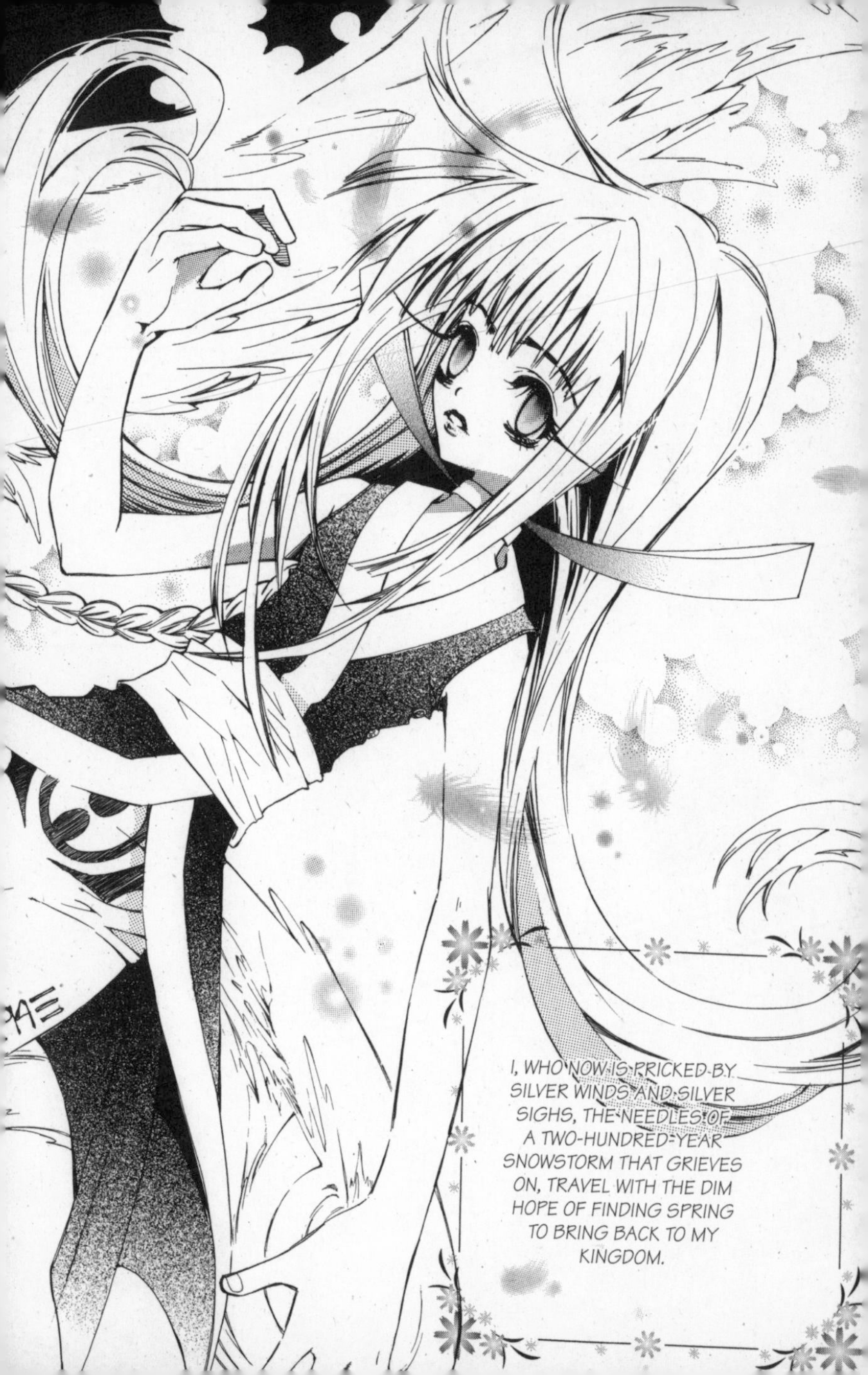
I, WHO NOW IS PRICKED BY SILVER WINDS AND SILVER SIGHS, THE NEEDLES OF A TWO-HUNDRED-YEAR SNOWSTORM THAT GRIEVES ON, TRAVEL WITH THE DIM HOPE OF FINDING SPRING TO BRING BACK TO MY KINGDOM.

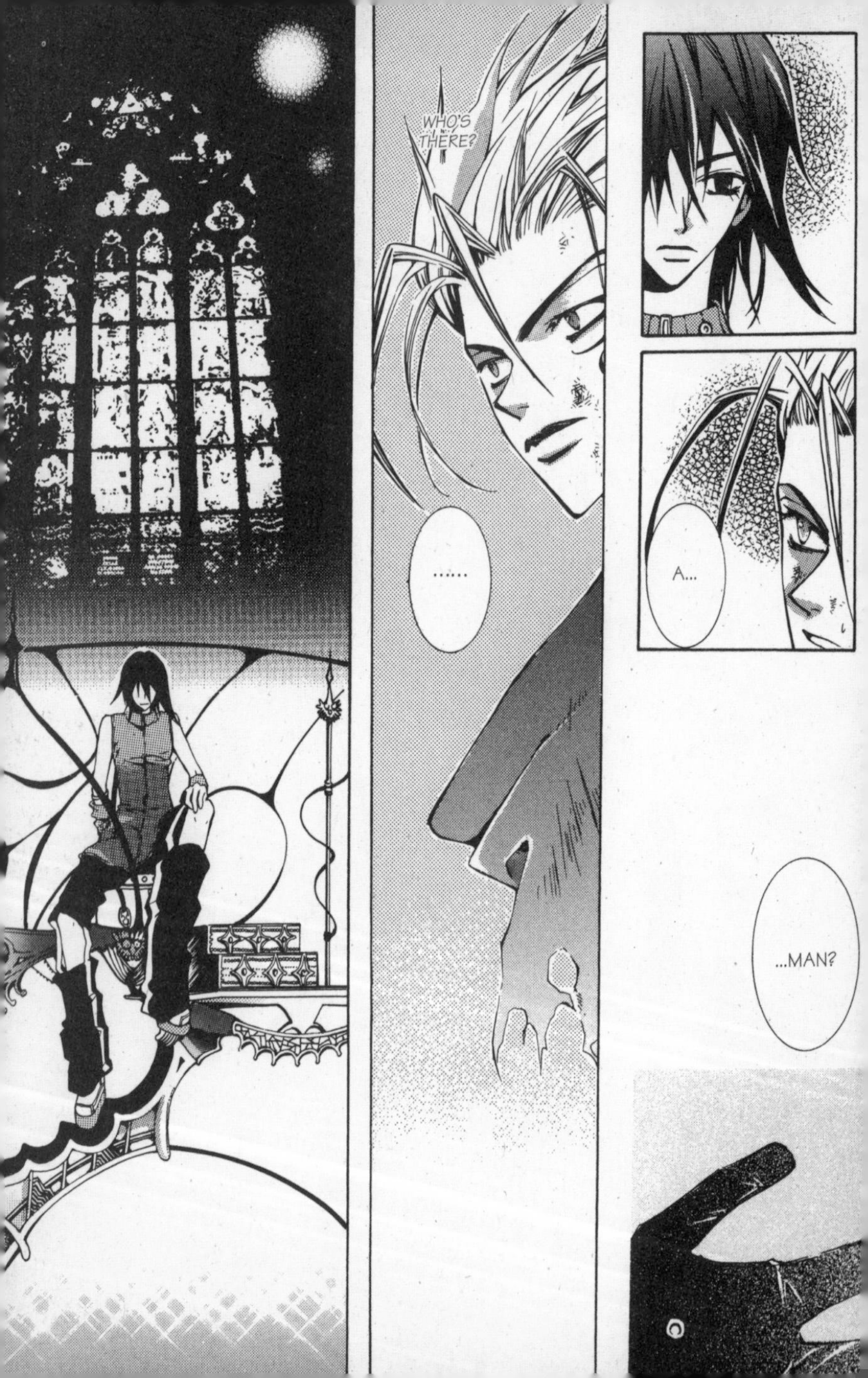
WHO'S THERE?
......
A...
...MAN?

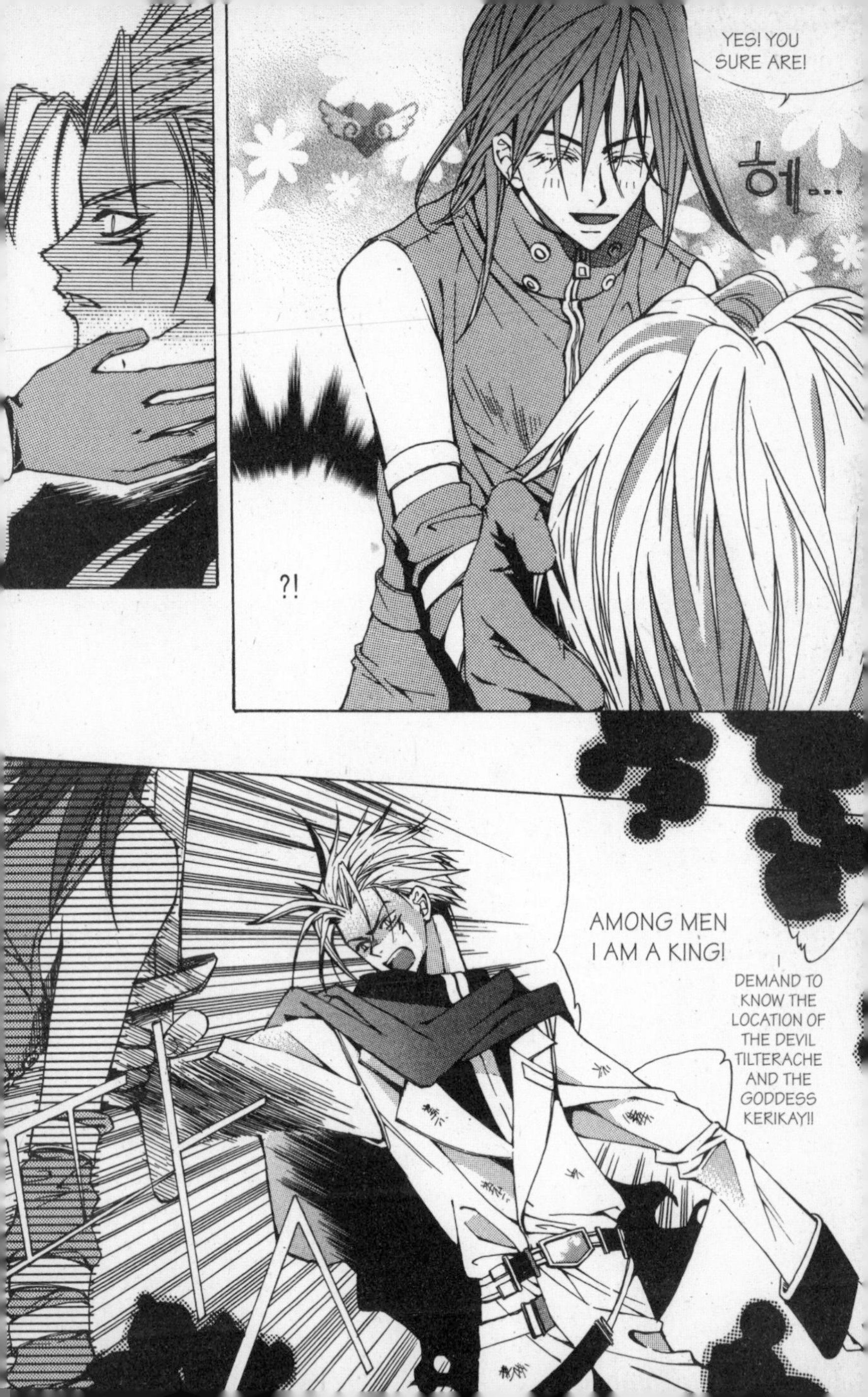
YES! YOU SURE ARE!
헤...
?!
AMONG MEN I AM A KING!
I DEMAND TO KNOW THE LOCATION OF THE DEVIL TILTERACHE AND THE GODDESS KERIKAY!!

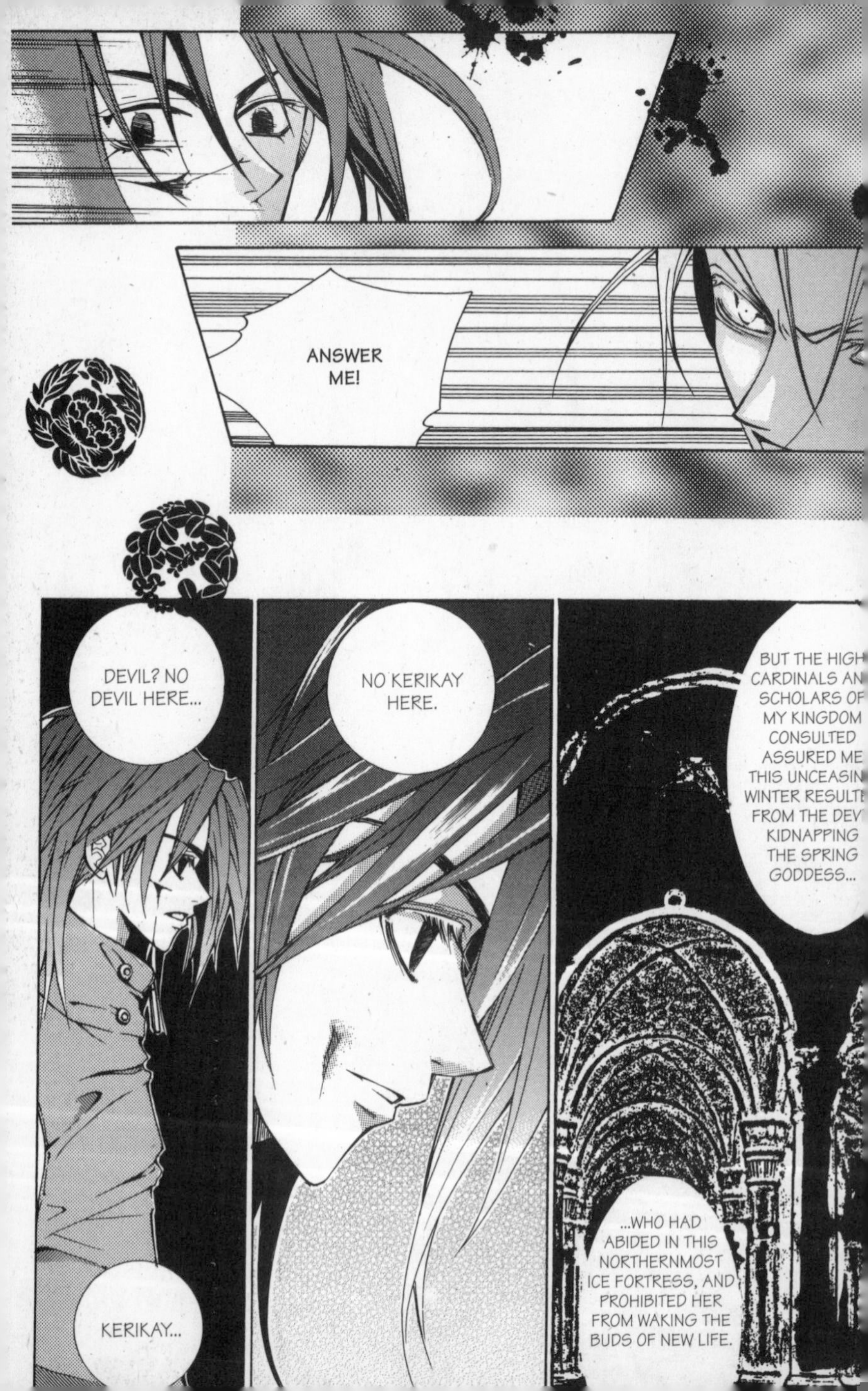
ANSWER ME!
DEVIL? NO DEVIL HERE...
KERIKAY...
NO KERIKAY HERE.
BUT THE HIGH CARDINALS AN SCHOLARS OF MY KINGDOM CONSULTED ASSURED ME THIS UNCEASIN WINTER RESULTE FROM THE DEV KIDNAPPING THE SPRING GODDESS...
...WHO HAD ABIDED IN THIS NORTHERNMOST ICE FORTRESS, AND PROHIBITED HER FROM WAKING THE BUDS OF NEW LIFE.

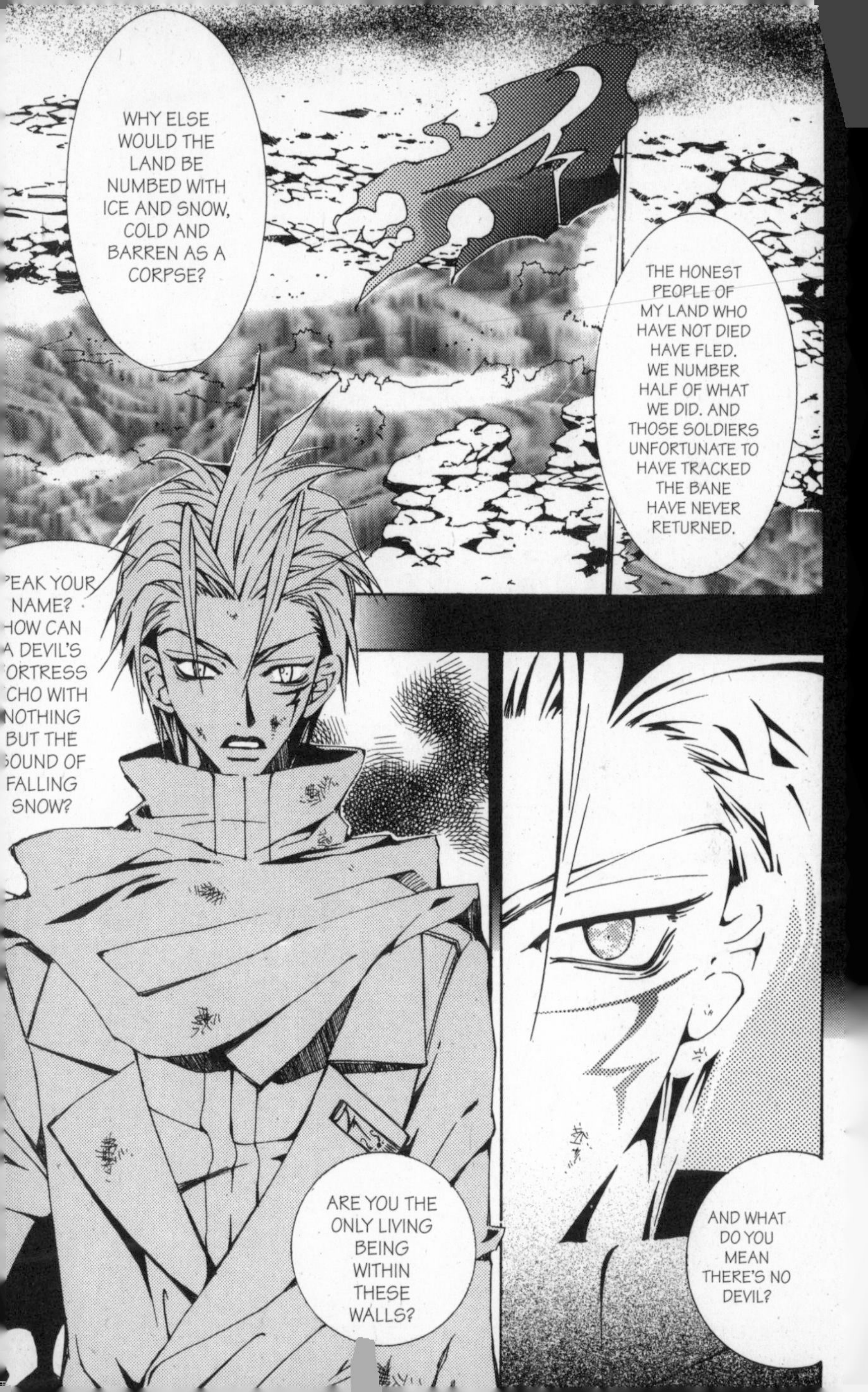
WHY ELSE WOULD THE LAND BE NUMBED WITH ICE AND SNOW, COLD AND BARREN AS A CORPSE?
THE HONEST PEOPLE OF MY LAND WHO HAVE NOT DIED HAVE FLED. WE NUMBER HALF OF WHAT WE DID. AND THOSE SOLDIERS UNFORTUNATE TO HAVE TRACKED THE BANE HAVE NEVER RETURNED.
EAK YOUR NAME? HOW CAN A DEVIL'S ORTRESS CHO WITH NOTHING BUT THE OUND OF FALLING SNOW?
ARE YOU THE ONLY LIVING BEING WITHIN THESE WALLS?
AND WHAT DO YOU MEAN THERE'S NO DEVIL?

POOR THING. YOU'RE A CAPTIVE, AREN'T YOU? IF YOU SPEAK FREELY, I'LL REWARD YOU WITH SAFE PASSAGE TO MY LANDS.

BUT YOU MUST ENUNCIATE EVERY DETAIL.

THERE'S NEVER BEEN A DEVIL HERE, YOUR MAJESTY.

......

I REALLY DUNNO ANYTHING

YOU CAN STAY AS LONG AS IT PLEASE YOU, YOUR MAJESTY.

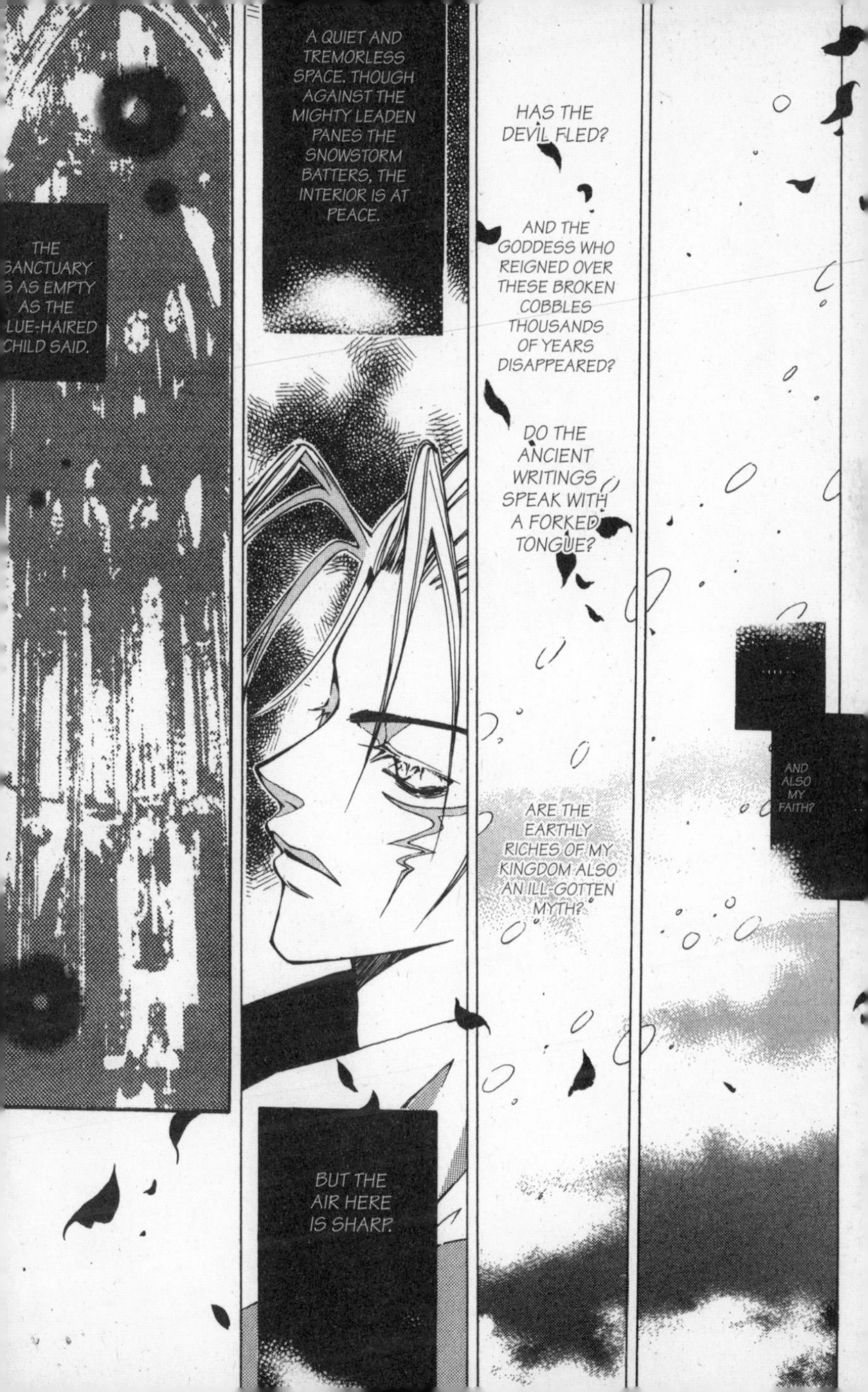

THE SANCTUARY S AS EMPTY AS THE LUE-HAIRED CHILD SAID.
A QUIET AND TREMORLESS SPACE. THOUGH AGAINST THE MIGHTY LEADEN PANES THE SNOWSTORM BATTERS, THE INTERIOR IS AT PEACE.
BUT THE AIR HERE IS SHARP.
HAS THE DEVIL FLED?
AND THE GODDESS WHO REIGNED OVER THESE BROKEN COBBLES THOUSANDS OF YEARS DISAPPEARED?
DO THE ANCIENT WRITINGS SPEAK WITH A FORKED TONGUE?
ARE THE EARTHLY RICHES OF MY KINGDOM ALSO AN ILL-GOTTEN MYTH?
......
AND ALSO MY FAITH?

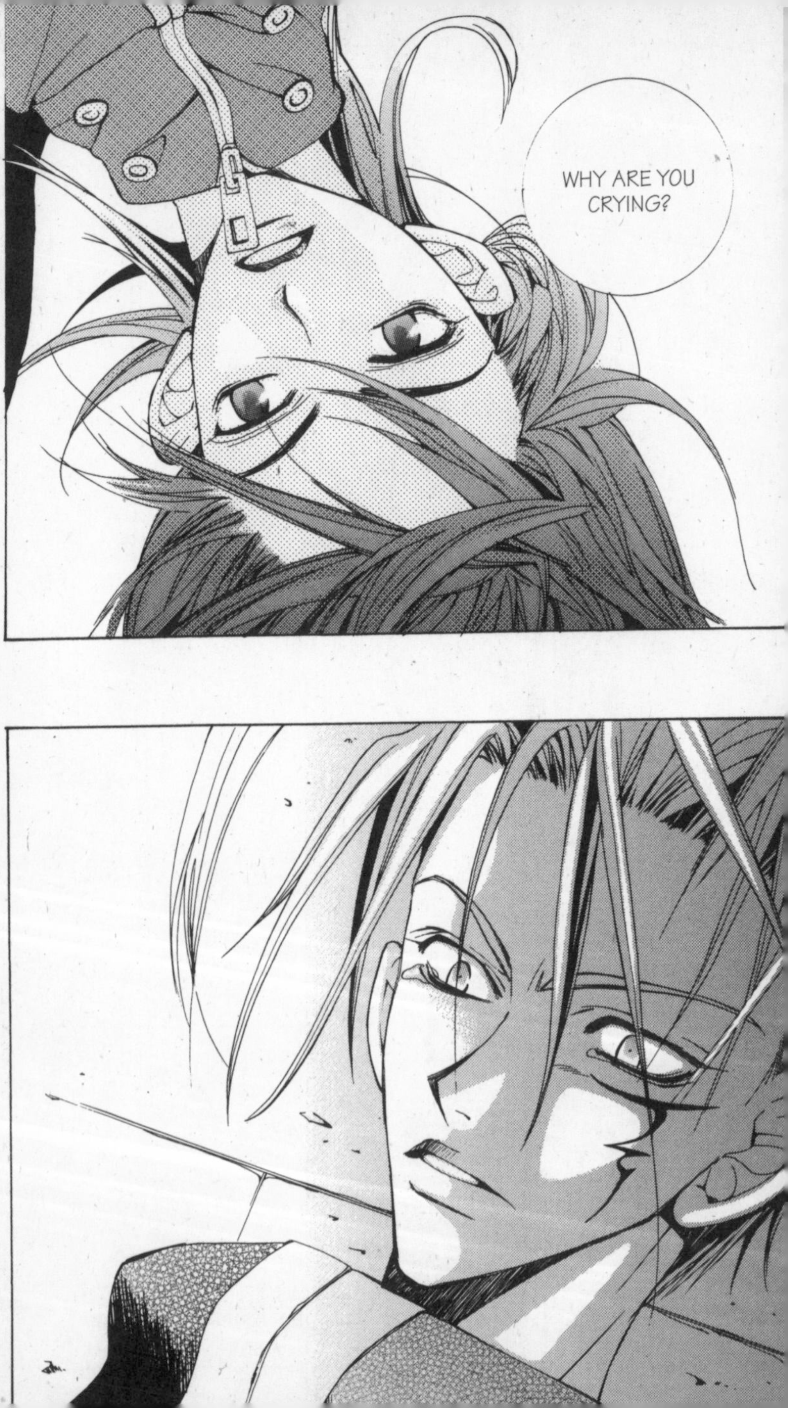
WHY ARE YOU CRYING?

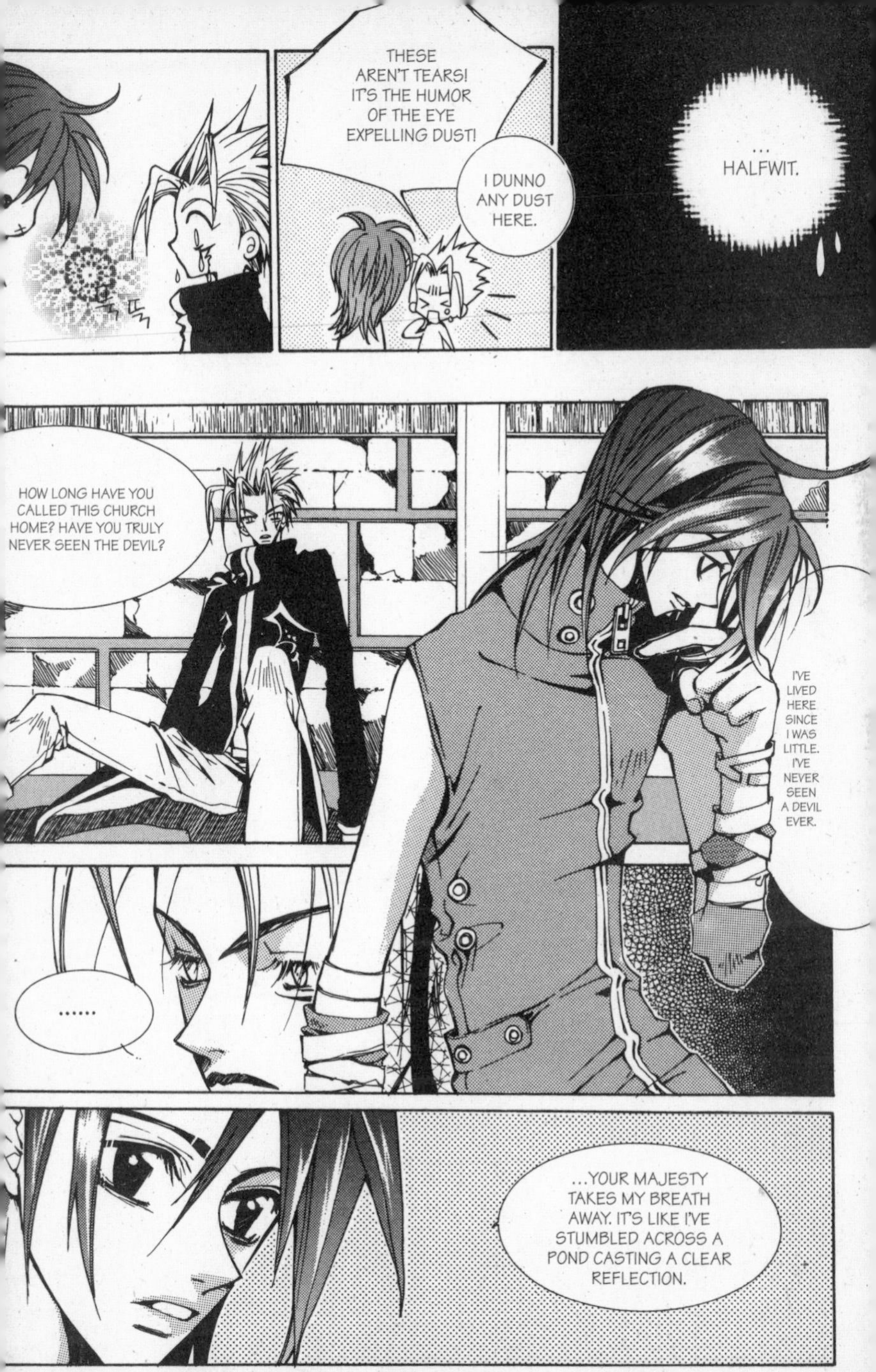

THESE AREN'T TEARS! IT'S THE HUMOR OF THE EYE EXPELLING DUST!
I DUNNO ANY DUST HERE.
... HALFWIT.
HOW LONG HAVE YOU CALLED THIS CHURCH HOME? HAVE YOU TRULY NEVER SEEN THE DEVIL?
I'VE LIVED HERE SINCE I WAS LITTLE. I'VE NEVER SEEN A DEVIL EVER.
......
...YOUR MAJESTY TAKES MY BREATH AWAY. IT'S LIKE I'VE STUMBLED ACROSS A POND CASTING A CLEAR REFLECTION.

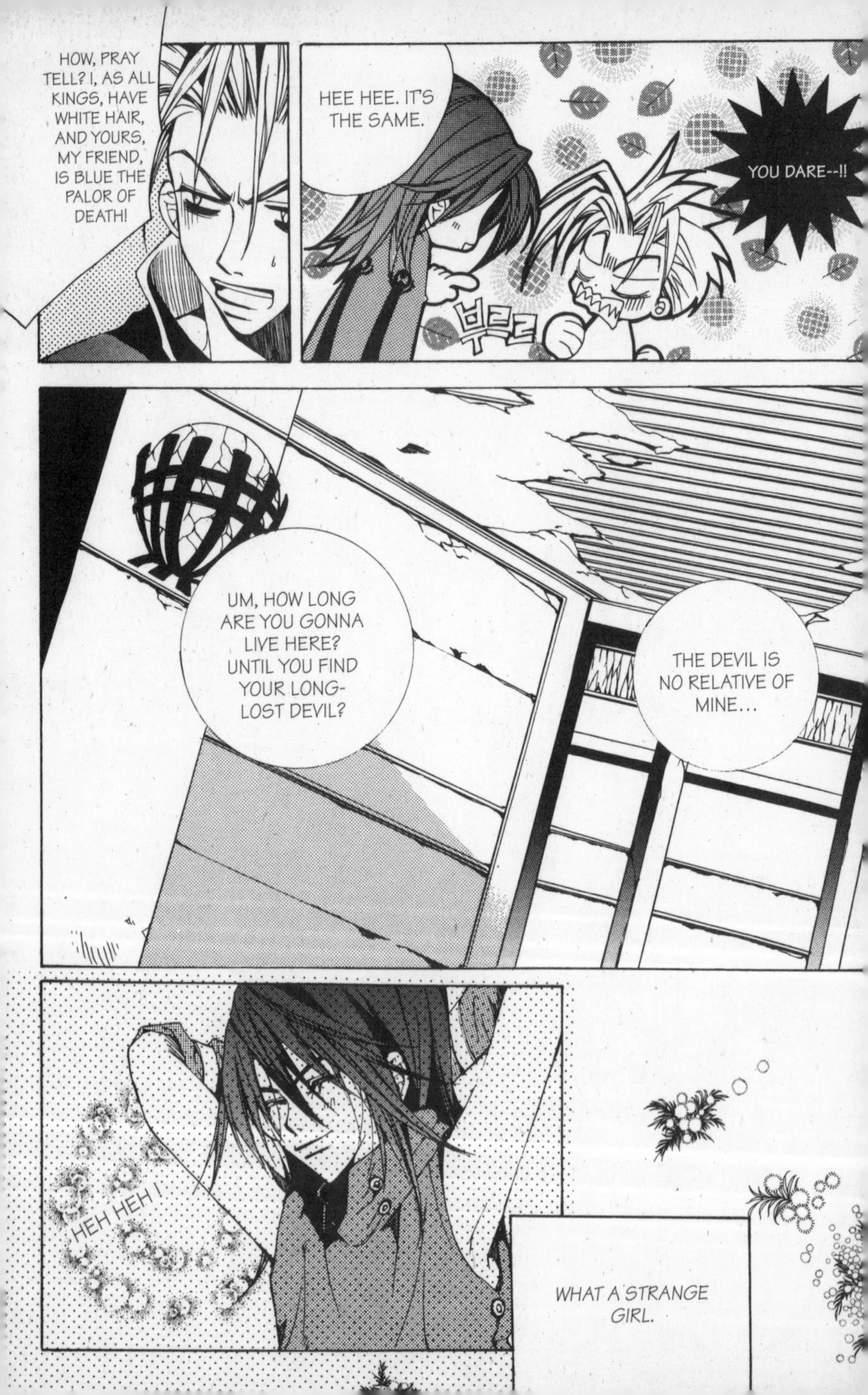
HOW, PRAY TELL? I, AS ALL KINGS, HAVE WHITE HAIR, AND YOURS, MY FRIEND, IS BLUE THE PALOR OF DEATH!
HEE HEE. IT'S THE SAME.
YOU DARE--!!
UM, HOW LONG ARE YOU GONNA LIVE HERE? UNTIL YOU FIND YOUR LONG-LOST DEVIL?
THE DEVIL IS NO RELATIVE OF MINE...
HEH HEH!
WHAT A STRANGE GIRL.

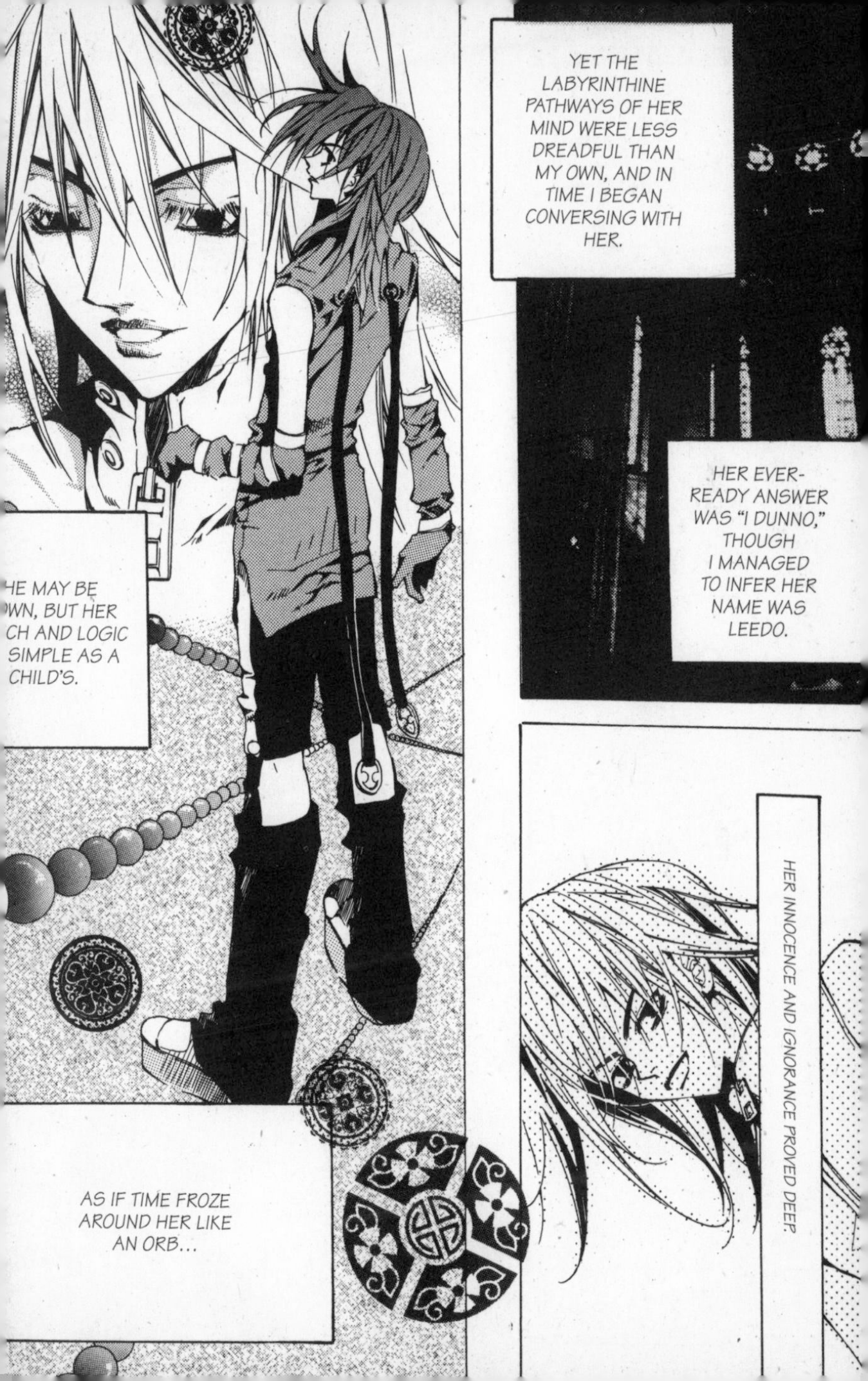
HE MAY BE WN, BUT HER CH AND LOGIC SIMPLE AS A CHILD'S.
AS IF TIME FROZE AROUND HER LIKE AN ORB...
YET THE LABYRINTHINE PATHWAYS OF HER MIND WERE LESS DREADFUL THAN MY OWN, AND IN TIME I BEGAN CONVERSING WITH HER.
HER EVER-READY ANSWER WAS "I DUNNO," THOUGH I MANAGED TO INFER HER NAME WAS LEEDO.
HER INNOCENCE AND IGNORANCE PROVED DEEP.

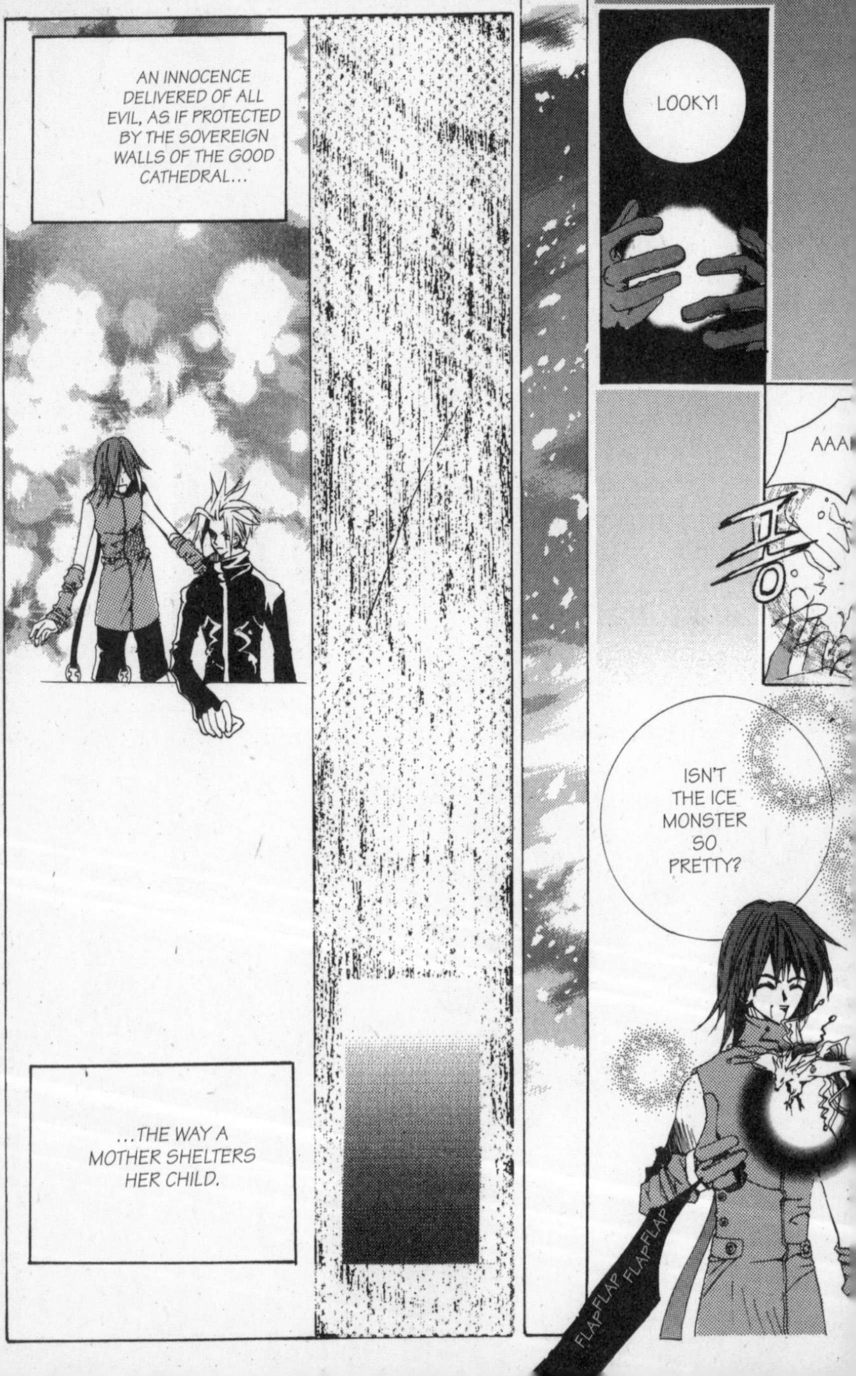
AN INNOCENCE DELIVERED OF ALL EVIL, AS IF PROTECTED BY THE SOVEREIGN WALLS OF THE GOOD CATHEDRAL...
...THE WAY A MOTHER SHELTERS HER CHILD.
LOOKY!
AAA
ISN'T THE ICE MONSTER SO PRETTY?
FLAPFLAP FLAPFLAP

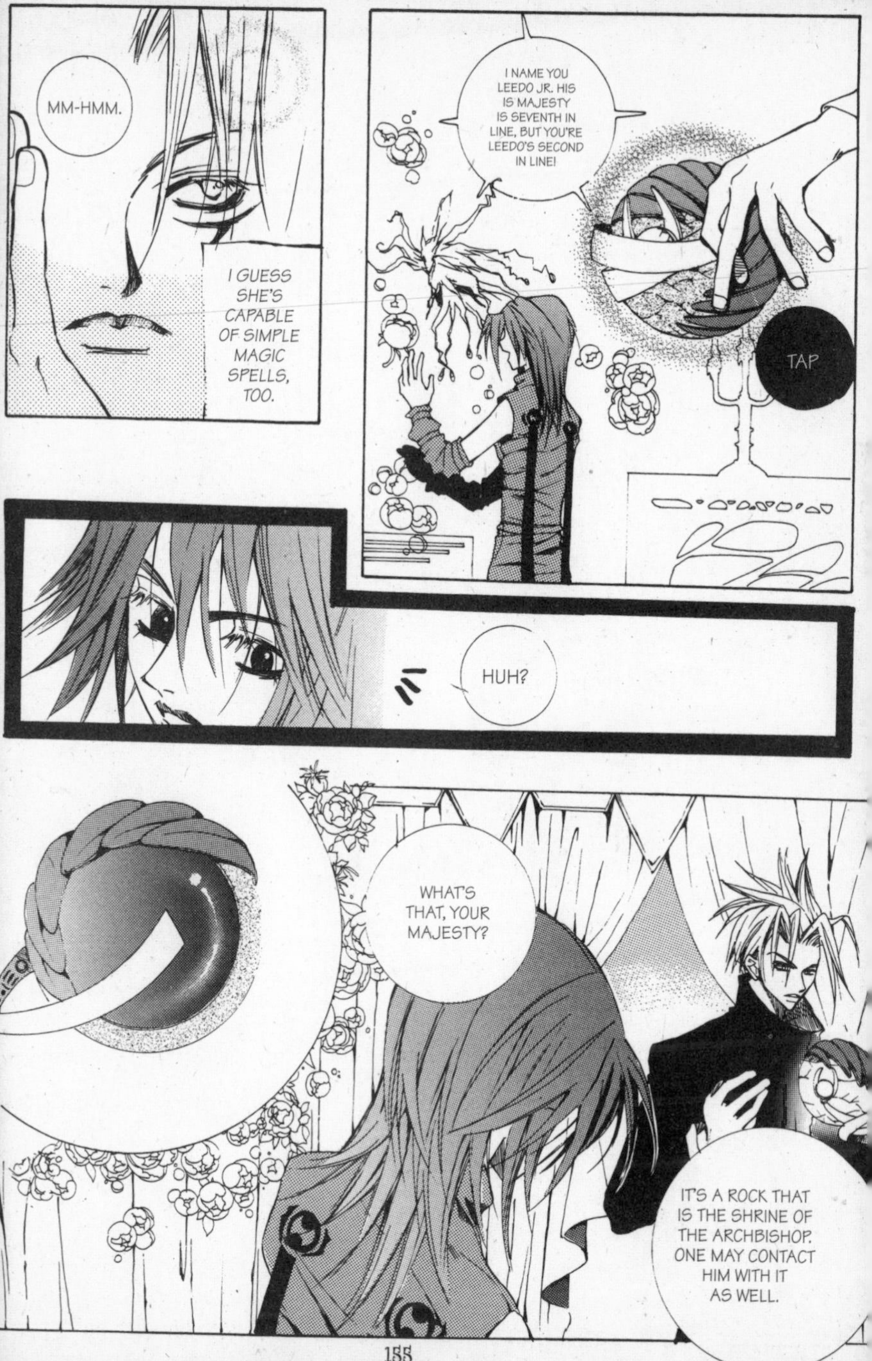
MM-HMM.
I GUESS SHE'S CAPABLE OF SIMPLE MAGIC SPELLS, TOO.
I NAME YOU LEEDO JR. HIS IS MAJESTY IS SEVENTH IN LINE, BUT YOU'RE LEEDO'S SECOND IN LINE!
TAP
HUH?
WHAT'S THAT, YOUR MAJESTY?
IT'S A ROCK THAT IS THE SHRINE OF THE ARCHBISHOP. ONE MAY CONTACT HIM WITH IT AS WELL.

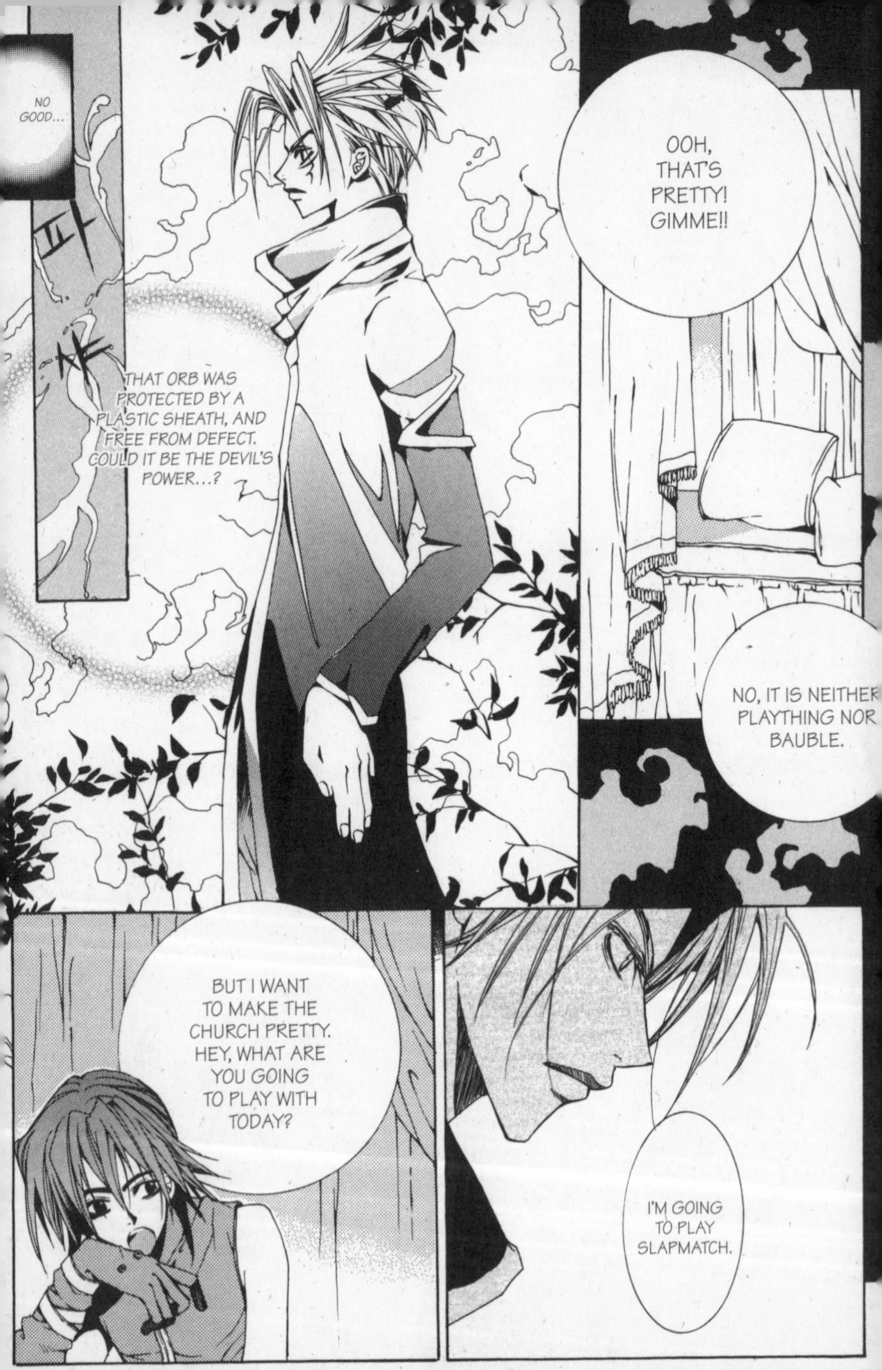
NO GOOD...
THAT ORB WAS PROTECTED BY A PLASTIC SHEATH, AND FREE FROM DEFECT. COULD IT BE THE DEVIL'S POWER...?
OOH, THAT'S PRETTY! GIMME!!
NO, IT IS NEITHER PLAYTHING NOR BAUBLE.
BUT I WANT TO MAKE THE CHURCH PRETTY. HEY, WHAT ARE YOU GOING TO PLAY WITH TODAY?
I'M GOING TO PLAY SLAPMATCH.

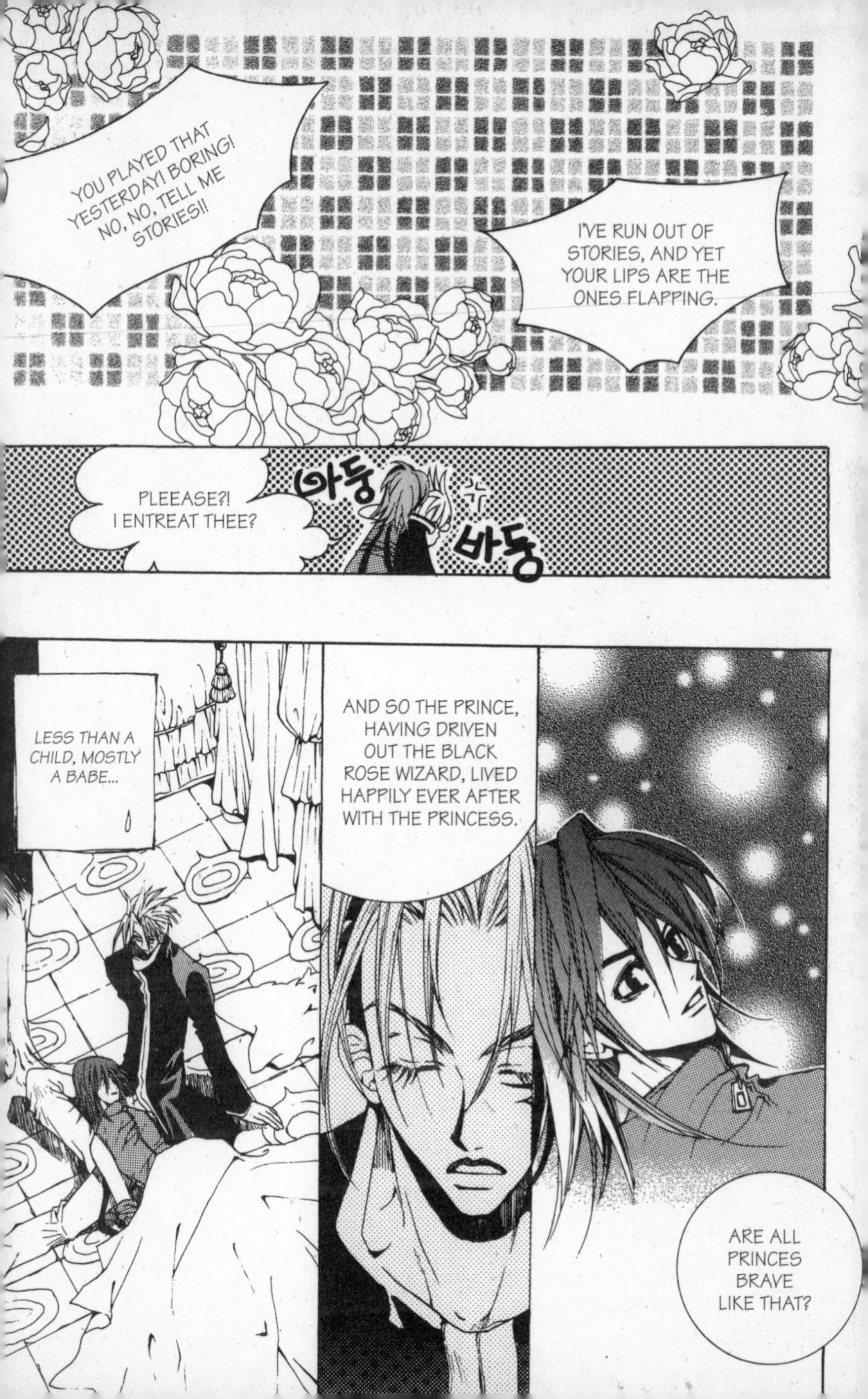

YOU PLAYED THAT YESTERDAY! BORING! NO, NO, TELL ME STORIES!!
I'VE RUN OUT OF STORIES, AND YET YOUR LIPS ARE THE ONES FLAPPING.
PLEEASE?! I ENTREAT THEE?
바둥
바동
LESS THAN A CHILD, MOSTLY A BABE...
AND SO THE PRINCE, HAVING DRIVEN OUT THE BLACK ROSE WIZARD, LIVED HAPPILY EVER AFTER WITH THE PRINCESS.
ARE ALL PRINCES BRAVE LIKE THAT?

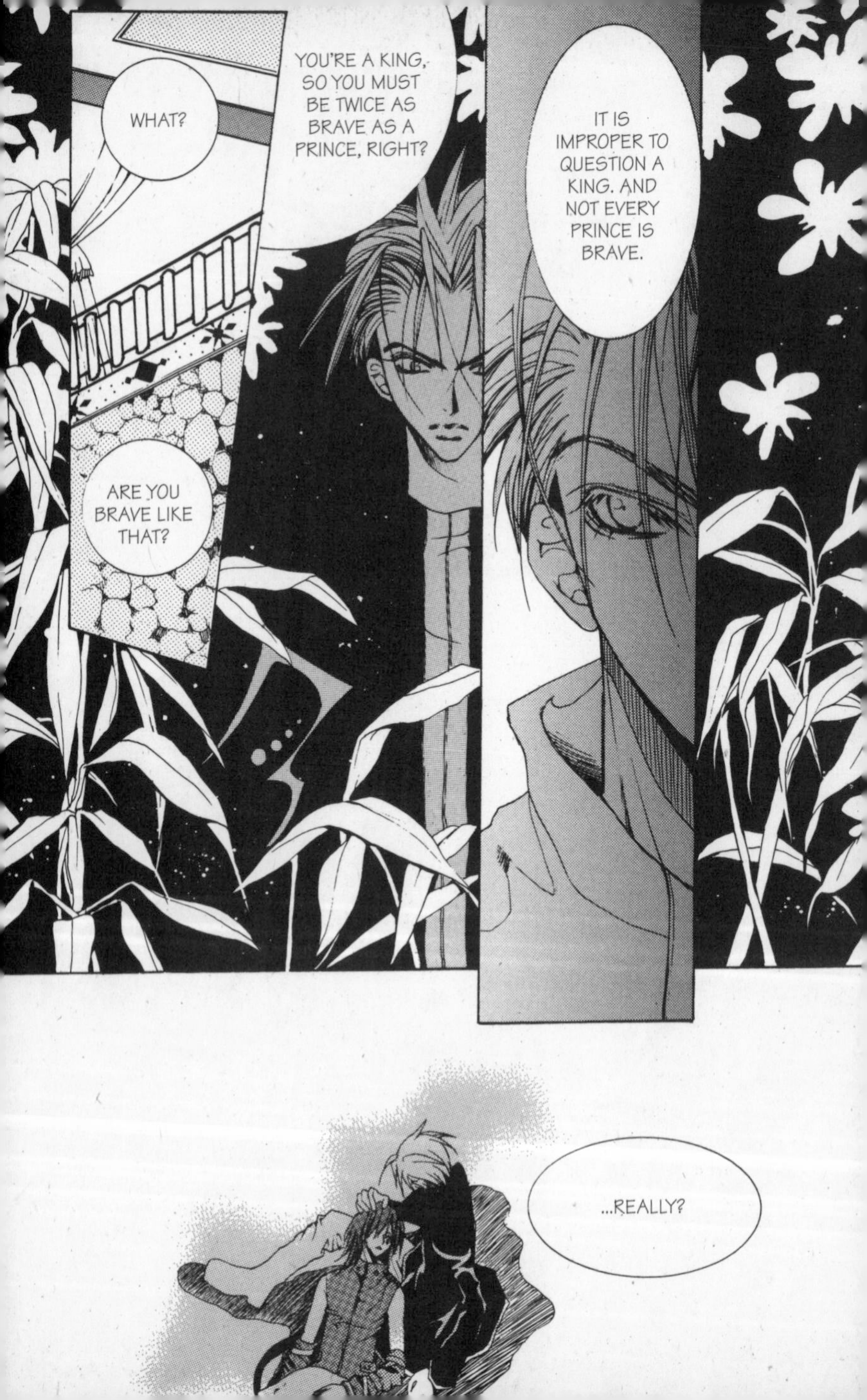
WHAT?
ARE YOU BRAVE LIKE THAT?
YOU'RE A KING, SO YOU MUST BE TWICE AS BRAVE AS A PRINCE, RIGHT?
IT IS IMPROPER TO QUESTION A KING. AND NOT EVERY PRINCE IS BRAVE.
...REALLY?

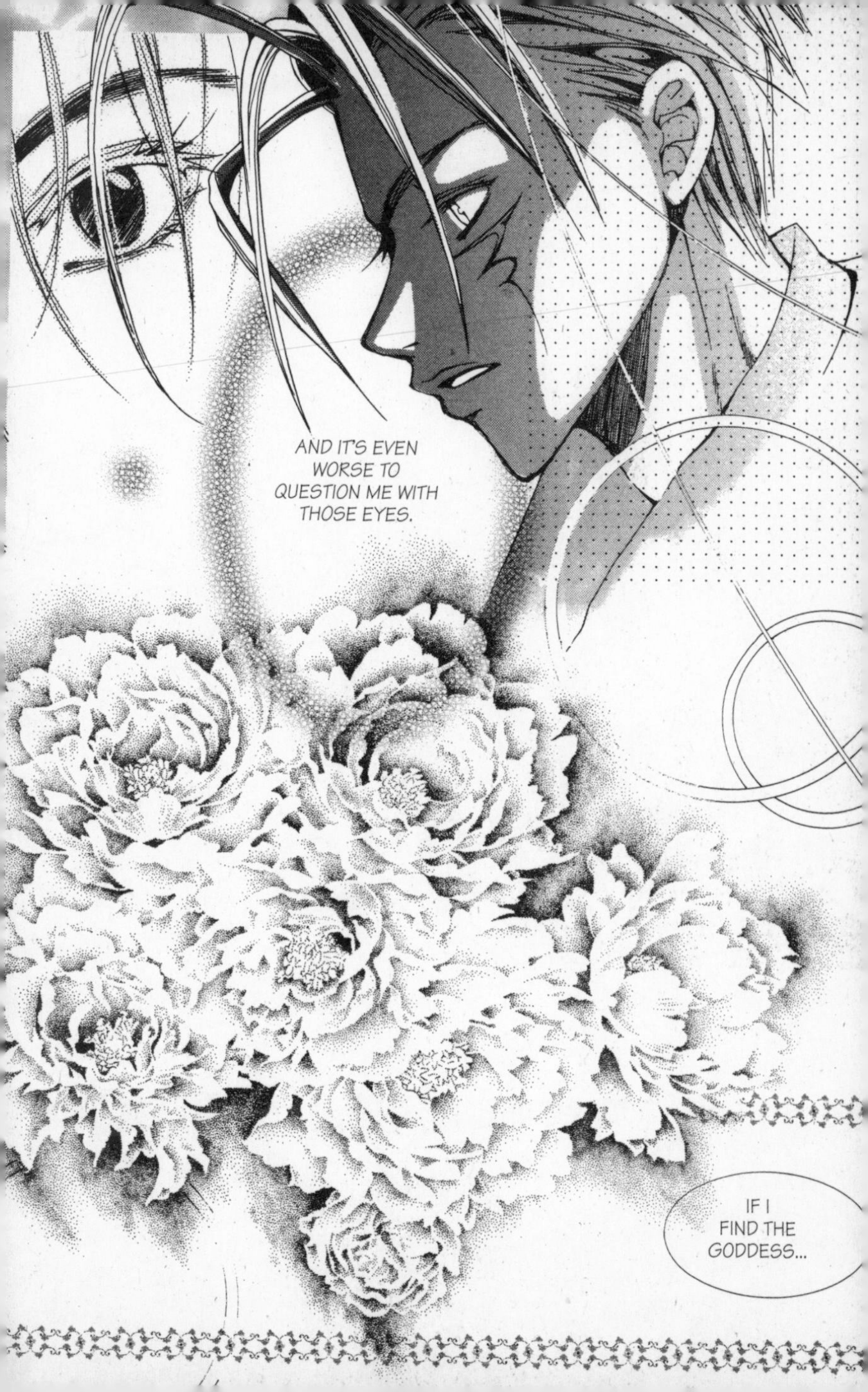
AND IT'S EVEN WORSE TO QUESTION ME WITH THOSE EYES.
IF I FIND THE GODDESS...

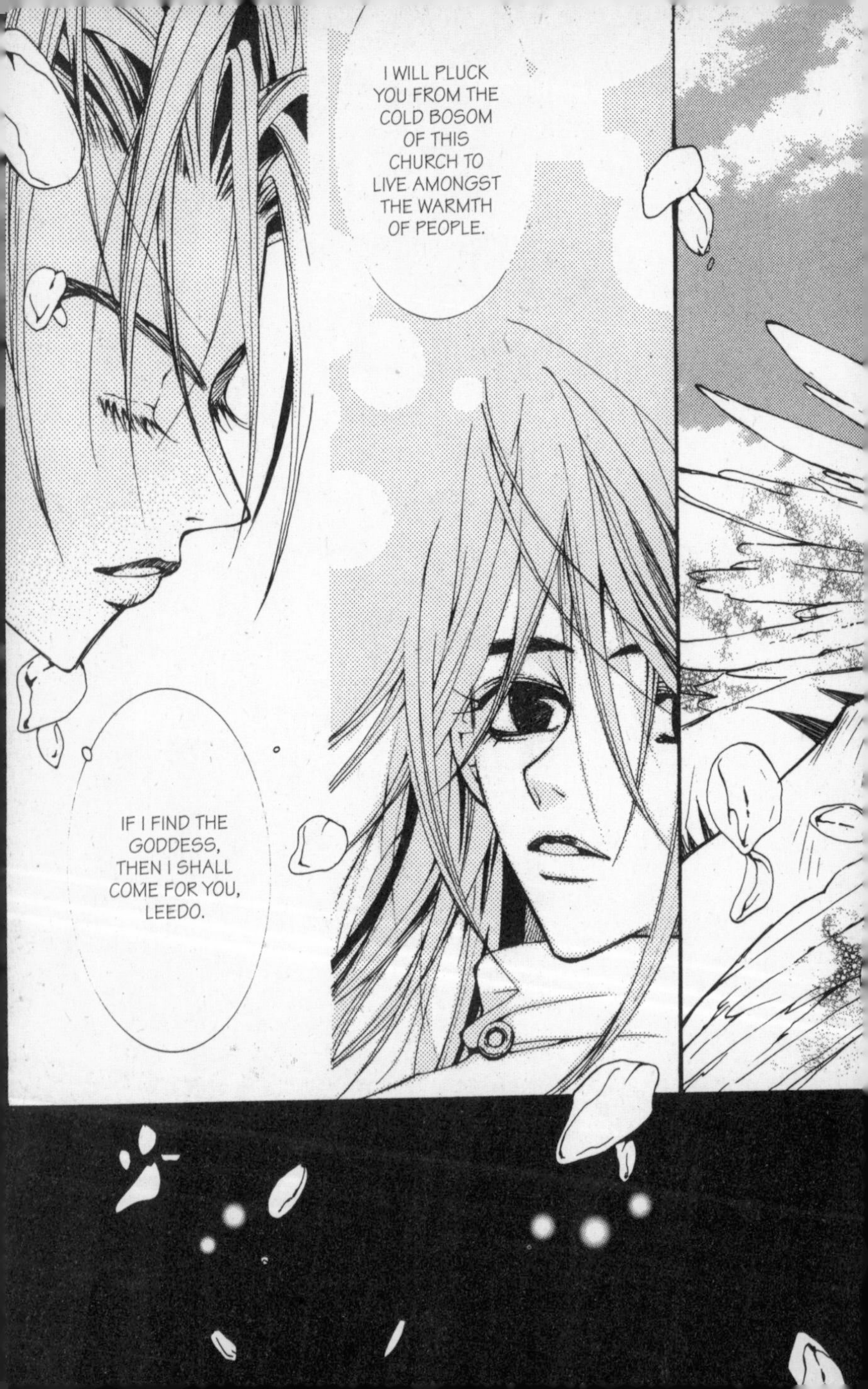
IF I FIND THE GODDESS, THEN I SHALL COME FOR YOU, LEEDO.
I WILL PLUCK YOU FROM THE COLD BOSOM OF THIS CHURCH TO LIVE AMONGST THE WARMTH OF PEOPLE.

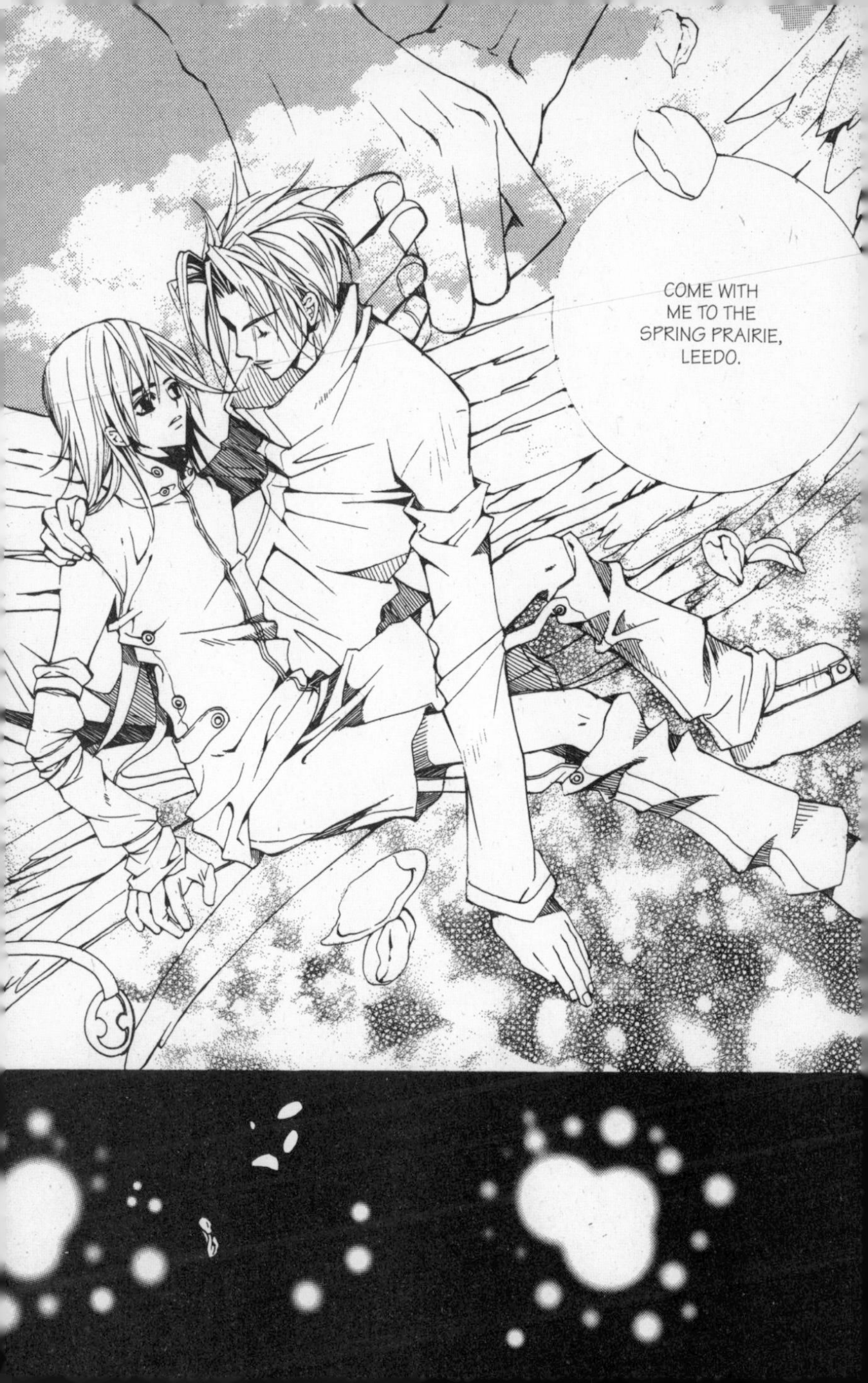
COME WITH ME TO THE SPRING PRAIRIE, LEEDO.

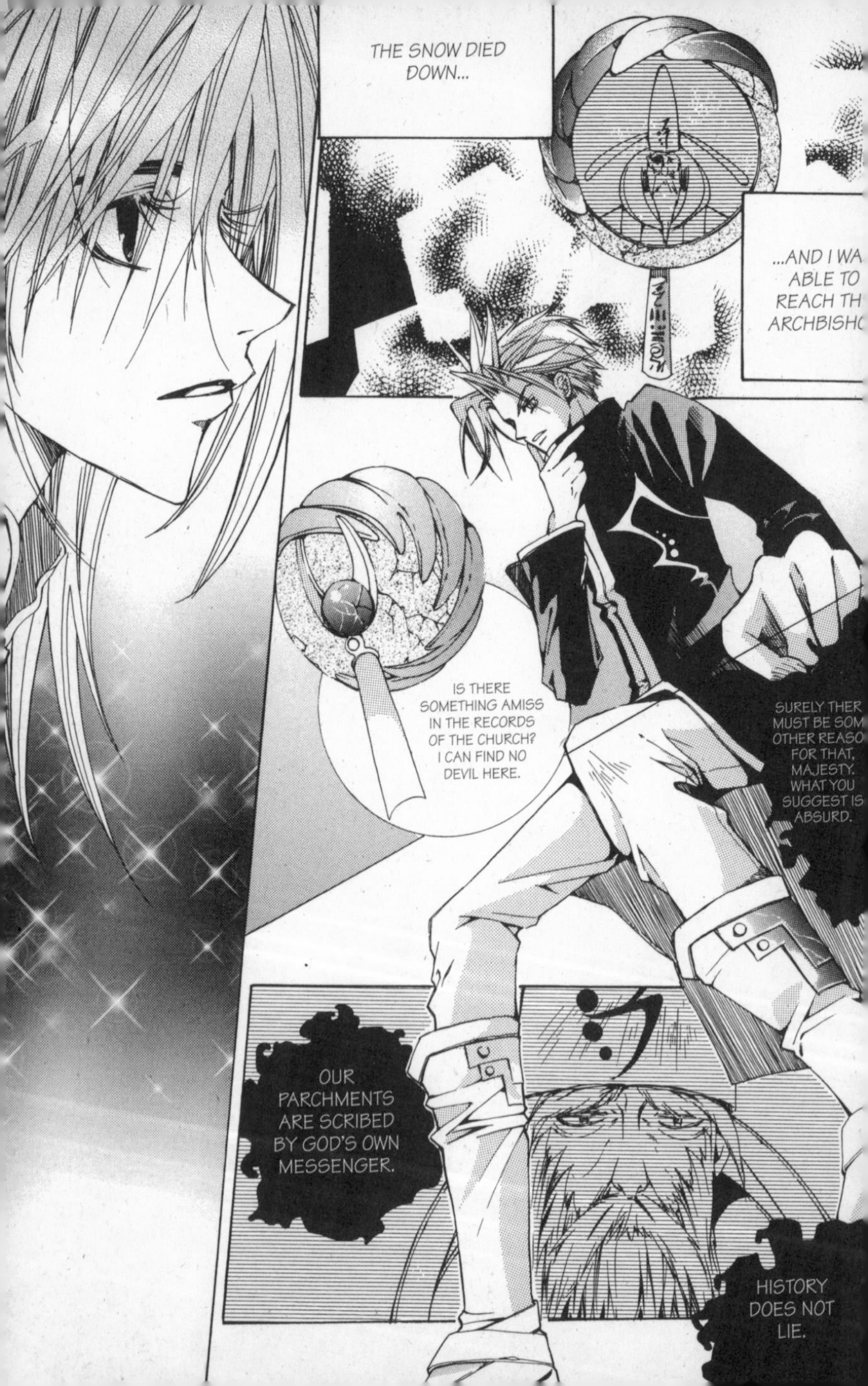
THE SNOW DIED DOWN...
...AND I WA ABLE TO REACH TH ARCHBISHO
IS THERE SOMETHING AMISS IN THE RECORDS OF THE CHURCH? I CAN FIND NO DEVIL HERE.
SURELY THER MUST BE SOM OTHER REASO FOR THAT, MAJESTY. WHAT YOU SUGGEST IS ABSURD.
OUR PARCHMENTS ARE SCRIBED BY GOD'S OWN MESSENGER.
HISTORY DOES NOT LIE.

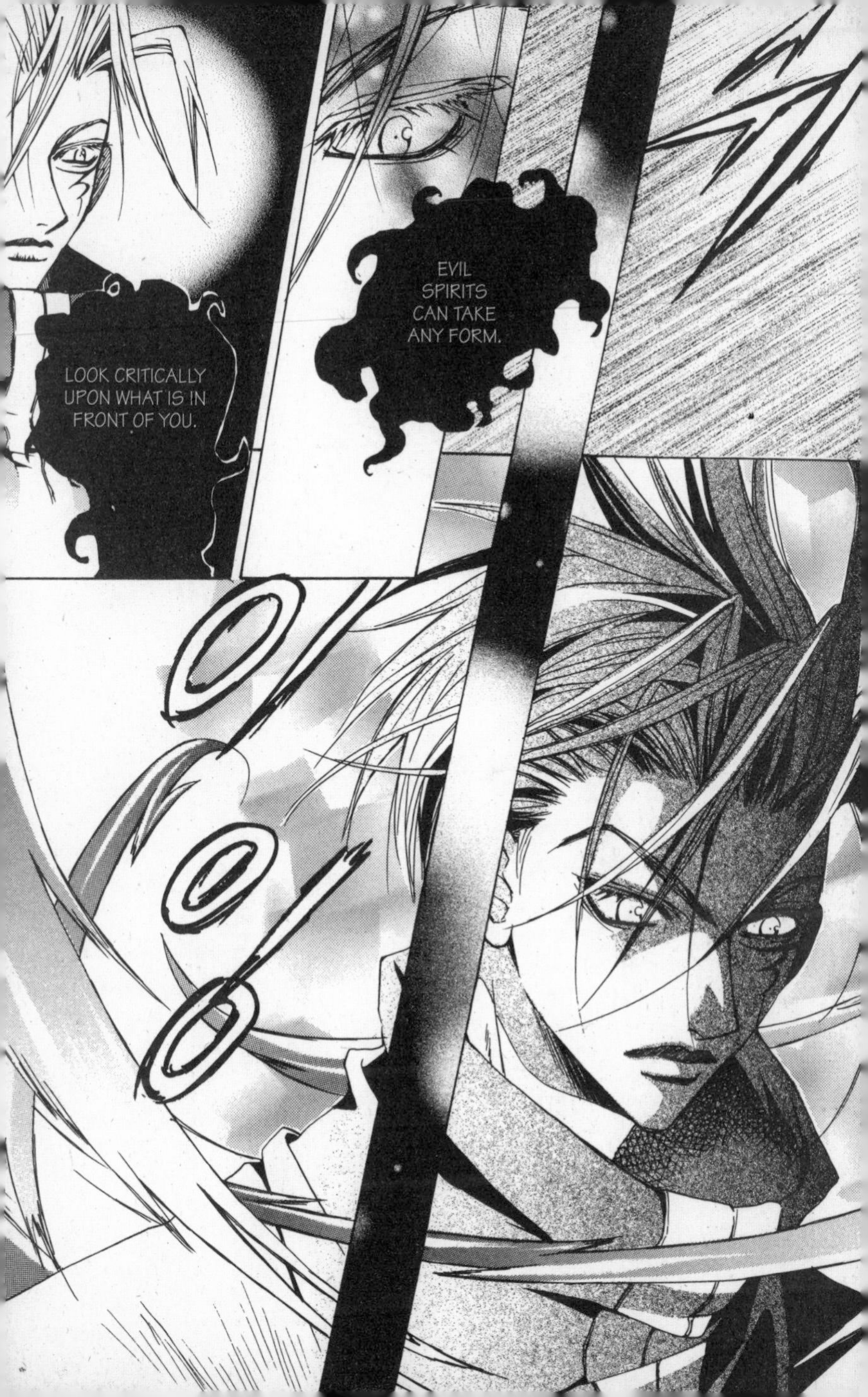
LOOK CRITICALLY UPON WHAT IS IN FRONT OF YOU.
EVIL SPIRITS CAN TAKE ANY FORM.

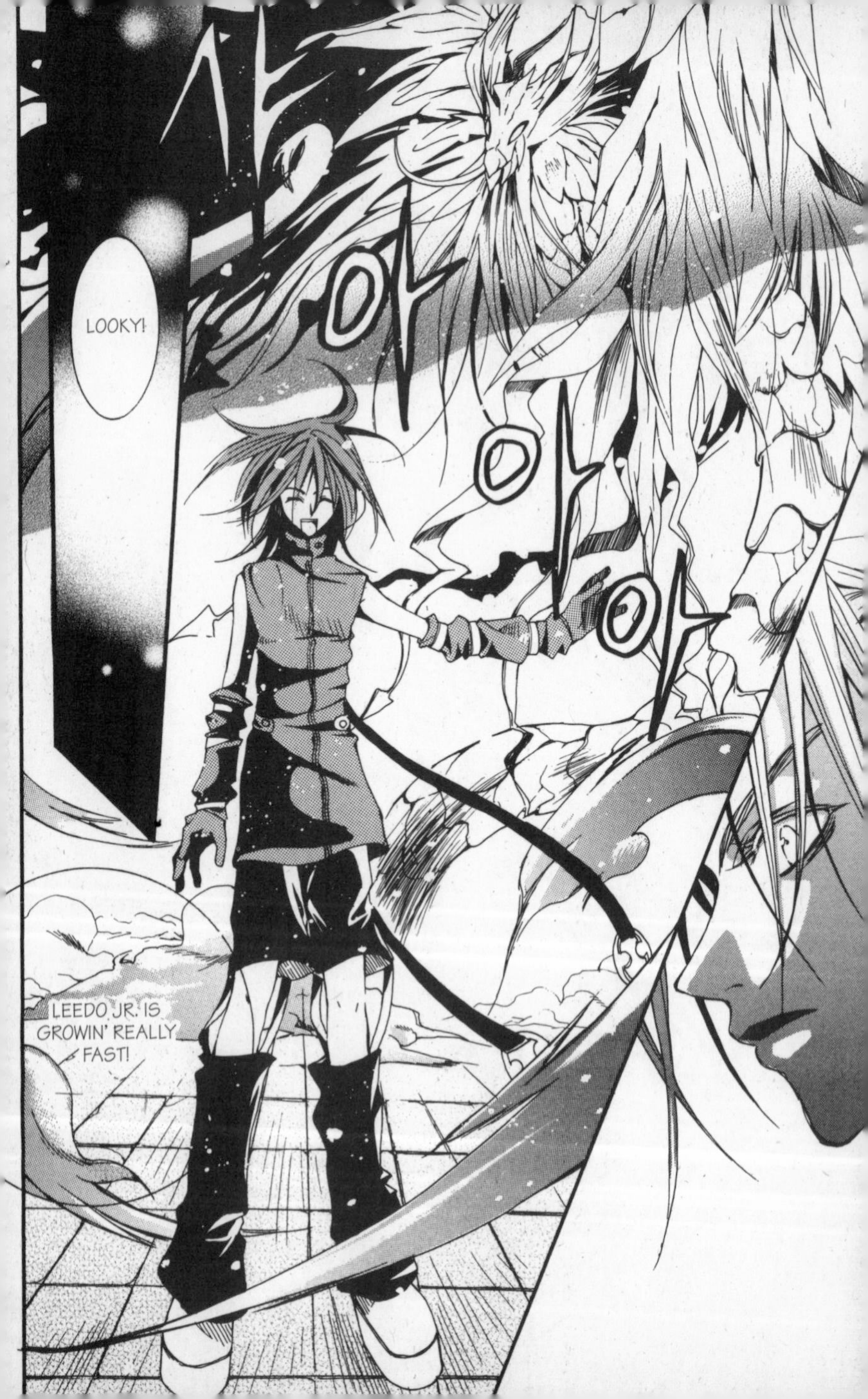
LOOKY!
LEEDO JR. IS GROWIN' REALLY FAST!

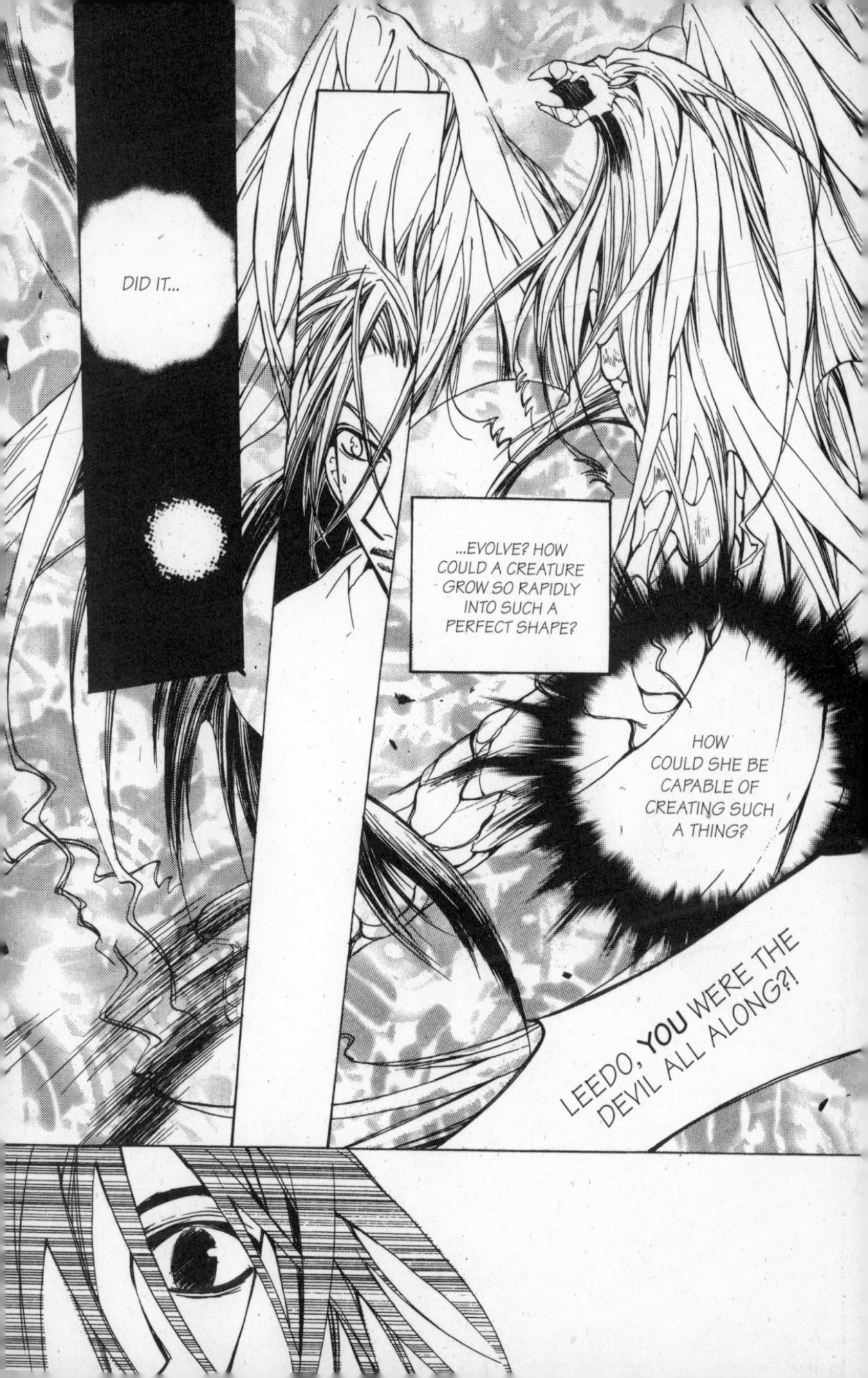
DID IT...
...EVOLVE? HOW COULD A CREATURE GROW SO RAPIDLY INTO SUCH A PERFECT SHAPE?
HOW COULD SHE BE CAPABLE OF CREATING SUCH A THING?
LEEDO, YOU WERE THE DEVIL ALL ALONG?!

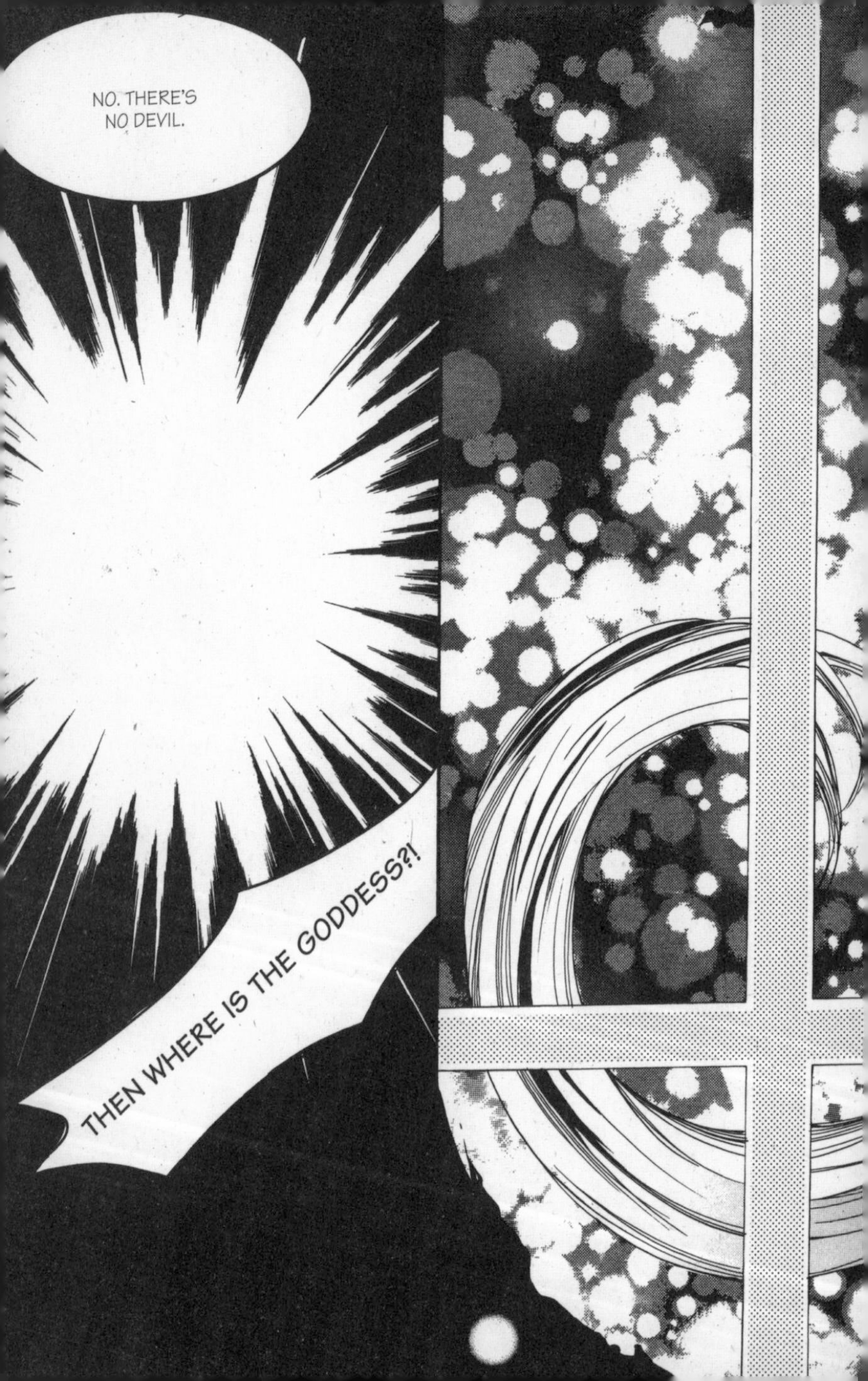
NO. THERE'S NO DEVIL.
THEN WHERE IS THE GODDESS?!

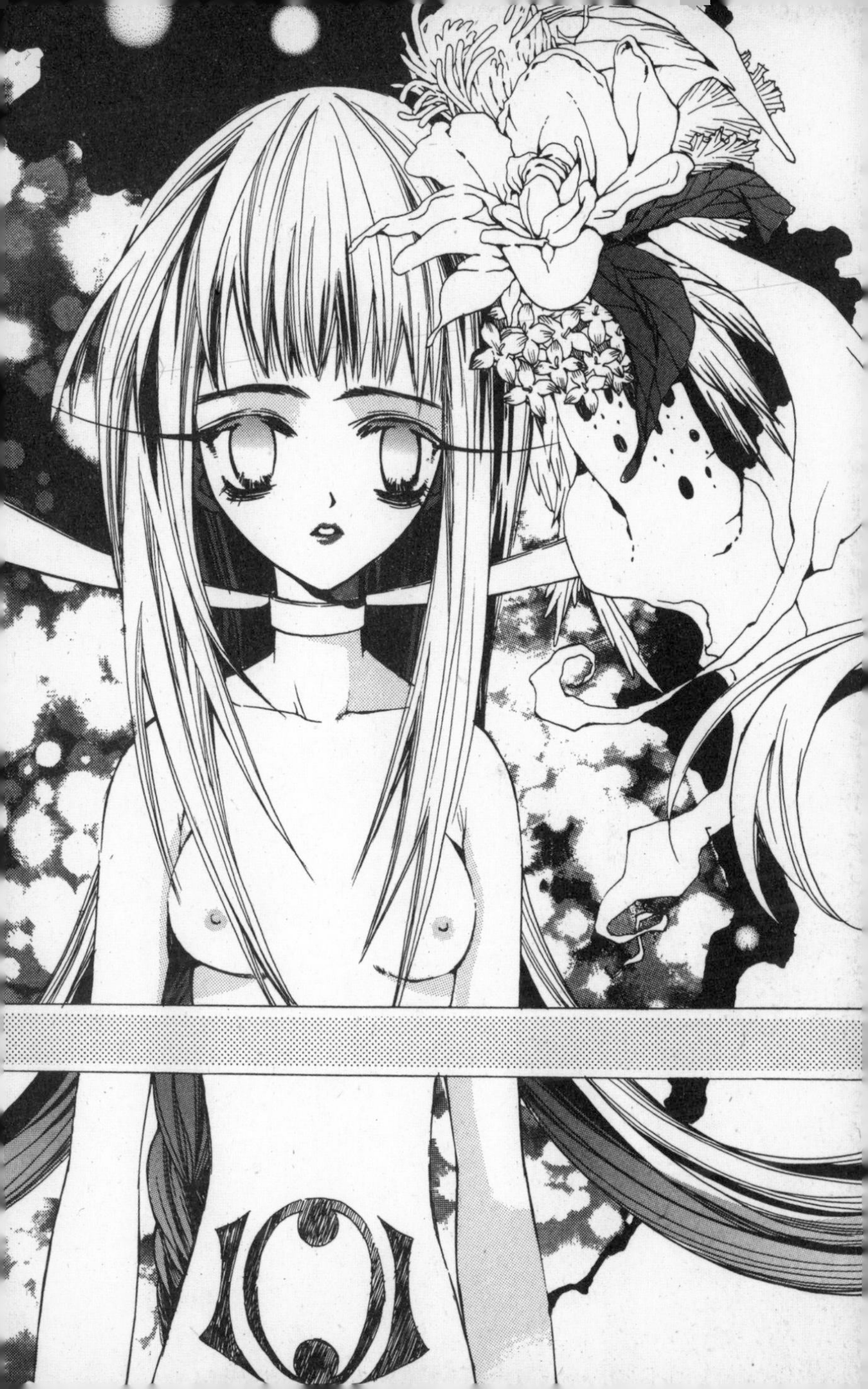

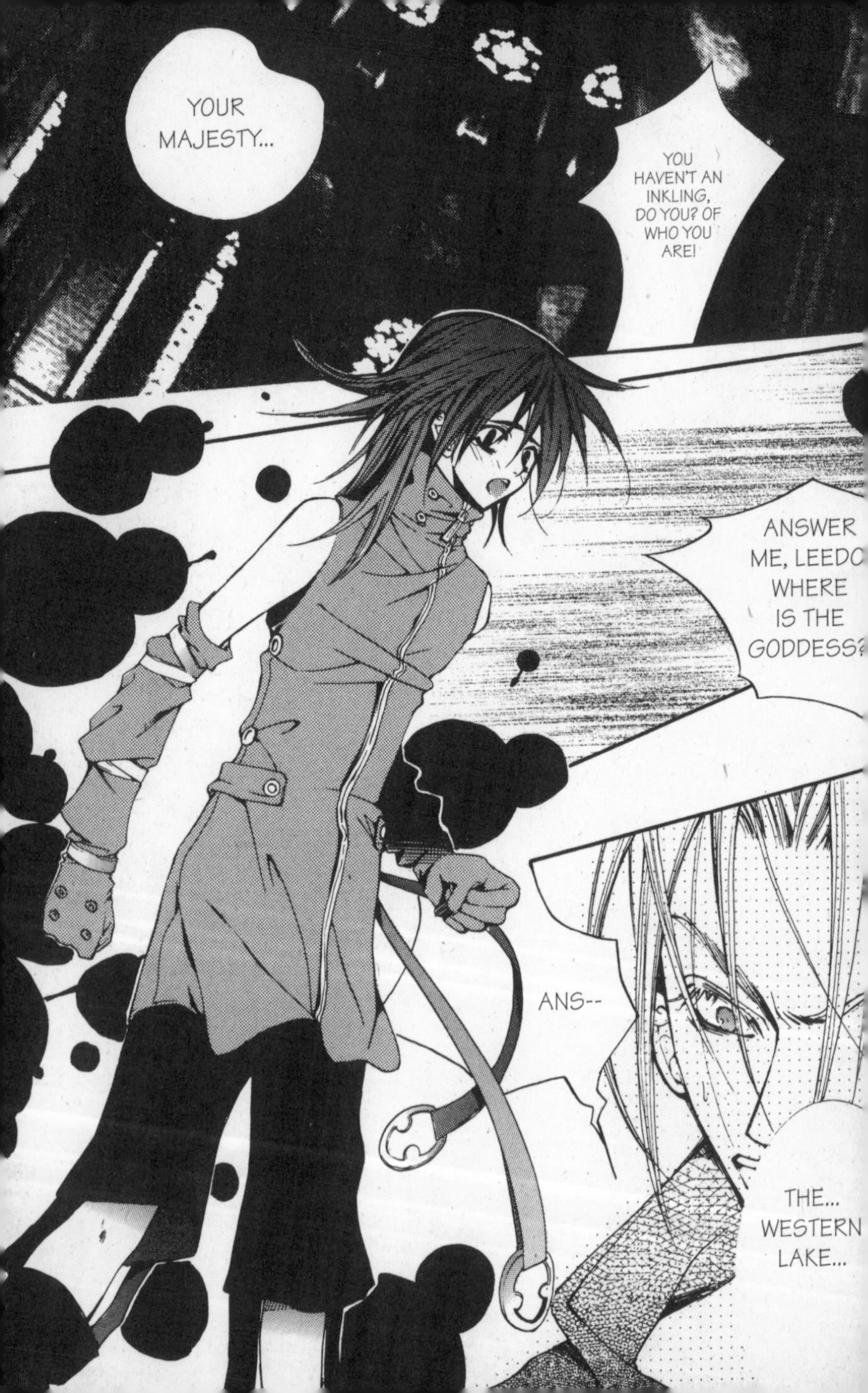
YOUR MAJESTY...
YOU HAVEN'T AN INKLING, DO YOU? OF WHO YOU ARE!
ANSWER ME, LEEDO WHERE IS THE GODDESS?
ANS--
THE... WESTERN LAKE...

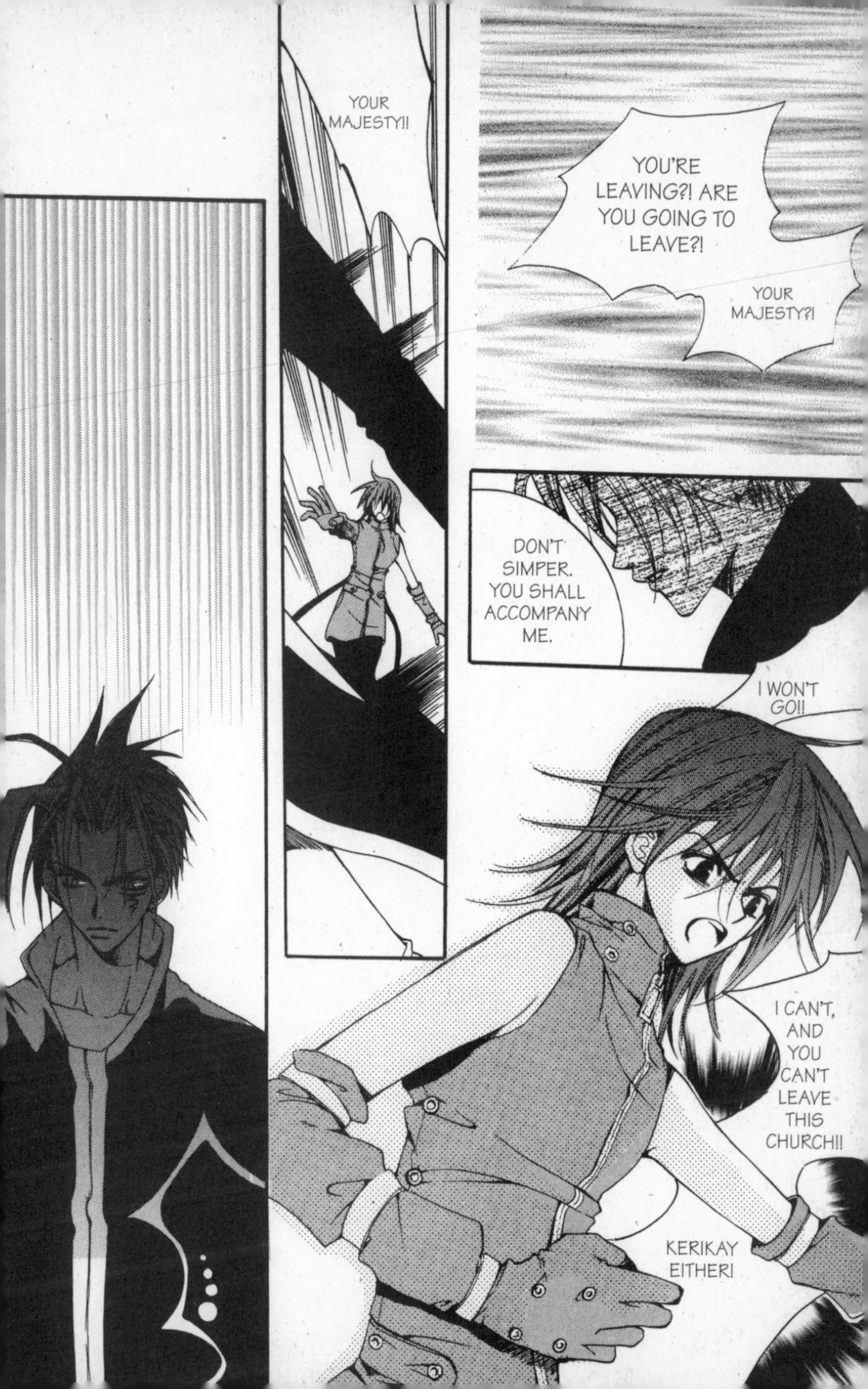
YOUR MAJESTY!!
YOU'RE LEAVING?! ARE YOU GOING TO LEAVE?!
YOUR MAJESTY?!
DON'T SIMPER. YOU SHALL ACCOMPANY ME.
I WON'T GO!!
I CAN'T, AND YOU CAN'T LEAVE THIS CHURCH!!
KERIKAY EITHER!

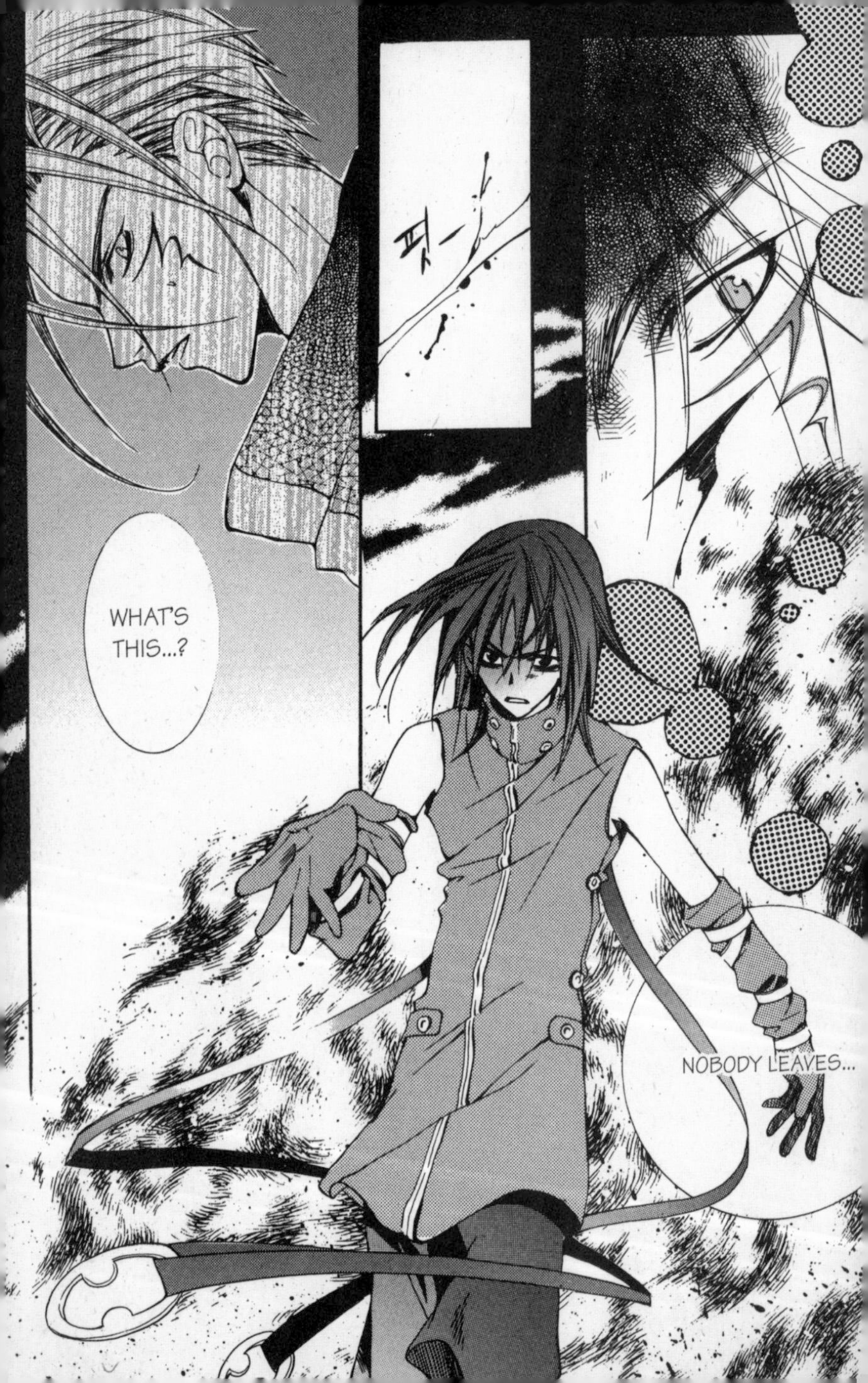
WHAT'S THIS...?
픽ㅡ
NOBODY LEAVES...

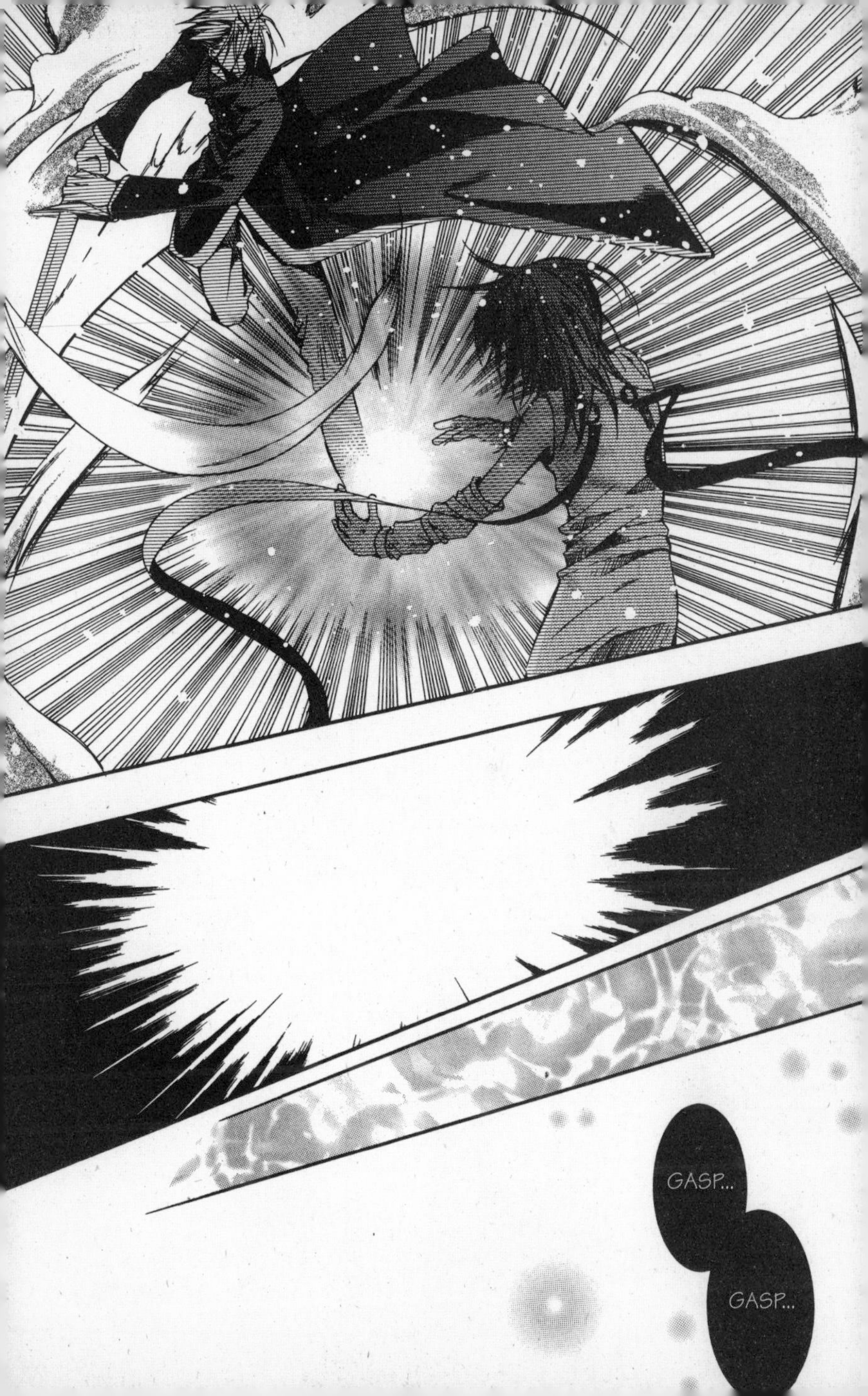
GASP...
GASP...

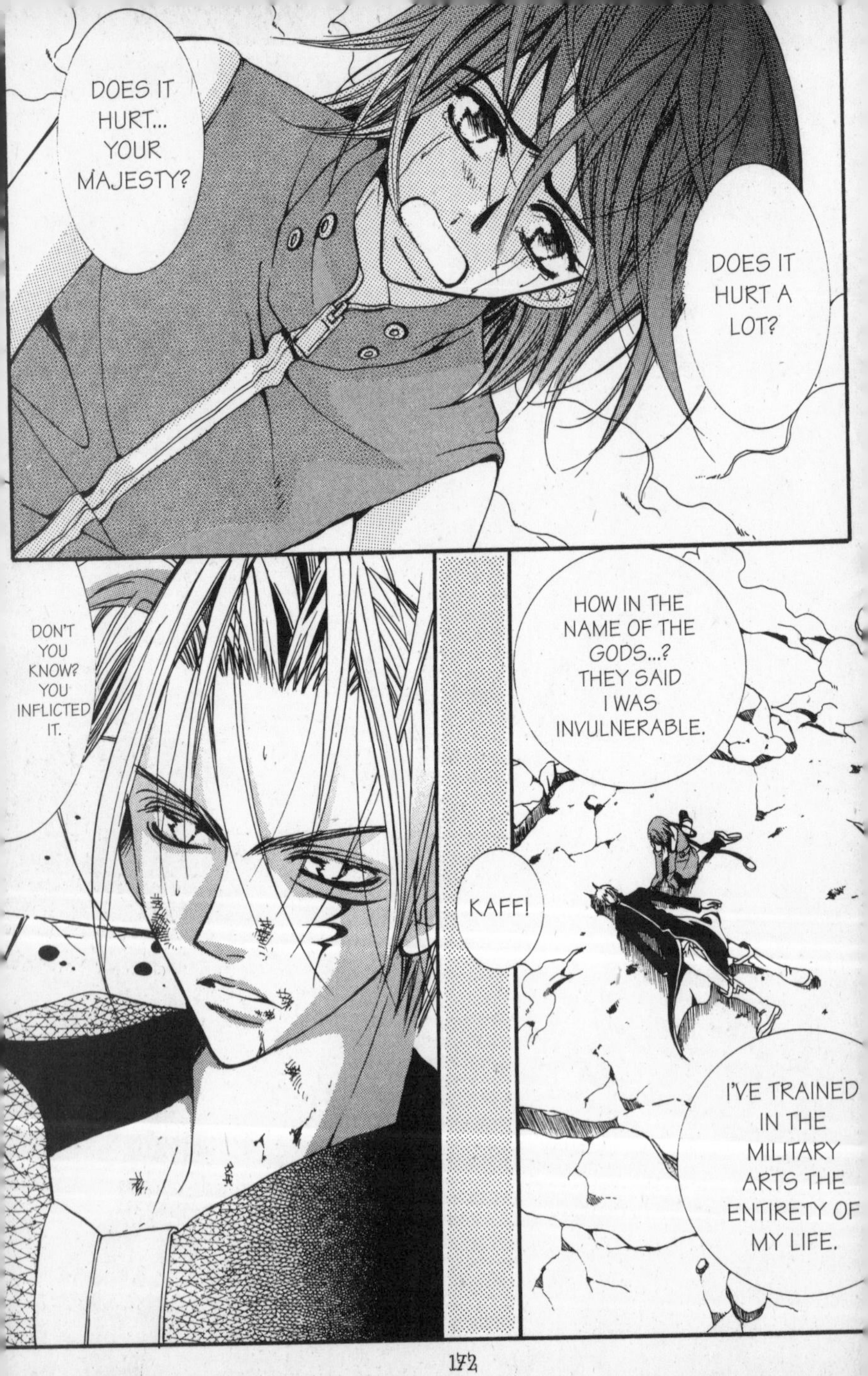
DOES IT HURT... YOUR MAJESTY?
DOES IT HURT A LOT?
DON'T YOU KNOW? YOU INFLICTED IT.
HOW IN THE NAME OF THE GODS...? THEY SAID I WAS INVULNERABLE.
KAFF!
I'VE TRAINED IN THE MILITARY ARTS THE ENTIRETY OF MY LIFE.

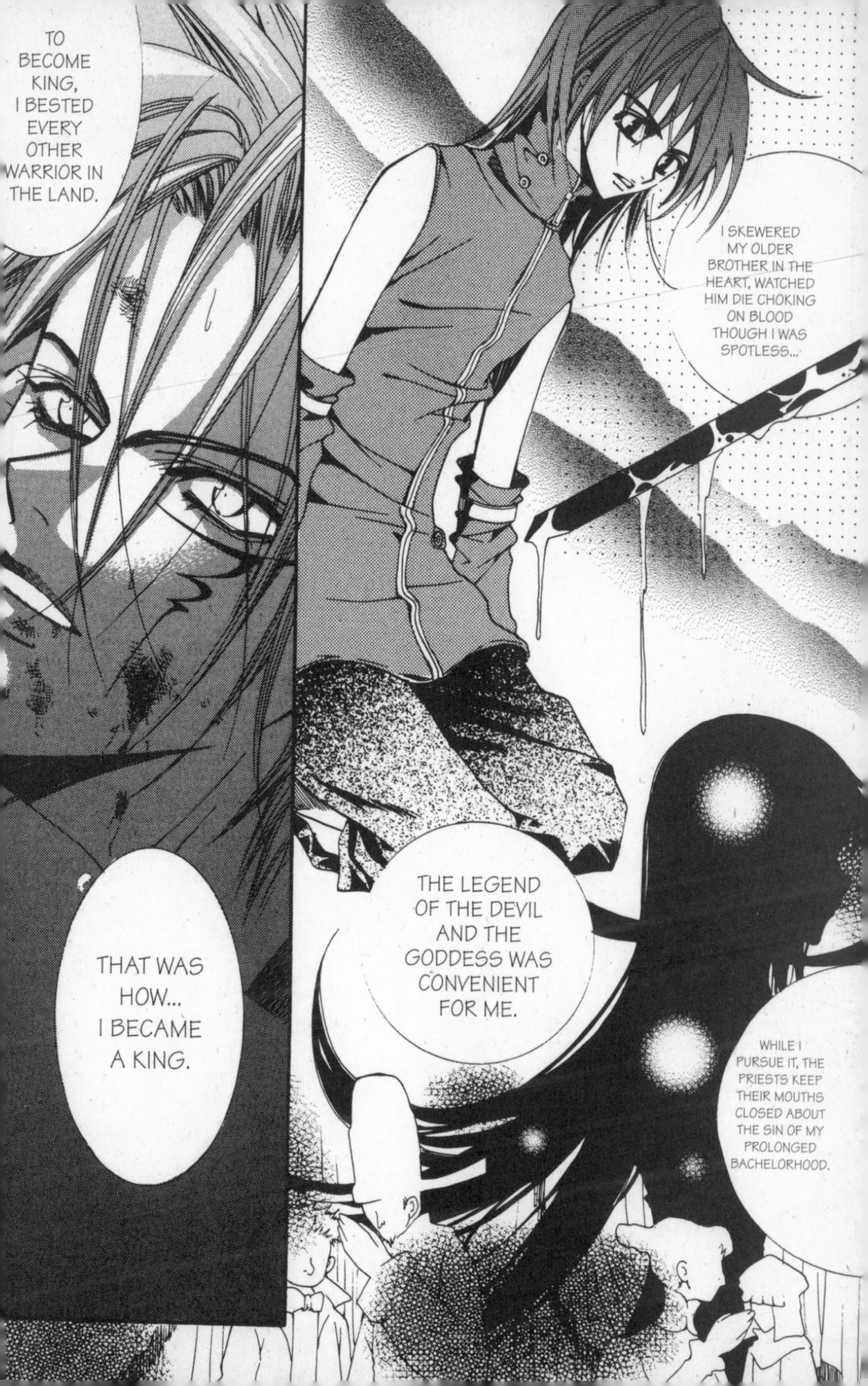
TO BECOME KING, I BESTED EVERY OTHER WARRIOR IN THE LAND.
THAT WAS HOW... I BECAME A KING.
I SKEWERED MY OLDER BROTHER IN THE HEART, WATCHED HIM DIE CHOKING ON BLOOD THOUGH I WAS SPOTLESS...
THE LEGEND OF THE DEVIL AND THE GODDESS WAS CONVENIENT FOR ME.
WHILE I PURSUE IT, THE PRIESTS KEEP THEIR MOUTHS CLOSED ABOUT THE SIN OF MY PROLONGED BACHELORHOOD.

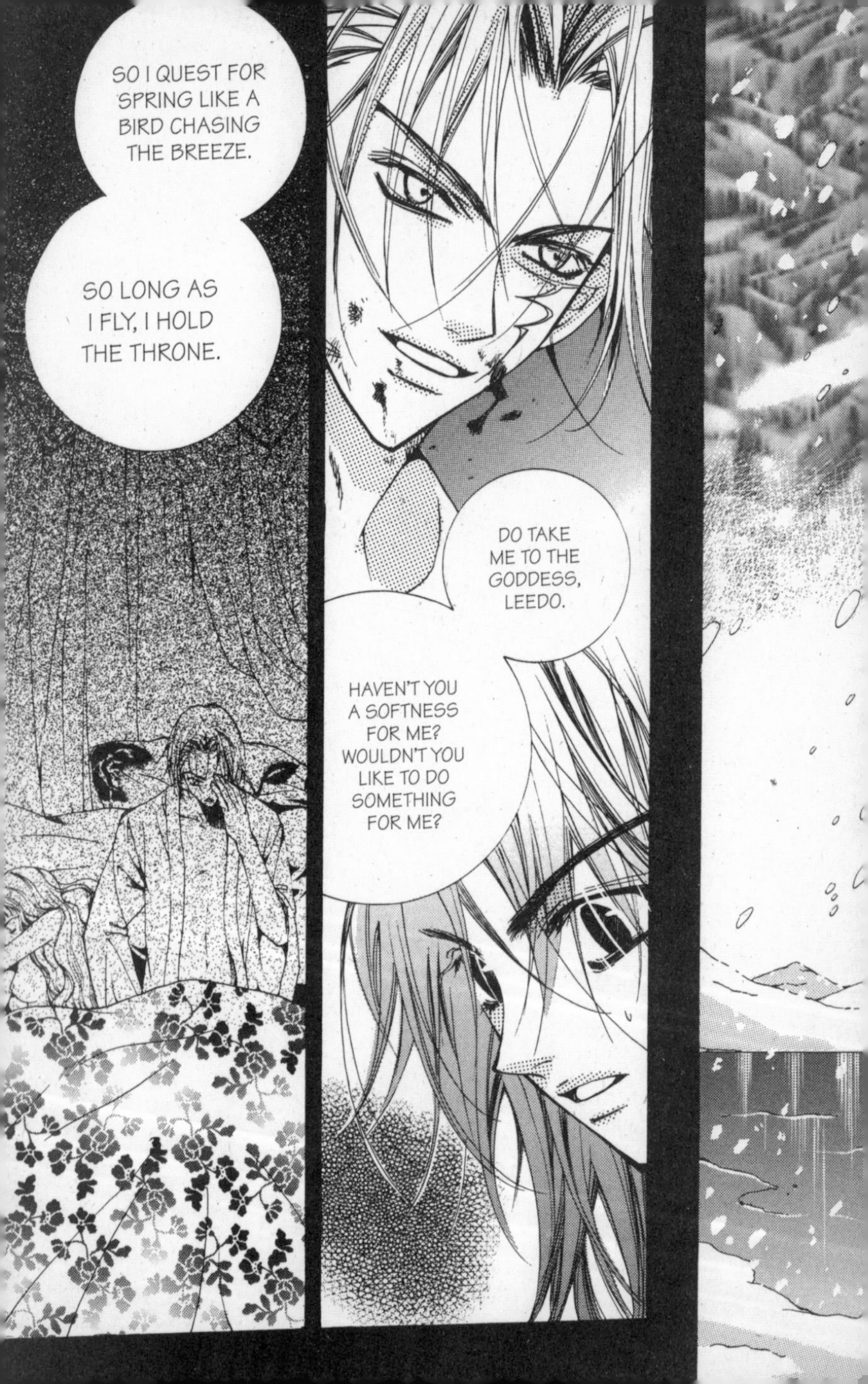
SO I QUEST FOR SPRING LIKE A BIRD CHASING THE BREEZE.
SO LONG AS I FLY, I HOLD THE THRONE.
DO TAKE ME TO THE GODDESS, LEEDO.
HAVEN'T YOU A SOFTNESS FOR ME? WOULDN'T YOU LIKE TO DO SOMETHING FOR ME?

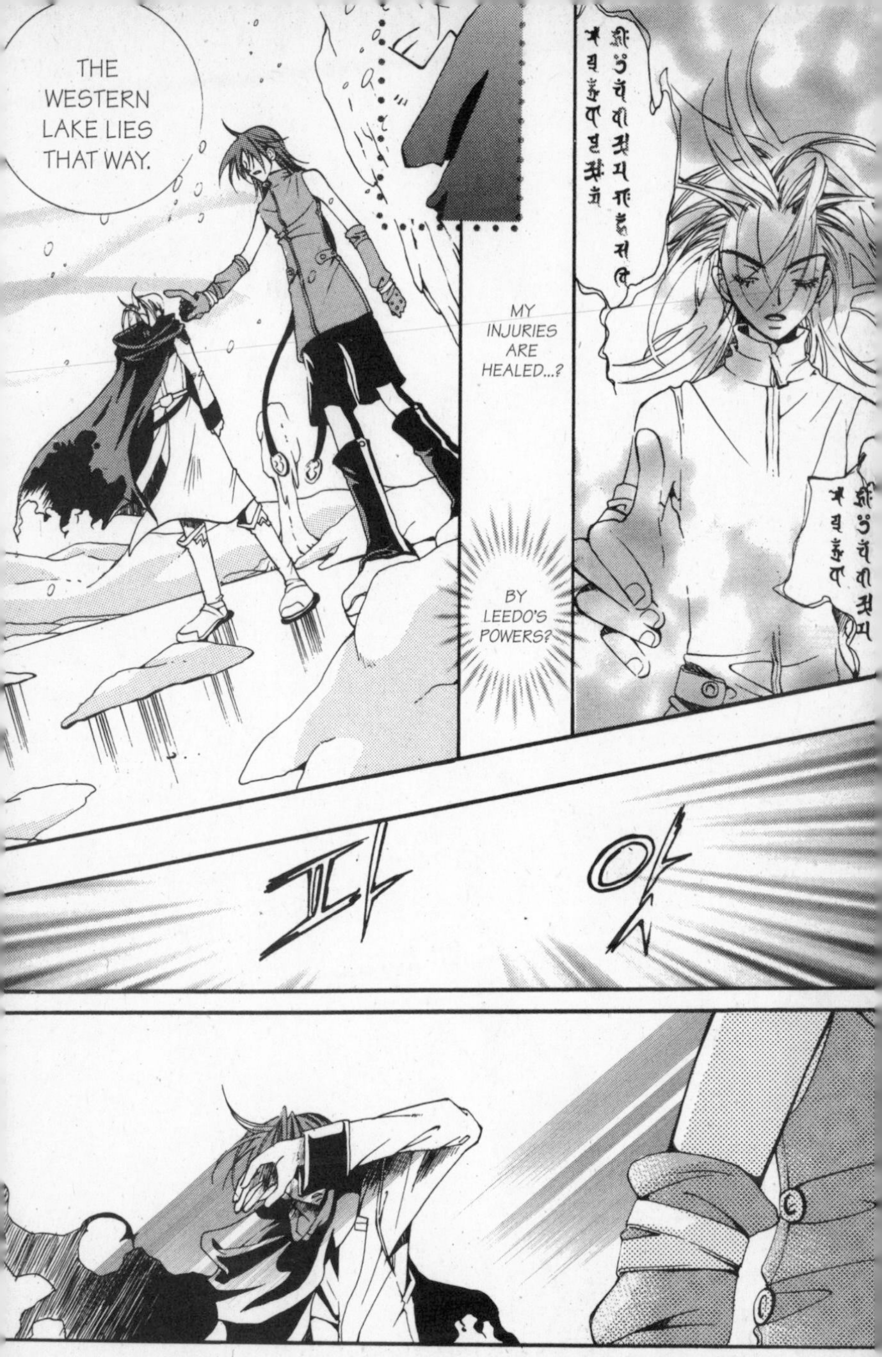
THE WESTERN LAKE LIES THAT WAY.
MY INJURIES ARE HEALED...?
BY LEEDO'S POWERS?
파앙

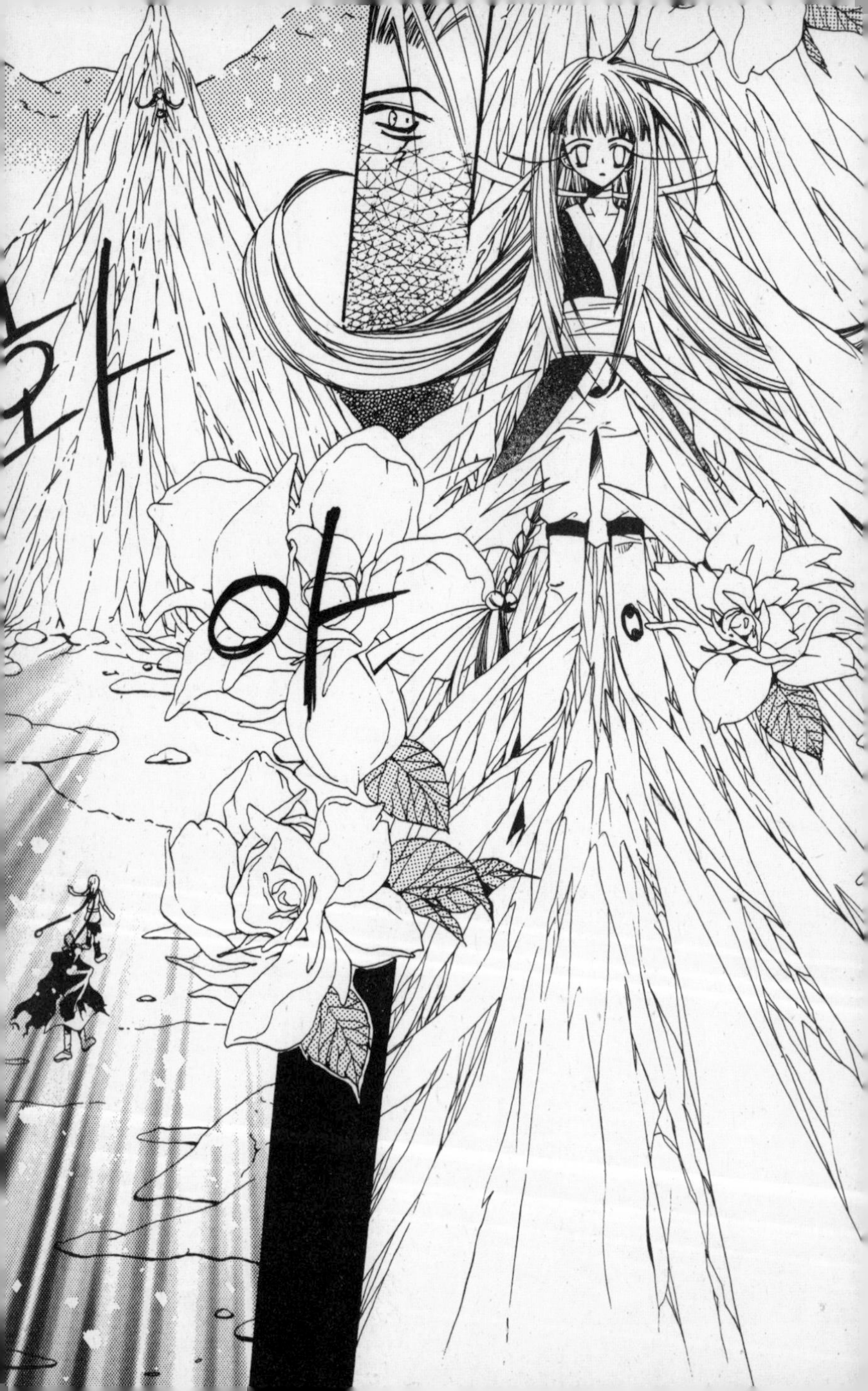

화아

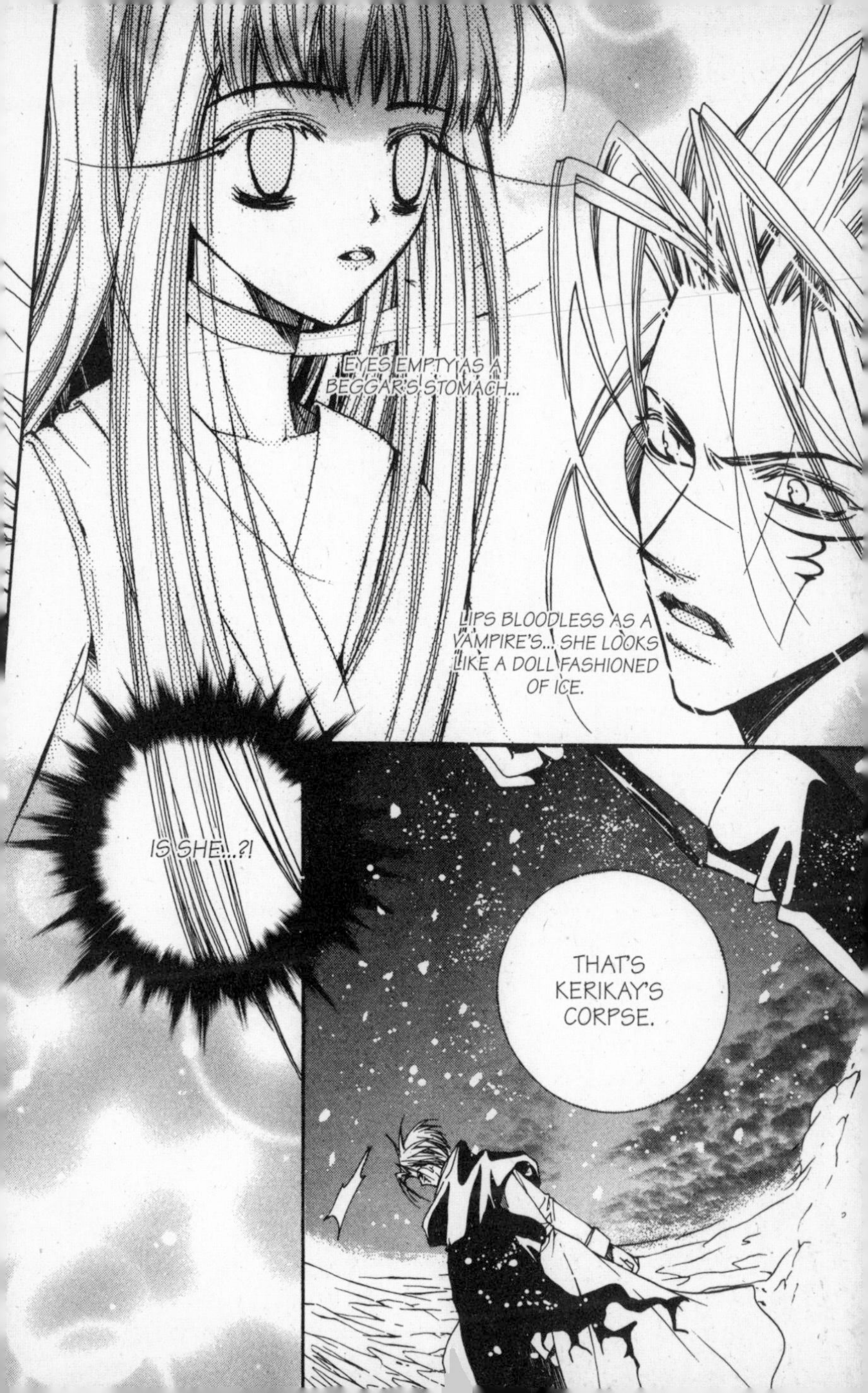
EYES EMPTY AS A BEGGAR'S STOMACH...
LIPS BLOODLESS AS A VAMPIRE'S... SHE LOOKS LIKE A DOLL FASHIONED OF ICE.
IS SHE...?!
THAT'S KERIKAY'S CORPSE.

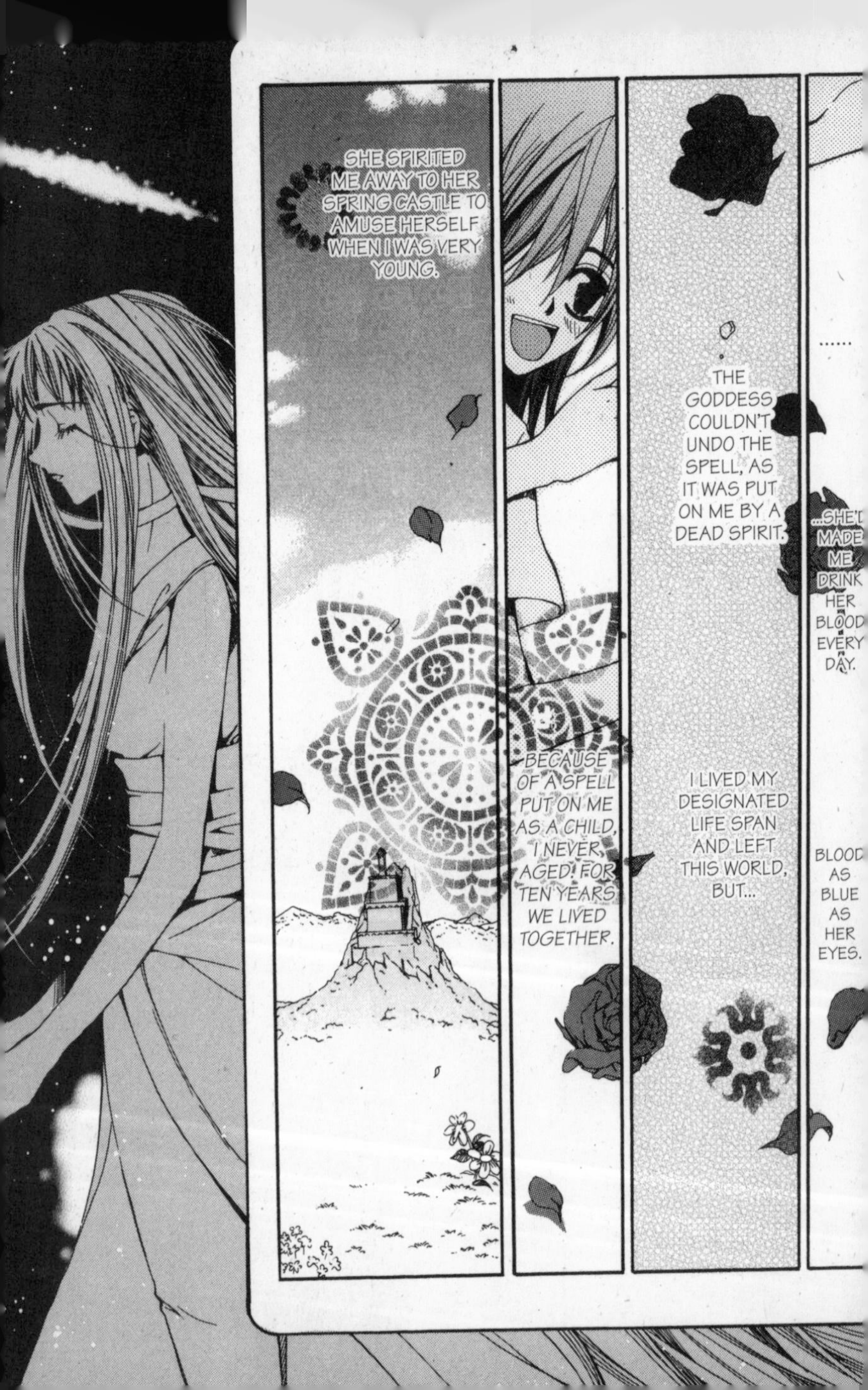
SHE SPIRITED ME AWAY TO HER SPRING CASTLE TO AMUSE HERSELF WHEN I WAS VERY YOUNG.
BECAUSE OF A SPELL PUT ON ME AS A CHILD, I NEVER AGED. FOR TEN YEARS WE LIVED TOGETHER.
THE GODDESS COULDN'T UNDO THE SPELL, AS IT WAS PUT ON ME BY A DEAD SPIRIT.
I LIVED MY DESIGNATED LIFE SPAN AND LEFT THIS WORLD, BUT...
......
...SHE'D MADE ME DRINK HER BLOOD EVERY DAY.
BLOOD AS BLUE AS HER EYES.

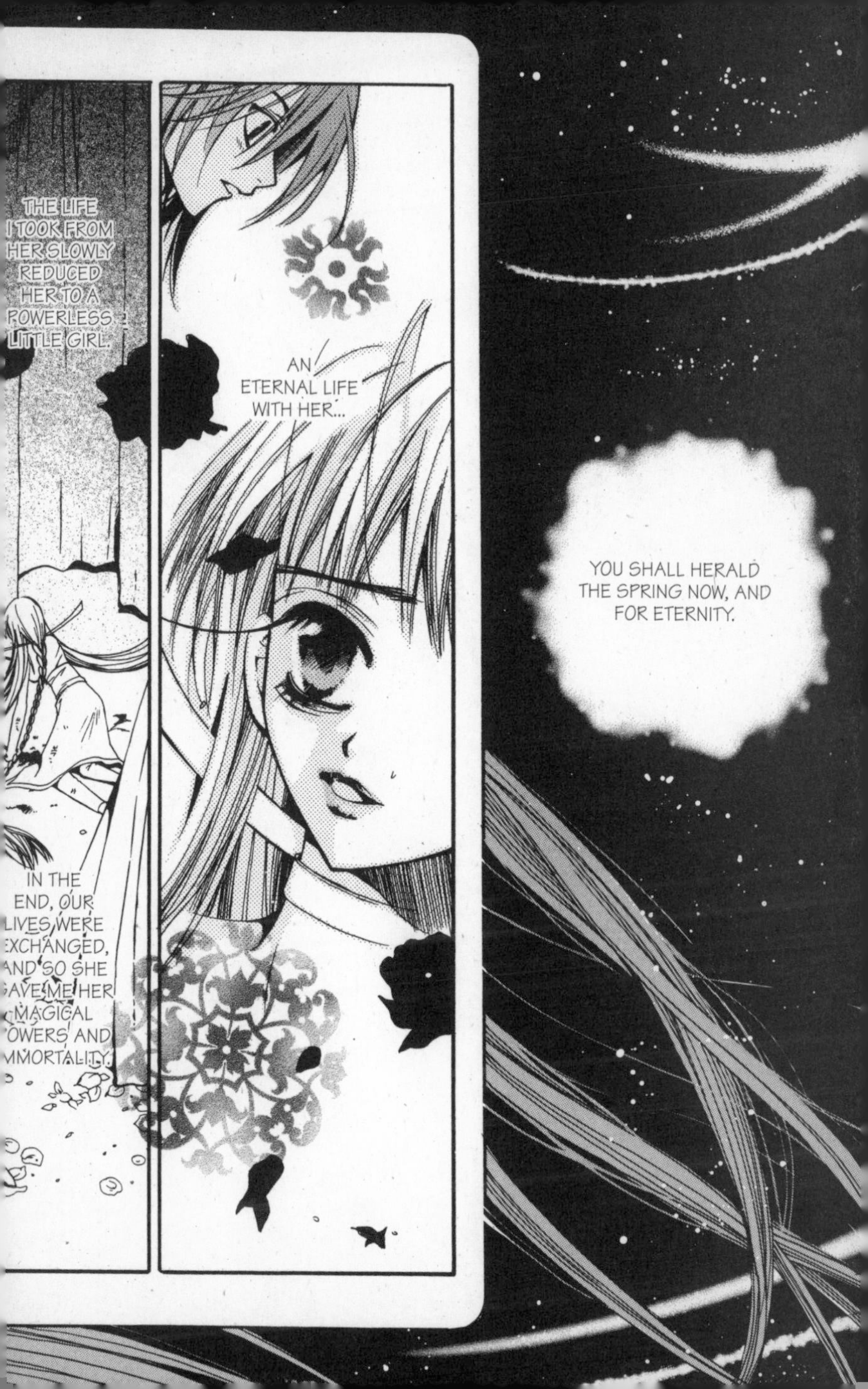
THE LIFE I TOOK FROM HER SLOWLY REDUCED HER TO A POWERLESS LITTLE GIRL.
IN THE END, OUR LIVES WERE EXCHANGED, AND SO SHE GAVE ME HER MAGICAL POWERS AND IMMORTALITY.
AN ETERNAL LIFE WITH HER...
YOU SHALL HERALD THE SPRING NOW, AND FOR ETERNITY.

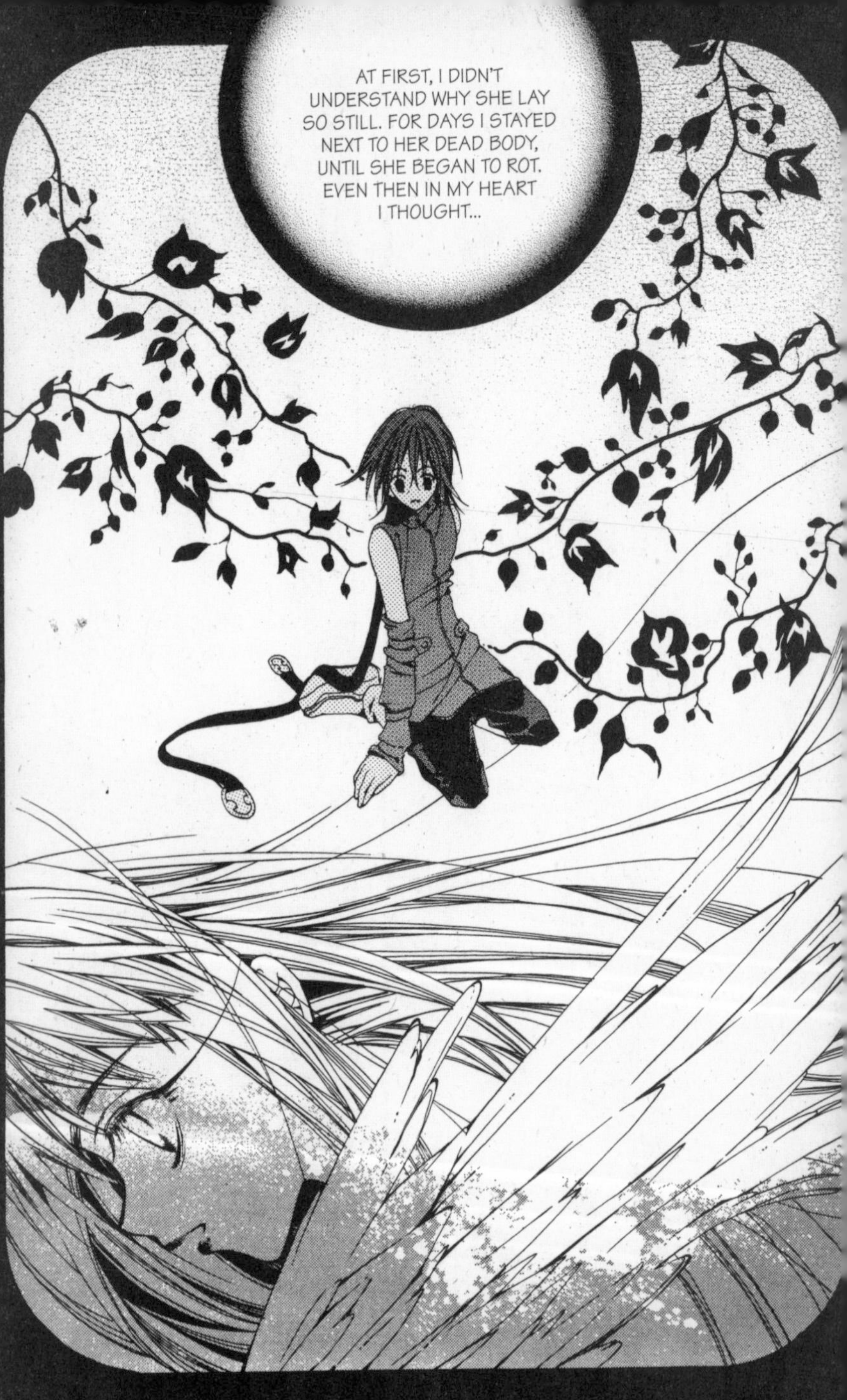
AT FIRST, I DIDN'T UNDERSTAND WHY SHE LAY SO STILL. FOR DAYS I STAYED NEXT TO HER DEAD BODY, UNTIL SHE BEGAN TO ROT. EVEN THEN IN MY HEART I THOUGHT...

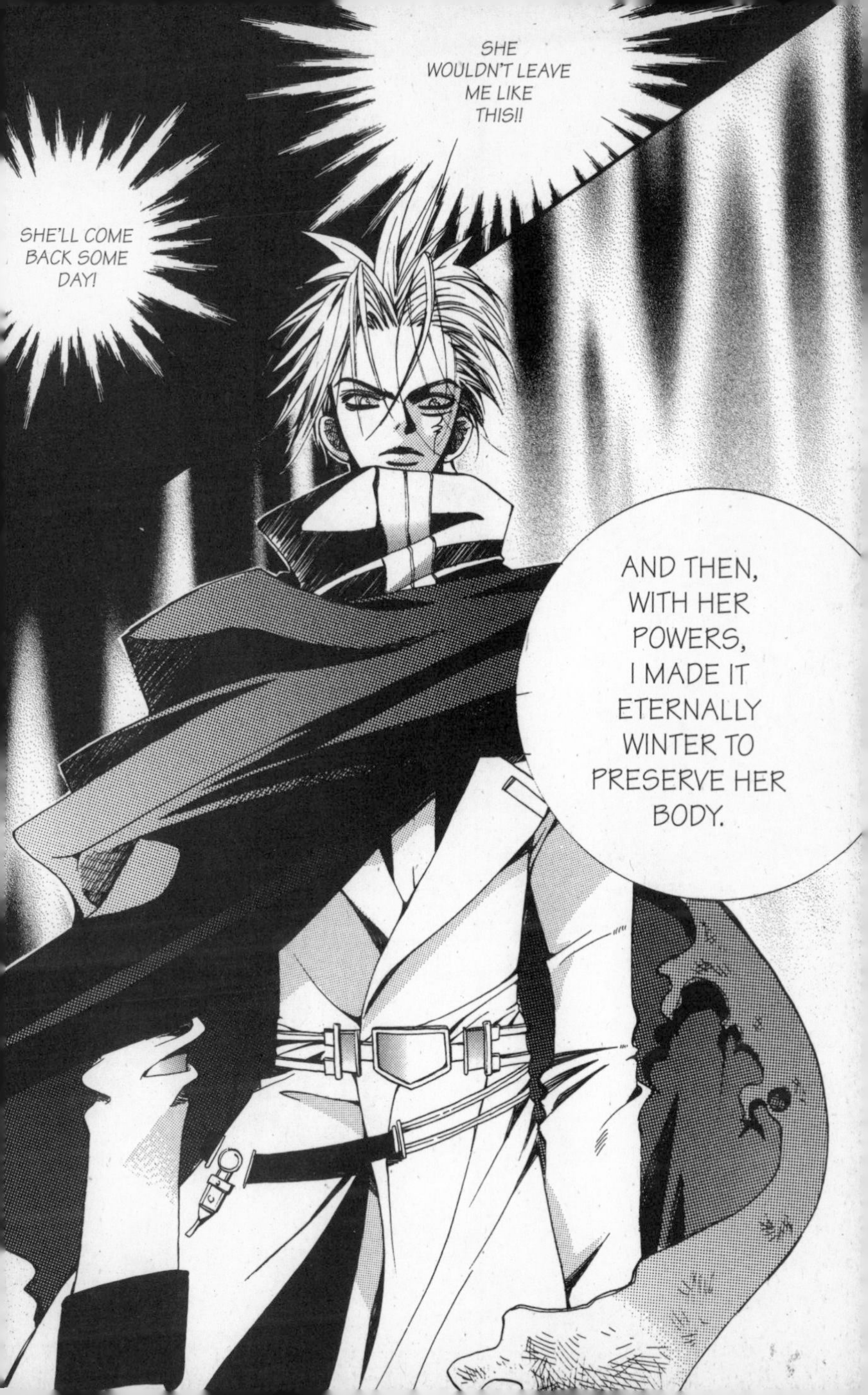
SHE WOULDN'T LEAVE ME LIKE THIS!!
SHE'LL COME BACK SOME DAY!
AND THEN, WITH HER POWERS, I MADE IT ETERNALLY WINTER TO PRESERVE HER BODY.

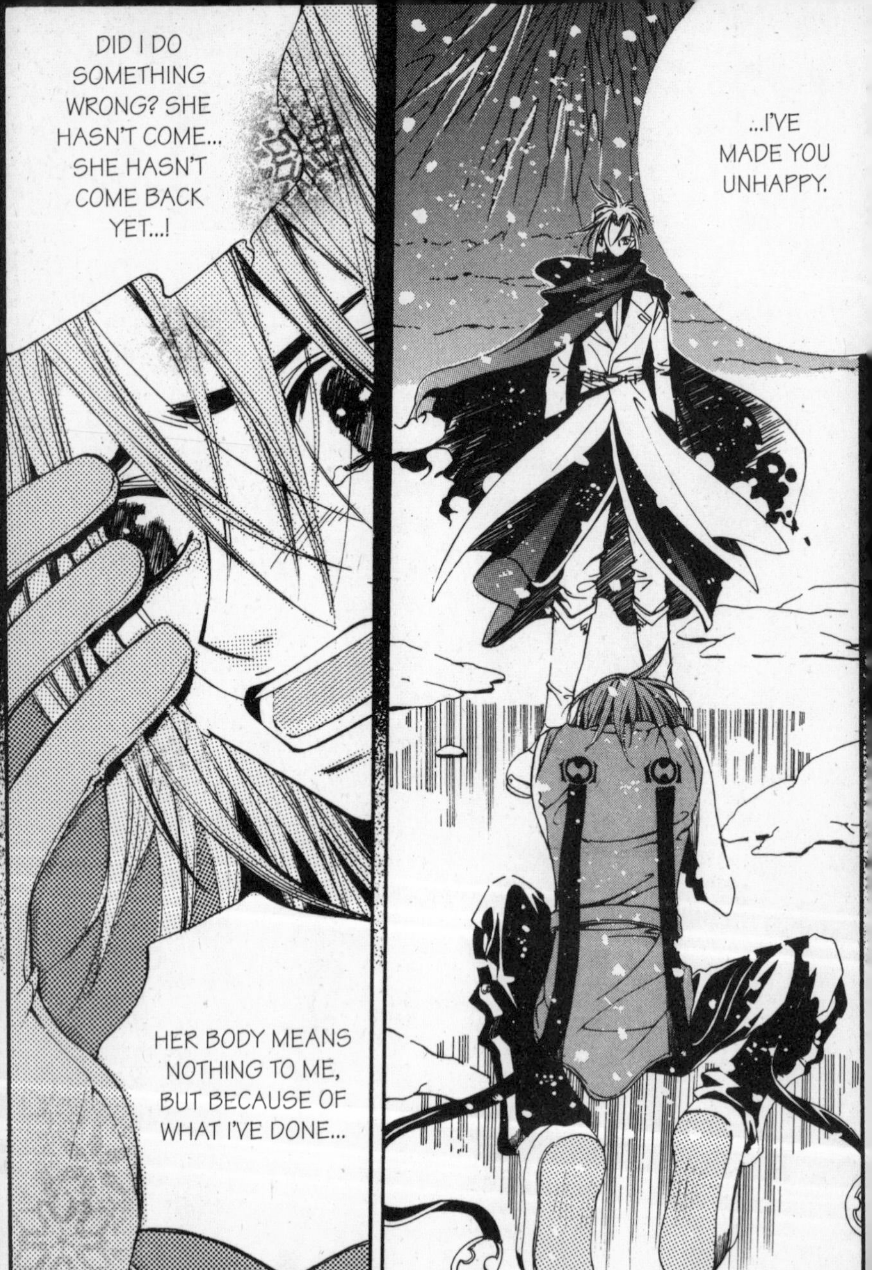
DID I DO SOMETHING WRONG? SHE HASN'T COME... SHE HASN'T COME BACK YET...!
HER BODY MEANS NOTHING TO ME, BUT BECAUSE OF WHAT I'VE DONE...
...I'VE MADE YOU UNHAPPY.

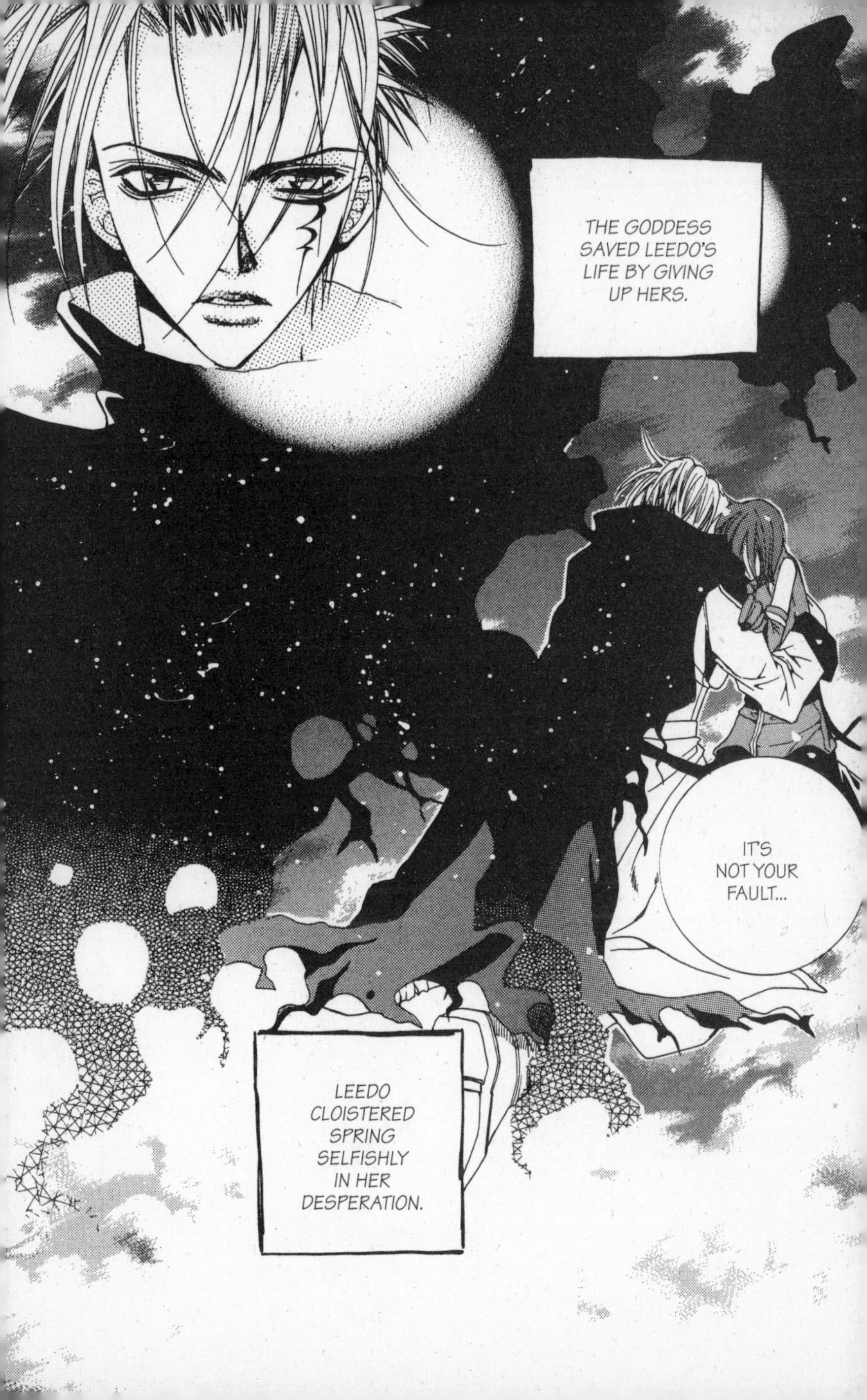
THE GODDESS SAVED LEEDO'S LIFE BY GIVING UP HERS.
IT'S NOT YOUR FAULT...
LEEDO CLOISTERED SPRING SELFISHLY IN HER DESPERATION.

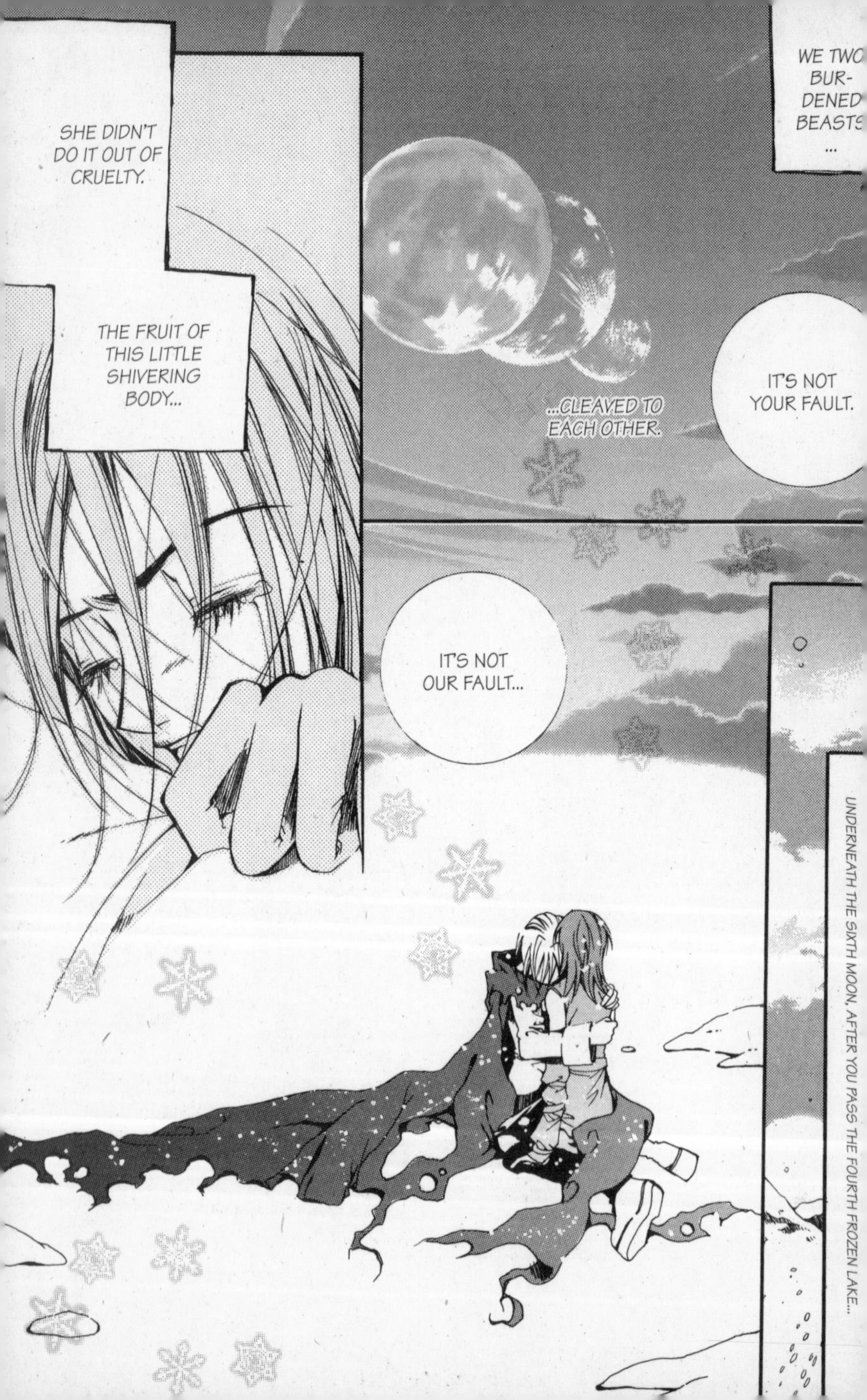

SHE DIDN'T DO IT OUT OF CRUELTY.
THE FRUIT OF THIS LITTLE SHIVERING BODY...
WE TWO BUR-DENED BEASTS ...
...CLEAVED TO EACH OTHER.
IT'S NOT YOUR FAULT.
IT'S NOT OUR FAULT...
UNDERNEATH THE SIXTH MOON, AFTER YOU PASS THE FOURTH FROZEN LAKE...

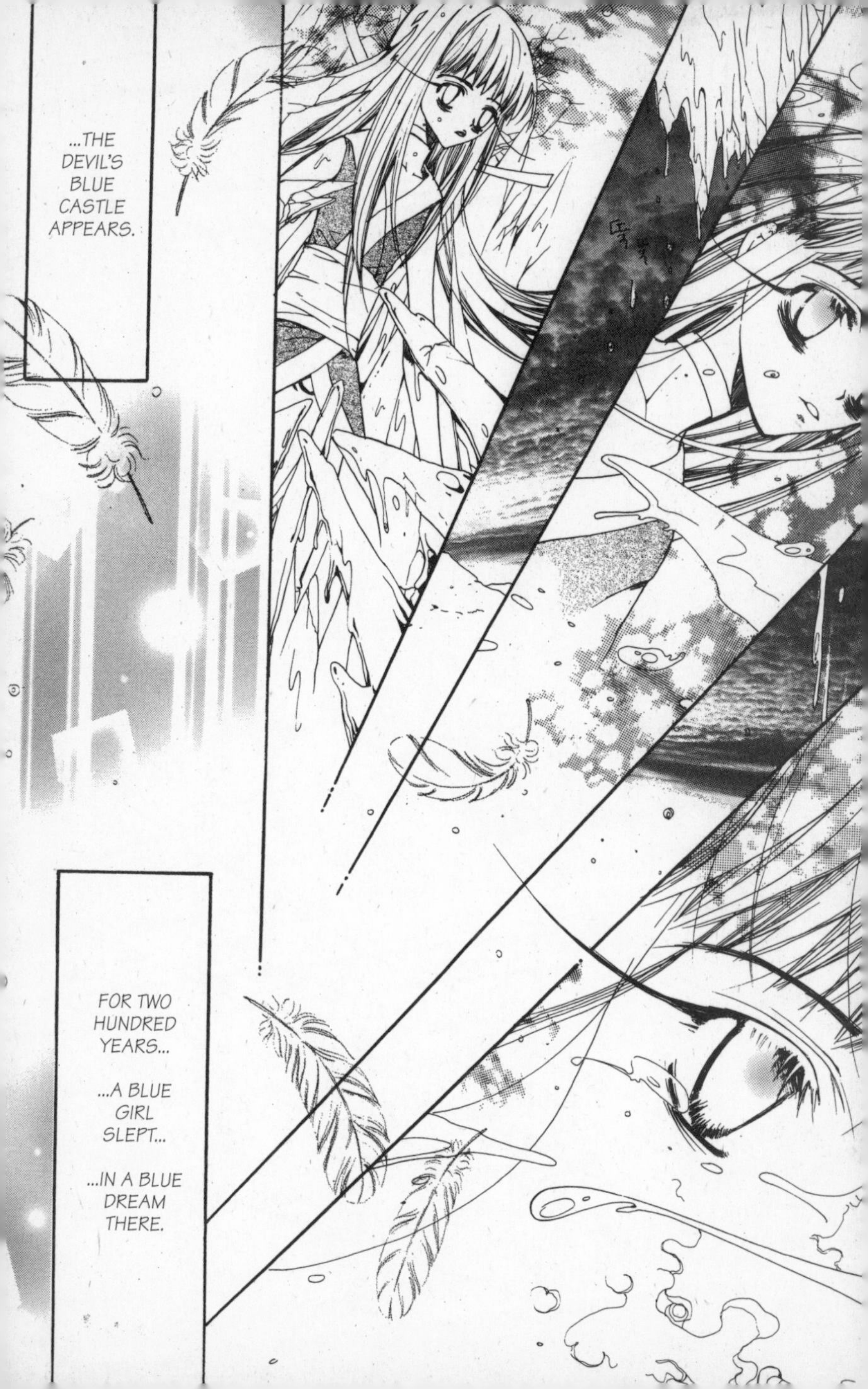
...THE DEVIL'S BLUE CASTLE APPEARS.
FOR TWO HUNDRED YEARS...
...A BLUE GIRL SLEPT...
...IN A BLUE DREAM THERE.

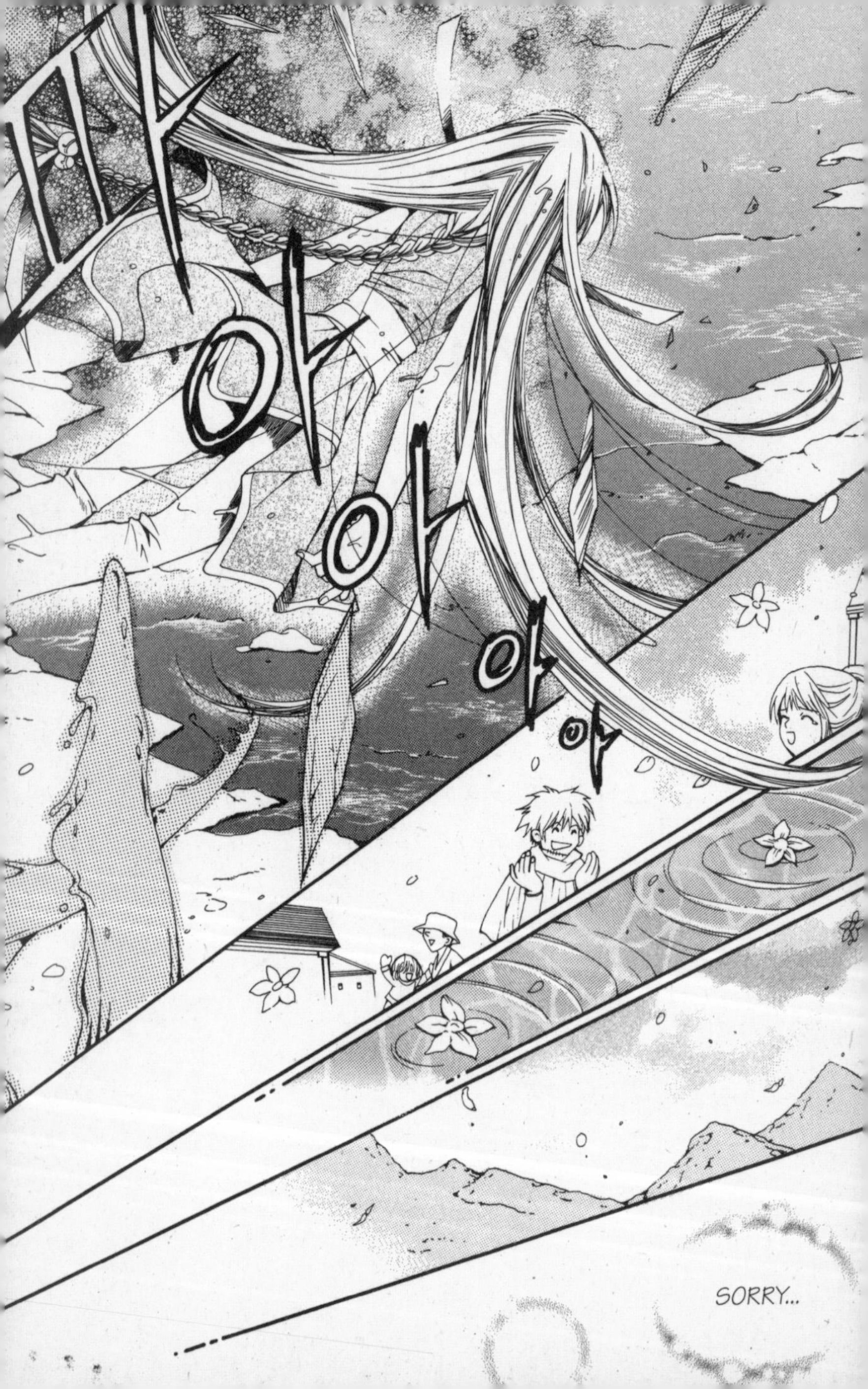
꺄아아아아
SORRY...

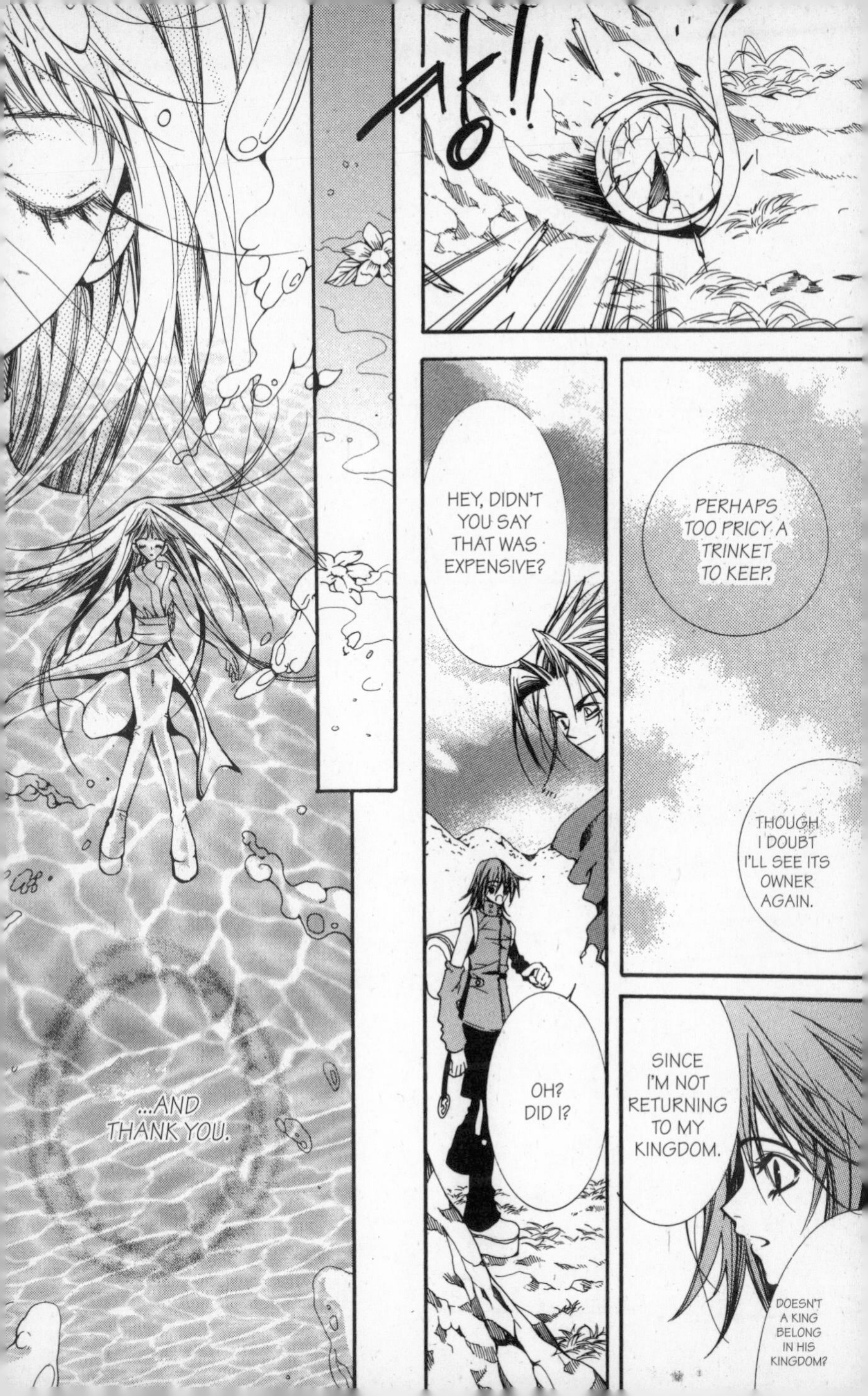
...AND THANK YOU.
HEY, DIDN'T YOU SAY THAT WAS EXPENSIVE?
OH? DID I?
PERHAPS TOO PRICY A TRINKET TO KEEP.
THOUGH I DOUBT I'LL SEE ITS OWNER AGAIN.
SINCE I'M NOT RETURNING TO MY KINGDOM.
DOESN'T A KING BELONG IN HIS KINGDOM?

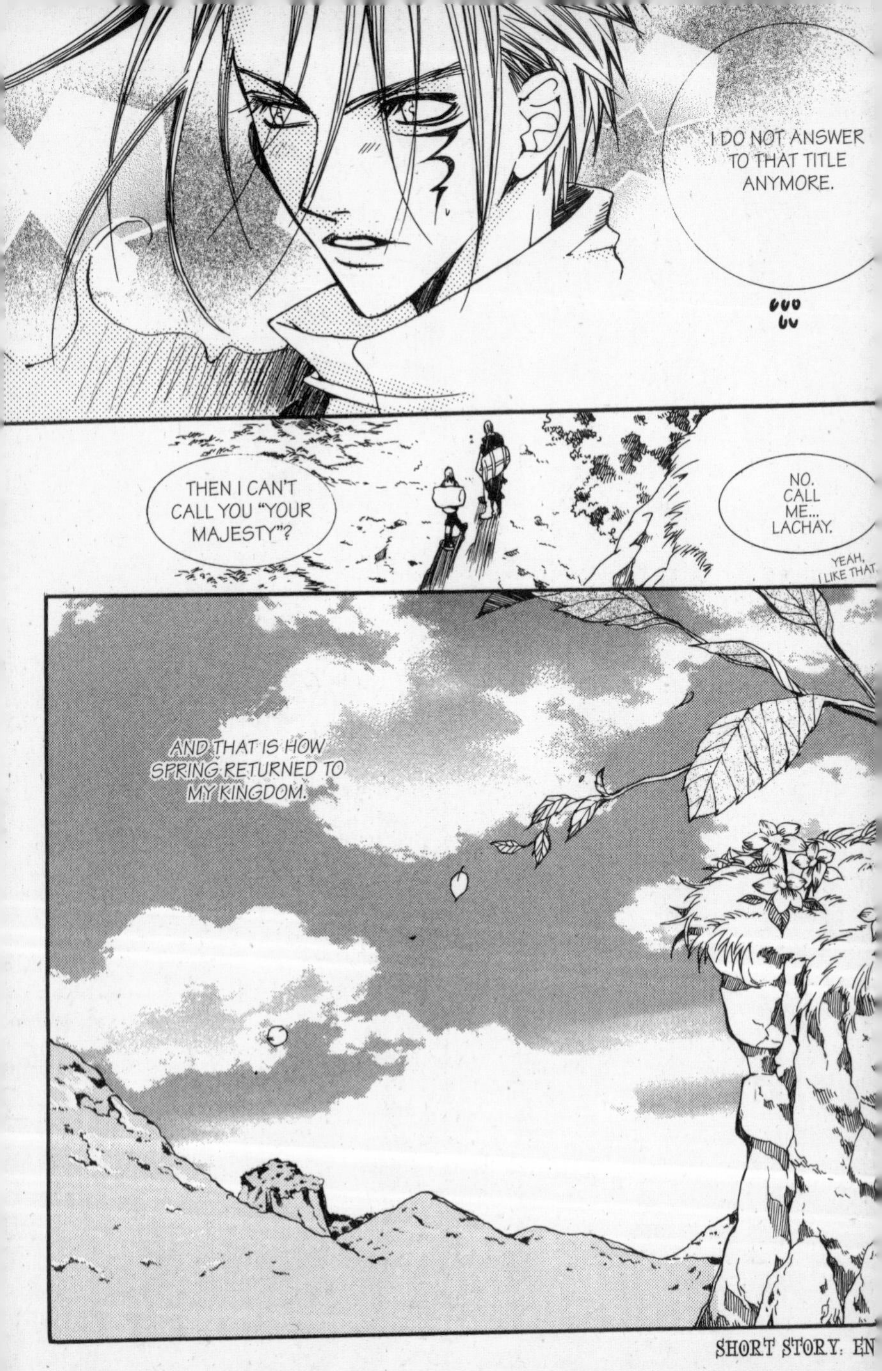
I DO NOT ANSWER TO THAT TITLE ANYMORE.
THEN I CAN'T CALL YOU "YOUR MAJESTY"?
NO. CALL ME... LACHAY.
YEAH, I LIKE THAT.
AND THAT IS HOW SPRING RETURNED TO MY KINGDOM.

SHORT STORY: EN

PRICELESS: THE END ♥